£5.00

CASS LIBRARY OF AFRICAN STUDIES

GENERAL STUDIES

No. 128

Editorial Adviser: JOHN RALPH WILLIS
Department of History, University of California, Berkeley

Politics and Society in South Eastern Nigeria 1841–1906

Politics and Society in South Eastern Nigeria 1841–1906

A Study of Power, Diplomacy and Commerce in Old Calabar

KANNAN K. NAIR

Department of History,
University of Malaya

FRANK CASS : LONDON

First published 1972 in Great Britain by
FRANK CASS AND COMPANY LIMITED
67 Great Russell Street, London WCIB 3BT, England

and in United States of America by
FRANK CASS AND COMPANY LIMITED
c/o International Scholarly Book Services, Inc.
P.O. Box 4347, Portland, Oregon 97208

Copyright © 1972 KANNAN K. NAIR

ISBN 0 7146 2296 6

Printed in Great Britain by
Clarke, Doble & Brendon Ltd.
Plymouth

TO THE MEMORY OF

MY MOTHER

Contents

Illustrations

Maps

List of Abbreviations

Ag.	Acting
Asst.	Assistant
B.T.	Board of Trade (British)
CALPROF	Calabar Provincial Papers
C.O.	Colonial Office (British)
Confid.	Confidential
C.S.O.	Colonial Secretary's Office (Nigeria)
D.C.	District Commissioner
F.O.	Foreign Office (British)
Govt.	Government
H.B.M.	His/Her Britannic Majesty
H.M.G.	His/Her Majesty's Government
H.M.S.	His/Her Majesty's Ships
H.M.S.O.	His/Her Majesty's Stationery Office
H.Q.	Headquarters
J.A.H.	Journal of African History
J.A.S.	Journal of the African Society
J.H.S.N.	Journal of the Historical Society of Nigeria
J.R.G.S.	Journal of the Royal Geographical Society
n.	footnote
Parl. Pap.	Parliamentary Papers (British)
P.R.G.S.	Proceedings of the Royal Geographical Society
U.P.	United Presbyterian Church of Scotland

Preface

Historical interest in Old Calabar is a product of various factors. For nearly 500 years from the first visit of the early Portuguese missionaries, Calabar has had one of the longest unbroken contacts with Europe of any port on the West African coast. It was a flourishing emporium of trade and one of the first ports on the Nigerian coast to make the transition from slave to palm oil trade. Its people, in particular the Efik, were famous in the eighteenth and nineteenth centuries among the trading people of the Oil Rivers. Calabar was the first site of Christian missionary endeavour on the Bight of Biafra. In time it rose to become the first headquarters of the British consul on the Bights of Benin and Biafra and the first capital of the Oil Rivers Protectorate.

The history of Calabar has, however, not hitherto received any special attention; historians interested in the trade and politics of Southern Nigeria have focused their attention on Lagos, Benin, Itsekiri, Brass, Kalabari and Bonny. The present work attempts modestly to sketch the outlines of political and social development of Calabar during one of the most crucial periods of its history. It does not pretend to do more than fill a vacuum in our knowledge and understanding of the southern Nigerian coast.

However, while previous studies which have peripherally touched on Calabar have seen external factors as the most dynamic force in the nineteenth century history of the area, the present work draws attention to the interaction between the external agents of change (supercargoes, missionaries and consuls) and the changes that were going on in the internal political, social and economic structure of Calabar society.

This study hence attempts to develop the argument that the nature of Efik-European relations cannot be analysed except with reference to the interactive effects of the internal rivalries between the towns, changes in the lineage structure, and the role of socio-economic and political institutions such as Ekpe.

The political and social history of a trading state can hardly be considered without constant reference to movements in the economy. Clearly, a major factor that made for change and development in Calabar was the trade in palm oil. One social effect of the oil trade was that greater integration was necessitated between the town-dwelling slaves and the free members of the houses; the fact that plantation-dwelling slaves were not similarly acculturated led to much social unrest. Also, the Ekpe fraternity whose membership was once drawn exclusively from amongst the nobility (or free born members of the houses) underwent a revolutionary development as it began to admit liberated slaves into its ranks. It is further argued in this study that many of the social reforms which took place in Calabar in the mid-nineteenth century and which the Christian missionaries happily attributed to their own endeavours were in fact consequential upon the development of the palm oil trade.

The political results of the expansion of the oil trade are best seen in the stimulation it provided to commercial and political rivalry between the major towns, namely Duke Town and Creek Town. The Calabar political system was a segmentary or acephalous one, although each town was more or less centralized in its government. The kings of these towns in the middle decade of the nineteenth century, Eyamba V and Eyo II, tried to consolidate their power by increasing their trade and securing the favour of the extra-territorial agents. It was this internal rivalry between the kings that best explains why missionary influence went deeper in Calabar than in most other parts of Southern Nigeria. However, King Eyo, unlike King Eyamba, exploited the oil trade, astutely contained the ambitions of the supercargoes, moderated the zeal of the missionaries and handled wisely the new and old ideas that were flowing through the life of the community at this time.

With the death of Eyo in 1858, the centre of effective political power moved from the Efik kings to the supercargoes and the consuls. It is argued here that the decline in Efik political leadership cannot be explained merely in terms of a consolidation in the position of the supercargoes and consuls, but also by an economic stress which is shown to have occurred in the river in the 1860s. It was largely the fact of economic stress that made it difficult for Efik political leadership to redress shifts in the balance of power between the European and Efik traders. European traders found in the trust system of trade a means of weakening the Efik polity.

The stress also altered the internal distribution of political power between the various towns, and within the towns between the principal lineages. The last quarter of the nineteenth century witnessed a movement by Henshaw Town to secede from Duke Town, and further segmentation of the Duke house.

The climax of more than half a century of active British political and socio-economic activities was the imposition of the colonial order. The loss of self-determination by Efik kings had important implications for political and social change. They were no longer in control of what changes to accept nor were they in a position to effectively direct the course of political and social development. Efik political and social organization underwent modification: the kings were stripped of their powers over external relations, and Ekpe as a political and judicial organization gave way before a new judicial system. Efik political agents, who formed part of the new power structure, emerged with authority not derived from traditional ranking in society. Colonialism altered the framework by which the Efik interpreted and evaluated the desirability of change in a western direction.

Though enmeshed in a new economy, the Efik, however, maintained rearguard control over certain areas, especially land tenure and the economic position of the Efik as middlemen. After 1891, when the colonial administration tried to break the control of the Efik and the hinterland chiefs over the middleman system and extend its political authority to the hinterland, the Efik offered sturdy resistance to British penetration. The early resistance to colonialism in Calabar would seem to be largely economic rather than political in nature.

A few difficulties encountered in the writing of this book ought to be mentioned. In the first place, as this book grew out of a specialized doctoral thesis it will inevitably lack a macro-approach. Secondly, since society is a living whole, every part bound to every other, developing through a process of change, all that one can do in a study of society is to select from the infinite variety of processes and activities what seem the significant movements and formative forces in an endless transition. Thirdly, while historical data for the period 1846 to 1856 is abundant in the accounts of missionaries and traders, and for the colonial period in the official papers, there are necessarily gaps in time which are difficult to fill. Hypotheses and circumstantial evidence have had to be used sometimes where documentation was found to be deficient. There is a paucity of material for the history of the Calabar hinterland. There is also the problem of inadequate statistical data relating to the volume and value of the trade of the port. The extent of our knowledge about the history of Calabar will thus depend on how well these limitations can be overcome.

Department of History,   K.K.N.
University of Malaya,
Kuala Lumpur.
1972

Acknowledgements

I acknowledge with delight my academic debt to several scholars on whom I leaned heavily for generous suggestions, friendly assistance and patient indulgence. In the University of Ibadan, where I wrote my doctoral thesis, my first debt is owed to the head of the Department of History, Professor J. F. A. Ajayi, my supervisor, whose detailed critical appraisals and guidance helped me attain clarity of ideas. My obligations are heavy to Dr. R. J. Gavin, of the Department of History, Ahmadu Bello University, for much intellectual stimulation; I owe much to Professor J. B. Webster (head of the Department of History, Makerere University College), Professor E. U. Essien-Udom, head of the Department of Political Science, University of Ibadan, Professor Father J. O'Connell (of the Department of Political Science, Ahmadu Bello University, Zaria) for their constructive criticisms, their many personal kindnesses, and their constant encouragement which sustained my morale. I am grateful to experts in particular fields for advice, particularly to Mr. G. I. Jones (Jesus College, University of Cambridge), Mr. R. Horton (Institute of African Studies, Ibadan), Dr. E. J. Alagoa (University of Ibadan) and the late Professor J. C. Anene (formerly head of the Department of History, University of Nigeria, Nsukka) for kindly placing at my disposal the benefits of their intimate knowledge of the Oil River states.

I also owe a very considerable debt to several informants (names appear in the footnotes) on whose time I trespassed and whose patience I tried with naïve queries during the field work in Calabar. They extended me their traditionally splendid hospitality, helped me realize the structural complexities of Efik society, and assisted me with their formidable memories in drawing up genealogical tables of their families.

In expressing my sincere gratitude to the several scholars for their valuable advice and for the scrupulousness with which they examined the drafts of this study, I should naturally absolve them from all responsibility for any errors of fact, judgement or interpretation that may still survive in the book.

I am deeply appreciative of the cheerful and courteous co-operation of the staff in the repositories of the Africana and Serials Sections of the University of Ibadan Library, the National Archives at Ibadan and Enugu, the Customary Court of Calabar, and The

Hope Waddell Institute; my labours while burrowing through their records were considerably expedited by the staff. Finally, I am deeply grateful to the Commonwealth Scholarships and Fellowships Plan under which sponsorship I had the good fortune to spend three years (1964–1967) researching in Nigeria and without which this book would never have been written.

K.K.N.

I

Structural Organization of Calabar Society

It was once notoriously fashionable to believe that most African societies in the pre-colonial period had suffered little social change, and that their histories were for the most part motionless ones. Such static empirical models are, however, today subject to substantial suspicion. The historical experience of Calabar does suggest that there were significant structural changes in its society during the eighteenth and the pre-colonial decades of the nineteenth centuries; that these changes established an important condition for the consequential development of the society, and finally, that in terms of the magnitude of change it might be argued that these changes were as significant as those which occured during the colonial period.

A Segmentary Political System

The Nigerian coastline on which the Atlantic Ocean breaks its surf is intersected at its easternmost point by an estuary. This estuary, twelve miles wide at its mouth and stretching northwards for more than thirty miles from the ocean, is flanked by banks of alluvial mud. Skirting these banks are tall mangrove trees, with their myriad of coiling roots and suckers, parasites, and lace-like tracery of leaves, reaching up for the sun. Here and there the banks are broken into by numerous creeks, the mouths of which are partially obscured by an overhanging sky of green mangrove foliage. A few islands, crowned and draped with forest, break the monotony of the unruffled waters of the estuary. Into the estuary two rivers, the Cross and the Calabar, empty their muddy waters.

At the head of the estuary were situated the trading settlements of Old Calabar, amongst the most important and bustling trade emporiums on the coast for nearly three hundred years. The name 'Old Calabar' is probably of European derivation, whereas the African population knew it as Efik, Efik Eburutu or Iboku. There are two theories about the origin of the name Old Calabar; the first being that it was taken from the (New) Calabar River, so named from the town of the Kalabari Ijaw. The second is that it was derived

1

from the Portuguese 'Calabarra' (or Kalbonger, Calabaros or Cala-pongas), meaning 'the bar is silent', an obvious reference to the calm waters of the estuary. Based on these two theories, the hypothesis is advanced that through some error the name Calabar was applied to the Cross River estuary, which was finally called 'Old' Calabar to distinguish it from the Kalabari River, which then became known as 'New' Calabar River.[1] Barbot described Old Calabar as being well furnished with villages and hamlets and 'good civilized people', and it had the greatest share of any European traders on the coast. Trade went on slowly, several ships lying there for between eight and ten months.[2] The population figures of the settlements at Old Calabar in 1858, as given by traders, were: Duke Town, 4,000; Henshaw Town, 120; Qua Town, 100; and Creek Town, 3,000.

Duke Town (Atakpa, or present-day Calabar), the first town of any size on the approach of the river from the ocean, is located between two hills on the east bank of the estuary. The anchorage is excellent; the holding bottom is nineteen feet deep and the surrounding hills offer shelter from prevailing winds. The Qua and Efut settlements lie behind Duke Town. At this point the Calabar estuary, a thousand yards wide, twists sharply twice. Just above Duke Town on the same side of the bank is situated Old Town (or Obutong). On the west side of the estuary live the Ibibio (or Egbo-sharry) and Oron people. Following the course of the estuary northwards and turning left into a long meandering creek, motionless except for the tide, one approaches Creek Town, about four miles from Duke Town. The Cross River, which flows west of the Calabar River in a somewhat parallel direction, is dotted with several settlements, the largest of which are Ikot Offiong (Ekricock), Ikoneto (George Ekricock), Adiabo (Guinea Company), Okoyong, Mbiabo, Itu (Old Ekricock), Umon and Akunakuna; on a tributary of the Cross River, just above Itu, is situated Enyong. On the upper reaches of the Calabar River, about ten miles north of Creek Town, lies the town of Uwet.

The political system of Calabar might be thought of as a federation or conglomeration of loosely-knit towns. Each town was a political unit with a territorial basis, its head having jurisdiction over his own town or house and representing the founding ancestors of his particular family. Each maintained its own administration and had the right to enforce sanction on others. Both these factors point to the fact that each of the towns was recognized to be politically equivalent. The relations between the major towns—Duke Town, Creek Town and Old Town—were in the order of inter-town dealings. Thus, they were in their political relations similar to European nation states in the eighteenth and nineteenth centuries. Political power was ultimately resident in the segments rather than in a central government.

The segmentary nature of the Calabar settlements might be illustrated and explained by reference to their early histories. The original inhabitants of Calabar are said to be the Qua (or Kwa, Akpa) and the Efut. They preceded the Efik who, however, are said to have later eclipsed them in numbers and importance.

The Qua claim to be of Ekoi origin, connected with the Ikpai branch of the Ejaham Ekoi, from the forest areas in the Cameroons.[3] They are believed to have been expelled from their original habitat by the Ekoi whose river the Qua fishermen poisoned while fishing.[4] A widely believed Qua tradition has it that following a dispute between a chief, Eta Ntison, and his son, Ikeng Ita, the supporters of each party migrated independently to found the settlements of Big Qua Town and Akim Qua Town. The two Qua communities—which exist to this day—remained ignorant of each other's existence until the Efik discovered them. Probably owing to the separate course of their early histories, the land tenure system of the two Qua communities differed. Land at Akim Qua, for example, was communally owned and each year it was reapportioned by the chief, the Ntoe, between the families who tilled it; land at Big Qua came to be owned individually by the founder families.[5]

The highest functioning unit recognized by the Qua was the town in which a number of family groups lived together. The Intelligence Report on the Qua, by E. C. Alderton, claims that in the 1930s, when it was written, the Qua clan occupied an area of about 60 square miles and had a total population of 3,000. There were nine Qua towns.[6] The authority for the control of the town was vested in the paramount head of each Qua settlement called the Ntoe.[7] It is an indication of the segmentary nature of the political system of the Qua that each Qua town recognized its own Ntoe, and that each Ntoe was independent and was advised by a council of elders recruited from among the family heads (esinjo).

The Efut[8] are believed to be an offshoot of the Bantu speaking people in the neighbourhood of the Rio del Rey (Usha Edet) in the Cameroons. The Efut left their original habitat in seven canoes and arrived at the Nigerian coastline. They founded the seven Efut towns of Abua, Ekondo, Ibonda, Ukem, Idundu, Nkpara and Ifako.[9]

The Efik were the last group of migrants to Calabar. Count de Cardi, writing in the late nineteenth century of the murder of certain English sailors in 1668, mentioned that the incident occurred prior to the arrival in the river of the Efik.[10] This would place Efik occupation of Calabar toward the end of the seventeenth or at the beginning of the eighteenth century.

A detailed account of Efik migration into the region has to be left to another occasion as it lies outside our present concern.[11] Efik tradition relates that following a civil war[12] in their original habitat in Ibibio land[13] (possibly Uruan), the Efik abandoned their old home in search of a new one. Two waves of migration are recognized; one settled at Enyong and the other at Creek Town (Ikoritungko). Creek Town was thus the original metropolis of the Efik at Calabar. From Creek Town the Efik migrated to Adiabo. Other areas occupied by migrating Efik groups included the Mbiabo settlements of Mbiabo, Mbiabo Edere, Ikot Offiong and Ikoneto.

The migrating Efik called themselves Eburutu Efik, since they claimed to have descended from Eburutu Otung Ema. The genealogy of the Efik gives some indication of the descendants who founded the various Efik settlements. It may be summarized as follows:

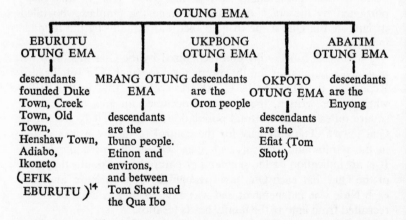

OTUNG EMA

EBURUTU OTUNG EMA		UKPBONG OTUNG EMA		ABATIM OTUNG EMA
descendants founded Duke Town, Creek Town, Old Town, Henshaw Town, Adiabo, Ikoneto (EFIK EBURUTU)[14]	MBANG OTUNG EMA descendants are the Ibuno people. Etinon and environs, and between Tom Shott and the Qua Ibo	descendants are the Oron people	OKPOTO OTUNG EMA descendants are the Efiat (Tom Shott)	descendants are the Enyong

The word 'Otung' is clearly an Ibibio word meaning compound or household. 'Otung Ema' means compound or household or family of Ema and it strengthens the argument of Ibibio origins of Efik.

The arrival of the Efik at Calabar coincided with a boom in the slave trade. Barbot stated that on his first voyage to the coast in 1678 he met an English ship which had spent ten months in Calabar and had obtained three hundred slaves.[15] In another passage he recorded that in April, 1698, the *Dragon* collected 212 slaves and was engaged in a valuable trade there. A long list of notables was involved in the trade.[16]

With the boom in the slave trade, new settlements were founded lower down the river in commanding positions to cut off rival settlements from the shipping. An internecine struggle in Creek Town caused several families, for instance, to descend a few miles and settle at Old Town.[17] Old Town was thus the first Efik settlement on the Calabar mainland. Though a number of families are said to have migrated to Old Town, Archibong Ekondo was attributed to be the leader of this wave. Ekondo, who subsequently became king of Old Town, is said to have descended from the Adim Ati (present day Ikang) and Batem Atai (present day Otu) families. He was succeeded to the kingship by Tom Robin of the Nkpo Atai (present day Etaknkpa) family. The origin of Old Town is thus linked with these families. The migration was said to have occurred at the time when Nsa Effiom, the eldest son of Effiom Ekpo (son of Ekpo Ibana), was ruler of Creek Town.[18]

Another wave of migration from Creek Town founded a settlement lower down the river than Old Town. This was Duke Town, or as Europeans called it, New Town. According to legend, Offiong Okoho (the elder) and Effiom Okoho, condemned twins who had been hiding in a bush just outside Creek Town, were responsible for the founding of Duke Town. While out on a fishing excursion, they came across an estuary and exclaimed Atakpa ('main river'), later the Efik name for Duke Town, which lay beyond the estuary. Since they were refugees from Creek Town they decided to move into the newly discovered town. They were followed by other families, but the Ambo, Cobham and Eyo families remained at Creek Town. One portion of the Cobham family, however, later moved to Duke Town during the reign of King Eyo I.[19] With the advantageous location of the new town for trade, having the ships at anchor in front, and free access to all parts of the surrounding country, it was destined to eclipse both Old Town and Creek Town.

The Efik settlements were segmentary in nature and, as illustrated above, for the most part rivals in trade. The Efik polity was not a single monarchy uniting different families under one paramount king (it was so only at the time of the Great Duke Ephraim who ruled between 1814 and 1834), but a conglomeration of loosely-knit towns each with its own rulers. K. O. Dike referred to these towns as 'republics',[20] but the term does not appear to be an adequate description, for the heads of these towns in the nineteenth century were referred to as 'kings'. Though in traditional Efik society no such position was recognized it became a de facto feature that the various heads were made kings by the European traders. The fact is that the Efik state was neither a monarchy nor a republic, and it is best perhaps to drop both terms. The term 'conglomeration of loosely-knit towns' is considered to be the safest description of the Efik state at the end of the eighteenth and during the nineteenth centuries. Indeed, loosely-knit towns as they were, they could still be monarchies or republics, depending on the election system or the amount of relative power wielded by the head of the town or house.

Segmentary Lineage System

The towns were further divided internally into a number of lineages, and each lineage was internally differentiated into smaller segments with localized areas of political activity. They competed for prestige, economic gain and political influence, but united as part of the larger political system for certain activities. The lineage, like the town, was thus a political unit. Political loyalties were spoken of in the idiom of kinship, and the political composition of the lineage was explained by reference to ancestry and descent.

The family system of the Qua was somewhat similar to that of the Efik, in that it was organized into certain wards. A group of families related by blood or adoption lived in one or more compounds. They elected family heads (esinjo) according to seniority of age. The office of head was non-hereditary and was not confined to any one branch or household. Nor was blood relationship with the previous head necessary. However, only free members could become heads, but if there was no suitable free born, a slave member could be chosen as regent until a free born was able to assume the position. The powers of the heads were not autocratic and were restricted to the distribution of land between the families, the hearing and settlement of civil disputes and the acting as advisors to the Ntoe.

It was noted earlier that the Ntoe was vested with the authority to control the town. He was generally elected by the kingmakers, who constituted the elders of the royal (or free) families. The most senior of the elders, if his conduct in the past had been exemplary, was generally elected the Ntoe. He received no tax or tribute from the esinjo, all revenue derived from land rents and produce being distributed among the family members by a treasurer elected for the purpose. Only in cases of serious financial crisis facing the town did families contribute to a special fund. The Ntoe possessed powers to expel any of his advisers if found unworthy of his office and alone possessed the right to wear a special garment made from the iroko tree bark.

Among the Efut, too, the smallest social unit was the family. Its headship went from father to eldest son, or in default of a son to a suitable free born member of the family. The family heads formed the village council, and the most suitable (in terms of age, experience and conduct) of their number was elected by the village to be the village head. A clan head was also elected, but these offices were not confined to the members of any one family, though free birth was essential.

The powers of the village council included in their administrative capacity the regulation of land tenure, the harvesting and planting of crops, and the making of by-laws. The village council also acted as a higher court if the various family heads could not settle disputes for themselves. It also dealt with offenders against the council weal. Criminal penalties and civil judgements were enforced by the Efut Ekpe on payment of fees to the society. The details of the Efut Ekpe, so far as they may be discovered, appear to be broadly similar to that of the graded Ekpe of the Efik, a fact much emphasized by Efut informants who believe that the Efik probably learnt of Ekpe from the Efut, whom they brought under their influence in many ways.

It is, however, in the Efik political and social organization that one discovers the best illustration of a segmentary lineage structure. One also discovers in studying the Efik settlement pattern and the lineage structure that the most characteristic feature of the system is the development of plutocratic and locally dominant kin groups.

The Efik social system was (and is) lineage-based, the component lineages being derived as the ramifications of the two great maximal lineages of the founding ancestors, namely Ema and Effiom Okoho. It should be noted that in the Efik political system, kinship (or blood relationship) was of paramount importance. The strong tradition of genealogies preserved by Efik families is an indication of the fact that a man's position in society depended on whether or not he could trace his lineage to the founding ancestor (akwa ete kiet) of the house (ufok) to which he belonged. If he could trace no such relationship either patrilineally or matrilineally, he remained an alien or stranger. It will be seen from the structural genealogy of the Efik below how the main lineages (wards) in the Efik towns were (and are) integrated with their outlying village settlements. The genealogies, collected from Chief Ene Ndem Ephraim Duke during an interview on 4 December, 1965, have been cross-checked with other informants and compared with those reproduced in *The Hart Report*. In both sketches the families are shown in capitals.

(*a*) *The Ema Group:*

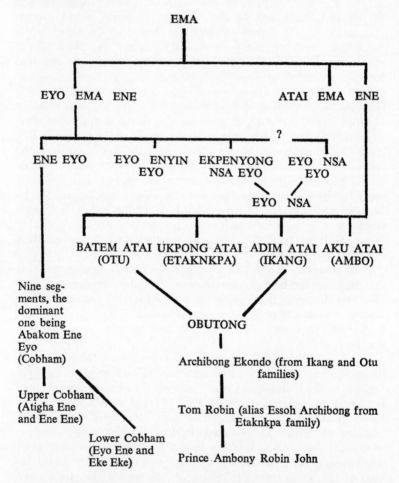

The Ekpenyong Nsa Eyo and Eyo Nsa Eyo segments also claim relations with Effiom Ekpo through the Odo segments; see table (*b*) *The Ephraim Group*. This extension is controversial, and some informants claim that it is part of the Eyo family's move to claim legitimacy for themselves by linking their ancestry with that of the other Efik.

(b) The Ephraim Group:

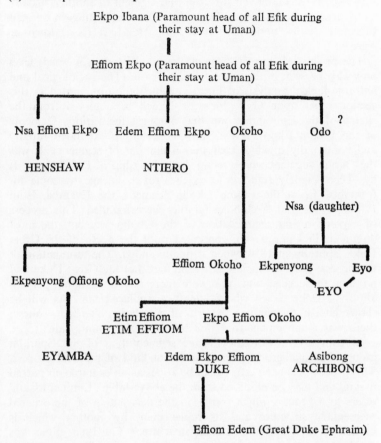

Ekpo Ibana (Paramount head of all Efik during
their stay at Uman)

Effiom Ekpo (Paramount head of all Efik during
their stay at Uman)

Nsa Effiom Ekpo   Edem Effiom Ekpo   Okoho   Odo   ?

HENSHAW   **NTIERO**

Nsa (daughter)

Effiom Okoho   Ekpenyong   Eyo

Ekpenyong Offiong Okoho   **EYO**

Etim Effiom   Ekpo Effiom Okoho
ETIM EFFIOM

EYAMBA   Edem Ekpo Effiom   Asibong
            DUKE   **ARCHIBONG**

Effiom Edem (Great Duke Ephraim)

The Eyamba family, founded by Ekpenyong Offiong Okoho, is
made up of three sub-families: Ekpenyong Offiong Okoho, Mbang
Offiong Okoho, and Abasi Offiong Okoho.

It will be noted from these two tables that the Efik political
structure expanded unevenly; not all of this expansion took place
in the eighteenth century. Lineage segmentation was not accompanied by great disturbance of the social order. Rather, it was
brought about by a gradual movement of people from those places
where resources were lean to those where they were in abundance.
Towns such as Duke Town, which became prosperous owing to
their strategic situation with regard to European trade, attracted

population from the less wealthy towns; also within lineage segments, there was a movement from one segment to another, usually as a result of marriage. Jones has illustrated this movement (which he calls 'population drift') for Henshaw (Nsa) town or ward.[21]

The process of lineage segmentation at the town (or ward) level may also be seen in the case of Duke Town. (The sociological and anthropological analysis of lineage segmentation attempted in this section relies upon G. I. Jones.[22]) It will be observed from the sketch of the Ephraim group that amongst the various segments of the Effiom Ekpo lineage, the Okoho group expanded rapidly and continually divided itself into a number of segments. It was the Okoho segment which retained the kingship of Duke Town. It has been vaguely referred to as the 'royal' lineage by some informants. From the Effiom Okoho segment, the Eyamba, Etim Effiom, Duke and Archibong families were founded. This process of expansion and segmentation of the Okoho segment, the most dominant in Duke Town, continued until the death of the Great Duke Ephraim in 1834, when it finally ended. The termination of the process may be attributed to the fact that the Great Duke had no sons to succeed him; nor were there any outstanding personalities in Duke Town who might have replaced him. As will be shown later in the chapter, the drift of population altered its course; there was a movement from the towns to the countryside.

In comparison with the lineage segmentation of the Ephraim group, the Ema group offers a different kind of political process. This process has been referred to by Jones as an example of 'partial fission' and may be observed from the above table. 'Limited fission' refers to a process which results in the destruction of the original segmentary structure and its replacement by another which is limited to a part of the original structure.[23] The Ema group was divided into two major segments: the Eyo Ema Ene and Atai Ema Ene segments. The Eyo Ema Ene segment divided itself into four segments, but two of them—the Ekpenyong Nsa Eyo and Eyo Nsa Eyo—came together to form the Eyo Nsa (or Eyo Honesty) ward. The Ene Eyo segment secured the kingship of Creek Town and expanded into nine segments, the dominant one being Abakom Ene Eyo. However, Ene Eyo could not expand as rapidly as the Eyo Nsa-Ekpenyong Nsa segments because the latter were also associated with the Effiom Okoho ward of Duke Town. The result was that the Ene Eyo lost the kingship of the town to the Eyo Nsa-Ekpenyong Nsa segments. The Abakom Ene Eyo segment, which gave its name to the Cobham wards in Duke Town and Creek Town, was split into two parts as shown in the sketch. The other segments did not split but moved to Duke Town. The Eyo Enyin, however, disintegrated as a political unit. The Atai Ema segment showed an example of limited political fission. The three segments of the Atai Ema—Batem Atai, Ukpong Atai and Adim Atai— came together to found Old Town (Obutong).

Agnatic and territorial distinctions were thus important in Calabar; local communities were organized on the basis of agnatic kinship and residence. Among the Efik some towns (wards) were known by the name of the founder. The traditional offices of village or town heads were confined to lineal descendants of the founding ancestors of these towns. This pattern was also characteristic of Bonny and Kalabari before the mid-eighteenth century and at the time of King Pepple and King Amarakiri.[24] Though wards were segmented into other units or segments, these were ultimately co-ordinated by a genealogical system of descent from the founders. This pattern of descent, clearly defined in Efik, was not emphasized in the Delta societies, including that of the Eastern Ijaw which shared the Efik tradition of agnatic descent from a single founder.[25] In Kalabari (New Calabar), ideas of descent from a single founder were of little consequence to the political or social process. In the latter, it was diversity rather than the unity of origin which was stressed.

The House System

Each Efik settlement was made up of large but compact villages of several compounds. In the centre of each compound stood the house of the compound owner, surrounded by those of his wives, servants and dependent relatives. There is some degree of variation in the structure of these compound houses as shown in the figures overleaf.

The enlarged households themselves were grouped together in lineages called 'house' (ufok).[26] An Efik house was a group of men patrilineally related to an immediate male ancestor, the wives of these men, their sons, their wives and unmarried daughters. Thus in the Calabar model, the house was only another name for a lineage, for a lineage was a subdivision of a clan, or of a sub-clan, whose members claimed to be able to trace their descent genealogically to a founding ancestor. In the nineteenth century they included household slaves as well. Several houses having patrilineal ties with each other were grouped together into towns (wards). There are, however, no visible boundaries to a ward, but it does seem that the ward was an important social and political unit. Whether the extension of the term 'house' to apply to towns was an eighteenth- or nineteenth-century feature is not clear. Waddell, for example, used the words towns (ward) and family interchangeably; G. I. Jones elaborates a kinship structure which consists of minor, major and maximal lineages corresponding to residence units of sub-section, section and wards.[27]

The origin of the Efik house is still uncertain. The hypothesis may be advanced that the system grew naturally from the patriarchal character of the social organization. For tradition has it that the Efik family groups recognized a common paternity even before they arrived at the estuary of the Cross River. It may be postulated also that the lineage kinship organization of the houses adapted itself to trade when the Efik entered into the Atlantic slave trade. If this hypothesis is valid, then the argument of Jeffreys that the house system in Calabar was a 'direct product of, and response to, the European slave trade'[28] may require modification.

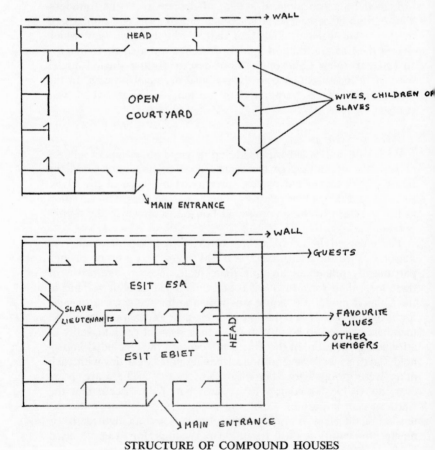

STRUCTURE OF COMPOUND HOUSES

The house system depended for its economic existence on corporate control of assets under the stewardship of the head of the house, who was called the etubom. The etubom was normally the oldest male of the lineage or house. He had a great deal of influence over the rest of the members. All trade transactions of the members of a house were conducted through the etubom; he negotiated with European traders and enjoyed a lion's share of the trade. He had judicial powers in disputes arising among the members, managed the financial affairs of the house and received a share of the profits of the land. Wealth and ability were important attributes of the office. A house head who possessed only mediocre abilities had generally to rely on the support of a brother or son with greater ability. Incompetence could easily disqualify an etubom from continuing in office or reduce him to a figurehead.

Thus, although accounts speak of the domestic powers of an etubom, there was a method of checking the abuse or excesses of the office holder. It might be asked how a house could depose an etubom if the etubom was traditionally regarded as the father or etenyin of the house. The explanation is that the etubom was himself a descendant of the ancestor just as much as any other true agnate of the family. It was only by traditional fiction, natural to the patriachal system, that his position as head came to be. It follows, therefore, that it was possible to produce someone to represent the founding ancestor, and by some fiction the person chosen was regarded as the embodiment in the flesh of the ancestor.[29] But, in fact, the post of etubom was so vital to Efik tradition that the etubom could not be summarily dismissed from office in the absence of the most grave and weighty reasons. In addition, a house council normally aided the etubom in the administration of the house. No outside force interfered with the internal self government of the houses or towns, unless invited by them to do so. Where there was a clash between two houses an appeal was made to a third house, but where arbitration failed, open hostilities resolved the outstanding issues.

One of the points of departure between the history of Calabar and its Delta neighbours was in the political and social development of the house systems. Though the Kalabari and Bonny houses may have begun like Calabar as corporate groups of kin tracing descent to common founders, in the eighteenth century they developed into what Jones has referred to as 'canoe houses'. The canoe house was a compact, well organized trading and fighting corporation, capable of manning and maintaining a war canoe.[30] Each of these canoes was equipped with a cannon fore or aft, a complement of fifty paddles, with drummers, musketeers, helmsmen and a war captain.

The helmsman and the captain was generally the house chief, unless he was disabled by infirmities of age, in which case drummers conveyed the chief's commands to the men. The canoe house segmented into sub-houses far more than the Efik house did. Jones stated that expansion in the case of the canoe house was by carefully planned segmentation into one or more new canoe houses.[31] The new house was economically independent of, but politically subordinate to the main house. The canoe houses were therefore small and their size more closely defined. In the Kalabari segmentary system, the house that was an offshoot of the parent house was said to have been able to reverse its rank order if it became powerful and wealthy enough.

By contrast, the Efik house was 'half way' between the canoe house system of Bonny and the family organization of the hinterland. Unlike the Delta system, the Efik house was closely related to land-holding rights in addition to trade. And unlike the social organization of the hinterland, it was not only organized on the basis of descent groups, but included those who were no more than fictionally related to the agnatic members of the houses. It also bore strong relationship to external trade.

The Ekpe

If Calabar was essentially a lineage society, there were also associations in the form of organized corporate groups in which membership did not follow automatically from birth or adoption into a kin or territorial unit. The most important of these associations was the secret society Ekpe. Each of the ethnic communities in Calabar had such a society. It must be emphasized that the secret society did not function as a central institution of government in the Calabar political system. Each settlement had its own branch of the society and they functioned more or less autonomously. The segmentary pattern of settlements was, therefore, hardly modified or brought into any kind of effective unity. Societies of lesser importance than Ekpe were the obon, which possessed five grades and functioned primarily as a burial society and honoured deceased members with memorial services; the ekpri akata, which met at night in November, December and January to sing songs and report gossip to the villagers; and the unam odak, literally 'animal of money', membership of which was obtained either by sacrificing a close relative or by handing over one's material wealth.

The Qua Ekpe owed its origin to the Ekoi among whom it was called Mgbe. It was a graded society and admission into it was secured by the purchase of these grades. The following were the grades of the Qua Ekpe in their order of importance: idaha, asian, otuk-antam, mambo, etere, okuakama, dibo, and ebunko.[32] Each of the grades had their own heads, but they had all to come from members of the first grade, idaha. Only a 'full-blooded' Qua was allowed to purchase the idaha grade. The asian grade could be bought by a wealthy slave in exceptional cases; generally, however, slaves and Europeans were able to purchase all the grades except the idaha, asian and otuk-antam.[33] The Ntoe, as the head of Ekpe, was also head of the idaha grade. Here was an essential difference between the Qua and Efik Ekpe. Whereas the Ntoe was the supreme head of both the Qua Ekpe and the town, the supreme head of the Efik Ekpe, the Eyamba, could not claim by this virtue alone rights to administer his country in the way the Ntoe could. Information relating to the Efut Ekpe is at best scanty, but it is possible that many of the Efut were members of the Efik Ekpe.

According to legend, the Efik Ekpe (or Egbo in its anglicized spelling) also owed its origin to the Ekoi in whose folklore it was first mentioned. 'Ekpe' is Ibibio and Efik for leopard, and Talbot believed that the name of the society must have originated from an association of those who worshipped this dreaded animal in the bush. Jones suggests that there is nothing in early accounts or in its modern survivals to support the view that it involved 'human leopard' beliefs and activities.[34] It is said to have been brought to Calabar by a certain Archibong Ekondo who purchased it from the Ekoi. Ekondo later sold it to Calabar. The esoteric ritual of the society concerned the spirit of the forest, which was on occasions brought out into the town and paraded about by masqueraders, and then returned to its abode (ikot ekpe) in the forest. This praeternatural being, symbolized by the masquerader, was a mystic figure never seen by the uninitiated. The chief masquerader had a number of lesser beings or messengers (idem ikwo) who executed his behests. These lesser beings, symbolized by dancers, wore masked costume (idem ikwo) or raffia, a bell around the waist, and brandished a long whip to thrash the uninitiated who came their way.

In the affluent conditions of Calabar society, Ekpe was modified to accommodate wealth by changing it into a graded association. The two highest orders, which may be called titles as distinguished from grades, were those of Eyamba and Ebunko. Five grades were normally recognized. They were in their order of importance, nyamkpe,[35] okpoho, okuakama, nkanda and a fifth grade which was made up of lesser grades, namely mboko, mboko mboko, mkpe, mbakara and edibo. The eyamba title, which was later bought for life by King Edem Ekpenyong Offiong Okoho (Eyamba V), was

confined to Duke Town and more specifically to the Eyamba (Offiong Okoho) family. It was occasionally leased to others: these
holders were King Edem Archibong (Eyamba VIII) and Orok
Edem or King Duke IX (Eyamba IX). (It was after King Duke's
reign that the British Government moved in and took Calabar over
as its protectorate.) Informants point out that kings who were not
also holders of Eyamba generally bought the nyamkpe grade.[36]
However, the first two holders of eyamba title were both from
Creek Town; they were Essien Ekpe Oku of Ambo (Eyamba I)
and Ekpenyong Ekpe Oku of Ambo (Eyamba II). Ekpenyong
Effiong Okoho of Duke Town was Eyamba III, while the first
eyamba title holder who was also a king, was Effiom Edem (Great
Duke Ephraim) who became Eyamba IV. The other title, ebonko,
said to be equal in importance to eyamba, was lodged in Creek
Town, and came to be specifically identified with the Eyo family.
Each of the grades had a head, called obong, who had control
over the plays, masquerades, drums and equipment belonging to
that grade. The obong who took charge of the fifth grade was called
obong mboko.

The numbers and names of the grades were inconstant. Antera
Duke made no reference to grades in the society, but from his
reference to 'King Egbo' it can be inferred that there was some
senior grade.[37] It is recorded that, in 1828, there were five grades;[38]
in 1853, ten grades;[39] in 1858, eleven grades;[40] and today, about
twenty-three.[41] It is possible to theorize about the growth of these
grades. In good times, when wealth was abundant, more grades
were usually created by the top title holders both as a means of
increasing the wealth of the society and as a means of making it
more difficult for those at the bottom rungs of the ladder to climb
their way up to the more influential ones. In bad times, intermediate
grades were probably abolished in order to make it easier for
aspiring members to jump from one grade to another.

One important factor in the corporate feeling and perpetuation
of the Ekpe consisted of sharing the fees paid by new members of
the different grades. In the late eighteenth century titles of Ekpe
were purchased by payment in slaves. Antera Duke recorded in
his diary that in August, 1787, one Jimmy Henshaw paid for the
title of 'King Egbo' four Calabar afaws (slaves).[42] Holman in 1828
stated that the fees for five grades amounted to 1,250 'white copper
rods' and 300 'Iron bars'.[43] Waddell stated that during the mid-
nineteenth century a person joining the highest rank paid an entrance fee to every member which amounted to nearly a hundred
pounds, there being a thousand members.[44] Initiation fees were not
the only source of payment made to Ekpe. Ekpe also raised revenue

from the imposition of fines and the collection of fees for settlement of cases.

Membership of the higher grades of Ekpe, particularly of the highest grade, was an investment. Having made the highest grade one received a share of the fees paid by all who subsequently became members of these grades. Apart from receiving the lion's share of the fees and fines paid to Ekpe, the members of the higher grades were also entitled to returns on each of the grades they had purchased before they reached the top grades. The rich thus became richer. It was this possibility of perpetuating their wealth which explains why families did not like to lose a title that one of their members had bought. On the death of such a member, when the title went out of the family, another member of the family would immediately pay Ekpe to keep the grade. In this way the family escaped the possible curses of later generations.

Apart from the factor of prestige involved, membership of Ekpe assured the members of the grades an income for life. It was an investment which yielded enormous dividends. The system of distributing dividends was a flexible one. Normally, the heads of the various grades met and set aside a lion's share for the eyamba and obunko. The rest of the money was divided among the five heads of grades; each head kept some of the dividends for himself and distributed the rest among other members. No money was generally put aside into a sinking fund for exigencies. This was, however, not true of the Ikoneto Ekpe which had a sinking fund out of which expenses for celebrations or other miscellaneous activities, or loans, were made to members.[45]

Since the fees for purchasing the hierarchy of titles were fixed, it followed that only the most affluent could rise to the top offices. Membership was at first open only to free men and later to slaves. Women were not admitted to the fraternity. Whilst free men could climb to the highest of its several grades of honours, the so-called slaves were confined to the lower ones. Waddell's reference to the possibility of boys being initiated into the lower grades[46] would seem to indicate that there were no specific restrictions regarding age. Any head of Ekpe could initiate an Efik man into the fraternity provided the person to be initiated could afford the entrance fee.

Strangers (non-Efik) could also be initiated into the order. This practice was prevalent (and might have begun) during the super-cargo days. It was to the advantage of supercargoes to be members of the organization since they could appeal to the fraternity to recover debts due to them by the African traders. Captain Burrell of the vessel *Heywood* of Liverpool was said to have held the rank of yampai (nyamkpe).[47] In December, 1874, Harry Hartze of

Matilda, an agent of the firm Messrs. Thomas Harrison of Liverpool, bought Ekpe titles up to nyamkpe from King Eyamba VIII and other members of the Ekpe.[48] J. B. Walker of Hope Factory in Calabar bought the same grade in 1878. Non-Efik members enjoyed the rights, claims and immunities of the grades into which they were initiated but they could not become heads of the grades. Under normal circumstances (in the absence of controversy) a non-Efik was initiated into Ekpe only after the obongs of the fraternity had met and consulted together; if the Eyamba or ebunko were not notified of the initiation it became invalid. Slaves were also initiated into the lower grades of Ekpe after a time if they were wealthy enough to buy them. Tradition has it that some of the wealthy kings of Calabar, such as the Great Duke Ephraim, at times bought Ekpe titles for their enterprising slaves in order to encourage them to greater industry.[49] The fraternity made the members—free, slave or stranger—an exclusively organized body within Efik society.

The sense of exclusiveness was achieved in several ways. Explicit restriction of entry into the grades, based on the ability to purchase Ekpe grades, made the members aware of their pre-eminent position and all the privileges that went with them. Ekpe members became a group apart from the rest of society. It made them honoured members of a society upon which they could rely in times of need. The sense of exclusiveness was expressed in the ceremonial functions of Ekpe. The fraternity's important mask dance and festivities were confined to members alone (though less important dances were open to all spectators), and this gave the initiated, as it were, a feeling of cultural unity. The uninitiated had to flee from the path of the masqueraders, and severe punishment was levied on those who dared to violate the custom. Ceremonial exclusiveness was also expressed in the funerals of Ekpe members. It is claimed to be an unwritten law that in any locality no Ekpe members should be buried unless some other members were present.[50] Apart from the fact that there was an element of respect involved in this custom, it is likely that it was also a device for preventing foul play.

Functions of Ekpe

The chief political importance of Ekpe was that it brought together into a single organization all the wealthy and leading gentry in each local community.[51] Authority over others could only be exercised through Ekpe. Therefore, all who mattered in society had to be members of the fraternity. No man, however rich, could hope to go against the collective and organized will of the society. The path to social advancement, recognition, and power lay in the membership of this body. This point may be most powerfully illustrated by reference to the traditional position of a king in Calabar society. Unless the king was head of Ekpe, or at least an important member of it, he had no greater authority in the society than other titled members. It followed from this that he had not vested in himself, as king, any political authority. All such authority was derived from his position as an important member of the fraternity.

As importance began to be attached through usage to the office of king, the upper grades of Ekpe formed the nucleus of what became known as the king's council or cabinet.[52] No mention is made of a council of town heads exercising authority over the local community at the end of the eighteenth century when Antera Duke was writing his diary. In the nineteenth century, the members of the cabinet were the heads of different families who held high position in Ekpe, and though they had only advisory powers the king could never hope to be an absolute autocrat. At the same time, since Ekpe was a veritable oligarchy, factional disturbances, civil strife and internecine squabbles which threatened the peace ran counter to its wishes. The elite of wealth felt a common compulsion to preserve the stability of society, neglect of which might endanger their own position. Disputes between families were also arrested by Ekpe before a crisis developed into large scale civil disorder.[53] In the days of the slave trade, Ekpe endeavoured to keep the slaves disciplined and orderly so that the public peace was not disturbed.

Ekpe was also used as a means of bringing the hinterland people who lived in the Cross River within the orbit of Calabar influence. This was done by selling Ekpe honours to those who dwelled outside Calabar. Those who purchased the grades became the obong Ekpe of their respective areas and could use the fraternity to obtain control over others in the district. Since they had bought these honours from Calabar, they always remained subject to the control and direction of the Ekpe in the metropolitan towns. In this way the powers of the Calabar towns extended to the interior.[54] The process by which the Ekpe society dealt with those who flouted its authority was referred to by the Efik as 'blowing Ekpe'. But Ekpe influence began to wane with the development of the palm oil trade. By the middle of the nineteenth century the Cross River towns had begun to shake off the influence of the Calabar Ekpe.

The legislative and judicial functions of Ekpe were derived from the political control that it maintained over the society at large. Ekpe made the laws and executed them, and was regarded by European traders as the only judicial authority in Calabar. It affected action by the application of a number of severe sanctions which have been outlined by Jones.[55] Waddell stated that it was the second grade of the society, the so-called 'Brass' Ekpe, which was responsible for law enforcement. A yellow flag of this grade was attached to property sealed by Ekpe.[56]

Contemporary European observers of the nineteenth century, particularly the missionaries, were often critical of the organization. They exaggerated the excesses of the fraternity and overlooked some of its beneficial aspects. The functions of Ekpe outlined above were perhaps the more apparent, but others should be mentioned. Jones has stated, for instance, that the grading of members on a basis of wealth in effect established a 'means test' for those seeking social advancement, and caused members of society to expand their wealth in a manner which was socially beneficial.[57] By making it socially and politically necessary for the wealthy to join the society, the wealth of individual men was spent purchasing its ranks. This distribution of wealth amongst members checked the rapid growth of independent powerful men who could split society between them. Also, Ekpe distributed power to a large group and to persons who had little or no power individually. The fact that it included most of the adult males in the community widened the franchise and gave representation to all families. In the nineteenth century, however, the divisions which Ekpe perpetuated between the slaves and the free, and between the rich and the poor, weakened Calabar society.[58]

Economic and Political Rivalries

The most significant and enduring feature of the political history of Calabar for much of the nineteenth century was the continuous struggle, both between towns and within each town between the different lineages or houses. This might to some extent be considered inevitable in a segmentary lineage society where the members of a group defined by reference to a particular genealogical level of segmentation, retain a certain group unity against members of another such group. For example, the members of a group descended agnatically from a particular man about five generations back might see themselves as a unit as against all the agnatic descendants of that man's brother. Such a state has been referred to as one of 'balanced opposition' since each such group maintained a relationship of actual or potential opposition to one another.[59] Where all inter-group relationships are conceived of in terms of the lineage, such antagonisms, if sufficiently intense, might have far reaching results upon the political stability of the society.

The rivalry was both commercial and political in character. As trade was the life blood of both the houses and towns, each sought to secure as large a share as possible of European trade. Political power was thus very largely determined by the degree of monopoly over external trade. For the house, and, by extension, the town which commanded extensive trade and amassed wealth, generally found itself in a powerful position to extend its influence or assume ascendancy over others which were economically less fortunate. The volume of trade done with Europeans was thus an important index in determining the power position of the Calabar houses and towns vis-à-vis one another. The heads of the houses and towns derived most of their political power from the fact that they monopolized economic power, for it was they who represented their houses and towns respectively in their external relations with European traders. To them, too, the European traders looked to arrange the conditions under which they traded. No one could trade outside the system in which the house head and the king were responsible for all trade transactions. In order to see more clearly the way in which control over European trade strengthened the position of the house heads and kings, it is necessary to dwell briefly upon the system of trade in Calabar.

When a trade vessel arrived at the estuary, the master was expected to send up for an Efik pilot and a fee was collected from the vessel for the service of escorting it safely into Calabar. In Calabar the sum of twenty-five coppers per registered ton of a ship, whether piloted or not, was charged.[60] Failure to observe the ceremony of employing a pilot could, in cases of competition, produce disagreeable results.[61]

Since the wealth of the etubom and the king was derived almost exclusively from their activities as middlemen (rather than as land owners or producers), a determined attempt was made to keep the Europeans out of African society. For, if the European trader was allowed to penetrate into the country and gain direct access to the interior markets, it was feared that he would completely undermine the middleman functions of the Efik. It is important to point out that the European supercargoes were themselves keen to stay on the hulks, away from the shore. Apart from guarding aginst endemic illnesses, they also dreaded the 'smokes' (harmattan) season toward the turn of each year. During this period the entire country was enveloped in exhaled vapour or dense fog which Europeans believed was injurious to their health. Normally at this time the traders went further down the estuary; if it was necessary for them to remain at the harbour, they tried to repel the vapour by fumigating the vessels with tobacco. The hulks generally had a house built over them to protect the crews against the weather.

Thus, to the advantage of both European and Efik traders, the 'trust' or credit system of trade was introduced. The system may be summarized as one under which European traders advanced a considerable amount of goods on trust to an Efik chief in exchange for an equivalent value of slaves (or palm oil) to be delivered by a specified date. The goods given on trust might consist of gunpowder, cloth, iron goods, utensils and alcohol in various forms. Barbot, writing of Calabar's trade in 1678, stated that the most current European goods used to purchase slaves and elephants' tooth in Calabar were iron bars, copper bars, blue rags, cloth and striped Guinea cloth of many colours, horse bells, hawk's bells, rangoes, pewter basins, tankards, beads and copper armlets. All goods in the seventeenth century were reduced to copper bars; for instance, a male slave was equal to thirty-eight, and a female slave thirty-six or thirty-seven copper bars.[62] With the trust obtained, the Efik chief organized a journey into the interior country where the producers of slaves or oil were paid part of the trust goods in exchange for the commodities. Trust, therefore, was an outlay of capital with its attendant risks and gains.

The profits made by the Efik middlemen and the Europeans in this system of trade were scandalously high. Europeans deflated the prices and exaggerated the value of the trade goods they handed over to the Efik middlemen. The latter made a profit because they themselves paid ridiculously low prices for the goods of the hinterland producers. This capital enabled the chiefs to own a fleet of canoes, make handsome profits and keep Europeans out of African society. Where the supercargoes were concerned, the trust system of trade enabled them to buy cheaply and sell expensively (often making many times the original price paid for the produce). It also enabled them to entrench themselves in a position where they could have a say in local politics and trade without unduly having to risk malaria and other endemic illness. Thus the system had its benefits where both parties were concerned.

Apart from the payment of trust, European traders often gave Efik chiefs a 'dash'[63] (or tip) as reward for their services. The dash was intended by them to sustain the chief's goodwill. Antera Duke's diary contains innumerable examples of these dash payments. The dash was seldom paid in money, but generally consisted of a puncheon of rum, a quantity of tobacco or an assortment of several marketable articles. It was paid before the trade transactions commenced. Smith states that it was an important aspect of trading to know how to make presents judiciously.[64]

In addition to these payments, all European ships had to pay a duty to Efik kings for the privilege of trading. It was known as comey (perhaps derived from 'custom').[65] The quantity of comey to be paid was calculated by the capacity of the vessel and was a considerable source of revenue. Part of it was expended by the Calabar kings on maintaining good relations with those communities which might interrupt trade links with the hinterland markets— it was the king's duty to keep the peace so that trade could prosper —and the rest was shared between the leading Efik traders. Europeans who paid comey viewed it as a payment which safeguarded their vessels and trade against molestation or interference. The proportion of comey paid to the various Efik kings at different times is a good indication of the value of trade done by each town with the European traders. It also illustrates the power position of these towns vis-à-vis one another. It was only after the payment of these various dues that trade could commence.

The dependence upon the European traders as a source of political and economic power over the rest of their countrymen made for intense commercial and political rivalry between the various etubom and kings. As a result of the trade arrangement described above, only the etubom and the kings had direct relations with the European traders. While the etubom supervised the trade of his own house, the king regulated the trade of the house and the town from which he came.

It has been earlier noted that in Calabar certain lineages grew more rapidly than others. The European traders appointed the king from among the members of the lineage who did most trade with them. The favoured lineage was generally the largest one in the town. The lineage from whence the king came was known as the 'royal lineage'. Thus in the nineteenth century, the Duke lineage (and more particularly the Offiong Okoho lineage) was the royal lineage of Duke Town, and the Eyo lineage enjoyed a similar honour in Creek Town. This system of royal lineages was highly unrealistic in that the traditional political philosophy of the Efik accepted every family born of a free stock as a royal family. In Duke Town there were more lineages than there were in Creek Town, and the result was that tension between lineages was correspondingly greater in the former than it was in the latter. For this reason the political evolution of Duke Town differed from that of Creek Town.

The title 'king' owed itself to European traders. It must be noted that contrary to other views on the subject, the position of a head of the town, whatever he may be called, was traditional in Efik society. Each of the larger Efik towns had a head. He was designated 'king' by the European traders; it is untrue, therefore, to state that the position was entirely untraditional to Efik polity. With the development of trade, the title was more than an honorific one used in recognition of the de facto power of the heads of the towns. But the title carried no implications of monarchy. A trader, Grant, was quoted to have stated that Duke Ephraim, one of the greatest traders of Calabar at the beginning of the nineteenth century, preferred to use the title 'Duke' because he considered it higher and more expressive of power than that of 'king'.[66]

While lineages rivalled each other for trade and wealth, towns manœuvred amongst themselves to cripple their rivals and gain dominance over the trade of the river. The jockeying for political power and monopolistic control over European trade was naturally more pronounced during a period of general trade depression. Until further work on the slave trade is done, it might be safely concluded on the strength of available surviving manifests of slave vessels that the closing decades of the eighteenth century constituted one such period.

The reasons for the decline of Calabar as a slave port may be briefly surmised. It was said that the English in the West Indies regarded slaves from Calabar as rebellious, and therefore preferred the Fanti of the Gold Coast.[67] In particular, slaves of Efik or Ibibio origin were notorious for their ferocity. However, there are two other more plausible reasons for the decline of Calabar as a slave port. One could have been the high comey charged there for vessels using the harbour. Figures are only available for the early nineteenth century. Adams estimated the value of the Bonny comey at about £150 a vessel compared with £250 at Calabar.[68] On account of these exorbitant duties Calabar lost its share of the slave trade to Bonny.[69] The other plausible reason for the decline of the slave trade at Calabar was that, with the cessation of inter-tribal conflict on the Rio Real, Kalabari and Bonny were able to supply slaves more speedily and in greater quantities than Calabar.[70]

It is significant that the decline of the slave trade in Calabar coincided with an increase in the rivalry between the major trading settlements. In 1767 there was strong competition between the English ports of Bristol and Liverpool in the trade to the coast of Africa. A letter from Calabar dated 12 August, 1767 described the scarcity of slaves at Calabar and its results:

We had a tolerable good passage of three weeks and five days. There are now seven large vessels in the river, each of which expects to purchase 500 slaves, and I imagine there was seldom ever known a greater scarcity of slaves than at present, and these few chiefly from the low country. The natives are at variance with each other, and in my opinion, it will never be ended before the destruction of all the people at Old Town, who have taken the lives of many a fine fellow . . . I now flatter myself, I shall be an assistant in revenging the just cause of every poor Englishman that have innocently suffered by them.[71]

In that year the jealousy between Old Town and Duke Town reached its crescendo. Old Town, by virtue of being the first Efik settlement on the mainland, claimed monopoly over the trade of the coast. It wanted to receive all comey paid by European vessels and was determined that Duke Town should trade with Europeans only through it. Duke Town, which had been established after Old Town, was, however, far more populous than Old Town and refused to trade through the latter town. Duke Town desired to overthrow the monopoly of Old Town and to receive comey payments from the European traders. A plan was said to have been arranged between Duke Town and the commanders of vessels that lay in the river to destroy Old Town.[72] The vessels were the *Indian Queen*, *Duke of York*, *Nancy*, and *Concord* of Bristol, the *Edgar* of Liverpool, and the *Canterbury* of London. The captains of these vessels were quite willing to strengthen their position and destroy Old Town's efforts to entrench itself in a monopolistic position vis-à-vis European traders.

On the invitation of Duke Town, therefore, the commanders of the vessels jointly sent several letters to the inhabitants of Old Town, and particularly to Ephraim Robin John, the principal chief of the town. In these letters the European merchants stated their readiness to arbitrate between the two towns if the inhabitants of Old Town came on board. The Old Town people were offered security and protection. Having no idea as to the real purpose of this hospitality, the inhabitants of Old Town joyfully accepted the invitation. The three brothers of the chief, Ephraim Robin John, and twenty-seven other persons, sailed in nine canoes to the *Indian Queen*. They were dispatched from thence to the *Edgar* and afterwards to the *Duke of York*. In the meantime, the people on board the other canoes were either distributed on board, or on canoes lying close to the ships. The crew of the *Duke of York*, aided by the captain and mates, and armed with offensive weapons, fell upon their unsuspecting guests and chained them. Their canoes were sunk, and the attendants either seized and killed, or drowned. The other ships repeated these atrocious acts. Duke Town inhabitants, who had hidden themselves in the bushes by the waterside, embarked in their canoes and butchered the people of Old Town when they tried to get away. About three hundred inhabitants of Old Town lost their lives. The Duke Town people obtained the principal chief of Old Town from the Europeans by exchanging him for a slave, and decapitated him. The brothers of the chiefs and the attendants who were captured were sold into slavery.[73] This sale of the Old Town people destroys the Efik claim that they never sold a fellow Efik into slavery.

The destruction of Old Town in 1767 left Duke Town and Creek Town the principal trading settlements of Calabar, and the foci of trade on the river. As the dominant middlemen, it was through them that all the inland trade in guns and merchandize passed. They waxed strong and powerful and were able to play the tyrant over the hinterland. The coastal city states which emerged as most successful were those whose wealth enabled them to make the greatest use of firearms. There is no mention of the import of gunpowder and firearms into Calabar at about 1670, when Dapper and Barbot wrote their accounts, and it may therefore be supposed that the imports first took place after this date.

It was through this trade in and use of firearms that Eyo Nsa of Creek Town was able to establish himself as one of the greatest traders and rise to the position of king. Eyo Nsa, an extremely brave man, won his title of King Eyo I[74] after his heroic victories over the enemies of the Efik, in particular the Adiadia people who claimed to be the original inhabitants of Creek Town. He also destroyed pirates who seized Efik canoes which went up river for trade. It was also under Eyo's stern rule that one part of the Cobham family which had been engaged in a dispute with him left Creek Town for Duke Town. Contemporary accounts state that Creek Town prospered because it had the 'best and most indefatigable' traders.[75]

The centralization of power at Duke Town

In 1814, following the death of Eyamba III, there ascended to the throne of Duke Town one of the most illustrious kings of Calabar, the Great Duke Ephraim (Effiom Edem Ekpo Effiom). The greatest trader in Duke Town, he soon aspired to a monopoly of the trade with Europeans over all Calabar. He came to the throne at a time when the transition from the slave trade to the oil trade was taking place. He exploited the new trade fully and set about first to consolidate his position within Duke Town. He ruled that all houses in Duke Town which traded with Europeans should henceforth do so through him. In addition, he gave out loans to his people to engage in the oil trade and market their produce through him. He also bought up all the grades of Ekpe, including the eyamba title, and entrenched himself in a powerful position not only with his own people but with European supercargoes as well. All trade was conducted through him, and any attempt to evade doing so met with stern action. The Duke family, for instance, quarrelled with the Henshaws who then lived along the present Marina (site of Cobham Town). The Henshaws had wanted to remain outside the Great Duke's trading system. The immediate cause for the quarrel is generally related to the erection of certain pillars in the ndem Efik shrine,[76] but there can be little doubt that what stimulated the conflict was the trade system.

The Great Duke attempted to subject the oil producing towns of the Cross River to his intimidation and control. He sent up armed vessels to force oil out of the inhabitants and sold it to the Europeans. He did not permit his position as a middleman to be undermined by allowing Europeans to settle on the coast, much less undertake exploratory voyages into the hinterland where the oil markets were located. These markets were at Ikpah, Nwaniba, Ifiseyon, Umon, Itu, Enyong, Akunakuna and Ikot Anang (see frontispiece). Trading sheds, erected by the river bank at strategic points, collected the oil from neighbouring peoples and stored it till the canoes arrived to take it away.[77] The canoes that were used to sail up to the markets, differed in size and capacity for storing oil and were managed by about thirty pullers each (chiefly slaves).

Both Duke Town and Creek Town grew rapidly in size, wealth and importance compared with other Efik towns. Both were near good anchorages and were the chief depôts for the slave and oil trade. Like Eyo I in Creek Town, who earned his name 'Honesty' on account of his integrity and fair dealing in trade, the Great Duke, too, was meticulously careful in his relations with European traders. The latter, too, respected and feared his influence over his tradesmen. For this reason, the European traders were careful to retain the goodwill and patronage of the kings. They gave Eyo two additional coppers for the oil he sold.[78] To Duke Ephraim, described as 'one of the most powerful chiefs on the western coast of Africa',[79] they gave one-third more than they did for oil bought from others and also provided him with a better assortment of trade goods.

With the development of these towns, the centralization of political power in Calabar moved a stage further. Having consolidated his position in Duke Town, the Great Duke Ephraim set about declaring his sovereignty over all Calabar. He could achieve this only by defeating the wealthy Eyo I, his rival in Creek Town. The Great Duke, therefore, used his position as eyamba to bring a trumped-up charge against Eyo and hauled him up before Ekpe to answer it. It was alleged that Eyo I was not of royal birth and was not, therefore, entitled to be king of Creek Town. Eyo I had, however, been given as wife a girl from the royal Ambo family.

But Duke Ephraim urged that this did not make Eyo I royal. What exactly was meant by 'royal' in this case is not clear. Ekpe never- theless proceeded to fine Eyo I an enormous sum of money and reduce his wealth and power by that means.[80] There is no doubt that the facts represented by Ekpe are subject to debate. The real reason for destroying Eyo I in this manner was, of course, to cripple him financially so that his position in the politics and trade of Calabar would thereby be weakened.

After the destruction of the economic and political viability of first Old Town, and then of Creek Town, Duke Town emerged as the most dominant trading settlement in Calabar during the period. The political power of Calabar was centralized at Duke Town under the Great Duke, who was at this time between forty and fifty years of age.[81] Later kings and European traders in Calabar looked back upon the reign of the Great Duke with nostalgia, characterizing it as the golden epoch of Calabar history.

The colonization of the hinterland

One of the great achievements of Great Duke Ephraim was that he initiated the colonization of the immediate hinterland of Calabar. The hinterland referred to is that area lying behind Calabar called Akpabuyo and Odukpani.[82] Oral testimonies (our main source)[83] which relate the way in which Akpabuyo, the larger and more im- portant of the two areas, was discovered to be fertile are interesting. It is said that a fisherman named Ayai Iyo, an Idua from Oron living close to the area had, once, while fishing in an adjoining river, carelessly thrown on the land the skin of a coco yam; to his amazement, he discovered several days later that this had grown into healthy roots. He then excitedly rushed to King Eyamba III (Egbo Young Offiong) bearing the coco yam. However, it was under the aegis of the next ruler, the Great Duke, that the coloniza- tion of the area may be said to have really begun.[84]

The Great Duke forthwith invited all the Efik houses in Calabar to occupy as much land as they desired at Akpabuyo. The call began a movement imbued with something resembling the Ameri- can frontier spirit of the early nineteenth century. Each house sent forth its men by canoes and on foot, in large and small companies, to stake their claims to any extent of land. Land thus claimed was to be the right of the founding houses, and each house cordoned off and demarcated its area by fences; it became recognized as, for example, Duke land, Eyo land, Obutong land, Cobham land. There was practically no house in Calabar which did not make the 'pilgrimage' to Akpabuyo.

It is difficult to account for this rush to the hinterland. One theory is that the new land gave promise of a large area of palm trees which could be tapped. At a time when the slave trade was declining and Bonny was becoming a great slave market, it made good sense for Calabar to move into the oil trade. It must be noted that the Efik and other communities had for long dealt also in the products of the soil. Palm oil had been exported from Calabar alongside slaves for a long time. Adam estimated in 1823 that Calabar exported annually 700–800 tons of palm oil, besides barwood.[85]

Another theory is that the new land was meant primarily for growing foodstuff. It is not known whether there was a general increase in the price of foodstuff at about this time; however, the planting of coco yam related in the tradition above might have a symbolic significance. But whether the first instinct was to gather oil for export or grow staple necessities for consumption, there is no doubt that eventually both were done. Staple food items such as yam, coco yam, coconuts and maize were said to have been grown while oil was extracted from the palm trees that grew wild as in most other parts of the Cross River and Ibibio land.[86]

A third theory is that the colonization of the hinterland was prompted by the need to find work for slaves after the abolition of the traffic in human cargo. The kings of Calabar intimated to the traders and missionaries prior to and in 1846 that the surplus slaves, left in the Calabar towns following the Anti-Slave Treaty, had to be profitably employed in agriculture. The colonization of the hinterland was one way in which this could be done.

The chief labour force on the newly acquired 'plantations',[87] which were probably established circa 1830 (Duke Ephraim died in 1834), consisted of slaves. The slaves who were sent away into the plantations were among those who were bought from the interior for sale to European slave traders. Since the more manpower a house possessed the greater was its ability to occupy and farm land, it is possible that those slaves who could not be sold for various reasons, or incorrigible slaves, were the first to be sent to labour on the plantations. Houses like Duke house, which had more slaves, were able to occupy more land than others. In the absence of statistics, it is impossible to ascertain either the acreages held by each house, or the number of slaves who were thus sent.

It must be remembered that the trade in palm oil (which developed with the slave trade) was at this time neither regular nor considerable. The general demand for palm oil in England at this time was low, and the prospects for its development in the early nineteenth century appeared unpromising. Individual shipments were usually less than ten casks or puncheons, even in the middle of the oil season.[88] However, the high price which was being offered in Europe for the commodity during the years of the Napoleonic Wars—about £60 a ton—encouraged greater efforts to export the oil.[89] At the same time, the competition offered to Calabar by the increased export of slaves by Bonny (which was more suitably situated for the slave trade) encouraged Calabar chiefs to increase their export of oil. But the fact that the oil trade in the Bights was in the hands of private European merchants from the start, and the imposition of high import taxes on it in England in the war years,[90] arrested its development. It was not until the 1830s, with the expansion of manufacturing in Europe, that any large demand for tropical commodities was created. Hitherto an end product in itself, the palm oil was now used as raw material in several large industries, for example, in the making of tin plating, soap, confectioneries, candles.[91] Also in the 1830s legitimate trade, hitherto left to merchants to establish, became the concern of both philanthropists and the British Government.

The result of these developments on the Calabar economy was far reaching. Palm oil was a commodity increasingly sought after by slave trading Europeans; and although it was not till the 1850s that the expected increase in the oil trade took place, the demand for it was nevertheless not falling.[92] Palm trees which grew wild at Akpabuyo now had a cash value and oil fetched good prices. Though the export of slaves was generally more profitable than that of oil, Calabar found it highly profitable to export both commodities, the main source for oil being the plantation areas, the Cross River and Ibibio land. After 1841, however, the export trade of Calabar was predominantly in oil. The transition from slave- to oil-exporting produced much social and political change in Calabar and it is to this that attention must now be directed.

REFERENCES

1   The names Calabar or Old Calabar were not applied to the Cross River till the Dutch maps of the seventeenth century. The earliest mention of Calabar occurs in an account by John Watts in 1668 entitled *A true relation of inhuman and unparalleled actions and barbarous murders of negroes or moors, committed on three Englishmen in Old Calabar in Guiney.* The next reference occurs in the table of a ship's cargo of slaves sold in the Leeward Islands in 1681 by the Royal African Company, where £8 9s. 9d. a head was paid for seventy-four 'Old Calabar negroes and many women'.

2   J. Barbot, *A Description of the Coasts of North and South Guinea*, Book 4, pp. 382–83.

3   It is said that the Qua got their name from the Portuguese traders who called them thus after one of the chiefs Oqua, with whom they opened trade negotiations. Okwa is still a common name among the

people of Qua Town. In Efik, Qua Town is called Akwa Obio (Big Town). See also D. Forde and G. I. Jones, *The Ibo and Ibibio-speaking Peoples of South-Eastern Nigeria*, Ethnographic Survey of Africa, Part 2 (London, 1962), p. 90.

4   The Intelligence Report on the Qua, while agreeing that they originally came from the forest areas of Ekoi country, states that they left their old homes on account of local warfare and scarcity of food; E. C. Alderton, 'A Report on the Qua Clan', contained in N. Mylius, 'A Report on the Calabar Division with special references to the Efik Clan', dated 5 March, 1932; C.S.O. 26/3, file No. 27627, Vol. 2.

5   His Highness Ntoe Ika Oqua II, interview, 18 November, 1965; and Chief E. Imona, *Chieftaincy in Calabar, the Status of Big Qua Town and the Origin of Akim Qua Town*, p. 9.

6   Vide also M. D. W. Jeffreys, 'Some Notes on the Ekoi', *The Journal of the Royal Anthropological Institute*, Vol. 69, 1939.

7   Although the Ntoe was generally a male, the trader Hutchinson states that between 1850 and 1854 the 'kingdom of Qua' was governed by a queen, who was a sister of the former king; T. J. Hutchinson, *Impressions of Western Africa*, p. 128. Vide also Waddell, *Journals*, Vol. 8, entry for 1 July, 1850, p. 20.

8   Vide E. C. Alderton, 'A Report on the Efut fragments in the Calabar Division with special reference to their representation in the Efik Native Authority', dated 21 January, 1933, in Mylius, op. cit.

9   His Highness Muri Edet and natural rulers of Efut, interview 6 December, 1965.

10 M. H. Kingsley, *West African Studies*, Appendix I, 'A Short Description of the Natives of the Niger Coast Protectorate with some account of their customs, religion, trade, etc.', by M. De Comte C. N. Cardi, p. 566. Cardi claimed to have quoted from tradition.

11 Vide *Report of the Enquiry into the Dispute over the Obongship of Calabar*, by A. K. Hart. This report is hereafter referred to as *The Hart Report*; M. D. W. Jeffreys, *Old Calabar and Notes on the Ibibio Language*, also A. E. Afigbo, 'Efik Origin and Migrations Reconsidered', *Nigeria Magazine*, No. 87, December, 1965, pp. 267–280; and a review of the article by M. D. W. Jeffreys, 'Efik Origin', *Nigeria Magazine*, No. 91, December, 1966, pp. 297–299.

12 Vide D. C. Simmons, 'An Ethnographic Sketch of the Efik People', in D. Forde (ed.), *Efik Traders of Old Calabar*, p. 3.

13 There is some linguistic proof that Efik is a dialect of the Ibibio language, and that it separated from the other only within the last few centuries. Simmons notes that a comparison of 195 Ibibio and Efik words on the Swadesh basic vocabulary list revealed 189 cognates (95.89%), and that this high percentage indicates recent separation of the two languages; D. Simmons, 'An Ethnographic Sketch of the Efik People', in D. Forde, op. cit., p. 2. For linguistic references, vide H. Goldie, *Principles of Efik Grammar and Specimens of the Language*; I. C. Ward, *The Phonetic and Tonal Structure of Efik*; D. Westermann and M. A. Bryan, *The Languages of West Africa*, where the Ibibio-Efik group is shown to have six dialects; J. Greenberg, 'Studies in African Linguistic Classification, I. The Niger-Congo Family', *Southwestern Journal of Anthropology*, Vol. 5 (1949), pp. 78–100, where Efik is classified in the Central Branch (Cross River Langu-

ages) of the Niger-Congo family; and M. D. W. Jeffreys, *Old Calabar* et seq., which is a study of Efik and Ibibio.

14   The missionaries state that they found the Efik calling themselves not Efik but Eburutu Efik. H. Goldie, *Efik Grammar* et seq., p. 58. Vide also M. D. W. Jeffreys, *Old Calabar* et seq., p. 26n.

15   J. Barbot, *A Description of the Coasts of North and South Guinea*, Book 4, p. 383.

16   Ibid., pp. 381–82, 465.

17   P. A. Talbot places the date of this migration at c. 1650; P. A. Talbot, *The Peoples of Southern Nigeria*, Vol. 1, p. 185. This dates does not, however, agree with de Cardi's observations.

18   For the genealogical relationship of the families to other Efik families see Appendix A, in this volume. Chief Ene Ndem Efik Duke, interview, 4 December, 1965.

19   See pp. 10–11.

20   K. Onwuke Dike, *Trade and Politics in the Niger Delta, 1830–1885*, p. 31.

21   G. I. Jones, *The Trading States of the Oil Rivers*, pp. 192–93.

22   Ibid.

23   Ibid., pp. 194–96.

24   Ibid., p. 205.

25   Ibid., p. 55.

26   G. I. Jones and D. Forde, op. cit., p. 91.

27   For a detailed discussion of Efik lineages vide G. I. Jones, 'The Political Organization of Old Calabar' in D. Forde (ed.), *Efik Traders* et seq.

28   M. D. W. Jeffreys, *Old Calabar* et seq., pp. 56–59.

29   Vide *The Hart Report*, Chapter 16, which deals with the question of deposition of an etubom.

30   G. I. Jones, *Trading States* et seq., pp. 55–57; vide also his *Report of the Position, Status and Influence of Chiefs and Natural Rulers in the Eastern Region of Nigeria*, p. 36; and his review of K. O. Dike, *Trade and Politics* et seq., in *Africa*, Vol. 27, No. 1, January, 1957, p. 84.

31   G. I. Jones, *Trading States* et seq., p. 56.

32   The wealth criteria which the Efik political system stressed does not seem to have been important in the Qua system. There have been Ntoe who were too poor to have houses of their own; Chief Asuquo Edet Okon, interview, 25 November, 1965.

33   Chief Asuquo Edet Okon, interview, 25 November, 1965.

34   P. A. Talbot, *The Peoples of Southern Nigeria*, Vol. 3, p. 779; Jones, 'Political Organization' et seq., p. 136.

35   It was only when a member had reached this grade that he was considered fully initiated into Ekpe, following which he normally wore a peacock feather in his hat.

36   Chief Ene Ndem Ephraim Duke, interview, 9 December, 1965; Effiom Ukpong Aye, interviews, 17 and 21 January, 1966.

37   Antera Duke diary, in D. Forde, (ed.) op. cit., entry for 31 August, 1787, p. 59.

38   Holman, *Travels in Madiera, Sierra Leone, etc.*, p. 392.

39   H. M. Waddell, *Twenty-Nine Years in the West Indies and Central Africa*, p. 313.

40   T. J. Hutchinson, *Impressions* et seq., p. 141.

41 *The Hart Report*, p. 54.
42 Antera Duke's diary, in D. Forde (ed.) *Efik Traders* et seq., entry for 31 August, 1787, p. 59. Afaw was probably Efik for ifan (ofo) or 'slave'.
43 Holman, op. cit., p. 392.
44 H. M. Waddell, *Twenty-Nine Years* et seq., p. 313.
45 Chief Etim Ekpenyong, interviews, 1 and 3 December, 1965.
46 H. M. Waddell, *Twenty-Nine Years* et seq., p. 313.
47 Holman, op. cit., pp. 392–93.
48 For details of the agreement, which throws light on the nature of non-Efik membership of the Ekpe, vide *The Hart Report*, pp. 59–60.
49 Chief Ene Ndem Ephraim Duke, interview, 23 November, 1965.
50 Udo Ema, 'The Ekpe Society', *Nigeria*, Vol. 16, 1938, p. 316.
51 Ekpe was divided into the following branches. Creek Town and Old Town each had its own Ekpe shed. Duke Town had to share a lodge with Creek Town because it was not one of the original Efik settlements in the sense Creek Town and Old Town were.
52 Chief Ene Ndem Ephraim Duke, interview, 23 November, 1965; *The Hart Report*, p. 57.
53 H. M. Waddell, *Twenty-Nine Years* et seq., pp. 448, 580, 591.
54 Chief Michael Henshaw, interview, 19 January, 1966; Waddell, *Twenty-Nine Years* et seq., p. 265, describes an occasion when some 'persons of consequence' from a 'far away country' had come to purchase Ekpe honours at Calabar.
55 G. I. Jones, 'Political Organization' et seq., pp. 142–3.
56 H. M. Waddell, *Twenty-Nine Years* et seq., pp. 503; vide also T. J. Hutchinson, *Impressions* et seq., p. 143.
57 G. I. Jones, 'Political Organization' et seq., p. 146.
58 Vide Chapter 2.
59 For a full treatment of these relationships, see the excellent account of John Beattie, *Other Cultures*, passim, but principally chapters 7 and 9.
60 T. J. Hutchinson, *Impressions* et seq., p. 257.
61 Bold, *The Merchants and Mariners African Guide*, p. 75.
62 M. Kingsley, *West African Studies*, pp. 627–628. The reference to monetary currency shows that from an early period the trade was not based on barter. Bardot gives the value in copper bars of articles brought by European slavers as follows: 1 iron bar was equivalent to 4 copper bars; 1 bunch of beads to 4; 5 rangoes to 4; 1 tankard to 3; 1 basin to 4; 1 yard of linen to 1; 6 knives to 1; 1 brass bell to 3. The prices of slaves, also given in terms of copper rods, ranged between the following: men, between 40 to 48 per head; women, between 28 to 36 per head; boys, between 20 to 40 per head; and girls, between 17 to 30 per head, Barbot, op. cit., p. 465.
    For a typical slaver's account in the eighteenth century see, E. Donnan, *Documents Illustrative of the History of the Slave Trade to America*, Vol. 2, p. 529.
63 Winwood Reade, *Savage Africa*, p. 22, derives the origin of the word 'dash' from the Portuguese 'das-me' (give me). Hugh Crow in his *Memoirs*, p. 276, states that a more probable, albeit speculative, etymon would be the English 'dash of rum' since this was usually given to the African traders by European ships.
64 J. Smith, *Trade and Travels in the Gulf of Guinea*, p. 187 and p. 193

for articles generally solicited by chiefs, head slaves or pilots of
vessels.

65 T. J. Hutchinson, *Ten Years' Wanderings Among the Ethiopians*,
p. 18.

66 Hugh Crow, *Memoirs of the late Captain Hugh Crow of Liverpool*,
p. 272.

67 E. Donnan, *Documents Illustrative of the History of the Slave
Trade to America*, Vol. 1, p. 108. M. Cowley and D. P. Mannix
discuss the changing likes and dislikes of slave buyers in *Black
Cargoes: a history of the Atlantic slave trade, 1815–1865.*

68 H. Crow, op. cit., p. 43; Capt. J. Adams, *Remarks on the country
extending from Cape Palmas to the River Congo*, p. 245 and p. 248.

69 J. Adams, op. cit., p. 143.

70 Ibid., p. 253; G. I. Jones, *Trading States* et seq., p. 46.

71 G. Williams, *History of the Liverpool Privateers*, p. 535. The massacre of Old Town described here relies upon the account given of the
incident by G. Williams, op. cit., pp. 536–38. Also, Capt. J. B. Walker,
'Note on the Old Calabar and Cross Rivers', *Proceedings of the
Royal Geographical Society*, Vol. 16, 1871–72, p. 136. One informant,
Chief Ene Ndem Ephraim Duke, recalled a book written by a European entitled *Tappe Tappe*, which is said to contain a vivid account
of the massacre, and of Tom Robin of Old Town. This publication
could not, however, be traced.

72 G. Williams, op. cit., pp. 536–37.

73 Vide ibid., pp. 537–38.

74 Some informants point out that Eyo Nsa was not king since he did not
belong to the royal family. See pp. 27–28.

75 Bold, op. cit., p. 79.

76 Chief Joseph Ewa Henshaw, interviews, 10 December and 14 December, 1965.

77 Chief Michael E. Henshaw, interview, 18 November, 1965.

78 Bold, op. cit., pp. 78–79.

79 H. Crow, op. cit., p. 272.

80 At his request the informant's name has been withheld; vide also
H. M. Waddell, *Twenty-Nine Years* et seq., p. 310.

81 H. Crow, op. cit., p. 272.

82 Akpabuyo lies fifteen or twenty miles from Calabar, and is close to
the town of Ikot Nakanda. Odukpani is situated about the fifteenth
mile stone on the Odukpani road, which continues northwards to
join the roads to Afikpo and to Enugu. Tradition has it that the word
'Akpabuyo' is derived from the words 'akpe' which meant 'river'
while 'abuyo' was probably derived from the name of the fisherman.

83 Chief Ene Ndem Ephraim Duke, interview, 23 November, 1965; Chief
Etim Ekpenyong, interviews, 1 December and 3 December, 1965.

84 The story is told that the Great Duke killed Ayai Iyo in order to
keep from others the secret about the land. There is an Efik proverb
which goes 'Generosity killed Ayai Iyo'.

85 J. Adams, *Remarks* et seq., p. 143 and p. 247.

86 Anne Martin, *The Oil Palm Economy of the Ibibio Farmer*, p. 9.

87 Whether the term 'plantation' or 'farm' or 'farm settlement' best
describes these areas is a matter of preference.

88 P. J. Maguire, *Liverpool Trade List, 1801–1804*, Vol. 1, (1801), p. 147,
cited in N. H. Stilliard, 'The Rise and Development of Legitimate

trade in Palm Oil with West Africa', unpublished M.A. thesis, Birmingham, October, 1938, p. 9.

89 *Parl. Pap.*, 1816, Vol. 6 (506), p. 12.

90 The European merchants in England complained that the import tax on oil, £6 6s. 8d. per ton, was exorbitant and only allowed a narrow margin of profit; *Parl. Pap.*, 1816, Vol. 6 (506), p. 13.

91 Vide Greaves, 'Modern Production Amongst Backward Peoples', *Studies in Economics and Commerce*, L.S.E., No. 5 (London, 1935), p. 24, cited in N. H. Stilliard, op. cit., p. 12.

92 Figures for the import of palm oil into the United Kingdom between 1830–1853 may be gleaned from the *Parl. Pap.*, 1845, Vol. 46 (187), which shows the annual import into the U.K. from West Africa, 1790–1844, and from *Parl. Pap.*, 1854, Vol. 45 (296), which covers the period 1844–53. As these figures are collectively for West Africa, it is not possible to ascertain what the Calabar contribution toward the aggregates was. See figures in N. H. Stilliard, op. cit., p. 60.

II

Social Change, 1841–56

Missionary literature available for the period 1841–1856 tends to give the misleading impression that social change and development in Calabar was primarily due to missionary enterprise. In reality, however, the effect of missionary work was limited for a number of reasons. It is the argument of this chapter that the most far-reaching changes in Calabar in the nineteenth century are the result of factors set in motion in the internal structure of society largely by changes in the economy. The transition from slave to oil trade as the primary export commodity, carried through without great dislocation to the economic life of the community, was attended by remarkable social and political developments. These changes did not often proceed in the way one would have expected. Calabar became a 'closed' society. It left room for wealthy town slaves to acquire importance within the houses; but at the same time people became more status conscious. These social developments are discussed in this chapter, while the political developments during the period are examined in the next chapter.

The Scottish Presbyterian missionaries and Sierra Leone emigrants, whose importance is by no means denied, came to Calabar at a time when Efik society was being restructured. They spent most of their time discussing the very issues which troubled men's minds, notably the increase in wealth which the oil trade brought to Efik middlemen. The achievements and failures of the Presbyterian Church may be interpreted in relation to the undercurrents of social change brought about by the internal factors.

Naturally, it was a period of strain and stress in the social system even if the economy was not unduly dislocated, a period when far reaching changes proceeded rapidly in certain areas of traditional life. Such social conflicts provided some opportunity for missionary endeavour: certain changes were conceded, but the most notable effect was the growth of witchcraft filling gaps which Christianity was not adapted to fill.

Structural change engendered by the oil trade

The period of transition from the slave to the oil trade cannot be established with any chronological precision. All that we know is that in Calabar the slave trade began to diminish in importance by the last quarter of the eighteenth century, and oil began to be shipped early in the nineteenth century. The transition, which must have begun sometime during this period, was, however, completed with the colonization of the hinterland plantations of Akpabuyo and Odukpani and with the increase in oil exports from Calabar in the early nineteenth century.

The transition to the oil economy was attended by remarkable structural changes in the society. It gave genesis to a differentiation between two categories of slaves. One, consisting largely of the 'floating' Ibo and Ibibio slave population left over in the various towns following the transition to the oil trade, was sent to the hinterland plantations to provide the labour force necessary for the collection and transportation of the oil. The greatest need of the houses in the days of the oil trade was manpower. Men had to be employed to collect the oil and handle the transport of the bulky produce to the markets that had sprung up along the rivers. From these collecting points the oil had to be taken by canoes to the coast. The more helpers a house mobilized, the greater was its ability to meet the increasing demands for oil at the coast and the greater its assurance of success in competing with other houses for the same. As a matter of expediency and sound economic planning, the slave population was rapidly mobilized and absorbed into the new economic milieu.

The other category of slaves consisted of those who stayed on in the towns and who were employed by the house heads to prosecute the trade at the coast. The town-dwelling slaves who became traders, unlike their plantation-dwelling brothers who were engaged in agricultural pursuits, were rapidly absorbed into the membership of the houses. They also enjoyed a measure of close relationship with the free agnates of the houses. The difference between the rate at which these two categories of slaves were assimilated into the social structure provides the essential clue to an understanding of the social forces operative in Calabar society in the middle of the nineteenth century. It was the dissatisfaction engendered by the social dichotomy which accounted, for instance, for the upheavals of the early 1850s.

The structure of Efik society was further complicated by the incorporation of 'strangers' into the houses. These were persons who had done homage to the free head or any other important free member of a family. Many of them were not Efik by blood relationship, nor were they slaves bought by Efik slave holders. They were persons who had voluntarily settled in Calabar, and attached themselves to one of the powerful Efik nobles in order to obtain security for their persons and property.

Incorporation of slaves and stranger elements into the membership of the houses was a revolutionary development. The houses had originally consisted only of the immediate family, dependents of the headmen and of adult kinsmen. But with the transition to oil export, the houses became increasingly heterogenous and cosmopolitan in nature. The term ekpuk (or lineage), which was used to express blood relationship, virtually disappeared among the Efik, and was replaced by the term ufok, as a considerable proportion of the population was no longer related by blood. Consequently, the Efik began to speak of themselves as members of a particular house, meaning that they were born belonging to a specific person. This statement did not necessarily imply any blood relationship.[1]

Alongside the system of agnatic kinship, there grew up a hierarchy based on fictional kin relations. Slaves remained outside the traditional rank system (which was preserved by members of the agnatic lineage), but were related in a fictional way to the free agnates of the lineages. The master was referred to as 'father' (ete) and the wives of the master as 'mothers'. Use was made of the old idiom of blood ties and of descent from a single founder, but in reality the relationship was not deep. The emphasis in a system of fictional kin relationship was on 'social' rather than physiological fatherhood. The father of the house was not the real father of the slave, except in a 'social' sense. This distinction was of particular importance in a segmentary society organized on patrilineal lines like Calabar. In such a society, every man belonged to a specific descent group; a very high value was attached to any man who had a son or sons to carry on the line. But while stupid or lazy slaves were weeded out in the sorting machines of the house system, the more enterprising or intelligent were propelled to the top of the social scale. Nevertheless, all slaves shaved their heads in symbolic representation of dropping their old relationships and assuming new ones. Once they became members of the Efik households, they took on the names of their masters and lost their own. To some extent it was an expediency enabling the European traders to recognize which master or house a particular trader represented. But it was also symbolic of the social relationship between the master and the slave, which in some respects approximated to that between father and son. Though slaves came to bear Efik surnames they were not strictly Efik citizens, but their children born on Efik soil were accorded that status.

The houses in the days of the oil trade were therefore units of trade, not kinship units. The traditional structure of the house during the slave trade era was one based on kin relationship. Although etubom and individual members of the houses bought slaves to perform domestic chores, the latter were not considered as integral members of the households, which consisted almost exclusively of true agnates. In the days of the oil trade, although the same words formerly used to describe traditional kinship relationships were employed for the new fictional relationships, the social structure of Calabar had become far more complex.

The trade in oil, unlike the trade in slaves, was non capital-intensive. Wealth became an attribute of individual enterprise in that it could be acquired by all and sundry. The slave trade, if we are to accept Antera Duke's diary, was chiefly prosecuted by the nobles and other people played no active role in its conduct. The method by which the slave trade was carried on—the trust system —created a small group of merchants who enjoyed liberal credit with the European traders, and monopolized a tremendous amount of wealth and power. Antera Duke's diary has considerable evidence to show that the nobles were the heads of kin groups, or etubom, who headed the houses. The oil trade permitted wealth to be made and diffused among a larger group, and by the most able rather than by those who owed their wealth to their noble status. It was for this reason that the houses had deemed it advantageous to have as large a number of workers as possible.

The trading system of the houses was designed to increase the affluence of their members by a 'built in' system of incentives which ensured their economic prosperity. The provision of incentives was necessary, for the prosperity enjoyed, or misfortunes suffered by members had an effect on the economic situation of the house as a whole. Initially, slaves traded on behalf of their masters and received a part of the proceeds as reward. When a slave had, over a period of years, faithfully served his master by considerably fattening his treasury, the master showed his gratitude by permitting the slave to trade on his own account and keep all, or a large fraction of his income. In addition, slaves might be allowed to work on the family land and trade the proceeds at the markets. Alternatively, a portion of the land might be leased over to the slave who would be required to make a yearly tribute to the master in return for the right to continue farming on the land. The ownership of the land, however, was always vested in the house. There does not seem to have been any hard and fast rule in the economic relations between slaves and their masters, but the recognition that wealthy slaves were an asset to the masters was important, for it attached a special premium to rich slaves.[2] The trader A. A. Cowan wrote:

. . . the more intelligent the chief, the more he encouraged his followers to become traders on their own account. Every male, as he came to show promise, would receive a gift of so much trading cargo. If that was squandered he rarely got a second chance, but if, on the other hand, it was turned over with interest he would probably be set up in a larger way and have several slaves handed over to him as well as additional capital. The Head of the House took as much interest in seeing such hench men were well paid for their produce as in his own case. He actually benefited from the trade done by his adherents, but apart from any direct gain, the wise chief recognized that the more his people prospered, the stronger the House of which he was the Head.[3]

Wealthy slaves not only contributed to the wealth of the house by their talent in commerce, but also employed, as it were, a 'self propagating' mechanism to increase their own income and that of their house. This system consisted of the hiring or purchase of other slaves to work and trade on their behalf. All wealthy slaves had a host of other slaves employed by them to conduct their trade. These bought slaves of wealthy slaves were subject to the supreme master (the etubom) of the house to which they were attached. Their numbers increased the social esteem in which the etubom was held, for the existence of a large affluent slave population was an index not only of his own wealth and strength but also of his liberal and generous character.[4]

One important effect of the trading system of the houses in the nineteenth century was the growth of wealthy and influential slave and stranger elements in the Calabar towns. By virtue of the fact that they considerably outnumbered the free agnates of the houses to which they belonged,[5] they cast an enormous influence over the other members. The houses, in the nineteenth century, came to rely on the wealth of the slave and stranger elements, whose sheer numerical superiority was an indicator of prosperity and economic viability. The free members of the houses not only constituted a minority, but were often also the poorer section of the total membership. This position was particularly true of the larger houses such as the Duke house. The plausible explanation is that as more slaves were freed in Duke Town, the slave composition of the Duke house was greater in proportion to that of other houses.

Of the galaxy of important slave personages who are said to have emerged in the Duke house in the mid-nineteenth century, one of the most prominent was Iron Bar (otherwise called Coffee Edem Iron Bar Duke or Ekpo Edem). The name 'Iron Bar', says Coffee Edem's grandson, arose from an incident that took place on board a merchant vessel. The captain of the vessel, who was to supply

Edem with goods, lost his keys in the toss of a wave. He was, there-fore, unable to get the goods out of the locker. Edem broke open the iron bar of the goods store, and in appreciation of his strength, was nicknamed 'Iron Bar'. His wealth came from his trade in oil, blackwood and ivory from the Ekoi area. He also carved calabash and decorated brass trays which he imported from abroad. The story is told that his first master, the Great Duke, had allowed him the use of a large area (about 300 acres) at Akpabuyo for farm-ing. It is a measure of the territorial extent over which Iron Bar's influence held sway that five villages in the Calabar area looked to him as their leader. These villages were Ikot Ndakara, Ikot Edem, Ndakara Anwa Enang, Atimbo and Ikot Edet Archibong.[6] Another notable who achieved fame, but was not of free descent, was Black Davies (Effa Etim Effiom) of the house of the Great Duke.

It may be asked why, although slaves obviously enjoyed high social and economic status toward the end of the eighteenth cen-tury, that it was only in the 1850s that a powerful and rich class of slaves emerged in the Calabar towns. The practice of bestowing honours upon enterprising slaves, by creating for them the kind of situation necessary for the accumulation of wealth, had begun actively only in the days of the Great Duke. It must have taken a long time for a slave family to build up a reserve of wealth, as it was only by sheer work and keen commercial acumen that wealth could be accumulated. Heads of prosperous houses seldom inter-fered in the distribution of their slaves' property. The property of a dead slave, as a rule, went to his children who continued to stay in the father's compound and enjoyed or perpetuated the estate inherited. Over a period of time therefore, a slave descendant might inherit a vast estate and strive to accumulate more wealth for the next generation.

In the case of freemen, the prospect of capital accumulation was not as bright, for upon the death of the head of a family, his estate was rapidly divided into numerous parts and distributed among the several claimants. It will be noted in the next chapter how the vast estate of the Great Duke was rapidly parcelled out among the hundreds who laid claim to it. Large scale capital accumulation was prevented by the inheritance patterns of polygamous and egali-tarian systems. Success was attained through individual effort and rarely through the wealth of one's father. Achieved status re-mained, during one's lifetime, personal to its holder; it was shared with children but as there were generally many claimants the share of each was correspondingly reduced. The oldest child had the first share of movable property; land was, however, rarely divided between heirs. For this reason, a rich, inventive capitalist class composed of free citizens of the Duke house could not emerge. From such a situation, bedevilling the free class, the slaves greatly benefited. Having no challenge to their legitimacy, the slaves who became heads of certain of the Duke house families worked on the lands given them by the Great Duke; they even assumed the headship of certain Duke families. It is said, for instance, that the headship of the Effiom Edem family had been monopolized by slaves and not by blood relatives of Effiom Edem. The author has been told that this was also the case with the Umo Edem family of Duke house. The Queen Duke, sister of Effiom Edem and head of the Umo Edem family, died without issue. Her blood relatives tried to seize the headship of the family and to oust the slave element but this manœuvre failed, and since then the headship of the family has always remained with the descendants of the original 'slave' group. Similarly, Iron Bar was said to be at one time (though not without dispute) head of the Ekpo Edem family.

The Plantation Slaves

In contrast to the affluence of the town-dwelling slaves, those who were employed by the houses to work on their plantations at Akpabuyo and Odukpani remained relatively less prosperous. The plantation slaves, living and labouring as they did far away from the towns where the nobility resided, not only formed a separate community, but had little or no contact with the houses. Indeed, they were not incorporated into the membership of the houses in the way the town-dwelling slaves were, nothwithstanding the fact that the plantation slaves paid allegiance to the heads of houses and were subject to the nobility of the towns. They remained only as members of the lineage plantation settlements, cut off from European intercourse and trade, and without opportunities for raising themselves into the economic and social positions attained by many of the town dwelling slaves.

Such a situation would have been remedied earlier, but the slave workers in the lineage plantations had not organized themselves to rise as a compact body. At first, only outcasts and criminals were sent away to these plantations to provide the labour force, but by the middle of the nineteenth century the plantations had become much better organized. Each of the Calabar houses had their own farms at Akpabuyo, Qua, Odukpani and other areas. The houses appointed their village plantation heads from among the trusted slaves and charged them with the orderly conduct of the slaves who lived in barracks. Some of the plantation slaves were far more trusted (and trustworthy) than some of the blood descendants of freemen who lived in the plantations. The latter had no superior authority to act on their own accord, and had to solicit the favour of the village heads (always slaves) who acted as caretakers of the lineage plantations.

Also, it was not until the middle of the nineteenth century that a strong willed leader of great influence emerged among the slaves to give expression to their discontent. Such a man was Eyo Okun, the best known of a handful of other leaders of the Blood Society. So powerful was his position among the thousands of slaves belonging to the plantations of the Eyo household that the Eyo kings found it necessary to acknowledge his position by employing him as an adviser. The nobility neglected their slaves' views at their peril. There were instances in Efik history when the plantation slaves were summoned in order to defend a king or to save the life of a king when threatened, or to act as a decisive political force, but it must be noted that slaves never became involved in the political rivalries of their houses until they felt that their interests were endangered.[7] The Eyo house relied fully on Eyo Okun to manage its plantations. Further, Okun was an adviser and a power behind the throne of several Eyo kings of Creek Town. Not being free born, he could not, however, aspire to high political office.

A complex social system

The fact that the various houses came to depend upon slaves for their wealth and well-being was one of momentous importance in determining the social framework of Calabar society in the middle decades of the nineteenth century. The nobility, who had as a measure of expediency incorporated slave and stranger elements, were not, however, willing to sacrifice their superior social status. Thus, there was established an extraordinarily complex social system in which there were two sets of social values. In one classification a wealthy slave was socially accepted as a 'gentleman' and any manual worker a 'boy'. But alongside this classification a different gradation emerged. The members of the so-called 'royal families' maintained an attitude of superiority, based on birth, to the slave and ex-slave classes. Persons who were not able to trace their genealogy along agnatic kinship lines to the 'royalty' were deprived of the right to elect, or succeed to the office of kingship or heads of houses. But, as Jones points out, the fact that nobles alone could aspire to political office did not mean that only they were engaged in Efik politics. Wealthy slaves and others were also involved. Their names appear in treaties[8] and some of them were the most influential members in their houses and towns.[9] They often acted as advisers to the kings, and were permitted to become heads of families if there were no free agnates to succeed to the office. A slave, like a freeman, was a member of a corporate organization and 'the longer he remained in it, and the more closely he was able to identify his interests with those of his master and his master's lineage and in the general community', the more his status improved both within the lineage and in the general community.[10] But a rich slave, like Iron Bar, was never fully free, nor could he, as Waddell noted, deny the claim of his deceased master's family on him; but no one asserted it, and no one else dared call Iron Bar a slave.[11]

Thus one of the results of the social changes attending the altered economic position of the slave members of the houses was the emphasis that came to be placed by the nobility on status, rather than class (in the economic sense), as the determinant criterion of one's social standing. In the history of the relations between slave and free elements in Calabar, nothing has been of more decisive import than the way in which the Efik nobility tried to encourage a division of society based on birth. In the early twentieth century, this defence was given institutional expression by the creation of an 'Efik Royal Fraternity', an aristocratic movement drawing its membership only from those Efik who were thought to have lineal connection with any of the great founding fathers of the Efik.[12] And this was precisely at a time when economic factors were dictating greater integration of masters and slaves in the houses. Efik society became partially stratified into 'overlapping' divisions of free born and slave.[13]

The process of assimilation of slave elements into the lineage structure in Calabar was not completed either in the towns or, still less, in the plantations. This situation contrasted sharply with that in Kalabari (Owame, or New Calabar) and Bonny where attempts to integrate slaves with the rest of the community were more successful. To understand why the history of the relations between slaves and their masters in Calabar differed remarkably from that of her neighbours, it is necessary to refer briefly to the political history of the delta states in the nineteenth century. Bonny and Kalabari competed with each other for trade, with the result that these two states were always in a state of intensive military and economic rivalry. The effect of this fierce rivalry was of momentous importance in determining the nature of the house system. Though the Kalabari and Bonny houses may have begun like Calabar as corporate groups of kin tracing descent to common founders, in the eighteenth century they developed into what Jones has referred to as 'canoe houses'. The canoe was an expensive craft to maintain. Food had to be bought from the hinterland. The financial questions therefore had to be handled well. Funds derived from a system of house taxation, the work bars, customs bars and other revenue from trade, were administered by the chief to main-tain and expand the houses. If the chief failed to do this judiciously, he was, like King William Pepple of Bonny and his predecessor, deposed by the members of the house. Since fierce competition between houses weeded out the weak, the compulsion to mobilize all resources possible to maintain and expand the houses was cor-respondingly high. In such a situation terms like freemen and slaves ceased to have meaning. The chief, whose task it was to keep the house, had to be an able man; it did not matter whether he was free born or slave born. Thus the heads of canoe houses were men of ability rather than men of noble (free) birth.

In Kalabari, it may be said that acculturation was brought about consciously by the activities of two institutions—the ekine and the koronogbo. Ekine conducted a massive integration drive to make it socially necessary for all who had amassed wealth and some power to become accomplished members of the culturally orientated ekine. One ought not to overlook the immense social pressure that came to be applied on non-members. The only prerequisite for joining the ekine was an ability to learn the various skills involved in the masquerade dances—something incumbent on anyone, irres-pective of birth. Ekine developed a system of grades—junior and senior; but given the nature of its activities, people who reached the top of the social ladder had necessarily become deeply ac-culturated people. The other society, koronogbo, was an instrument for terrorizing the poorly acculturated, and for encouraging them to learn the Kalabari language, so that they might be rewarded, by ekine, with social status.

The ekine masquerade and the koronogbo went beyond the capacity to master the language and the movements of the dance. Both movements and drum-calls were linked with the myths of the gods. They reflected the idealized version of Kalabari culture, and were commentaries on social roles and behaviour in Kalabari towns. In short, ekine attempted a general social incorporation that related a man to society and to the ancestors, to the human and to the divine that penetrated the human. The Kalabari house thus provided a system designed to assimilate the alien element. The 'open criteria of citizenship' (with its emphasis on common culture and residence), was the key to the vastly successful integration of slaves in Kalabari society.[14]

Much has already been written by historians of the eastern delta about the successes and achievements of King Ja Ja (a slave bought from Amibo) to indicate the high social mobility Bonny society offered its slaves. The real differentiation in the membership of the houses of Kalabari and Bonny was on a basis of function and achievement.

Aristocracy versus meritocracy

In Calabar, however, the question of full citizenship gave rise to an intense but non-violent struggle between the aristocracy of birth and those of slave origin. Unlike their Kalabari and Bonny counterparts, the Efik nobility fought to retain the importance of free birth in the corporate kinship units as the basis of social snobbery. In other words, the emphasis came to be placed on the closed criterion of descent as the basic qualification for full citizenship.

Status in the affluent society of Calabar in the 1850s was no doubt expressed through the acquisition of material goods. Those who had money spent it on acquiring attractive pieces of furniture or other assorted knick-knacks. Wealthy chiefs lived in large prefabricated houses imported from Liverpool and other places. Imported houses were normally equipped with antique furniture and utilities, such as sofas, chairs, mahogany tables, sash windows, decorative clocks, barrel organs, china and stoneware.[15] Some Efik even abandoned their traditional attire of the ofong isin (waist cloth) and ofong idem (top gown) and took to the fineries of Victorian dress. If the final effect was in some respects like and in other respects curiously unlike a Victorian household, that was not surprising. The imported houses gave prestige to traders and impressed both their African and European trading partners. The Efik were after all a trading community and those who imported foreign goods had to give status to the articles they imported.

The fact that slave labour produced much of the prosperity of the 1850s was scarcely admitted, even if recognized by the nobility. While economic factors encouraged social integration within the houses, differentiations based on birth were encouraged within Efik society at large. Ekpe, more than any other institution, made a clear distinction between those of slave ancestry and those of free birth. Indeed, as Jones stated, Ekpe made no differentiation between chattel and other slaves:

> There existed in Old Calabar a convention that no person born in the place could be sold out of it, that he could be treated as a chattel slave. But Egbo disregarded such distinctions. In its view a slave had no rights against his master any more than a woman had against her husband. A master could treat his slaves as he liked (it was 'no matter for Egbo'), and so could an Egbo agent, in

anything that could be represented as the maintenance of Egbo discipline.[16]

By admitting slaves to the lower grades of its ranks and denying them full membership of the higher grades which it reserved exclusively for freemen, the Ekpe exposed itself nakedly as a defender of the nobility against the pretensions of those of slave origin. Originally a voluntary association for mutual protection, Ekpe had later become an oligarchy, its higher grade members ruling solely for their own especial benefit.

While the trade in palm oil brought prosperity to freemen and slaves, it did not reduce the social distance between the former living in the Calabar towns and the latter dwelling on the plantations along the Calabar and Cross rivers. Except for those employed in the Calabar households, slaves were looked upon as a source of cheap labour; to that extent the new economy bred a more oppressive type of slavery. The resentment of the plantation slaves arose, among other factors, from the fact that they had not been fully incorporated or assimilated into the local communities of the towns as members of the lineage plantation settlements.

It was during this period, when the rising slave class tried to use the inbuilt hierarchical structure of the slave and the freeman to produce a stable and secure meritocracy in place of the old aristocracy of birth, that the Christian missionaries came to the country. The missionaries belonged to the Scottish United Presbyterian Church. Hope Waddell, who led the exploratory mission in April, 1846, was accompanied by Samuel Edgerley, an English printer, and his wife; Andrew Chisholm, a mulatto carpenter; and Edward Miller, a Negro teacher. They abhorred many of the customs of the Efik and determined to end them.

The missionaries shared with the slaves the view that Ekpe was an instrument of class oppression. Hope Waddell's strictures on Ekpe must be taken seriously for he reflected the opinions of an oppressed but rising class in Calabar society. His words on certain occasions might well have been those of the oppressed majority:

> It is so rude as scarcely to be a substitute for a government. Its members may perpetuate any enormity in their own homes, families and farms over their children, wives, and slaves and great oppression generally towards others not members. In a word it is such as might have originated in the most broken and ruined condition of human society or among gangs of robbers.[17]

Waddell's conviction that Ekpe was designed to perpetuate the division between slaves and free classes was strengthened by the

E

absence of any Ekpe laws to grant freedom to slaves. The nearest approach of the slaves to freedom was to obtain it by the purchase or gift of Ekpe titles from their masters. But the privileges were of little consequence compared to those of the great nobles:

> They [the top ranking Ekpe members] on the other hand who have them in the highest degree are more than free; they are ennobled, and their privileges give them power and opportunities incompatible with the liberties of others not similarly favoured.[18]

His prescription for correcting the ills of the society was not to incorporate slaves more completely into the government, but to weaken the strength of the institution. This naturally offended the Efik nobility. The slaves began by attacking the Efik customs which required, upon the death of a king or prominent person, the sacrifice of a number of slaves, servants, courtiers and wives. The greater the importance of the freeman who died the greater the number of heads that rolled in his honour. The custom had the sanction of the traditional belief that the next world resembled in its social structure the present world and a king needed retainers to go with him. To neglect to provide for the dead king would arouse the spirits to avenge the insult thereby suffered and they would return to earth to claim a few lives. The custom also became a means for the houses to display their wealth, and as such, the terrifying competition in sacrificing slaves in gigantic numbers obviously led to an abuse of the custom.

Slaves who managed to escape from immolation fled to the countryside and established their own community on the Qua River. In 1850–51 the slave population of the Qua plantation, thoroughly disgusted by the wanton reduction of their numbers by brutal means, decided to mobilize their strength to rival and defy the Ekpe association of the freemen. The Ekpe was chiefly responsible for the funeral arrangements of the freemen or nobles who died, and hence was instrumental in securing slaves to be sacrificed on such occasions. The slaves founded the Order of Bloodmen (nka iyip) and its members bore the name of 'Bloodmen'. It was organized in grades like the Ekpe and drew its membership both from the plantations and from the Calabar towns; indeed, from all those who were in need of protection against the oppression of the Ekpe. The oath which the Bloodmen took on the mingled blood of their members, and which gave the movement its name, created solidarity and trust between themselves. The missionary Goldie gives a description of the oath taken by the Bloodmen in Creek Town at the time of the death of Eyo III in 1861: 'Ekpenyong Oku, a headman of the town, proceeded to administer the oath. He pulled up the skin of the wrist and cut it, drawing a drop or two of blood, which was mixed with that in the plate, and the individual took out of the blood one of the seeds, which has a symbolical signification with them, ate it, and then dipping the tips of his fingers in the blood, put them to his mouth . . . the administrators made a formal address to the blood, charging it to look and avenge the violation of any breach of the covenant.'[19] As well as inspiring mutual trust, it is also possible, as one writer has suggested, that the blood oath might have been intended to remedy the lack of agnatic ties between freemen and slaves. Further incidents of human sacrifices occurred in February 1850, at Duke Town following the death of two notables. The missionary Anderson, left in charge of Duke Town, felt that 'a united moral force on the part of all the white people in the Neighbourhood whether missionary or trader was fully warranted if not imperatively called for on behalf of the insulted, injured, bleeding humanity'.[20] On the following day, a meeting convened at the mission house and attended by ten captains, three surgeons, and the missionaries Edgerley and Anderson, considered the steps to be taken to prevent further human sacrifices on the death of Calabar dignitaries. After the conclusion of the meeting a procession, consisting of nineteen white gentlemen, called on King Archibong and King Eyo and threatened to break off all intercourse with them if an Ekpe law to forbid recurrence of sacrifices was not passed within a month.

The supercargoes and missionaries next formed a permanent Society for the Suppression of Human Sacrifices in Old Calabar (later renamed Society for the Abolition of Inhuman and Superstitious Custom and for Promoting Civilization in Calabar, or S.A.I.S.C.), and for the prevention of destruction of human life in any way, except as the penalty of crime. A meeting had been held, on board the *Celma* on February 12, between the Calabar authorities of the two towns and the Europeans; at its conclusion the two kings, Eyo and Archibong, and twenty-six of their principal men signed a document to abolish forever, by Ekpe law, the practice of human sacrifices in Calabar.[21] On February 15, the regular and authoritative Ekpe law was proclaimed in both towns. In Duke Town it was proclaimed by Creek Town officers ,and in Creek Town by the Duke Town officers, the two towns having mutual oversight of each other for the observances of the law. It was then published in all the towns of Calabar.[22] In November 1850, John Beecroft, the British consul, not only gladly agreed to join the S.A.I.S.C. but even added that if Eyo and Archibong had any difficulties implementing the laws the S.A.I.S.C. had made for Ekpe

to enforce, he would bring warships to their aid. Of this one writer
has remarked:

> Thus social reforms which the rulers of Calabar under pressure from
> missionary reformers agreed to carry out became matters which the
> consul undertook to enforce by the navy of an outside power . . .
> both traders and the consul took advantage of this desire of mis-
> sionaries for combined intervention in African society to weaken
> the African states without pursuing the objects the missionaries had
> in mind.[23]

The question may be posed: how did the supercargoes and the
missionaries come to think the measure possible in terms of Calabar
politics?

The moral pressure of the supercargo community was an important factor in the missionary campaign against human sacrifice.[24] Although supercargoes superficially supported the missionaries on humanitarian questions, it must be pointed out that it was
in their own interests to do so. Since the commerce of European
traders and their relations with the interior network of trade were
in the hands of the Efik, ramifications of local politics had reper-
cussions on trade. The funeral customs observed at the death of
every king or notable meant a consequent stoppage of trade. It was
in the interest of supercargoes, therefore, to work for the termination of the custom. They naturally supported the missionaries in
this cause.

The fact that there was between 1850–1851 already an internal
movement among the plantation slaves to end the custom of human
sacrifice is of decisive importance in evaluating the claim of the
missionaries that the abolition of human sacrifice represented a
signal achievement of the mission. Historians have generally overlooked the existence in Calabar of a body of opinion favouring
reform of one nature or another, and the extent to which this was
crucial to the attitudes adopted by the Efik kings and missionaries.
King Eyo's attitude to slavery, for instance, was perhaps also that of
a politician in a society where the institution of slavery was under
fire. Both the supercargoes and the missionaries had been in the
Calabar river area for some time and knew the politics of the
place quite intimately and, as will be evident in the next chapter,
they were heavily involved themselves in Calabar politics. It is
reasonable to assume that they would have become aware of a
local movement among the slave population against the oppression
of plantation slavery. If this view is credible, the conclusion might
be drawn that force was used to tip an already swinging balance.
The complexity of human situations makes it extremely unlikely
that a heavily laden balance can be reversed without undermining

the bases of society. The speed with which the abolition of human sacrifice was secured by the missionaries can be understood only in terms of the changes already going on in the social structure.

One of the immediate problems following the legal abolition of human sacrifice was that slaves began to flee from the houses, making it necessary for the nobility to have recourse to strong measures. In June, 1850, for example, Waddell received a message from Young Eyo that the latter's father was obliged to 'blow Ekpe' (meaning that he instructed Ekpe) that henceforth every such offender would be punished with death.

Waddell was obviously torn between supporting measures which sought to emancipate slaves and measures intended to retain the goodwill of the ruling nobility. Eyo made clear to Waddell the difficulties he had had when the slaves disregarded minor punishments and took undue advantage of the security given them by the Ekpe law against human sacrifice. Slaves apparently proved difficult to control without strong laws; they misbehaved toward one another, the older slaves often flogged the newer ones with coneskin whips 'a fathom and a half long and cut their flesh all to pieces'.[25]

Waddell had in 1850 outlined a plan that would improve the conditions of household slaves so that it would make it unnecessary for them to escape.[26] He urged slave holders to improve the conditions of domestic slaves, exercise patience with them as God was patient to all, and when they had to punish slaves for some real crimes to do so with reason and justice. He believed in letting the best slaves work out their own freedom and attain some respectable position in the country as reward for their good behaviour. This would, he believed, encourage others to conduct themselves well. But these plans were never satisfactorily worked out.

The politics of the lineages provided at once the reason and the opportunity for slaves to express their resentment against the entire pattern of social stratification. It must be stressed that the demonstration of the Bloodmen was not a slave 'revolt' designed to overthrow the political authority of the lineage heads. It was essentially a movement calculated to bring to an end the immolation of slaves and to assert the rights of plantation-dwelling and poorly-acculturated slaves against the wealthy town-dwelling cliques who controlled, or more usually vied with each other to control the politics of the lineages. It was primarily the tensions within the lineage system, particularly those between the head and the potential heir, and those between the heirs and the successful amongst their father's slaves and servants, that afforded the Bloodmen an opportunity for effectively checking the excesses of the nobility.

Most of the tensions between and within lineages arose from charges of the use of witchcraft. It was during the period of rapid economic development that traditional relationships in society began to break down, and that witchcraft, especially sorcery, got out of hand. Traditional 'controls' and the 'rule of law' gave way to other forms of social control. People attributed changes or events they did not favour to the supernatural powers of persons they disliked. Ordeals were visited not only upon slaves but also upon freemen suspected of having resorted to witchcraft for political reasons.

In Calabar it was believed that there were two kinds of witches: white witches (afia-ifot) and black witches (obu-bit), these latter possessing the power to cause mysterious deaths, and therefore believed by the Efik to be the most dangerous. The white witches might be called upon to protect one's person and property and were therefore not harmful.[27] It might be added that pregnant mothers guarded against witchcraft, whilst the barren lifted the bane of sterility by using witchcraft, and illness and death were attributed to some curse. Family members feared one another, and distrusted other families. Reinforcing this belief in magic was the Efik concept of a double soul in men, one of which dwelled constantly in the body, whilst the other was capable of being sent forth to possess some wild animal in the bush. This soul, possessing the chance to inflict 'clandestine wickedness', would destroy the neighbour's goats or cows in the disguise of a leopard, or drag people underwater after assuming the form of a crocodile.[28] Since the belief in witchcraft was related to the belief in sorcery, and most misfortune was traced to the work of witches or sorcerers, it is easy to understand the hysteria of fear caused from time to time and the treatment meted out to the practitioners. As sorcerers were considered prospective or actual murderers they had to be put to death. The normal way to do this was to subject them to a trial by ordeal. The results of such tests, intended to prove guilt or innocence, were often disastrous.[29] The most common kind of ordeal was one which involved swallowing a poisoned bean, called esere[30] or Calabar bean. There is little doubt that the person who administered the nut to the accused could determine whether the latter survived or died by the mode of administration.[31] The magic potion, prepared to a certain formula, was certain to cause agony; however, an excessive or a deficient dose merely produced vomiting. Some claim that if the bean had been previously boiled the consequences were painful but never fatal. Other variants of the ordeal included the thrusting of a needle or fish bone into the eye, the rubbing of 'alligator pepper' into the eye, or the pouring of boiling oil over the hands in order to test if the hands scalded (considered a definite proof of guilt). The 'alligator pepper', said to resemble the ginger lily (ntuen-ibok) seeds, and as hot as spice, consisted of tiny seeds made into a medicinal potion and placed into the eyes of the accused. If he was guilty, his eyes would feel so hot that they would appear to be falling out, but if innocent of the charge, the pepper would have no effect on him.

Normally, the services of a local medicine man, or abia idiong, were required to detect the witch. The abia idiong also had other functions in society: he predicted success in farming and trading operations and administered idiong, which was a method of getting relief from sickness or a process of finding out if one would recover from ailment. The normal procedure was to call in an abia idiong or some such diviner who would order a white basin to be filled with water. This would be placed in the open yard so that the medicine man might observe the reflection of the sun. If the spirit of the sick man could not be prevailed upon to enter the basin but fled away to the sun after flitting around the basin, the abia idiong would conclude that the sick man would die. Another, who professed medicinal powers, would place a leaf of a certain bush in the patient's hand to make him vomit; if that effect were produced he would recover, otherwise he would die.[32]

Ordeals of this nature naturally placed the alleged criminal at the mercy of the officials in charge. Since the man who administered the esere could save or destroy the accused, he was in effect the judge. Witchcraft was no more than trickery by which men and women outwitted their neighbours, or a peg on which to hang notions that their neighbours were turning against them. The accused submitted to the tests in order to have the peace of mind resulting from being acquitted of the charge (everyone believed in the efficacy of the tests), and cleared of suspicion. As Lowie puts it:

> Under the hectoring suggestion of the chief and her social environment the accused is no longer certain of herself and solves the mental conflict by willingly submitting to the ordeal.[33]

Lowie says in this connection that reported cases of confession demand attention. It is easy to understand that a woman unable to bear the physical agony of the boiling oil should end the torture by admitting her guilt. But, asks Lowie, how do we account for someone who says he assumed a different figure and killed another, for example, or the wife who owned to preventing a sore on her husband's ankle from healing because every night a snake issued from her mouth to lick the wound?

The logical device for finding the evil-doer followed from the deep psychic projection of the cause of one's troubles outside oneself. Witchcraft tended therefore to be psychologically important while the Supreme God remained metaphysically important. It is easy to see that the propagation of the practice of witchcraft became important as a means of expressing the unresolved social and political tensions of the community. The death of every king, for example, plunged the town into confusion and terror with its esere ordeals, since the question of succession normally led to a struggle between various interested groups for power.

The death of Archibong I in 1852 occasioned one of those frequent tensions in the Duke lineage system. Accusations were made by and against the town dwelling relatives and rivals of the deceased king. Two hundred Bloodmen came into the town to prevent the sacrifice of slaves and the strangling of wives frequent on such an occasion. The Duke and Eyamba parties accused each other of having used witchcraft to kill the late king. Archibong's mother, Obuma, attributing her son's death to witchcraft, began to coerce the late king's wives to prove their innocence in the usual way, that is by 'chopping nut'. Obuma had also called in the Bloodmen, with whom Archibong had wisely cultivated cordial friendship, in order to avenge the death of the king. Obuma's real intention was to use the Bloodmen to destroy the Eyamba family, and in particular Mr. Young, his ruthless brother Antero, their niece Offiong, and other members of the Eyamba family. At length, when a high ranking woman was accused, she exercised her right to challenge an opponent and called upon Mr. Young to suffer the ordeal with her. The latter made his escape on board a vessel to Creek Town, while the other Eyamba members took refuge elsewhere, including the mission house.

The Bloodmen did not interfere in the proceedings. Instead, they stood by in their hundreds to witness the death of one after another of the members of the Duke and Eyamba parties as the two accused each other of having premeditated the death of the king. Obuma was herself challenged to take the ordeal but not wishing to risk doing so, set off the heads of six casks of gunpowder that she had in her house to silence the request. For several days Duke Town was in a state of anarchy; order was restored eventually only by an invitation to Eyo to intervene. The Bloodmen returned to their farms after all parties had 'sworn mbiam that no more persons should die, in any way, for the late king'.[34] Mbiam was supposed to be a mysterious power by which the Efik swore. The Efik had great faith in this form of oath because it was believed that mbiam had the power to punish liars.[35]

There is little doubt that the Order of Bloodmen had achieved some of its objectives. No further funeral sacrifices on a large scale occurred; in 1857, when a slave was killed, the Bloodmen success-fully demanded the offender and he was delivered up to justice. Through non-violent means, the Bloodmen had begun a social revolution for equality between all men, irrespective of their birth. In 1863 the Bloodmen were even able to win court cases against the nobility and Nyampa. They did not, however, manage com-pletely to destroy the traditional belief in witchcraft. The legal abolition of the poison ordeal was contained in the second article of the treaty of 21 January, 1856 signed at Old Town by five of its chiefs. It read simply, 'That the use of poison nut as an ordeal, unless by the concurrence of the chiefs of the other towns . . . be abol-ished . . .' This treaty was ineffective, and another along similar lines was entered upon on 6 September, 1878, by King Archibong III and his chiefs. The third article of this treaty read: 'Anyone admin-istering the Esere Bean whether the person taking it dies or not, shall be considered guilty of murder, and suffer death.'

However the reports of the District Officer of Eket in 1910 and 1912 give some indication that witchcraft activity continued into the present century. M. D. W. Jeffreys gives ample evidence of the frequent occurrence of witchcraft trials and accusations in the Calabar area during other periods. Under the British administration, as now, to call a person a witch was, and is, actionable, and Jeffreys states that the Efik and Ibibio got over this difficulty by using the circumlocution 'the people of the night'.[36]

Missionaries and social change

In studies of social change, where the element or unit to which change is attributed can be clearly identified, it is fairly easy to differentiate between internal and external causes of change. One of the difficulties in studying a structurally and otherwise complex society such as Calabar is the frequent interaction between internal and external causes of change. It is extremely rare that single causes are followed by single effects so that the search for an understand-ing of social change is by no means an easy task. When, therefore, the missionaries claimed credit for the weakening of traditional religious beliefs they were treading on rather uncertain ground. It can be contended, with sufficient justification, that there appears to be a close correlation between the decline in traditional religious values and an increase in the affluence of the community.

A good illustration of this is provided by the relative importance of the office of the priest of the ndem Efik during periods of trade depression and prosperity. It must be realized that the ndem and the priest who administered to it were of great socio-religious significance to Calabar society. The ndem, centred around the cult of Anansa Ikang, was prayed to by all for forgiveness from crime, for the fertility of the land and the peace of the country, for prosperity in commerce and farming, and for similar favours.[37] Entire communities sacrificed to the ndem on the banks of a river or at a crossroads where, it was believed, the spirit was likely to pass more often. At first, these sacrifices consisted of the lives of freemen. Missionary accounts speak of albinos being offered as sacrifices. The present Efik claim that this would have been hardly likely, for ndem would not accept men of supposedly 'impure' characteristics, and neither would slaves have been acceptable sacrifices. Later on, however, such humble creatures as cows, fowls and sheep were offered to the ndem. The ceremony in the case of a cow was as follows: a fat cow was taken to the river mouth and, after a brief ceremony, was thrown into the river. All present made their wish. If the cow sank and did not rise to the surface, the wish had been granted; if, however, the cow floated the converse was true. The divine oracles would then be consulted, and the sacrifice repeated.

So important was the ndem to Efik cosmology that it found a place in the political system as well. It was the ndem priest who performed the traditional ritual ceremonies during the coronation of the king. Only when the ndem priest had placed the crown, called ntinya (made from a special type of rope, elephants' teeth and other types of ornament), on the head of the king did the latter become acceptable to the people as their legitimate head.

It is amazing that while the acquisition of wealth had become a major preoccupation of the Efik, the office of the ndem priest had by 1847 'fallen into disrepute, and the emoluments . . . [were] . . . so trifling that only a decayed gentleman . . . [could] . . . be found to accept the honour. A poor, little, old man, who often got his dinner as an alms at the mission house, was the dignitary at the time of which we write'.[38] At about the same time the use of certain ritual symbols began to wane. Chief Cameron is said to have remarked in 1849 that the Ekpenyong symbols had been removed in his part of the town and thrown into the river, a story confirmed by Waddell's houseboys who saw them floating in the creek.

In the 1850s—a time of prosperity—little heed was paid to the ndem Efik. From the description of the ndem cult, it may be concluded that it was predominantly an earth cult. This cult referred to the whole community (living and dead) in their relationship to the land. The decay of the land cult points to the emphasis on trade among the Efik—this was something relatively original in West Africa where the earth cult was extremely important amongst peoples, for the earth nourished the living and contained the dead thus symbolizing the continuity of the community. The relationship between the fortunes of trade and the vigour with which traditional deities and supernatural powers were worshipped are apparent.

In the missionary records for the 1860s—a period when the trade was declining with falling oil prices—there was a revival of ndem worship. Society based on the booming oil trade found itself in difficulties during periods of depression or stagnant trade and countered the loss of its self confidence by turning to the worship of the ndem. Anderson, who makes several references to the ndem in his diary for 1862, states that in April of that year a 'Calabar Sunday' was observed and that sacrifices were made to the ndem.[39] In June, 1862, King Archibong and the Duke gentlemen sacrificed an albino slave girl down the river in the neighbourhood of Parrot Island (generally chosen for this purpose) for the ndem Efik.[40] Another entry for 16 April, 1862 in Anderson's diary reads:

> Great sacrifice made to Ndem Efik today—I suppose on account of the fire last Saturday. Some say that a new high priest of the Ndem has been installed.[41]

On 20 April, 1862, Anderson recorded:

> Spoke seriously today to King A. [Archibong] after public service was over, about the wickedness and foolishness of trusting to anything, save God himself, as a protection from fire, famine, sickness, or any other evil. He pleaded that the worship of, or rather by Ndem Efik had been taught by God to the fathers of the Calabar people, just as He had taught the fathers of the white people to worship in Bible fashion.[42]

Though direct evidence is inconclusive, it is possible that other beliefs also diminished in importance as more energy was expended in trade. Among these might have been those related to magical medicine (ibok usiak owo),[43] the ndok,[44] and reincarnation[45] (ufiak emana). The evidence seems to point to the fact that the observance of Efik rituals corresponded to the flux of economic change.

Secondly, it must be remembered that change takes place at a different pace in different spheres: it can take place rapidly in politics and economics and less rapidly in areas like marriage customs, traditional religious beliefs and rituals. So, too, the elements in syncretistic practices vary—modern elements dominating more in some practices and traditional in others. One result of the conflict between traditional religion and Christianity in Calabar was that three elements of belief continued to exist simultaneously in the minds of most Efik. These were the cult of the ancestors, magic, and Christianity. This was possible because Efik religion, like most other West African religions, may be described as 'polytheistic', after Geoffrey Parrinder.[46] In most of these religions, there was little reluctance to accept new gods or cults as there were no narrow doctrinal divisions or jealous gods. Consequently, Christianity was accepted along with Efik religion, but to borrow a phrase from Williamson, they were 'religions at two levels'.[47]

In so far as there were theological similarities between the teachings of Christianity and the body of traditional Efik beliefs, these were confined to the belief in a Supreme God, and in the existence of the soul. However, it must be pointed out that the missionaries preached the gospel without determining from their audience whether the message being put across was properly understood. What the Efik people received and assimilated depended on their own background and patterns of thought, and on the personality and message of the preachers. Much of the missionary preaching in Calabar was 'sterile intellectualism', unrelated to the world in which the Efik lived.

It must be noted, on the charge of inconstancy of African Christians and their doubtful allegiance to the religion which they confessed, that it is wrong to deplore a want of spirituality where there is incomplete doctrinal comprehension. The Efik developed a peculiar fidelity to the church and to 'traditional religion'. To pray to Jesus and to Abasi (the Efik God) was the same thing, since it was from God that the traditional medicine man or priest eventually derived his powers. It would not be irrelevant to mention here that the culture of the African was too frequently judged, not in the light of the authentic Biblical message, but on the contrary, in the light of the civilization which is called Christian. From the indentification 'Christian civilized' the consequence is drawn 'African pagan'.[48]

For some individuals, Christianity filled the vacuum left by the decline of the old system of ritual beliefs. To others, however, the religious vacuum only led to an increase in the practice of witchcraft. It is possible that Christianity did not wholly replace the old traditional religious beliefs largely because its doctrine could not adapt itself to fill all the gaps in traditional Efik society. Though some changes were conceded to the reforming missionaries, the most notable effect was the growth of witchcraft.

Thirdly, wherever the missionaries were able to achieve some degree of socio-cultural change it was not only due to missionary propaganda per se, but also to a body of opinion within Calabar society which favoured reform, or at least was not hostile to missionary reforms which did not threaten the self interests of Efik 'progressives'. King Eyo, one of the most colourful and intriguing kings with whom the missionaries cultivated close friendship, headed one such group. He nevertheless exercised care to sanction reforms only in those areas of life where tradition had ceased to be of importance. It was precisely in such areas that the success of the missionaries was greatest. Eyo agreed to ban the worship of sacred symbols[49] and the indok spirits,[50] and categorically stated that he had no sympathy with the abia idiong practitioners (medicine men).[51] He also outlawed human sacrifice, restricted trial by ordeal to public trials, outlawed Sabbath markets, permitted twin children to live and afforded them a place of refuge from the angry and diehard 'traditionalists'. He also called a halt to the practice of killing wives and slaves at the funerals of kings and the nobility, permitted women to go about clothed and sanctioned the proper burial of slaves.

He undoubtedly acted in the full awareness of the need to change the old foundation of society and to face the test of the new times. But he was also aware that some values of traditional Efik life had to remain valid if Efik society was to be preserved and have continuity. He often warned the missionaries many times that they could not hope to have everything done at once as if by a miracle.[52] He spoke of the difficulties he would have with his old chiefs if he sanctioned reforms over and above those they were willing to accept. In 1846 he warned missionaries that already some of the old chiefs were beginning to ask why the king had given them a place to build a house, fearing that more missionaries would come and take the country away from them.[53]

Fourthly, it must be admitted that the missionaries themselves were uncertain and divided amongst themselves as to the best means of effecting social change. The journals of Hope Waddell contain details of several unpleasant exchanges between the missionaries, and many of these arose from very trivial causes. The chief grounds of criticism against Waddell seem to be two: his extreme parsimony, and the overbearing and dominating character of his personal relations with his fellow workers. Engagement in acrimonious and hostile remarks against each other, and failure to co-operate fully were in fact injurious to the mission's proper functioning. Waddell was a subtle politician; the missionary Anderson was impetuous in the early days, and did not see eye to eye with Waddell on several issues, but mellowed in his later years; but it was Edgerley who did the most harm to the early efforts of the church. On two occasions, in 1849 and in 1854, he angered the Efik by the mischievous and despicable manner in which he interfered with the sacred symbols kept in the places of worship.

It did not, however, take long for the missionaries to realize that it was futile to battle against the entire body of Efik traditions. They had of necessity to adapt themselves to the circumstances and confront the problems of the church in a realistic manner. One of the first of these problems was that of the eligibility of slave-holders to membership of the Christian church. If all slave-holders were kept out of church as a matter of principle, no Christian church would be formed in Calabar. Refusal to receive a believing disciple merely because he was a master of slaves was to deny his Christianity and excommunicate him from the universal church, to treat him as a heathen after he had been converted. Moreover, slaves outnumbered masters twenty-fold and their relationship with their masters was often complex. Freemen at times sold themselves voluntarily into slavery but, because of their former free status, could never be counted or treated as an ordinary slave; yet they were slaves. In one instance, a freeman who had sold himself to a certain Henshaw Duke, a magnate of Henshaw Town, later sold himself to King Eyo. This led Henshaw Duke to seek clarification of the situation from King Eyo and for some understanding on the subject. It was subsequently agreed that King Eyo might keep the man, while the slaves he took from Henshaw Duke were to be returned to the latter.[54]

Even where a slave had emancipated himself the situation was not a simple one. The neighbours of a master who had granted a slave his freedom might not acknowledge it, and by freeing his slaves, a master was not necessarily thereby free of his responsibilities. The freed slaves, having no master, had no protector and they could be picked up by someone and sold once again. Waddell stated that there was no regular means of emancipation in Calabar nor any law to protect the emancipated slave. He put it this way:

> Suppose I could succeed in persuading Young Eyo, the only one of our members in this town as yet much affected by this question, that he could free his slaves, but retain them on fair terms to do his work as free servants he and I would be equally at a loss to know how it should be effected, not in name and seeming only but in reality. It would amount to a re-arrangement of work and wages, under the influence of Christian principles, such as we have already laboured to effect, and no more. The fair terms must be his own, for they could not better themselves, though nominally free, by refusing his offers. He must give them work and pay of some kind or they cannot live. There is none other to do it.[55]

After 1856, or thereabouts, 'free papers' were granted by the British consul to slaves. These papers established the freedom of those slaves to whom they were given. A slave possessing such a paper could not be legally seized by anyone and made to work as a slave.

Arguments such as Waddell's are part of the rationale, something of a sophistry, adopted for eventually incorporating slave-holders and slaves alike into the church. The subject forms part of mission history which need not be entered into here. What is to be noted, however, is the strong pull exerted on the mission by public opinion in Calabar. The body of public opinion was an important element in the story of social change, for the debates and exercises engaged in were fundamental to the whole basis of society. It is a truism that a society would not accept social change over and above what would safeguard its interest and survival. The missionary had to be also a politician sensitive enough to distinguish between the shades of opinion of various categories of people.

If the missionaries stressed the indifference of the Calabar peoples to following the path of righteous living as the reason for the thin number of converts to Christianity, it should also be not forgotten that the rigid policy toward conversion adopted by the church was a factor to be considered.

Waddell's ideas on the subject, which largely determined the attitude of the church in Calabar during its formative years, were as follows:

> The first principles of religion must be first taught, though they may in themselves be inoperative to produce conversion; and the law must be preached till it is at last understood though it should be preached for years without making converts.[56]

When, for instance, in 1854, news reached Waddell in Scotland that a certain Ukpabio had been baptized, the first in Calabar, he was shocked. On his return to Calabar Waddell heard of more baptisms, particularly those of five schoolboys whose ages ranged between twelve and sixteen years. He was seriously troubled by the propriety of the measures in converting the boys and set about drawing a distinction between baptism and conversion, thus making it extremely difficult for the Efik to obtain baptism into the church. He believed it to be legitimate to decline receiving to immediate communion, in certain circumstances, persons who had been baptized. His chief argument was that only the rigid selection of the first members could ensure that the converts were able to give 'tone and character' to their cause. No one who had doubtful allegiance to the church was to be admitted. In this respect, Waddell believed in a small, utterly dedicated party influencing the whole of society.

The attempts of the missionaries to induce social change by altering the entire fabric of Efik society were certain to fail. Polygamy was one of the social institutions which the missionaries tried to undermine by insisting that polygamists could not be accepted into the church. It was derived from the principle that polygamy was opposed to the tenets of Christian marriage; Waddell would not compromise upon this principle.[57] It at once ruled out the nobility from membership of the church since it was the 'big men' who were the polygamists; 'the young men of the town could get none suitable, and were all taking up with street girls and keeping slave women for friends in private, whom yet they were not allowed to marry.'[58]

In the case of polygamy, as in other areas of social and cultural life, ignorance of the validity of traditional institutions made it easy for the missionaries to condemn what they did not understand. They failed to make a basic distinction between a marriage in which creation of a nuclear family was the predominant consideration, and a marriage which had the significance of propagation of the kinsfolk of both the participants. To transfer the undiluted monogamous life of an ideal Christian marriage to the Efik situation and to make it harmonious with the wider social system required important structural changes in society, and these changes were absent.

Polygamy was functional for the solution of a variety of problems in traditional life. It increased the numerical strength and wealth of the houses by enlarging the size of the extended family, the basic unit of society. The desire of every Efik was to rear a large family, not only because it increased the labour reservoir needed for a system of trade and farming, but also because it meant that the family benefited from the joint income of a number of kinsmen. Eyo was proud, for instance, that his father had forty children and that he himself had many wives. Large households were not only a symbol of prestige, but unlike western societies where such a situation would have meant an economic liability, they were an economic asset in Calabar. Waddell criticized polygamy as the wrong system to beget offspring, pointing out that half of Eyo's sixty wives were barren; in a Christian land they would have had two or three hundred children, every woman having her own husband. The argument appears to be that a woman does not bear any more, whether the marriage is polygamous or monogamous. African women do not, in their indigenous cultures, bear more than one child every two or three years. In monogamy, husbands are not shunned for so long.[59]

It is important to see here that Waddell was putting to Eyo an entirely different view of society, the state and Eyo's position. In effect, Waddell was talking of the nation whose power would be augmented by multiplication of its members, while Eyo was talking about the house. Waddell implied that Eyo's power would grow as the nation of which he was the king was enlarged. Eyo of course did not see it that way.

Polygamy was also a useful diplomatic device to enable chiefs to establish a network of friendly relations with key segments of their own lineage and with neighbouring chiefs. Eyo II, for instance, married wives from Ikot Offiong and Ibibio country. His successor, Eyo III, was the son of the Ibibio mother. Eyo also married off his daughters to the chiefs of the other towns as a means of retaining the allegiance of these chiefs to Creek Town. In Efik marriages, the fathers of the women became the husbands' brothers-in-law (ukot), or in Efik usage of the term, 'relations-in-law'. It is through the marriage system that the Efik kings sought to extend their political influence up the Calabar and the Cross Rivers areas.

The antagonism between monogamy and polygamy rested on a conflict of views and interests based on misunderstandings. The missionaries, for instance, interpreted the dowry system as one in which wives were 'bought'. This view was based on a misconception of the functions of the dowry. In a lineage society like Calabar, the dowry was a form of compensation to the kin group which had lost one of its female members who would now bear children for another lineage. The payment created a bond between the two lineages, helped determine the position of children in the social structure, and gave the husband certain rights formerly possessed by the kin of the bride. It created a healthy respect for the wife. The dowry was a form of security which ensured good behaviour on the part of both parties to the marriage. It created social stability; and by making it necessary to watch the morals of girls before marriage, it checked the increase in moral laxity.

It is for reasons such as those illustrated above that missionary endeavour to induce social change did not succeed as anticipated; indeed it often met with the resistance of the ruling nobility of the Efik towns. In this respect the resistance of King Eyo to conversion is a case in point.

Although King Eyo threw open his compound to the missionaries, acted as their interpreter, and consented to their social reforms when he thought them warranted and acceptable to his countrymen, encouraged them when they despaired, and listened to the admonitions of the missionaries with a patience and under-

F

standing that deeply touched their hearts, he never permitted the missionaries to consolidate their position. He knew that to turn into a radical reformer and be a pliant instrument in the hands of the missionaries was not only to court the hostility of his older and more conservative followers, but was also to allow missionaries to entrench their social and religious positions. He took a rational attitude toward Christian evangelism and the changes they espoused, in that he accepted only those which he thought were not hasty. He was intellectually convinced of the truth of many of the missionary teachings and did describe some Efik customs as 'fool things'.[60] These were, however, precisely those customs which were already losing their importance under the changing economic conditions.

There were other beliefs which were more difficult to shake off, and those were the ones which the rulers were determined not to surrender. The idea of equality with slaves was a disturbing concept to the chiefs of hierarchical societies for it struck directly at a key support of political power. For King Eyo and other freemen to seek baptism would be to place themselves on a level with the few converted slaves. It would undermine the sanction of awe and reverence which surrounded the person of the chief. In a society where slave holding was an important aspect of status, and political power to a large extent a function of number of followers, the egalitarian assumptions of Christianity were a disruptive force. In order to control the nature and pace of social change, Eyo was determined to place a check on reckless missionary zeal.

Eyo resisted conversion to Christianity and refused to give up polygamy. The reason for this was more political than religious. Eyo was careful not to offend the older people of the town. In the first place, he did not want to be embarrassed in the way the first king, Eyo I, was stripped of his position by the powerful Ekpe. Secondly, the Eyo II lineage, which had become the royal and legitimate lineage of Creek Town, was one which originated with Eyo II. At a time when the rights of a different Eyo lineage were being established, Eyo II feared that reckless social reforms would endanger the political fortunes of his lineage. Eyo was therefore irritated whenever the missionaries urged him in his internal affairs. Waddell wrote in his journal:

> . . . [Eyo] seemed rather chagrined that the white people should be urging him on in matters of internal government and seemed to insinuate that I had been rather precipitate, if anything, by informing the friends down the river so promptly of what had taken place and that he would like as well if such matters were left more to himself.[61]

In 1851 Eyo imposed restrictions on the movement of missionaries into the interior district. By these rules, the missionaries were
to secure Eyo's permission before they travelled to any part of
the interior. Traders were forbidden to accompany missionaries on
their journeys in order to safeguard the interests of Efik traders.
Nor might missionaries travel beyond a day's journey without a
guide. These restrictions were, on the whole, faithfully adhered
to,[62] but there were instances when Waddell conducted excursions
into the interior without obtaining Eyo's permission. Waddell
travelled short distances at a time, and at intervals as opportunities
offered themselves, ventured into neighbouring regions. He
stated that when he wanted to go to any town where he had not
been before he had always told Eyo, but did not deem it needful
to do so if he was only going again or merely boating about the
river. Eyo, however, insisted that he be kept informed about all
movements as even his brothers did. Waddell's musing that in
England he was not used to that kind of restraint received no
yielding from Eyo. Waddell added that he could not even get
people to accompany him on these expeditions or tell him anything about the river and its channels. He felt that they seemed
particularly desirous of keeping the white people from all acquaintance with the Egbo Shary side of the river where the oil markets
were held. But he believed that as the missionaries had no pre-
judices, and especially as they had no interest in the oil trade, they
should not be prevented from travelling freely.[63]

It was precisely his determination to control the nature and
pace of change which involved Eyo in a series of crises in his
relations with the missionaries. The missionary records after 1851
are full of 'horrifying stories' of the 'cruelties' and 'brutalities' and
of the 'disordered fleshly lusts' of Eyo. Admired by the missionaries until his refusal to be converted or to give up polygamy, Eyo
began after 1851 to be caricatured as 'a licentious despot' whose
way of life was 'simply abominable'.[64] In July, 1855, when Eyo
took on more wives, Waddell swore to be independent of him.[65]
This promise to get rid of Eyo's services to the mission was a turning point in the history of the mission, for hitherto Waddell had
heavily relied on Eyo for almost everything. On 2 September, 1855
Waddell had his last public Sabbath meeting in Eyo's yard; on the
following Sabbath he refused completely Eyo's aid as an interpreter, stating:

> The deplorable inconsistencies of his own [Eyo's] life and continued
> impenitence with the divine truths which he was the medium of
> communicating has long opposed my mind. His aid in this way was
> valuable as long as it was required. At first the incongruity of his

conduct with his teachings was not remarked, indeed not remarkable.
It was to be expected. But it is now remarkable and prejudicial. At
first useful his services have become useless or injurious; for he does
not himself believe, repent, obey.[66]

'Education' and social change

It is necessary to examine the extent to which 'education', as
the Christian missionaries understood it, was used as an agency to
promote social change.

A careful analysis will reveal that the education the Efik sought
had a strictly utilitarian or pragmatic intent. As a trading people,
the primary demand of the Efik was for a system of commercial
education which would produce artisans, clerks and men educated
in the life and language of the coast. The medium in which they
wished to receive instruction was English. On both counts—commercial education and literacy in the English language—the missionaries failed to satisfy the aspirations of the Efik and left them
bitterly disappointed with missionary activity in the field of education.

The Efik rulers had expected the missionaries to continue the
tradition of the merchants who taught the African traders to speak
English and instructed them in the proper accounting and management of trade returns. This tradition is amply reflected in the
diaries and writings of both African and European traders. The
diary of Antera Duke, written between 1785 and 1788,[67] the accounts
of Laird and Oldfield[68] and J. Adams[69] contain descriptions of
great numbers of people who had learnt to read writing (but not
print) from the captains of merchant vessels and to keep a regular
set of trade books. They also contain accounts of the practice of
the principal traders who put their sons on board the vessels, or
sent their sons to England, to learn trade customs and learn to
speak and write English though unable to write a word of their
own language.[70] An English trader, who has left for posterity a
glimpse of his impressions of the standard of literacy achieved in
English by the Efik during the reign of the Great Duke Ephraim,
wrote thus:

> Agreements of all kinds and promissory notes, and orders upon the
> officers of the ship are also given under your hands, on scraps of
> paper which they fold carefully up and tie in the corners of their
> handkerchiefs. A native trader doing business with ten or fifteen
> ships at the same time, whose transactions extend to every article
> of commerce they have, has an incredible number of these
> written documents or 'books', but I never knew a wrong book
> presented.[71]

Waddell has also remarked that he found the Efik extremely interested in the maintenance of trade books. After watching Young Eyo, son of King Eyo, write and copy into an account book the memoranda of business transactions which his father had made on slates, he confessed:

> They were neatly entered and all in English, and convinced that the teachers both for Duke Town and this place Creek Town must be really competent men. Neither Chisholm nor Miller were equal to this young man in writing and arithmetic; and no teacher here will maintain his standing among the people unless superior to even the best informed of the natives.[72]

It is a little known fact that long before the missionaries came to Calabar, the chiefs had established schools, and employed schoolmasters for the purpose of instructing in this art the youth belonging to families of consequence.[73] Oral tradition gathered in Calabar confirms that the Henshaw Town family had begun a school in a disused Ekpe shed, known simply as the Henshaw Town School, not only for the children of the Henshaw chiefs but for all children, slave and free. The chiefs had approached the trading companies to get a teacher for the school, and in later years Mr. Young (Egbo Young) said to be a man of good ability and knowledge of English, was one of the African teachers.[74] Mr. Young, a brother of King Eyamba, also maintained a regular journal of all state affairs in English.[75] West African teachers from elsewhere on the coast[76] and Europeans were employed by the Efik kings to keep their accounts and instruct their families in the art.

The missionaries did in the initial stages teach in English, but not for the reasons the Efik had in mind. In the first place, none of the missionaries knew Efik and therefore had to teach in English. Secondly, the whole orientation of their educational endeavour was geared not to the economic requirements of Efik society but to an ability to read the Bible. They hoped that through the Bible, the Efik would familiarize themselves with the religious and socio-moral message contained in it. Their intention was to use the long period of schooling to mould the character of young people[77] and inspire them to a robust Christian life. Increasingly pinched for funds, the missionaries sought the least expensive method of training pupils, and avoided technical and agricultural training which was costly in terms of personnel, money and equipment.

Commercial education was systematically replaced by a system of quasi-religious education. Since the school was conceived by the evangelists as the nursery of the chuch, it justified the large and essential place that education was given in the missionary enterprise. The result was the establishment of small schools of the simplest character, which taught little more than the rudiments of reading, writing and arithmetic; the scripture was the pivot around which the curriculum of the schools revolved. An examination of Waddell's school time-table in 1854 would demonstrate this:

> The school duties have been thus arranged open at 9 with prayers. Till 10 arithmetic classes for all. Then a few verses of scriptures are taught in Efik and repeated by all. Then reading and spelling Efik lessons in classes till 11 during which time every person separately repeats to his class teacher the verse previously given out by me. Finally roll called; absentees enquired after, tickets to the most worthy of each class, and prayer. Afternoon open at 3 with prayer. Then writing for all till 4 except Wednesday and Friday when the two highest classes had geography. At 4 scripture verses as forenoon given out and repeated. Till 5 reading English in classes from Primer to Bible, each class saying the verse to its teacher. At 5 a lesson in the Calabar cathechism. Hymn. Roll, tickets and prayers till 5½.[78]

The heavy emphasis placed on religious instruction[79] partly explains why the Efik, who were so keen to receive the missionaries, were not very enthusiastic in the early years to keep their children in school for long. As soon as the boys had learnt to speak, read and write a little English, sufficient to conduct small trade negotiations with the European traders, they were immediately removed from school and put into trade. An argument that demonstrates that education was considered as related almost exclusively to trade was the alleged Efik prejudice against female education. The Efik contention was that girls were not actively engaged in commerce and therefore were less anxious than the men for regular schooling.

When the missionaries turned away from teaching in English and concentrated on Efik as a media of instruction, a further blow was delivered to the hopes of the Efik elders. The intent of the missionaries was to translate the Bible into Efik so that it could reach a larger reading public. The Efik traders, not interested in the study of a language that was widespread, began to send slaves to the mission schools. The slaves, however, saw in formal education and in their association with the mission a new means of achieving recognition and identity. This factor explains the increasing, though irregular, attendance, of pupils in schools.

It is not necessary to recount here the rapid development of schools, the recruitment of teachers from overseas to provide the teaching staff in these schools, and the tremendous contribution of the missionaries to the publication and translation of books. The effect of all this endeavour was not immediately tangible. It is a sad comment on the attitude taken by the missionaries towards education that had the Efik been given the benefit of a commercial education they would have been a great commercial people.

Conclusion

It may generally be said of the missionaries that they were hampered in two ways in the adaptations they made. In the first place, they did not always understand the traditional system and, because they were horrified by some cruel customs, tended to condemn everything. Secondly, they were 'culture-bound' and wanted Christians in Calabar to reproduce the mode of life they were accustomed to seeing among Christians in Scotland. The ethnocentric approach to the problem of evangelization was a serious one, for the missionaries found it difficult even to disentangle the essential elements of Christianity from their European dress. They tried to introduce every aspect of English, or Western life right down to the Victorian skirt for the women. The concept of female emancipation for example, was more English than Christian. And, not least, the missionaries were competing with a traditional system of religion partly entrenched and partly changing, but which still looked very formidable to them—and that made it hard for them to be fair to traditional society.

Without denying the missionaries the credit due to them, it may be said that the most significant social changes in Calabar society were due to an internal restructuring of economic, social and political relationships. It was internal factors that were basically responsible for uprooting aspects of tradition no longer functionally related to the central characteristics of the social structure. External factors were not permitted to disrupt radically the evolutionary social changes through which the society passed. This was particularly true during the reign of King Eyo who showed most remarkably that it was possible to 'modernize' without becoming either 'westernized', or 'Christianized'. Nevertheless, the Efik were sensitive to the conflict between the old and the new social principles as they felt the discrepancy between the method of life required of them by the newly-emerging values and the traditional scheme of life to which they were accustomed.

REFERENCES

1 M. D. W. Jeffreys, *Old Calabar* et seq., Part 2, pp. 42–43.
2 Chief Thomas A. Effiom, interview, 21 December, 1965, and other informants.

3   A. A. Cowan, 'Early Trading Conditions in the Bight of Biafra',
    Part 1, *J. A. S.*, Vol. 34, 1935, pp. 399–400.
4   Chief Thomas A. Effiom, interview, 21 December, 1965, and Chief
    Michael Henshaw, interview, 19 January, 1966.
5   H. Goldie, *Efik Dictionary* et seq., p. 361.
6   Effiom Edem, interview, 15 January, 1966.
7   G. I. Jones, *Trading States* et seq., p. 189.
8   Vide, for example, the names of leading slaves such as Black Davies
    and Yellow Duke in the following treaties: 'Engagement of King
    Duke Ephraim, Duke Town, Old Calabar, October 19, 1855', E.
    Herstlet, *A Complete Collection of Treaties and Conventions*, Vol. 10,
    pp. 29–30; 'Additional Articles to the Treaty with the King and Chiefs
    of Old Calabar of 1851', 18 January, 1855, ibid., Vol. 10, p. 21;
    'Agreement, with Old Calabar: Fine for violation of a treaty, Dec-
    ember 7, 1867', ibid., Vol. 13, p. 21; 'Ratification of the Additional
    Article of 18th January, 1855 to the Treaty with the King and Chiefs
    of Old Calabar, of 15th February, 1851 for the protection of twin
    children, Old Calabar, April 25, 1871', ibid., Vol. 13, pp. 24–25;
    'Agreement with the King and Chiefs of Old Calabar (Duke Town)
    for the Abolition of Substitutionary Punishment, April 26, 1871',
    ibid., Vol. 13, p. 25.
9   G. I. Jones, *Trading States* et seq., p. 190.
10 G. I. Jones, 'Political Organization' et seq., p. 147.
11 H. M. Waddell, *Twenty-Nine Years* et seq., p. 318.
12 Vide *The Hart Report*, pp. 87–97.
13 G. I. Jones, 'Political Organization' et seq., p. 124.
14 The author is indebted to Robin Horton's 'From Fishing Village to
    City State' a paper read at an Institute of African Studies (Ibadan)
    seminar, 2 February, 1967. For a fuller treatment of the ekine see R.
    Horton, 'The Kalabari Ekine Society: a Borderland of Religion and
    Art', *Africa*, Vol. 33, No. 2, April, 1963; also G. I. Jones, *Trading
    States* et seq., pp. 67–68 and P. A. Talbot, *Tribes of the Niger Delta*
    et seq., p. 300ff.
15 H. M. Waddell, *Journals*, Vol. 7, entry for 2 September, 1849, p. 25.
    See a description of Eyo's house, for instance, in ibid., Vol. 1, entry
    for 11 April, 1846, p. 23. In the household of Etubom Eyo Nsa Eyo
    Ita, 13B Prince Street, Creek Town, I was shown a list of European-
    imported articles said to belong to either King Eyo II or King Eyo
    III. These included decorative clocks, picture frames, Victorian clay
    models, two cannons made by Ellis Scott & Son, Liverpool, a Portu-
    guese statue of a lady, and a photo of King Eyo II dressed in Victorian
    fashion. The etubom was unfortunately not able to identify the owner-
    ship of the other articles in the house, which included a week-date
    indicator with English postal rates inscribed on it, a large picture
    depicting Queen Victoria and her Empire, another of the Battle of
    Waterloo, a large crystal chandelier, coloured window panes and a
    windvane with a weather cock which also acted as a lightning con-
    ductor. A house built and furnished in the fashion of this etubom
    might have been little different from that of a Victorian home. For
    Waddell's description of Eyo II's house, vide his *Twenty-Nine Years*
    et seq., p. 244. Liverpool houses were in vogue at the time of the
    Great Duke Ephraim.
16 G. I. Jones, 'Political Organization' et seq., p. 148.

17 H. M. Waddell, *Journals*, Vol. 10, letter to Rev. George Blyth, March, 1855, p. 73.
18 Ibid.
19 H. Goldie and J. T. Dean, *Calabar and its Mission*, (Edinburgh, 1890), p. 199.
20 W. Marwick, *William and Louisa Anderson*, vide Anderson's diary entry for 6 February, 1850, p. 233; also reproduced in *U. P. Missionary Record*, 1850, pp. 105–10.
21 H. M. Waddell, *Twenty-Nine Years* et seq., p. 422; and W. Marwick, op. cit., see Anderson's entry for 12 February, 1850, p. 236.
22 H. M. Waddell, *Journals*, Vol. 7, entry for 19 February, 1850, p. 81; it was said that many of the Scottish churches, hearing these glad tidings, held special thanksgiving services on the second Sunday in July, 1850; Somerville to Waddell, Letter Book, Vol. 1, p. 572, cited in J. F. A. Ajayi, *Christian Missions in Nigeria, 1841–1891*, p. 65, n. 2.
23 J. F. A. Ajayi, op. cit., pp. 65–66.
24 H. M. Waddell, *Twenty-Nine Years* et seq., pp. 486–92, where discussions with the traders are set down. Though the question of morals and religion divided them and the missionaries, the supercargoes were willing to support missionaries on questions of humanity. Other circumstances from time to time, however, inflamed their hostility to the mission. Also, ibid., pp. 578–86, 609–11.
25 H. M. Waddell, *Journals*, Vol. 8, entry for 1 April, 1850, p. 6.
26 Ibid., Vol. 8, entry for 29 June, 1850, p. 19.
27 M. D. W. Jeffreys says that witchcraft is of two kinds, one from the high God and the other from man. Witchcraft from God confers complete magical power: such a person can cause a woman to give birth to twins. Witches can destroy any 'medicine' except the 'poison nut'. If the poison nut is knocked on their faces they die. Even smelling the nut is sufficient to cause death. A witch cannot die a natural death but must be killed by ibok. See M. D. W. Jeffreys, 'Witchcraft in the Calabar Province', *African Studies*, Vol. 25, No. 2, 1966, p. 98. See also Malcolm Ruel, 'Witchcraft, Morality and Doubt' in *ODU*, University of Ife *Journal of African Studies*, Vol. 2, No. 1, July 1965, pp. 3–27.
Mary Kingsley wrote: 'Witches are found from Sierra Leone to the Cameroons but they are extra prevalent on the Gold Coast and Calabar'; M. Kingsley, *West African Studies*, p. 175.
28 Vide Robert Lowie, *Primitive Religion*, pp. 33–34.
29 Kingsley states: 'In the Calabar district I have heard of entire villages taking the bean voluntarily because another village had accused it [of practising witchcraft] *en bloc*'; M. Kingsley, *Travels in West Africa*, p. 446.
30 Esere is described in Goldie's dictionary as the product of a vine; H. Goldie, *Dictionary of the Efik Language*, p. 90. According to the *Century Dictionary* (1904), Vol. 1, p. 488, it is defined as 'the seed of an African leguminous climber, Physostigma venenosum, a violent poison, used as a remedy in diseases of the eye'.
For a fuller discussion, vide F. W. Daniell, who was in Calabar in 1841, and stated that any person found guilty of a capital offence was usually forced to swallow a deadly potion. The condemned person, after swallowing the liquid is ordered to walk about until its

effects become palpable. If the accused is fortunate enough to vomit up the poison, he is considered innocent and allowed to depart unmolested. In local parlance, this ordeal is designated as 'chopping nut'. F. W. Daniell, 'On the Natives of Old Calabar, West Coast of Africa', *Journal of the Ethnological Society*, Vol. 1–2, 1844–50.

31 H. N. Waddell, *Journals*, Vol. 1, entry for 3 May, 1846, p. 46.

32 Ibid., Vol. 10, entry for 7 September, 1854, p. 40.

33 R. Lowie, op. cit., p. 36–37.

34 H. M. Waddell, *Twenty-Nine Years* et seq., p. 499.

35 Vide Waddell, *Journals*, Vol. 2, under various dates.

36 M. D. W. Jeffreys, 'Witchcraft in the Calabar Province', op. cit., pp. 95–100.

37 H. Goldie and J. T. Dean, op. cit., p. 43; and H. Goldie, *Memoir of King Eyo VII of Old Calabar*, p. 4. Waddell writes of the importance of the office of the priest, 'He had charge of the ndem Efik, or great Calabar juju. To him the chiefs of the land made lowly reverence while he made obeisance to none, and before him and his idol the convenants of tribes and families were sealed by oath'. H. M. Waddell, *Twenty-Nine Years* et seq., pp. 314–15, Goldie adds that the ndem Efik had as a tribute the skins of all leopards killed, and that should a slave take refuge in his shrine he belonged to the ndem Efik; H. Goldie and J. T. Dean, op. cit., p. 43.

38 H. M. Waddell, *Twenty-Nine Years* et seq., p. 315.

39 W. Marwick, op. cit., pp. 398–99; entry in Anderson's diary for 27 April, 1862, 'No gentleman save one at Church today, all the rest been offering a great sacrifice, this being Calabar Sunday'.

40 Ibid., p. 399; Anderson's diary entry for 14 June, 1862.

41 Ibid., p. 398.

42 Ibid., entry for 20 April, 1862.

43 This medicine 'for mentioning persons' was resorted to by a husband who suspected his wife of adultery and desired to learn the name of the guilty man. It also prevented a woman from giving birth until she had named her adulterous partner; for details, see D. Simmons, 'An etnographic sketch of the Efik people' in D. Forde (ed.), *Efik Traders* et seq., p. 21.

44 This ceremony, which in the past had some connection with the spirits of the dead, is held in November or early December, and it welcomes in a New Year. On this day, most people bathed their feet or bodies in the water to wash off the dirt of the preceding year; for details, D. Simmons, op. cit., p. 26.

45 If a child resembles a deceased relative the family considers the child to be a reincarnation of that relative. Simmons states that a concept known as akana (vow) postulated that before birth an individual promised God what he would be and do after he was born, whether he would be prosperous or poor, and how many years he intended to live. When the individual was born he fulfilled that promise; D. Simmons, op. cit., p. 20.

Oral testimony has it that a man was reincarnated seven times and not beyond. If an Efik child died a few days after birth, the popular suspicion was that the parents of the dead child were meant to be deceived by the child. Deep cuts were inflicted on the face and body, or a toe was cut off, in order that the child might be afraid to be reborn. The missionaries found it difficult to challenge the Efik notion that deformity was a freak of nature.

46 G. Parrinder, *West African Religion*, Chapter 2. G. I. Jones, accounting for the decline in the cults in the Eastern Delta areas, writes:

> The attitude of the African communities in the Eastern Region toward religious and magical beliefs was and is open-minded, empirical, and eclectic. As a result their religious cults were more unstable and liable to change than some of the other institutions. A cult was subject to popular feeling, that is, to fashion and when it had 'lost its power', that is, when most people had ceased to believe in it, it tended to disappear and to be replaced by another and more fashionable cult. This inherent instability rendered these religious beliefs very vulnerable in periods of rapid cultural change like the nineteenth century; G. I. Jones, *Trading States* et seq., p. 84.

47 S. G. Williamson, *Akan Religion and the Christian Faith*, Chapter 8.
48 Vide Thomas Ekollo, 'The Importance of Culture for the assimilation of the Christian Message in Negro Africa', *Presence Africaine, Cultural Journal of the Negro World*, June–November, 1956, Nos. 8–10, p. 87. These numbers of the journal contain papers read at the First Congress of Negro Writers and Artists held at Paris.
49 H. M. Waddell, *Journals*, Vol. 7, entry for 2 September, 1848, p. 25.
50 Ibid., Vol. 7, 19 November, 1849, p. 41.
51 Ibid., Vol. 7, 21 January, 1850, p. 70, and Vol. 8, 3 March, 1851, p. 70.
52 Ibid., Vol. 8, 3 October, 1850, p. 38.
53 Ibid., Vol. 1, 21 April, 1846, p. 35.
54 Ibid., Vol. 10, 10 September, 1854, pp. 40–41.
55 Ibid., Vol. 10, Waddell to George Blyth, March, 1855, p. 75.
56 Ibid., Vol. 10, p. 29, extract from Waddell to James Simpson of Annan, 25 July, 1854. Vide also Vol. 10, entry for 1 August, 1854, p. 32.
57 Vide H. M. Waddell, *Twenty-Nine Years* et seq., Appendix 5, pp. 688ff., 'Polygamy in Mission Churches'.
58 H. M. Waddell, *Journals*, Vol. 8, entry for 3 March, 1851, p. 71; Vide also Vol. 10, 6 December, 1853, and Vol. 1, 13 June, 1846.
59 H. M. Waddell, *Twenty-Nine Years* et seq., p. 487.
60 Agnes Waddell, *Memorials of Mrs. Sutherland of Old Calabar* (Paisley, 1883), p. 27, cited in E. A. Ayandele, *The Missionary Impact on Modern Nigeria, 1842–1914*, p. 20.
61 H. M. Waddell, *Journals*, Vol. 8, entry for 3 October, 1850, p. 38.
62 Only on one occasion, in 1861, a missionary, Thompson, threatened to call the gunboat to assert the liberty of the British subject to wander wherever he liked, and this provoked the rulers of Duke Town to attempt to expel him and the missionaries. The Foreign Mission Board censured the missionary severely; Somerville to Thompson, 21 June, 1861, and the resolutions adopted by the standing sub-committee, 20 June, 1861, both in *U. P. Letter Book*, Vol. 6, p. 463ff., cited in J. F. A. Ajayi, op. cit., p. 94, n. 4.
63 H. M. Waddell, *Journals*, Vol. 8, entry for 23 February, 1851, pp. 67–68.
64 Ibid., Vol. 10, 2 November, 1854, p. 47.
65 Ibid., Vol. 10, 18 July, 1855, p. 94, and Vol. 11, 2 September, 1855, p. 6.

66   Ibid., Vol. 11, entry for 9 September, 1855, p. 8. Waddell wrote of
     the difficulty of dealing plainly and pointedly with Eyo in conversa-
     tion: 'so prompt is he in reply, and so fertile in excuses, and so bold
     in denials and so plausible in yieldings'; ibid., Vol. 11, entry for 1
     May, 1856, p. 62ff.
67   This diary, which has only recently been brought to scholarly notice,
     was written by an Efik trader, Antera Duke, and contains entries
     made between 1785–88 in a large folio volume apparently given to
     him by an officer of a slave ship that called at Duke Town. The
     story of the discovery of the journal, and a reproduction of it in its
     original form and in modern English version, is given in D. Forde
     (ed.), *Efik Traders* et seq.
68   Macgregor Laird and R. A. K. Oldfield, *Narrative of an Expedition
     into the Interior of Africa*, Vol. 2, p. 395. They also quote the case
     of a captured slave, resident at Fernando Po, who had sent his son
     to England for his education (pp. 395–6).
69   J. Adams, *Sketches Taken during Ten Voyages to Africa Between
     the Years 1786 and 1800*, p. 40.
70   H. Goldie and J. T. Dean, op. cit., p. 92. The contents of several
     letters written by the Efik to Liverpool merchants are reproduced
     in G. Williams, op. cit., pp. 524–27.
71   J. Smith, op. cit., pp. 199–200. Also, H. Crow, op. cit., pp. 285–86.
72   H. M. Waddell, *Journals*, Vol. 1, 11 May, 1846, p. 48. Chisholm and
     Miller were on the mission staff.
73   J. Adams, *Sketches* et seq., p. 43.
74   H. Goldie and J. T. Dean, op. cit., p. 92.
75   H. M. Waddell, *Journals*, Vol. 1, 16 April, 1846, p. 32.
76   One example of such a man was Mr. Ferguson from the Cape Coast.
     He had been in the Niger Expedition and had at one time been hired
     by King Eyo to keep accounts of his trade dealings. When, however,
     Eyo's trade grew extensive the king hired an Englishman as a regular
     clerk; H. M. Waddell, *Journals*, Vol. 1, 16 April, 1846, p. 30.
77   James O'Connell, 'The State and the Organization of Elementary
     Education in Nigeria, 1945–1960' in Hans N. Weiler (ed.), *Erziehung
     und Politik in Nigeria*, Freiburg in Breisgan, 1964), p. 114.
78   H. M. Waddell, *Journals*, Vol. 10, p. 69, 'Report of the Creek Town
     Mission Station for 1854'.
79   As Oldham pointed out, the simple placing of religion as a subject
     into the curriculum was liable to create the utterly false impression
     that religion was a subject among other subjects and could be 'learnt'
     by the pupils; J. H. Oldham, 'The Educational Work of Missionary
     Societies', *Africa*, Vol. 7, No. 1, 1934. Vide also James W. C. Dougall,
     'The Development of the Education of the African in relation to
     Western contact', *Africa*, Vol. 11, No. 3, July, 1938, p. 313.

III

Internal Politics &
External Factors, 1841–58

The social transformation experienced by Calabar society in the 1840s and 1850s had profound political implications for the Efik rulers, namely King Eyamba V of Duke Town and King Eyo II of Creek Town. The political leadership of these towns encountered a dilemma of no little magnitude. On the one hand they found it vitally necessary to mobilize the support of the extra-territorial agents, namely the supercargoes, missionaries and the British consul, in order to strengthen the power positions of the Efik towns. On the other they realized the prudence of maintaining a modicum of political control over the influence of the extra-territorial agents on Calabar politics. The supercargoes, who had formerly been outside Efik society, gradually began to exercise a greater influence over the internal politics of the towns. The missionaries were actively introducing new ideas into the society, while the consul generally supported the supercargoes. However, strong Efik kings could hopefully rely upon the consul for support if the latter felt that such support would advance the interests of Britain.

It must be realized that in a segmentary lineage society, such as Calabar, each ward could conduct its politics independently of others. The test of political leadership in each ward consisted in part of an ability to judiciously build its own power position vis-à-vis the rest by manœuvring the extra-territorial elements. This invariably led to the stimulation of commercial and political rivalry between Duke Town and Creek Town under the leadership of Kings Eyamba V and Eyo II respectively. It can be successfully argued that missionary influence went deeper in Calabar because of the fact of internal rivalry. In this context, Eyo II emerged triumphant and re-established the political and economic fortunes of his town. Unlike Eyamba, Eyo was able to contain the political ambitions of the supercargoes and moderate the excessive zeal of the missionaries. More generally, political statecraft consisted of a wise handling of the old and new ideas that flowed through the life of the community.

Rivalry between Duke Town and Creek Town

In examining the stimulation of commercial and political rivalry between Duke and Creek Towns, it is useful to begin by studying the nature of the political process in both territories. The presence or absence of internal conflicts within the political systems was bound to weaken or strengthen a town in its relations vis-à-vis other towns.

In Duke Town there is sufficient evidence to suspect that the overwhelming pressure was to over-engage in politics and give only scant attention to trade. This was because the kingship of Duke Town was not customarily vested in a single lineage but was a matter for contest between the several lineages of the town. The death of a reigning king became an occasion for rivalry between the lineages to produce the successor. Thus when the Great Duke Ephraim died in 1834 without an heir it was an opportune moment for the Eyamba family to challenge the Duke family for the vacant throne of Duke Town. The Duke house, and in particular the Effiom Duke family, had been tremendously weakened by the loss of the Great Duke. The only substantial support that it received in its bid for paramountcy over the Eyamba was that of the Archibong family.

The Eyamba family emerged the successful party, and the new king of Duke Town was Eyamba V (Edem Ekpenyong Offiong Okoho). The attempts made by Eyamba firstly to remove any opposition to his reign and secondly to consolidate his position provide an apt illustration of his response to the particular kind of political situation that prevailed in Duke Town. He commenced his reign by a massacre of a great number of the Duke family to eliminate any potential threat to the longevity of his rule. Presumably, it was the secondary consequences of the contest for power which led some writers to state that Eyamba V was a 'usurper' to the throne of Duke Town.[1] The energetic repression of rival elements is not an uncommon political technique employed with varying degrees of success by those in power. Whether Eyamba V had been elected to the throne or had indeed usurped it, he certainly did not give Duke Town the strong political leadership that the Great Duke provided in his days. The unity forged between Duke Town and Creek Town, which had been a spectacular achievement of the Great Duke Ephraim, disintegrated when Eyamba V succeeded to the throne. Eyamba realized that in Duke Town legitimate authority consisted of two types, traditional and charismatic authority. If the latter can be defined as resting on devotion to the specific and exceptional sanctity, heroism or exemplary character of an individual person and of the normative patterns or order revealed or ordained by them, Eyamba V had little of it.

Traditional authority, on the other hand, rests on an established belief in the sanctity of immemorial traditions and the legitimacy of the status of those exercising authority under them. Such authority was largely a matter of personal loyalty owed to the person of the chief within the area of accustomed obligations. Eyamba believed in confirming his position and did so by hypocritically stimulating the loyalty of others on purely opportunistic grounds. It might be added that his fault was partly owing to a flaw in his character. A well built man with a good humoured face, open-hearted and cordial, he made a vain show of his wealth by lavishing presents among his friends and supporters. He lived a life of luxury, and to establish his status imported, among other things, a large handsomely furnished 'iron house' from Liverpool. It was a five-roomed house, measuring 40 by 30 feet, well carpeted, papered and painted and extremely well furnished with sofas, tables, mirrors, a canopied 'bed of state', and two chairs of state, gilded and cushioned.[2]

As a necessary adjunct to political authority and power, the kings of Calabar also purchased the eyamba title of Ekpe. The headship of this body carried by tradition the greatest civil authority and prestige. The purchase of the highest grade of Ekpe increased the authority of the kings and facilitated their work as rulers. This important point raises the issue of the nature of kingship in Calabar. Kings were not recognized as such by Ekpe authority; the former had authority and power only as holders of the eyamba title.[3] But unlike other kings who had purchased the eyamba title, Eyamba V obtained the title by paying the entire town for it. In return, the Eyambas were allowed to retain the ownership of the title. Waddell states that Eyamba's power had been much consolidated after his purchase of the eyamba title. The designation, Eyamba V, probably indicated that he was the fifth member of his house to become obong and eyamba.[4] Such an investment might have been a method of sustaining his political authority over his people. But vanity and extravagance, far beyond what he could afford, depleted his treasury. Duke Town was hardly the viable political and economic ward it had been during the days of the Great Duke Ephraim.

Contemporary with Eyamba V was Eyo II who emerged as the most dominant personality in Creek Town. Here, where kingship was vested de facto in a single lineage, namely the Eyo lineage, loss of trade through over-involvement in internal politics was reduced to a minimum. Unlike Eyamba, Eyo did not aspire to hold political office until he had made himself wealthy enough to do so, a fact that he could accomplish only by building up his trade.

Creek Town had been reduced to a state of economic stagnation during the rule of Eyo I, father of Eyo II. This ruin of the rich Eyo I was primarily engineered by Duke Town which had in 1770 collaborated with Creek Town to destroy Old Town. Eyo I was subsequently succeeded by one of his brothers, a rash, headstrong man with little mercantile ability or political acumen; he did little therefore to restore the broken fortunes of the Eyo house. It is reported that after 1820 (when Eyo I died) Creek Town was an area where 'bush grew in the courtyards of forsaken mansions and the tigers prowled through the grass-grown streets in open day'.[5] Most of the Creek Town families either retired to their farms or migrated to Duke Town[6] to settle under the aegis of the Great Duke Ephraim, the ruling king in that town. Eyo II was among those who migrated to serve under the Great Duke.

It was at Duke Town that Eyo, in the formative days of his youth, was schooled in the ways of trade and politics. He learnt from the Great Duke how closely politics was related to trade. He who stood foremost in traffic and wealth was powerful and could outrival all other claimants to political power. The Great Duke taught him a maxim which he steadfastly followed through his life, namely 'Keep to your trade, and your trade will keep you'.[7] He picked up in speech and writing (though not in print) a smattering of the English language, the lingua franca of trade in the river. He gained a valuable insight into the mechanism and nature of trading activities by working as a cabin boy on board English slaving vessels that sailed between Calabar, the West Indies and Liverpool. His experience in this triangular trans-Atlantic slave trading system must have left a profound impression on him.[8]

Upon his return to Creek Town (it is not known precisely when), Eyo was determined to rescue both the Eyo house and the town from economic and political stagnation. Putting into practice the lesson he had learnt from the Great Duke, Eyo lost no time in exploiting the oil trade of the Calabar and Cross Rivers to its fullest, as the Great Duke had done with respect to the slave trade. His chief concern was to end the dismal period of Creek Town history and to restore the past glory of the town as the original metropolis of Calabar, the focal point from which the waves of Efik migration had radiated to other areas. He urged his several brothers and half brothers, who lived in obscure independence on their properties, to join him in rebuilding the seat of their ancestors. Working quietly and unobtrusively, Eyo II built up the trade and prosperity of the town. He appeared to be the most powerful and ambitious contender for the throne for he had the economic power necessary for the creation of a viable political unit.

However natural it might seem that Eyo II should succeed to

the throne there were two important technical points that could not be ignored. First, Eyo II was not the eldest son among the thirteen children of Eyo I.[9] According to the patriarchal system of the Efik, the headship of a house or family was vested in the eldest male, and Eyo II could not legitimately claim to be administrator of his father's house even if he was the king of Creek Town. To the supercargoes, who had become influential king-makers in Calabar, only Eyo II was acceptable since it was their policy to choose the dominant personality in each town to be king. To overcome this technical difficulty and to satisfy the essentially patriarchal outlook of the Efik, the Eyo family decided to install as family head not Eyo II but his eldest brother, Efiok Eyo (Father Tom). The accounts of traders, which state that Eyo II was crowned by supercargoes, make little mention of the reaction of the other families to the accession of Eyo to the kingship. Clearly, foreign interference had broken the Efik law of succession, and although the Eyo family consented to the arrangement, the Otung family in Creek Town resented the crowning (it is not known for what reasons) to such an extent that part of the Otung family, led by Ekpo Ene Okpo, abandoned the town to join their kith and kin in Cobham Town.

The second technical point was that patrilineal descent was rated higher than matrilineal descent in the succession to the headship of a town. Here again tradition was broken because Eyo II's matri-lineal relations were the decisive factor in accounting for his eleva-tion to the throne. The Ambo family, which traditionally blessed the king of Creek Town, claimed that Eyo II would not have been recognized as a legitimate king by them if he had not been the son of a Mbarakom princess, namely Eyo I's wife. Eyo I had courted the hostility of the Ambo family, who refused to recognize him as king, since he could trace no genealogical relationship to them except through his wife, Inyang Essien, who was a Mbarakom princess. Eyo, in winning the favour of the Ambo family, thus became the first in the line of the dynasty of Eyo kings acceptable to the Ambo. In reality one Prince Okun Essien should have been elected king but he had died. The Ambo decided that Eyo Eyo Nsa, the grandson of their late monarch, was a good enough substitute.[10]

Eyo's ability to win the support of the supercargoes and over-come the technical difficulties in succeeding to the throne reflected the economic and political position to which he had risen in Creek Town. It naturally excited the jealousy of Eyamba V, who was particularly annoyed when Eyo successfully claimed the indepen-dence of Creek Town from Duke Town. The two towns were henceforth to have their own kings and be politically distinct units. Symbolic of this separation was the change effected on Ekpe. The headship of the body was vested in Duke Town, and more particularly in the Eyamba family, since Eyamba V had bought for ever the eyamba title. The rank of deputy head, obong obongko (ebunko or okpoho) was handed over to Creek Town. Eyo II thus became the first obong obongko of Ekpe following the political changes; the song composed in his honour by the Creek Town Ekpe sounded the trend of things to come:

> Okpoho Eyo Eyo Eyen Inyang
> Nkpo Mba Kiso Nkan Edem
>
> (Eyo Eyo the son of Inyang
> There are many more things in the future than in the past)[11]

The rivalry between Kings Eyo and Eyamba was of utmost significance in determining the course of political development in Calabar until the death of Eyamba V in 1847. Both towns competed for commercial supremacy, political power and for the favour of the extra-territorial elements in order to build up or buttress their respective political positions. But Eyamba could hardly match the political vision, diplomacy and wealth of Eyo. Finding himself left behind in the contest for power and commercial supremacy, the embittered Eyamba declared himself 'king of all black men'[12] and threatened to put Eyo in chains. Eyo prepared a great force of armed canoes and appeared unexpectedly at Duke Town. He dared Eyamba to arrest him, but the Duke Town king was taken aback and tried to mask his embarrassment by laughing it off as a joke. Duke Town was evidently not prepared for war, and Eyo left the town confounded at his cool audacity. Eyamba's declaration of himself as 'king of all black men' raises once again the alien nature of the institution of kingship. The essence of Eyamba's claim is that Eyo had been made king by the European gentlemen of the river. While this is true it may be argued that the criteria for appointment to the kingship as laid down by the European traders, viz. connection with a royal family and success in trade and wealth, formed part of the criteria for such appointment under the traditional constitution. Also, a weak man who might succeed to the kingship under the traditional constitution would find it difficult to rule the country even if he were to resort to traditional means of coercing his people. Although it is certain that the European's restricted idea of royalty did not agree with Efik notion, yet it cannot be denied that those who were elected kings were in reality the most dominant personalities in the towns. Thus, while the entire idea of an institution known as kingship was foreign to the

Efik, the person who became the king of the town was indeed the most powerful. The office of kingship had a special relation to European traders; in Efik tradition kingship had no real political significance since each head of a family group was traditionally equal to all other family group heads.

Eyamba decided to take the issue a step further by forbidding the captains of trading vessels to fire gun salutes to Eyo when the latter visited their ships. He even imposed fines on those who contravened his order. The rivalry between the two kings embarrassed the supercargoes, since Eyo demanded his honours as king and refused to transact trade with those who did not salute him. Since the trade of Eyo had become the most important in Calabar, the supercargoes could not afford to disregard the rights he claimed. To impress upon Eyamba and all others that he needed no leave from anyone to put forth his legitimate claim, he demonstrated his wealth by laying the street between his residence and the town house with hundreds of boxes of brass and copper rods, each worth five pounds sterling. He walked on these without even putting his foot to the ground.[13]

The anti-slave trade treaties

The political power and authority of Kings Eyamba and Eyo, as of other Efik kings, had their roots in external trade. The period of their reigns was one in which the transition from slave to oil export was in the process of completion. The external trade in slaves was no longer of any importance to the economy of Calabar. In 1841, a senior naval officer, William Tucker, reporting on Calabar to the Admiralty, stated that the slave trade there (Calabar) was of no importance.[14] External trade was chiefly in oil, a commodity which had been exported alongside with slaves from Calabar for a long time. By the 1840s it was found profitable to export palm oil rather than slaves since the Bonny port had successfully captured the slave market. Moreover, the demand for oil was kept up by those manufacturing industries in England which made use of it as a raw material in the making of several household consumption goods. Calabar was geographically situated in a strategic position in relation to the oil-producing area, for most of the oil came from the Cross River valley; the rest was sent down from the plantations at Akpabuyo and Odukpani. In the early days of the oil trade, the competition for oil was so great and the produce so scarce, that several ships had to make prolonged stays in the harbour to collect their cargo. Beecroft reported that, in 1830, three or four ships had to lay over for the palm oil season, some of them for as long as eighteen months.[15]

Hence, when the British were desirous of persuading the coastal rulers to sign the anti-slave trade treaties they found the most ready response in Calabar. The willingness of the kings to sign the treaty of 1841[16] warmed the hearts of the British. Indeed, far from being offenders of the provisions of the treaty, the Calabar community on several occasions played the part of informers to the British Navy on the movement of slavers. In December, 1842, for instance, they sent a canoe to warn Commodore Raymond at Fernando Po about the presence of French slavers and warships on the river.[17] J. Peters, in his evidence before the Select Committee on West Africa in 1842, stated that in Calabar there had been only one small cargo of slaves taken away within the last twelve months of that year, and that the trade was very much diminished. He attributed the absence of interest in slave dealing to the influence over the chiefs of masters of English vessels.[18]

The treaty system may be seen as an attempt by Lord Palmerston, who was at this point British Foreign Secretary, to enlist the support of the African ruling groups for an expansion of Anglo-African legitimate commerce.[19] Britain was eager to preserve and strengthen the Efik polity in order to enable the city state to maintain cordial commercial relations with its hinterland where the oil was chiefly produced, and to keep open the trade routes between the coast and the hinterland. Calabar readily collaborated with Britain in advancing British commercial interests because this was ultimately to its own material benefit.

In this respect, the history of British contractual relations with Calabar differed from that of the Delta states. In the case of Bonny, for instance, King Pepple of Bonny had refused to yield to the demands of the treaty-makers. Several agreements had been signed by the British with the Bonny rulers but none of these had been kept. Between 1836 and 1839 King Pepple had signed four agreements; three of them were ignored by his traders, while the one of 1837 was broken by the European traders. Trade in slaves at Bonny was still profitable in the 1840s, largely because the chief producing centre lay in the immediate hinterland of that port. So great had been Bonny's involvement with the slave trade that it feared the annual subsidy paid in compensation to the Efik chiefs would only be used to prosecute the trade with renewed vigour.[20] Naval power had to be used to force the Bonny rulers to submit to the demands of the British, a task in which the latter did not fail to enlist the opportunities provided by the internal weakening of the Bonny kingdom at about this time. The internal disintegration of the kingdom followed the death of Opubu.[21] The treaties signed at Bonny between 1836 and 1839 may be said to have signalized naval power as the new and disintegrating factor in Bonny society.

In Calabar, however, where the treaty stipulations were observed, African sovereignty was preserved inviolate by the kings. Despite the commercial and political rivalry between Eyamba and Eyo, the two kings took care to limit the expansion of the European trading frontier beyond the coast. They realized that if they slackened their vigilance over European traders and freely allowed them up the river, the middleman position they enjoyed would be utterly destroyed. Eyamba did not conceal the fears he entertained when Beecroft conducted explorations up the Cross River in 1841 and 1842. In 1842 he expressed apprehension that the exploration of the Cross River would lead to consequences injurious to the trade of his town. He added, 'I hear your country men done spoil West Indies. I think he want spoil our country all same.'[22] The Efik rulers wanted to keep Beecroft and the British out of the hinterland precisely because they did not want the supercargoes to upset the existing trade pattern.

Attempts to gain control over hinterland towns
No doubt the Efik traders wanted to do away with the large number of intermediary towns between Calabar and the oil producing areas. The Efik traders had little or no control over towns between the markets and the coast. Efik influence until the late nineteenth century had been confined to Itu, which was about thirty miles from Calabar up the Cross River. An Efik proverb, 'Asan Osim Itu ye Ukwa' (it reaches to Itu and Ukwa),[23] indicates that Itu and Ukwa marked the boundaries of the commercial sphere on the Efik. The latter proceeded no further up the Cross River than Umon (or Bosun)[24] nor were they permitted to do so by the Umon people, who commanded the river in this region.[25] Even the Efik language had been confined to a small area outside Calabar. For instance in 1884 Goldie, exploring the Cross River, found that after the town of Ikot Ana, Efik was of little use and he had to employ an interpreter.[26] Luke, in 1890, found that Efik was useless beyond the town of Ululemo, which was by water about a hundred and sixty miles up river from Calabar but only half that distance as the crow flew.[27]

Beecroft discovered that some of the intermediate towns, like Umon, were equally desirous of eliminating the monopolistic position of Calabar middlemen at the coast by allowing European traders to establish direct commercial contact with them. Eyamba probably knew Umon's wishes, for he tried to keep Beecroft away from the town by warning him that the Umon people would kill him, his slaves and kroomen if he went up the Cross River.[28] Bee-croft arranged a truce between Umon and Akunakuna, who had been quarrelling over a landing place for canoes; but on the subject of negotiating peace between Umon and Calabar there was no success, Beecroft being nearly shot in the process. Waddell stated that although no serious depredations had been committed on trading canoes from Calabar for a long time, the Umon people 'quash[ed] their teeth at Calabar and white people, the latter being all called by them Beecroft.'[29] Neither Eyamba nor Eyo were willing to allow European traders to help them break down the monopoly claimed by the intermediate towns who used their strategic positions to permit or frustrate Efik commercial ambitions. Umon, for in-stance, was an island in the centre of the Cross River. From its position, it commanded traffic on both sides and let no canoe pass up or down the river. It was an emporium of trade both for the river peoples and the Akunakuna toward the interior. Attempts to reduce Umon had led to military expeditions organized by the Akunakuna and others but these had been warded off by the power-ful Umon.

Eyamba was too weak to score a victory over some of these towns. His trade was in a bad way and he faltered in his com-mercial relations with the supercargoes. Moreover, his indiscriminate taking of trust weakened his position. In 1846 he was arrested and put in chains on board the brig *May*, as a debtor. Eyamba owed it thirty-five puncheons, or about twenty-five tons, of oil and the time for payment had long passed. Nothing else detained the vessel in the river, and its captain, having expressed loss of faith in the king's word, later released him on sureties.[30] Though Eyo too, in the ordinary course of events, was bound to be indebted, it was never serious enough to warrant his arrest. The situation resulting from the arrest of an important chief or king was not confined to the humiliation thereby inflicted by the trader. Its effect on the internal markets should not be overlooked. The news of the arrest of a defaulter, or even one who was not a defaulter, was often quickly relayed to the oil markets thereby injuring his character and standing as a trader. The price of oil immediately tended to rise, for oil must be had at any price to liberate the captive.[31] Nothing compensated for an unjust imprisonment on board a ship for no one would believe that it was wrongful arrest. The arrest of King Eyamba, himself a debtor, produced a great commotion in Calabar.

The arrest exemplified the extent to which the shortcomings of Eyamba's rule had affected the economy by 1846. Waddell, de-scribing the poor appearance of Duke Town, stated that the beach was lined with sheds filled with empty oil casks belonging to the shipping.[32] Old Town, which had been the original sovereign of the whole district called Calabar and strategically located to control trade,[33] had also gone into decay; its king, Acqua, aged and bedridden, was unable to assert his authority.[34]

It was therefore Eyo rather than Eyamba who was in a position to deal with the problem of the intermediate towns. Eyo's Creek Town prospered with the oil trade; missionary accounts speak of the bustling trade carried on in that town,[35] and of the greatly increased importance of Eyo II in the river. He had consolidated his position in Calabar by gaining the support of the supercargoes. His extensive trade in oil amounted to several thousand puncheons annually. His integrity and punctual honouring of promises for delivery of goods made him a favourite among the European traders. King Eyo possessed several thousand slaves who were engaged in either agriculture or trade and about four hundred canoes with a captain and crew for every one of them. In addition, he employed his people to reclaim waste lands, to found towns, and cultivate farms. All this gave him command of the rivers and channels of trade.[36]

Thus in 1846, when Eyamba waged a war against Umon to gain direct intercourse for Duke Town with Akunakuna and the people beyond by breaking the Umon corridor (which lay about eighty miles from Duke Town), it was Eyo who had to bring the war, so badly handled by Eyamba, to an end. In March of that year he re-established commercial links with Umon and promised the Umon traders gifts and annual presents as compensation for the regular comey he received from European traders. Eyo had earlier offered to bring Umon to its feet but the 'doughty monarch' Eyamba had wanted the glory for himself.[37] Eyo's triumph in restoring normal commercial relations between Calabar and Umon resulted in a further intensification of the rivalry between him and Eyamba.

Internal rivalry and attitudes towards missionaries

If the need for co-operative effort to keep European traders out of the hinterland superseded the rivalry between Kings Eyamba and Eyo, the same was not true of the missionaries. The Efik rulers had invited the missionaries in the hope that they would in some way strengthen their respective economies. The Efik kings were in particular keen on the diversification of the economy. They realized that although palm oil sold well there was potential danger in specializing in a single export commodity. They were keen to receive instruction in methods of agricultural skills and in the cultivation of such other crops as cotton and coffee. They were prepared to use slave labour to develop the agricultural potentialities of the hinterland and for that reason continued their purchase of slaves from the Ibo and Qua markets for use as domestic labourers. The Ibo slave market was the more extensive but the Qua market was the cheaper one. The former was, however, greatly preferred by Calabar chiefs owing probably to the range of choice it offered its customers.[38] The Efik rulers were also interested in spreading a knowledge of the white man's language. The degree of success in these areas has been discussed in the last chapter. What concerns us here is the economic argument for inviting missionaries to the country. Kings Eyo and Eyamba, in urging Commander Raymond (who had negotiated the anti-slave trade treaties) to send them people who could instruct their countrymen in these arts, stated:

> One thing I want for beg your Queen, I have too much man now, I can't sell slaves, and don't know what for do for them. But if I can get some cotton and coffee to grow, and man for teach me, and make sugar cane for me country come up proper, and sell for trade side I very glad. Mr. Blyth tell me England glad for send man to teach book and make we understand God all same white man do.[39]

King Eyo told Waddell, when the latter arrived in Calabar, that he was willing to devote some hundred acres of his territory to cotton cultivation if anyone showed him the way to go about it.[40] Thus the Christian missionaries were not invited to preach evangelism alone, but also to spread new skills so that they might be of material benefit to the people. Calabar was a trade emporium. What was urgently needed for this economy were men with the knowledge to keep accounts and records of transactions, to conduct trade negotiations in the language of trade, that is, English. What was needed from the missionaries was not so much their spiritual message as the provision of an education that had relevance and meaning to an intensely commercial community.

It was obvious, therefore, that each town was anxious to preserve a monopoly over missionary enterprise. No sooner had the missionaries arrived in April, 1846, than Waddell, the chief missionary, discovered that each town was keen to make itself the centre of missionary endeavour in Calabar. The agreement to receive missionaries into the town had been negotiated independently with the Efik rulers, so that when the mission arrived at Duke Town, King Eyamba believed that it was to his town alone that the missionaries had come to reside. When Eyamba subsequently heard that the missionaries proposed to set up schools in both

Duke Town and Creek Town, he expressed surprise and betrayed his jealous feelings towards Creek Town. Eyamba regarded the increased prosperity of Eyo and his town with envy, if not alarm. He thought it a new and strange thing for a missionary to live in two towns under two kings.[41] Beecroft had, in fact, to allay Eyamba's fears by assuring him that no harm would come to him as a result of missionary operations in Creek Town.[42] In the intense rivalry between the Efik kings, Waddell found that the missionaries became an issue no less important than commerce or the spread of political influence. He clearly foresaw the problems that might result from such jealousy:

> The jealousy and rivalry of the two kings of Calabar may be productive of good to the mission, but it will also be productive of great difficulty to those who conduct it. Eyo Honesty must have an equal proportion of every thing or will resent as a slight any inferiority.[43]

Initially, however, the missionaries benefited from the rivalry. The kings accorded them a most hospitable welcome to their part of the country, and enthusiastically encouraged them to help establish the mission. When the church had to be erected, King Eyamba, who held the eyamba title in Ekpe, immediately ordered to 'blow Ekpe' for the missionaries so that his people might, on an appointed day, work on the grounds allocated to the missionaries. He himself came to the site in an iron carriage to watch the building under construction.

King Eyo, rich and enterprising, made the most favourable impression upon Waddell. He had an excellent and amiable personality, and appeared to be fully alive to the benefits of the 'humanizing' influence of the missionaries. He spoke of God with the reverence of a true believer and even agreed with Waddell that his riches should be ascribed to the work of God's favour. Eyo stressed, in particular, the advantage that Creek Town hoped to derive from western education:

> You see every good thing we have come from the white people because they know more than we. They all get learning when young, but our children grow up like the goats till they are able to visit the ships when they begin to pick up a little and little after a time. So a school in our town to teach our children to saby book like white people will be very good thing.[44]

When Eyo realized that Duke Town too was the scene of missionary activities, King Eyo and his son, Young Eyo, requested the missionaries to have their establishment centred at Creek Town. Waddell, embarrassed for an explanation of the settlement at Duke Town, replied that the latter had been a matter of expediency. It

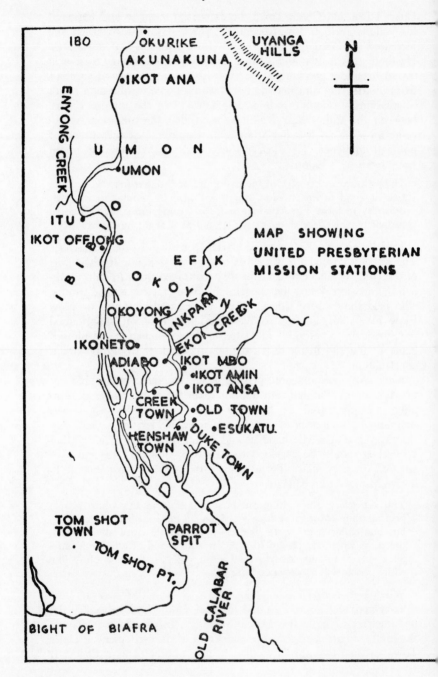

was to afford Mrs. Edgerley, suffering from a delicate state of health, a comfortable place to live on the shore. Young Eyo cleared about three or four acres of land, and urged the missionaries to build a large house in Creek Town as they had done at Duke Town. He added that he wanted Creek Town 'to be all the same as Duke Town' and that he did not think God loved Duke Town more than he did Creek Town. He even charged Waddell with making little of Creek Town since Waddell only built a small house there and had just one teacher for the whole town. He was particular that the teacher for Creek Town should be an Englishman ('a proper white man') as in Duke Town. Young agreed that Chisholm, the mulatto carpenter who had been appointed to teach in Creek Town, was a good man but he was not a 'proper white man' of Edgerley's kind in Duke Town. He wished that either Edgerley or Waddell would come to live in Creek Town.[45] Apprehensive of the influence that a small son had over his father, Waddell admitted feeling somewhat uneasy over the concern of Young Eyo.[46]

Missionary influence went deeper in Calabar than elsewhere in the Delta because of the rivalry and the willingness of the rulers to use traditional sanctions to show favour to the church. There is no doubt that in the early years Waddell believed that Duke Town was a more suitable area for the missionary headquarters. It was more populous[47] and closer to the estuary where the European ships came in with supplies and mail. Eyo, however, knew how to win the missionaries over to his side. He legislated on their behalf and gained their admiration. In a matter of about two years, to the chagrin of Eyamba, Eyo made Creek Town the centre of missionary activities in Calabar. But Eyo was always careful not to turn into a radical reformer and thereby lose the confidence of his people.[48]

The appointment of a British consul

It was at about this time that the third of the extra-territorial elements, namely, the British consul, was introduced into the politics of the river. The arguments of the supercargoes and of the Naval Squadron for the establishment of some form of British representation on the coast have been studied in other works; but it is necessary to state here that the Efik kings (particularly Eyo) were also instrumental in making appeals to the British government for the appointment of a British consul.

The concern of the Efik kings was presumably aroused by the fear of French activities in the Calabar area. The French had traded at Calabar for a long period. In 1830, for instance, John Beecroft complained that at Calabar, British merchants were hopelessly outnumbered by nine French slave trading vessels newly arrived in the river.[49] The French took advantage of their numerical strength to treat lightly the remonstrances of British merchants. Since the oil rivers were not British territory, a foreigner was still entitled to carry on the slave trade therein, or on the high seas, without interruption from British cruisers. The activity of the English cruisers was practically limited to their nationals and subjects of European powers that signed anti-slave treaties. France was not one of these countries.[50] The English traders had to face the competition offered by the French, and it was not always stifled in a peaceful manner. A British merchant in the Calabar River, Richard Cummins by name, had once to appeal to the navy for protection because a hostile French slaver had fatally shot one of his officers through the belly.[51] The 1840s witnessed a renewal of French activities, not only at Calabar, but all along the shore as well. In the Anglo-French rivalry of that decade, Africa had become a point of issue for both nations. The French aim was to secure preserves for her own political and commercial expansion.

The anti-slave treaties of Palmerston were related to the crusade for the development of Africa's external trade in legitimate articles. But they were also, and perhaps more closely, related to the policy of screening the coastline diplomatically against the encroachment of other European powers, notably France. British policy was one of drawing independent African states within the orbit of industrialized Britain by bonds of trade. French control over the area, it was feared, would frustrate this aim, and on a global level tilt the balance of power in Britain's disfavour. The French were successful in securing the repudiation of the rights claimed by the British, by virtue of Anglo-French agreements, to search her ships. Under a fresh agreement concluded after the abrogation of the previous one, each nation maintained her own cruisers for this purpose.[52]

In 1842 and 1843 French slavers called at the Calabar River. Beecroft sent a vessel of war, the *Rapid*, and took a slaver.[53] In 1843, the French man-of-war, *La Vigie*, threatened to blow up Calabar if it did not supply slaves to the French schooner, *Luiz d'Aubuquerque*. A protracted palaver ensued, and eventually the French agreed to take palm oil in lieu of slaves.[54] The renewed French trading on the coast resulted in an expansion of trade, from eleven million francs in 1840 to twenty-three million francs in 1846.

After 1846 the nature of French activities in Calabar underwent a change. French dealings with the local chieftains had a political intent quite exclusive of any commercial design. This intent could be properly described as the securing of political influence over

Calabar. The train of events began towards the end of August, 1847, when two French boats (the *Foque* and *Australie*) visited Calabar. The ostensible purpose of the visit was not commercial, but was to conclude a treaty pledging the Calabar people to abandon the practice of human sacrifice at funerals.

The negotiation that ensued between the French and King Eyo is worth recalling for it reveals to some extent not only the strong faith that King Eyo had in his English allies, but also the king's shrewdness and skill in handling the embarrassing situation. Eyo declared that the people of Calabar were 'Englishmen' and had signed treaties with England. In regard to the abolition of the practice, Eyo stated that it had already been done at Creek Town and that he was doing what he could to abolish it throughout the rest of the country. The French offered to supply bullocks to the Calabar people for their sacrificial rituals. Eyo replied he could buy bullocks himself if it was possible to use them rather than men for the purpose. When the French threatened to cease trading with Calabar if an end was not put to human sacrifice, Eyo replied, 'Very good, if your ships come for trade they can come as English ships do.'[55] Eyo accepted an invitation by the commodore and captain to visit them on board the French vessel but refused the offer to hoist a French flag on his canoe:[56]

'No, suppose I go in my own boat, I carry English colours; I be Englishman . . . if you will send for your own boat for me I can go in it and your boat can carry your colours; but my boat always carry English colours. When any ship ask me to go to it I go in that ship's boat, they send for me. So English and Dutchman do.'

An element of fear and distrust must have been present in Eyo's calculations. That the French had got possession of Gabon by treachery was not unknown. At one stage, Eyo was even said to have confessed that he was forced to carry on the slave trade with the French for a while against his wishes. The French had on that occasion gone up the river with armed vessels and threatened to ransack the town if Eyo did not procure slaves for them.[57]

Eyo pinned all his hopes on the English. The implicit trust that the English would do Calabar only good and no harm was a phenomenon shared by many of Eyo's countrymen. Also the missionaries, fearing that once French control over the area was established French missionaries might follow, had advised Eyo to resist the French.

An application to permit an English flag to be hoisted in Calabar was despatched to Captain Hope, then on board an English vessel H.M.S. *Bittern* in the river. No effect was given to this request.

Captain Hope explained that there was a treaty between England and France, in force till 1850, which provided that neither party should take any direct step towards appropriating the coast, without the knowledge of the other, and their going equal partners in it. Consequently, it was not possible to hoist the English standard without sending to the French commodore for the French standards to be hoisted at the same time.

Captain Hope expressed reservations about King Eyo's and the chiefs' understanding as to what would have been indicated by hoisting an English flag: 'I do not think that they meant to make over the country to us, but merely to put themselves under our protection.'[58] Eyo appeared to be searching for a legitimate answer to give the French. He had also, in 1847, applied directly to England for protection. Palmerston is reported to have immediately enquired of his Foreign Office clerks whether Britain had a treaty with Eyo. They replied that there was only a slave treaty. Palmerston was satisfied that this treaty prevented the French from taking Calabar under their protection.[59]

Eyo's request had also met with the support of the missionaries who had arrived in the river only three years previous to the French landings, and no doubt availed themselves of the opportunity to request the British government for protection of their mission activities. Waddell persuaded the church's Foreign Mission Committee in Edinburgh to approach the government with a plea to set up a protectorate in Calabar. They added that already 'this country is almost equivalent to an English colony.'[60]

In March, 1848, H.M.S. *Favourite*, under Commander Murray, came up the river bringing the answer of the British government to the request for protection over Calabar. Lord Palmerston's reply consisted of an assurance of the Queen's desire for the welfare of the people of Calabar; but, he did not deem it either necessary or desirable to grant their request. Rather, he hoped they would abolish the custom of human sacrifice. Governor Beecroft, at Fernando Po, was to accompany a British warship to Calabar as a counter demonstration against the French. Eyo, on behalf of the Creek Town people, gave the required pledge relating to human sacrifice.[61] A meeting of all the chiefs was subsequently held on board the *Favourite* at which the pledge of King Eyo was read; the Duke Town people were, with difficulty, made to say that they would also take steps to abolish the practice in their town as soon as possible.[62]

It is not unreasonable to assume that King Eyo's request for a British Consul provided the opportunity rather than the primary reason for the appointment of such an official. Palmerston was interested in the protection and development of British commerce along the coast. He had been displeased with the decision of the Hutt Committee, which declared itself against the continuation of the Squadron and in favour of an increase in diplomatic measures.[63] He was alive to the importance of British commercial interest in West Africa, and felt that without the Squadron British trade would most certainly suffer. (British economic interest in the Bights, which increased vastly with the development of the palm oil trade, was valued in 1840 at £1,000 per annum.) With the appointment in May, 1849 of Beecroft as Consul for the Bights of Benin and Biafra and the establishment of a headquarters at Fernando Po, Palmerston gave a definite shape to British policy on the Nigerian coast.

When Beecroft was appointed consul, his principal responsibility was to safeguard the commercial interests of the British in the area. British policy had been dominated by the commercial motive; the promotion and protection of British commerce in legitimate items of trade remained the crucial issue in British West African policy. Beecroft was instructed to travel from one river to another in a man-of-war and supervise the conduct of commerce. Some historians have stated that in 1849 the Foreign Office had, in all likelihood, no real territorial ambitions in West Africa, and that the British government and most thinking people alike were opposed to territorial empire for its own sake. Others have attached significance to the deletion of a portion of Beecroft's terms of appointment which read:

H.B.M's Government in establishing the Consulate in the Bights of Benin and Biafra, have no intention to seek Possession, either by purchase or otherwise of any portion of the African continent in these parts, nor of any neighbouring island.[64]

The removal of that statement, however, does not indicate territorial ambitions, but it does not exclude the possibility that territory might be acquired—that is significant. After all, the British were negotiating for the Danish forts on the Gold Coast and they would have taken over a fort at Whydah had they been able to arrange matters with the King of Dahomey. It would be incorrect therefore to argue that it was a period when political objectives were conspicuously missing from British discussion of African affairs.

Two factors, however, contributed towards a rather friendly reception by the Efik of the appointment of a consul entrusted with the responsibility of safeguarding British commerce. In the first place, the people of Calabar interpreted Beecroft's appointment as a fulfilment of their request for a British government representative to be stationed in Calabar. They entertained the hope that such a representative would defend and protect the state against the French and assist in the maintenance of the status quo. The British were evidently fearful that if the French traders got to work they would break the monopoly held by British traders, thus disrupting the trading system of the river.

Secondly, the choice of Beecroft for the consulship was of major importance in the Efik attitude towards the office. It is not necessary here to delve into the details of Beecroft's long and intimate association with the coast.[65] Suffice it to say that Beecroft had won the hearts and admiration of the coastal rulers, among whom he occupied an unrivalled position of influence and respect. The Efik potentates expressed no misgivings and accepted his appointment with no opposition. In addition, Beecroft's early actions appealed to the pecuniary interests of the local rulers, particularly in the matter of subsidies which had been promised but only irregularly paid to them. For example, the Efik kings received subsidies for only two of the five years promised. The subsidies were to be shared equally between Duke and Creek Towns, and normally consisted of swords, waist belts, long dane guns, brass rods and flint muskets.[66] Beecroft readily championed the cause of the Efik kings by making representations to the Commander of one of the British cruisers in the river, who immediately transmitted the message to Commodore Sir Charles Hotham.[67] The Efik kings interpreted Beecroft's speedy action as proof of his integrity and honesty of purpose; hence their confidence in him.

External factors and internal politics in Duke Town

By the 1850s the consul, supercargoes and missionaries had in the pursuit of their intentions begun to influence the course of Calabar's internal politics. There was to some extent a convergence in the motives of the consul and the supercargoes. The consul was interested in the maintenance of good government and therefore the creation of a strong and viable state. Consequently, he was prepared to support the African government so long as it was strong, but an internal crisis often led him to be drawn into economic and political disputes with rival claimants to the throne. The merchants were primarily interested in trade and their object was to bring pressure on Efik politicians to regulate commerce in a manner that benefited European trade. Trade could only prosper if society remained stable and functioned harmoniously. The missionaries were similarly involved with local political struggles, and at times resorted to the age-old political device of playing off one European agent against another.

In order to appreciate the desperate attempts made by the Efik kings to maintain their political and economic sovereignty against the heavy odds they faced, it is necessary to examine the influence exerted by the supercargoes, the consul and the missionaries on Efik kings in chronological sequence (so far as this is possible).

Duke Town was politically the most susceptible area, firstly because its kings generally relied upon extra-territorial agents for support, and secondly because it was more accessible to warships than Creek Town. The death of King Eyamba in 1847 further exacerbated an already uneasy situation in Duke Town. For nearly two years there was an interregnum, while a dispute raged between three contestants, namely Ntiero Ekpenyong Offiong Okoho (otherwise known as Young), Edem Odo of the Duke family, and Effiom Okoho Archibong Ekpe of the Archibong family.

The supercargoes could hardly conduct their normal trade relations in the absence of a regular king whose duty it was to arrange and negotiate all trade. In May, 1849, the supercargoes decided to cut short the rivalry between the contestants by electing a king from among them. A supercargo, Lt. Selwyn, commanding the *Teaser*, held a meeting with the missionaries and the masters of vessels in the river to ascertain a successor to the late king. The nominee of the Archibong family, Archibong Duke, owing to his connection with the Duke Ephraim line, was elected king. Young, on account of his age, ability and influence, was declared premier. The proceedings of the meeting at which Eyamba's successor was picked illustrates the extent to which the Duke Town chief feared the British gunboats:

> The meeting was held in our school room; and Lt. Selwyn having got all the information he wanted, at his request I [Anderson] sent for Archibong and Mr. Young. Both came attended by large retinues. None were allowed to enter the school room but the two chiefs. Being deprived of their armed men, they evidently thought some mischief was intended. They have an unspeakable dread of a man-of-war ship. It was with fear and trembling they took the seats provided for them. They felt much relieved when Lt. Selwyn told his errand—that he had been sent by the Queen to find out who is king of this country, and to pay him one of the instalments of coppers promised in the treaty made with Eyamba for the suppression of the slave trade in this river. After a little talk, Mr. Young gave up all claims to the kingship, and *accepted* the premiership. Archibong was then recognized by all present as king ...[68]

The dissatisfied Young professed himself 'king of all the black men, suppose Archibong be king for the white'. Eyo, who had consolidated his position, obviously thought little of Archibong I.[69]

H

He declared himself king of Calabar,[70] while Archibong I was ruler in Duke Town. Though the Duke Town gentry and some of the captains[71] were offended by Eyo's proclamation, no action was taken against him. The missionaries supported him in the hope that Eyo would use his powers to promote the spread of the Bible.

The consul was prepared to back up the political authority of King Archibong so long as he remained friendly to the British. A good illustration of this policy being translated into practice is the support given to Archibong when the latter experienced tremendous difficulty in settling the disturbances caused by the Bloodmen movement in 1851.[72] The supercargoes, thoroughly alarmed by the uprising, summoned a meeting on 31 January to discuss the upheaval. They resolved to represent to the consul that their lives and properties were in imminent danger of destruction, and to request the consul to interfere in the affair with a man-of-war.[73] Beecroft called a meeting on 12 February, after the slave demonstration had died down, to which King Eyo refused to come until expressly invited. Beecroft emphasized in his despatch the jealousy existing between Creek Town and Duke Town, and had, in fact, to send a boat to Eyo so that King Archibong would know that Eyo was coming at the request of Beecroft.[74]

At the final meeting on 15 February,[75] Beecroft supported the authority of Ekpe to the hilt and favoured the preservation of the political and social status quo of Calabar society. While stressing that he had 'no desire to aid the slave power to subdue an attempt at self liberation', he argued that Ekpe was the only government that could effectively rule Calabar. The Bloodmen, he said, had sworn fidelity to each other not only for the assertion of their rights, but also to secure such rights by the law of might; that is, by the seizure of property in the town. It was alleged that since it was known to the slaves that human sacrifice was forbidden, the fears they expressed were a camouflage for the anarchy, confusion and plunder intended by them.

The term of the agreement betrayed Beecroft's lack of feeling for the honest cause of the 'Bloodmen', namely, their right to live in security. Nowhere in the agreement was any guarantee provided for safeguarding the security and lives of the plantation slaves. It only confirmed the law abolishing human sacrifice, a law whose travesty was in fact the prime cause of the demonstration. Palmerston was thus justifiably annoyed with Beecroft for having taken such a firm stand against an evidently injured party. He expressed his disfavour of articles 2, 4 and 5 on the grounds that they were an attempt to suppress a genuine movement among the long-suffering slaves for emancipation. He saw no reason why British officers should inter-

fere between masters and slaves, or in regard to attempts being
made by slaves to regain their freedom.[76]

The agreement subsequently signed between the insurgents and
the Duke Town chiefs enacted:

Firstly, That the ancient Ekpe law of the country be strictly respected
and adhered to within the jurisdiction of Duke Town.

Secondly, That no armed bodies of men were to come into Duke
Town on any pretence whatsoever.

Thirdly, That no slave who had a master living should *chop blood*
with other slaves without special permission of the master.

Fourthly, That in the event of any slave belonging to any person
in the town and running away to the plantation, he or she should
be given up when demanded.

Fifthly, That all combinations among slaves for interfering with
the *correction* of any domestic servant by his or her master was
henceforth declared illegal.

Sixthly, That the law abolishing human sacrifice was confirmed and
that it be not so interpreted as to interfere with the action of the
criminal law [indigenous] of the country.

Finally, That should any article of the present treaty, or the law
for abolishing human sacrifice, be infringed, the injured party is
to apply for redress to H.M. Consul through any British resident
on the spot.[77]

The consul was aware of his delicate position in the Bights. He
valued his exalted position in the circles of the ruling nobility and
preferred to work through them in advancing Britain's interests in
the area. Furthermore, Britain, at this period, does not seem to
have had ambitions for permanent territorial possessions on the
shore. All that she was interested in was the exercise of informal
control, short of genuine territorial empire, which would help her
West African commerce. Beecroft felt that the security of British
trade was closely related to a preservation of the status quo. Ekpe
protected supercargoes against bad debtors, and for this reason
many of the supercargoes in the rivers had become members of
the society and purchased the lesser Ekpe grades. It was this society
that kept the peace, and ensured that the Calabar traders honoured
all the commercial agreements entered into with their European
counterparts. Naturally, Beecroft deemed it prudent that he should
keep the only effective instrument available to him going, while
seeking to allay the fears of those opposed to it. How that could
be done without in any way antagonizing the Bloodmen was a
problem that Beecroft could hardly be said to have settled. For
the moment, however, Beecroft had strengthened the political
leadership in Duke Town.

The death of King Archibong I on 4 February, 1852, provoked

a fresh wave of dispute between the Duke and Eyamba lineages. The premier, Young, abdicated and left the town in a 'state of anarchy'. The supercargoes lost no time in writing to Beecroft (on the day after Archibong's death) of their concern about the security of the large amount of British property which was in the hands of Archibong. Every hour, they begged, was of the greatest importance to them.[78] The turn of events afforded an opportunity for Beecroft to intervene in the domestic politics of Duke Town. Beecroft called upon the late Archibong's mother's family, Duke Ephraim, Young and the principal chiefs. King Eyo, who was also invited, arrived with a large retinue followed by five or six canoes. The result of the meeting was the election in April, 1852, of Duke Ephraim, a brother of the Great Duke Ephraim, who ought to have been king years ago. He was now poor but not without influence in the country,[79] and as Anderson believed, with an 'awful thirst for ardent spirit'. The missionaries emulated the supercargoes by attempting to consolidate their position in areas where the local rulers were weak. Their initial targets were Old Town and Duke Town. The totally indefensible manner in which some missionaries, particularly Edgerley, intervened in situations repugnant to their moral code exposed a certain streak of cruelty in the foreign religious order. In December, 1849, Edgerley made his way into the Old Town Ekpe shed and indiscreetly broke the sacred drum. It was an unfriendly act and one that aroused the hostility of the Efik towards the mission. Neither King Eyo nor any Calabar man would have committed such an act on pain of death. Edgerley attributed his action to an Ekpe man's flogging of a boy who was going through the town ringing the school bell. Waddell apologized for Edgerley's behaviour but, with little intention to yield any further, declared that he thought the Ekpe men at Old Town were also much at fault for molesting Edgerley's boy as this constituted an interference with missionary work.[80] In replying to the charge Eyo made it clear that Ekpe never meddled with Europeans, as the ship captains well knew, nor even with the Kroomen as they were not Calabar men; the boy however was a Calabar citizen subject to Ekpe laws. When the matter was reopened two days later, Waddell once again overlooked Edgerley's undue impetuosity[81] and 'managed to lay the blame on Old Willy Tom, the chief of the town'. Waddell's chief blame was a childish one, that Willy Tom had been away for several months in the plantations several miles off from the town when he 'should have been at home keeping his town, and not have left it for every man and Ekpe runner to do as he pleased and hinder the mission school'. Edgerley had, in a letter of apology to Waddell, acknowledged

with regret the transaction at Old Town and expressed sorrow for
the heat of temper displayed in King Eyo's presence. Commented
Waddell, 'The wrath of man cannot advance the work of God'.[82]

Edgerley repeated the misdemeanour in 1854 at Old Town. The
people of Old Town once again charged him with having violated
the sacred place of their god, Anansa, and upsetting what he saw
there. Edgerley admitted that he accidently broke an egg placed
in the house of worship; the egg, it must be noted, was an important offering made to the deity. Edgerley also added that he
saw laid upon a small table in the house 'four freshly cleaned
human skulls'. He attributed his intrusion into the house to
curiosity, and the subsequent proceedings to a challenge of a student
of his who had said some 'impudent things' to him after having
seen him examining the skulls. It is an indication of how indignant
the Efik were that Edgerley was followed from the beach to his
home by a crowd of about sixty 'infuriated fellows brandishing
sticks and cutlasses.' The crowd forced their way into his yard
and threatened his life and property. Edgerley immediately wrote
to Waddell who appealed to King Eyo that the complaint against
Edgerley was sub judice, and that the Old Town people had now
assaulted him committing thereby 'a more flagrant offence'.

The dispute resulted in a situation involving some interesting
dramatis personae: the ship captains, out to maintain their
supremacy at any cost; Edgerley, acquainted with the Efik language but a typical nineteenth century schoolmaster, self righteous,
overbearing and impossible; the Old Town people, especially the
young men, who saw the attack on the shrine as an opportunity to
get the oppressive Edgerley out; and finally, the subtle politician
Waddell, restrained yet firm, trying at once to maintain his relations
with Edgerley and with the people of Old Town.

A meeting called to discuss the issue was described as 'a sort
of trial, the first between a white man, or at least a missionary and
natives before a native authority that has yet taken place'. Edgerley
damaged his case in the line of defence he took. Relates Waddell:

He [Edgerley] did so in a loose rambling manner, and going over
much unnecessary ground and introducing irrelevant matter, thereby
affording them reason as no doubt they desired to go into old
stories and drag in many irritating things with which the present
meeting had nothing to do. And also he gesticulated so much and
imitated the actions and voices of the people so frequently brandishing his stock that the onlookers were sometimes laughing and sometimes surprised while I was excessively annoyed at the want of
prudence and dignity which all this manifested. At once he lost
his cause . . .[83]

Edgerley's failure to restrain his temper, his interruption of the speeches of others and his use of such abusive language as 'obukbo owo' (worthless people) embarrassed the missionaries present. At this point, the scheming ship captains saw an opportunity to speak of what a man-of-war would do if anything happened to a white man in Calabar, and referred to the events at Bonny. While Waddell, the politician, tried to shift the onus of the blame from the missionaries to the local rulers, he disagreed with the merchants and stated that he required nothing more than a return to sense and normal relations.[84] It would be an exaggeration to state that

> . . . the missionaries were incensed at this 'assault' on the Mission; moreover they could not forget the humiliation of a white man standing before an African king, Eyo, and judgement pronounced by the latter on a matter in which the white man did not come out well. The missionaries and traders felt that a decisive blow had been administered at their prestige and were bent on having it retrieved. The latter considered calling in a man-of-war.[85]

In point of fact, it was the missionaries who triumphed and the Old Town people who lost their case. Moreover, the calling in of a man-of-war was a threat made during and not after the 'trial'.

The argument that the missionaries intended to destroy Old Town and that they found a casus belli in the immolation of about fifty slaves (which had accompanied the burial of King Willy Tom of Old Town in February, 1854),[86] is a misleading one. There is no proof to suggest that the missionaries mobilized the support of the supercargoes and the consul against Old Town in respect of the infringement of the Ekpe law of 1850. If anything, the balance of evidence is in favour of the supercargoes having engineered the idea, and the consul having used the missionaries as a scapegoat. This view would be borne out by a close study of the events that led to and followed the bombardment of Old Town in 1855.

Two weeks before the arrival at Calabar of the acting consul, Lynslager, the supercargoes summoned a meeting on board one of the ships in the river, to which the missionaries were not invited. King Eyo, who was present, was against any use of force to settle the Old Town issue. He desired to fine the town twenty slaves and remove the interdict which forbade funeral obsequies. The supercargoes, on the contrary, were the ones who urged the arrest and deportation of two of the principal men involved, and the destruction of the town. The missionaries, who heard the news, objected to the burning of the town as an 'extreme measure unwarranted by any law or treaty and involving the innocent in sufferings with the guilty'.[87] Instead, they proposed that the guilty persons, six or seven in number, be seized and held bound to answer the charges and pay the penalty. Eyo agreed to this suggestion during a meeting held with the consul. Waddell refused to attend further meetings, 'having felt very uncomfortable at the feeling displayed by the trade gentlemen towards missionaries'.

In the final analysis, it was the attitude of the ship captains that was significant. Although the missionaries were anxious to punish Old Town for the violation of laws, they realized that the indiscreet behaviour of Edgerley accounted in part for the resentment of the people. It is unlikely that the missionaries were favourably inclined towards the virtual destruction of the town.

On 19 January, 1855, Old Town was shelled for nearly an hour by the war steamer *Antelope*, after which the kroomen and marines were sent on shore to set fire to every part of the town. Since the reason given for this destruction was the immolation of slaves, the Old Town people naturally believed that there must have been some collaboration between the missionaries and the supercargoes. Consequently, the feelings against the missionaries mounted high. Waddell protested against the action, and a Dutch supercargo, Captain Baak, responded: 'I hear now Mr. Waddell is the only man that wants to screen these people. So he does always set himself to cover up their crimes.' And yet it is true that Waddell was the one who was most openly vocal about Efik rituals and customs. As he wrote to his headquarters, the mission stood to lose by the results of bombardment.[88] Since the town was levelled to the ground, and left deserted and desolate, its people might well abandon the place entirely and leave for their farms or other places, and be lost to the mission.

On the other hand, the supercargoes had nothing to lose and all to gain. The town had declined from its former importance as a commercial metropolis, and was no longer of any value to shipping interest. The supercargoes could afford to bombard the declining and defenceless town and set an example to the other towns. In particular, the bombardment might well have been intended to frighten the chiefs of Duke Town, who were largely indebted to the ships, into paying their dues. It was from about this period that the consolidation of the position of supercargoes in the river might be said to have commenced.[89]

The bombardment of Old Town was taken up in the British Parliament. The missionaries wrote a long memorial to the British government on 2 October, 1855, and sent a deputation to present the memorial to Lord Clarendon.[90] In it, the missionaries refuted the allegation made by the consul that they were implicated in the proceedings against Old Town. They submitted that firstly, the extinction of the town was illegal, since there was no treaty between

Old Town and the British government regarding human sacrifice; secondly, it was undertaken despite the strong protest of the missionaries; thirdly, it had an injurious effect on the mission; fourthly, it tended to weaken the beneficial influence of the white man upon the African mind; and fifthly, the consul had prohibited the town from being rebuilt. In Calabar, Lynslager tried to secure the signatures of the Creek Town and Duke Town rulers to a document that was to state that the destruction of the town was beneficial to the country. King Eyo, on being advised by the wily Waddell, refused to sign the document.[91]

The British government decided to inquire into the disposition of the inhabitants of Calabar, and accordingly sent Consul Hutchinson in H.M.S. *Bloodhound* to the river. On 21 January, 1856, a meeting was held at Old Town to which the missionaries, kings, chiefs and gentlemen of Duke Town, Creek Town and Old Town, and supercargoes were invited. It was decided that if the Old Town gentlemen entered into a treaty with Britain solemnly undertaking to abolish human sacrifice, the use of the poison nut, and the practice of killing twin children, and to protect missionaries, the town would receive permission to be rebuilt on its former site.[92] At this point, however, the missionaries used their influence and pressure to secure for themselves as many concessions as possible. Old Town agreed to the conditions prescribed for the rebuilding of the town.

In 1856, there was another incident which showed that it was not at Creek Town, but at Duke Town that Europeans attempted to entrench their position. This incident was the declaration by the missionaries of the political independence of the Mission House in Duke Town.

To the missionaries, the mission house was a 'cell of civilization', a city of refuge, around which they gathered small bands of adherents. It housed the so-called 'criminals' and fugitives from Calabar laws, the unwanted and the ill cared-for persons of Calabar society. Youngsters were taken to the house by the missionaries to learn English, attend classes, live the lives of Englishmen, and to remove them from the 'traditional' environment.[93] It was hoped that constant touch with the missionaries would inspire young students to greater things, while making it possible for the missionaries to select the more promising lads for mission work. The students became the personal wards of the missionaries. Since religion was a matter of relations between persons, the missionaries saw that Christianity could spread in Calabar only by personal contact of love and fellow feeling between missionaries and converts.

The mission house set itself as an establishment above the law of the land.[94] Missionaries ceased to depend upon Ekpe as a machinery for enforcing reforms and preferred to rely upon their own resources. In 1856 matters came to a head. In May of that year, King Eyo sounded his own anxiety about the position assumed by the mission house and conveyed to Waddell the disagreement of one of his chiefs with the aims and doings of the mission house. It was even proposed that it would be better for Calabar if the church was built out of the town. If the mission house continued the practice of accommodating twin children and their mothers, which was hardly in conformity with traditional practice, there was no place for it in the town. Goldie pointed out to Eyo a sort of promise formerly made, that when the church was built, being a 'makara (European) house' and God's house, twins would be protected therein.

The Efik kings refused to accept as either desirable or tenable the thesis that the mission house ought to be independent of the state. In May, 1856, the king of Duke Town, Duke Ephraim, actually 'blew Ekpe' on the mission house. What had happened was that in November, 1855, two men and a woman were accused of having caused the death of a little boy by ifot (witchcraft), and were therefore called upon to submit to trial by ordeal. The missionary Anderson gave them asylum in the Duke Town mission house.[95] Refugee prisoners, after the destruction of Old Town in 1855, were similarly protected by the mission house. The action resulted in a controversy between the state and the missionaries and involved the larger questions of the relations between missions and the governments under which they served. The missionaries found it impossible to obey a civil authority which they declared was 'ungodly'. The decisive result as stated above was that King Duke Ephraim 'blew Ekpe' on the mission until it was ready to surrender the refugees to take the esere bean test. The decree stated that,

(a) no person was to go to any of the mission premises with provisions of any kind whatever for sale or dash (gift).
(b) all gentlemen who have children or slaves living on the mission premises must take them away to the town at once.
(c) no Calabar person was to visit the missionaries.
(d) no child must be sent or allowed to go to school.
(e) no gentlemen must allow meetings in his yard on Sabbath for the hearing of God's word; and none belonging to the town was to go to Church on Sabbath, or to meetings of any kind, with the Mission people.[96]

The markets were closed and church meetings failed. So effective was the Ekpe proclamation that no one came to church. When

Anderson approached the people they ran away 'as if they had seen a spectre'.[97] A few days later, on 14 June, 1856, the consul arrived in H.M.S. *Scourge* and heard the missionaries complain that Ekpe had been 'blown' on their house. The consul declared that the mission grounds had been made over to the mission for mission purposes 'for ever' by King Eyamba and his gentlemen. He added that the present action of King Ephraim was a violation of the stipulation entered into with the missionaries upon their arrival, as well as of the promises made to them before they came to the country. Ekpe was soon despatched to reverse the proclamation of 29 May and to announce the restoration of the liberty to visit the missionaries, attend school, go to church and supply provisions to the mission houses. The right of sanctuary of the mission house was affirmed and the interdict was lifted. And there was a naval force ready to enforce the decree.[98]

The controversy was highly significant from the point of view of Efik political and social history. It represented the desperate resistance of the Calabar people to the political and social consequences of missionary activity. Efik laws were disobeyed; a sanctuary was provided for those who ran away from them; and the powers and authority of the kings were grossly undermined. The controversy was also significant in that, instead of improving Ekpe from within, the missionaries were now breaking it from without by creating the nucleus of a new order.

External factors and internal politics in Creek Town

Unlike the weak kings of Duke Town and Old Town, Eyo II of Creek Town was strong enough to maintain his political and economic independence. His handling of the European agents differed from that of King Eyamba, Archibong I and Ephraim Duke who ruled contemporaneously in Duke Town. Eyo kept the friendship of the Europeans and was ready to yield to them up to a point, but not beyond. While he did not allow himself to be used as a pliant instrument for European designs, he was able to gain the support of European agents to strengthen himself, materially and morally, in his struggle to establish commercial and political hegemony over a wide area. Strong as he was, he knew the limits of his power and did not overstep the bounds of his traditional authority.

He put off pressures exerted upon him by the missionaries by telling them plainly that he could not use his influence to pass laws outside his town because no Calabar king had authority over those areas. An incident that occurred in 1850 is worth recalling in this respect. In March of that year, the missionary-organized Society for the Abolition of Inhuman and Superstitious Customs and for Promoting Civilization in Calabar (S.A.I.S.C.) called upon Eyo to settle the mischief of Old Town which had violated the treaty outlawing human sacrifice. Eyo refused to 'blow Ekpe' on Old Town, on the grounds that the law against human sacrifice had not technically been proclaimed there and hence was literally not binding on the town. The technicality of the matter was considered crucial because the Old Town Chief, Old Willie Tom, was absent from the Ekpe meeting which sanctioned the law. Eyo argued that though the law was morally binding on the chief, it was legally null and void in Old Town. It was morally binding because Old Town had sentimental relations with Creek Town since one of King Eyo's wives was a daughter of Old Willie Tom, but this did not supersede the legally independent status of the Old Town community. Indeed, any usurping of the authority of the Old Town king, argued Eyo, would be regarded as a violation of Ekpe principles, and would be met with by Ekpe penalties. Willie Tom and his chiefs had, therefore, to consent to the law before Ekpe could be sent to their town with it. The missionaries Edgerley and Waddell who were deputed to visit the king at his farm later obtained the consent of the Old Town king to the new law.

It is quite clear from this incident that Eyo was not prepared to enforce legislation in areas over which he had no traditional authority. In refraining from hurting the sensibilities of the Old Town chief, Eyo clearly demonstrated that political wisdom consisted not of a blind following of the old ideas that governed the community, but of wise handling of the new and old ideas that flowed through the life of the community.

As a politician, however, Eyo was prepared to legislate for the missionaries when the institutions to be reformed were fragile or already in a process of change. It is extremely important to note that the new laws that Eyo agreed to became at times an excuse for him to play the political game and to strengthen the authority of the Calabar kings over those areas which appeared to be drifting away from the metropolitan towns. There were, for example, certain areas in the hinterland which had been traditionally acknowledged as 'belonging' to the Calabar towns. Ekpe laws passed at Duke, Creek and Old Towns would normally be considered as applicable to the hinterland towns which were under the influence of the metropolitan towns. The Calabar kings, however, noticed that during the affluent days of the oil trade the hinterland towns were less prepared to accept the 'hegemony' of the metropolitan towns. When a situation of this nature arose, as illustrated below, King Eyo was only too willing to enforce missionary-inspired laws in an attempt to strengthen Efik 'hegemony' over reactionary peoples.

In September, 1850 Ebunda and Adiabo (Guinea Company) claimed that they were not 'Calabar people' and delivered an affront to Ekpe and the Efik kings by opposing the authority of the Calabar towns to legislate on their behalf. It appears that the Ebunda were a little colony from the Cameroons who emigrated to the region they occupied a number of years prior to the incident related, and had not been reckoned as properly Calabar people nor subject to them, though mingling, trading and dwelling with them.[99] They were protesting against the law seeking to do away with human sacrifice which the Calabar towns had legislated. This afforded King Eyo the opportunity to warn Ebunda and Adiabo of the consequences of a visit to them by the European man-of-war. This reference to a man-of-war should be explained: in the conference orginally held on the subject between the Europeans and Africans, it was agreed that if any place or party broke the Ekpe law and was too strong for African authority then the white people in the trade would be applied to for aid. If the latter were not able to secure its observance, then a man-of-war might be called in to settle the palaver with the 'refractory' people.[100]

Both Creek Town and Duke Town threatened Adiabo with the use of economic sanctions if she was determined to resist the introduction of the new law. The two towns would cease to trade with her and no longer would its inhabitants be regarded as Calabar people. Since Adiabo had no direct trade with the ships, it would obtain neither cloth, rum nor foodstuff. The palaver dragged on into the following month, October, with Adiabo positively refusing to accept the new law made in Calabar. Creek Town and Duke Town then declared what amounted to a boycott of Adiabo. Any Calabar man who traded with Adiabo was to be subjected to heavy punishment. The Adiabo people were not to travel beyond the boundaries of their town or farm, on pain of being captured and despoiled of all they had. Nor should they dare to trade in any article brought by the ships, wear fine clothes, drink rum, use tobacco, snuff, fire arms or salt. In a word, they were henceforth to be self-sufficient, and cut off from the fellowship of their country and deprived of intercourse not only with Calabar but with other towns as well. When the news was communicated to the Adiabo people, they were alarmed, and forthwith came down the river to beg for mitigation and mercy. They pleaded in extenuation that they believed that laws applied only to Duke and Creek Towns and not to the hinterland areas. Apparently in disbelief of the eagerness of Calabar to forbid human sacrifice, they suspected that the Efik must have been paid by the Europeans to consent to the law, and wanted part of the payment before they agreed to obey it.[101] Meanwhile, the Ebunda people had also submitted, and agreed to pay a fine for transgressing the Ekpe law against human sacrifice. It was ascertained that they had no right to plead exemption from the law because it was made known in their town by Ekpe drum. The fine proposed was ten slaves, but it was later reduced to eight. The affair not only represented an attempt by the Calabar towns to assert their political authority over the hinterland. It was also indicative of an interesting attempt to switch from a system of personal law to a system of territorial law.

There is no doubt that King Eyo's reputation and influence was beyond any question. Although he had no jurisdiction over Duke Town, he was often invited by Duke Town chiefs and others to interpose in any crisis that occurred there. When Duke Town was reduced to a state of anarchy following the abdication of the premier Young in 1852 (after the death of Archibong I), it was Eyo who succeeded in restoring peace and order. Anderson noted that King Eyo 'must have performed his part of the business with great skill and prudence', for had he not done so, his presence in Duke Town would have increased rather than hushed the storm.[102] Eyo's position in Calabar was powerful and influential for several reasons. He owned most of the slaves in Creek Town and a large number of the gentlemen in the town were dependent on him. Similarly, a number of Duke Town chiefs and people were under heavy obligation to him. The missionaries were another group which leaned upon Eyo's shoulder.[103] He had an overwhelming portion of the trade and wealth of the country, and his immense authority reduced the European ship captains to the status of humble servants. If the pattern of comey allocation to kings can be taken as a reliable indication of exactly where the trade was concentrated, in 1852 the supercargoes paid two-thirds of the total comey paid to Calabar to King Eyo, and the remaining one-third to King Ephraim Duke. Comey was levied at the rate of twenty coppers per registered ton of the vessel.[104]

Conclusion

A close study of the period 1841–1858 indicates the danger of over-generalizing the extent to which British paramountcy was established over Calabar. Duke Town, particularly after the death of Eyamba V, permitted the extra-territorial agents to gain a footing. Its disputes over succession to the throne, its dependence on the consul to maintain political equilibrium, its failure to resolve its domestic problems, and its generally weak political leadership admitted foreign intervention into its domestic politics.

On the other hand, King Eyo II of Creek Town took advantage

108   *Politics and Society in Old Calabar, 1841–1906*

of the rising oil demands to exploit that trade fully, and to con-solidate his position vis-à-vis Duke Town and the European traders. His effective political leadership and the general character of the Creek Town political process, where kingship was vested in a single lineage, ensured that foreign interference was reduced to the minimum possible in the circumstances of the day. Eyo yielded to Europeans where he found it necessary or unavoidable, but was tactful enough to restrain further European encroachment into his domestic affairs. He cultivated the friendship and support of the three extra-territorial agents—the supercargoes, missionaries and the consul.

A study of the period also indicates that while politics were closely related to trade, they were also largely influenced by the dominant personalities of the time. With the death of the powerful Eyo II in 1858, the political and economic fortunes of Creek Town began to decline and the town followed in the footsteps of Duke Town. The general weakening of political leadership, the setbacks in the fortunes of trade and the greatly consolidated position of the European supercargoes created stresses and strains which rendered the Efik towns less assertive, and more helplessly tolerant of foreign intervention in the following decades. The centre of effective political power began to move from the Efik kings to the supercargoes and the consul.

REFERENCES

1 H. M. Waddell, *Twenty-Nine Years* et seq., p. 311; G. I. Jones, 'Political Organization', op. cit., p. 128.
2 For a description and illustration of the iron house of Eyamba V, vide H. M. Waddell, *Journals*, Vol. 1, entry for 11 April, 1846, p. 22. One of the pillars of the house may still be seen in front of the ndem Efik shrine in Calabar.
3 Vide p. 19.
4 H. M. Waddell, *Journals*, Vol. 1, entry for 14 April, 1846, p. 26; and G. I. Jones, 'Political Organization' et seq., p. 158.
5 H. M. Waddell, *Twenty-Nine Years* et seq., p. 310. It is to be won-dered whether there were tigers in Calabar.
6 J. V. Clinton, 'King Eyo Honesty II of Creek Town', *Nigeria Maga-zine*, No. 69, August, 1961, p. 182.
7 H. Goldie, *Memoir of King Eyo VII* et seq., p. 8.
8 For Eyo's own story of his rise from being a 'pull-a-boy' in a canoe belonging to the Great Duke to his position as a powerful king, as told to Waddell, vide F.O. 2/19, No. 89, Hutchinson to Cotton Supply Association of Manchester, 20 November, 1857.
9 *The Hart Report*, pp. 107 and 195.
10 Vide ibid., p. 129.
11 Chief Etim Ekpenyong, interviews, 1 December and 3 December, 1965.

12 H. M. Waddell, *Twenty-Nine Years* et seq., p. 312.
13 Ibid.
14 F.O. 84/384, Vol. 2, No. 56, Tucker to O'Farrell, 30 July, 1841.
15 Vide *Extracts from Evidence taken before the Committee of Both Houses of Parliament Relative to the Slave Trade*, (London, 1851), published with two other reports in a publication of the African Civilization Society.
16 For a copy of the treaty, vide, E. Herstlet, *A Complete Collection of the Treaties* et seq., Vol. 8, pp. 978–79, 'Treaty with King Eyamba', 6 December, 1841.
17 F.O. 84/384, No. 56, Tucker to O'Farrell, 30 July, 1841.
18 See J. Peters's evidence in the *Report of the Select Committee on West Africa, 1842*, dated June 17, 1842, p. 354. Questions 5814–7.
19 For a study of the policy towards West Africa of Lord Palmerston, vide R. J. Gavin, 'Palmerston's Policy Towards East and West Africa 1830–1865', unpublished Ph.D. thesis, Cambridge, 1958; also his 'Nigeria and Lord Palmerston', *Ibadan*, No. 12, June, 1961.
20 This was the view of Tucker, who was ordered to negotiate the 1841 treaty with Bonny. This treaty failed to receive the ratification of Palmerston, and the old one of 1839 was forced upon the Bonny chiefs. But there is other evidence which maintains that the slave trade in Bonny, as at Calabar, had declined since the end of the 1930s. Vide, for example, the evidence of Commodore Broadhead in 1842 in *Parl. Pap.*, 1842, Vol. 11 (551), Part 1, Question 2557.
21 For details vide K. O. Dike, *Trade and Politics* et seq., pp. 68–71.
22 Beecroft assured Eyamba that his aim was purely scientific, not political; J. Beecroft and J. B. King, 'Details of Explorations of the Old Calabar River, in 1841 and 1842', *J. R. G. S.* Vol. 14, Part 2, (London, 1844), p. 260.
23 H. Goldie, *Dictionary of the Efik Language*, p. 361.
24 The Efik people call Umon 'Bosun'; Beecroft and King, op cit., p. 267. Beecroft met Calabar traders here in 1841 and 1842; p. 270.
25 H. Goldie, *Dictionary of the Efik Language*, p. 361.
26 H. Goldie and J. T. Dean, op. cit., p. 284.
27 J. Luke, *Pioneering in Mary Slessor's Country*, p. 131.
28 J. Beecroft and J. B. King, op. cit., pp. 263 and 266.
29 H. M. Waddell, *Journals*, Vol. 8, entry for 22 March, 1851, p. 74, referring to the Itu-Calabar feud of 'about ten years ago'.
30 For a description of the arrest and detention, vide H. M. Waddell, *Twenty-Nine Years* et seq., p. 274.
31 H. M. Waddell, *Journals*, Vol. 8, entry for 15 June, 1850, p. 18.
32 H. M. Waddell, *Twenty-Nine Years* et seq., p. 243.
33 Ibid., p. 251.
34 H. M. Waddell, *Journals*, Vol. 1, entry for 9 June, 1846, p. 65.
35 Vide, for example, ibid., Vol. 1, entry for 11 April, 1846, p. 20.
36 H. M. Waddell, *Twenty-Nine Years* et seq., p. 320.
37 For details of the war with Umon, vide ibid., pp. 286–7. Umon, henceforth, was friendly toward Calabar and the peace lasted: H. M. Waddell, *Journals*, Vol. 8, entry for 22 March, 1851, p. 73.
38 H. M. Waddell's evidence, *Minutes of Evidence taken before the Select Committee on the Slave Trade*, 20 April, 1849, questions 389–93.
39 King Eyo to Commander Raymond on board man-of-war *Spy*, 1 December, 1842, reproduced in H. M. Waddell, *Twenty-Nine Years* et

seq., p. 664. For King Eyamba's identical letter, dated 4 December, 1842, vide ibid., p. 663–4.

40   F.O. 2/19, No. 89, Hutchinson to Cotton Supply Association at Manchester, 20 November, 1857.

41   H. M. Waddell, *Journals*, Vol. 1, entry for 13 April, 1846, p. 26.

42   Ibid.

43   Ibid., 11 May, 1846, p. 50.

44   Ibid., 21 April, 1846, p. 35.

45   Ibid., 11 June, 1846, p. 66.

46   Ibid., 11 May, 1846, p. 48.

47   The population of Duke Town in 1846 was between 5,000 and 6,000, that of Creek Town, about 4,000; Waddell, ibid., Vol. 1, entries for 11 April and 13 April, 1846, pp. 22 and 26 respectively.

48   For a detailed treatment of the social and cultural changes wrought by the missionaries, and the pace at which Eyo was willing to sanction the reforms envisaged by the missionaries, vide Chapter 2 in this volume.

49   C.O. 82/4, No. 3, Beecroft to Nicolls, 17 November, 1830, cited in K. O. Dike, *Trade and Politics* et seq., p. 54.

50   W. N. M. Geary, *Nigeria under British Rule*, p. 70.

51   C.O. 82/1, Cummins to Lieutenant Bagley, 26 July, 1828, cited in K. O. Dike, *Trade and Politics* et seq., p. 54.

52   R. J. Gavin, 'Palmerston's Policy' *Towards East and West Africa, 1830–1865*, unpublished Ph.D. thesis, Cambridge, 1959–60, p. 152.

53   *Proceedings of the Anti Slavery Convention*, pp. 261–2, cited in K. O. Dike, *Trade and Politics* et seq., p. 68.

54   F.O. 84/495, No. 12, Encl. 2, Raymond to Foote, 10 January, 1842.

55   H. M. Waddell, *Twenty-Nine Years* et seq., p. 351.

56   For a description of the events vide ibid., pp. 350–52, and H. Goldie and J. T. Dean, op. cit., pp. 129–30.

57   H. M. Waddell's evidence before the Select Committee, 1849 et seq., p. 43, question 419.

58   Ibid., pp. 44–45, questions 443–47.

59   F.O. 84/710, Memo by Foreign Office clerk, December 6, 1847, Minute by Palmerston, December 8, 1847, cited in R. J. Gavin, *Palmerston's Policy* et seq., p. 156.

60   U.P. *Missionary Record*, 1848, pp. 28 and 56, cited in J. F. A. Ajayi, op. cit., p. 60.

61   E. Hertslet, *Treaties* et seq., Vol. 8, pp. 40–41, 'Treaty with King Eyo', 18 March, 1848.

62   H. Goldie and J. T. Dean, op. cit., pp. 132–3. Also, Commodore Murray to Commodore Sir Charles Hotham, March 24, 1848, in appendix to the Minutes of Evidence taken before the Select Committee, op. cit., 1849; extracts from H. M. Waddell's *Journals* in U.P. *Missionary Record*, 1848, p. 24ff., cited in J. F. A. Ajayi, op. cit., p. 60; H. M. Waddell, *Twenty-Nine Years* et seq., Chapter 19, p. 374, and Waddell's letter published in W. Marwick, op. cit., pp. 240–2.

63   Palmerston and Russell (then Prime Minister) set out to defeat the opposition that was mounting to the retention of the West African Squadron in 1850; R. J. Gavin 'Nigeria' et seq., *Ibadan*, No. 12, 1961, p. 26.

64   For the draft, vide F.O. 84/775, Palmerston to Beecroft, 30 June, 1849; cf. this with the final version, C.O. 267/211.

65   Beecroft's association with the coast was of long-standing significance. It dated back to 1829 when Nicolls, Governor of Fernando Po, employed him as head of the Department of Works. In 1834, when the settlement was evacuated, he became a merchant in the employ of Messrs. Tennant & Co., and after 1837, of Robert Jamieson of Glasgow. He undertook several exploratory voyages up the Delta rivers, and thus got to know personally the chiefs of the area. He acted as political agent to the British naval authorities at least on nine occasions between 1844 and 1849. When Spain reasserted her sovereignty over Fernando Po, Beecroft was appointed Governor of the island. This position he held when the British Government decided to appoint him Consul for the Bights in 1849. One contemporary wrote of him '. . . he is well known, highly respected, and possesses influence such as no white-man on the coast has ever obtained'. See F.O. 84/549, Nicolls to Barrow, 5 June, 1844, cited in K. O. Dike, 'John Beecroft, 1790–1854', *J. H. S. N.*, Vol. 1, December, 1956; vide also C.O. 267, No. 211, and F.O. 84/775, Palmerston to Beecroft 30 June, 1849. Also *Parl. Pap.*, 1842, Vol. 84, cited in J. C. Anene, *Southern Nigeria in Transition, 1885–1906*, p. 29.

66   CALPROF 5/1, receipt of presents by King Eyo and King Archibong, August 21 and August 22, 1851.

67   For Waddell's evidence, see his testimony before the 1849 Select Committee, op. cit., question 285.

68   W. Marwick, op. cit., p. 216; entry in Anderson's diary dated 28 May, 1849.

69   Anderson stated that Archibong I was, when compared with Eyo, 'young, inexperienced and rash'; W. Marwick, op. cit., p. 224; entry in Anderson's journal sent home, 22 August, 1849. Also Anderson's articles in U.P. *Missionary Record*, February, 1851.

70   H. M. Waddell, *Journals*, Vol. 7, entries for 6 January, p. 67 and for 8 January, 1850, p. 68. There is, however, unfortunately no evidence which indicates the effectiveness or consequences of this declaration.

71   It was possible that the supercargoes felt their support for Eyo, if given, would put them in bad relations with the Duke Town gentry.

72   The genesis of the slave movement is discussed in Chapter 2, in this volume.

73   CALPROF 4/1, Vol. 1, (or F.O. 84/858), Charles Calvert, on behalf of the masters and supercargoes of the Old Calabar River, to Beecroft, January 31, 1851, and covering letter of even date.

74   F.O. 84/858, Beecroft to Palmerston, 4 March, 1851.

75   A full description of the negotiations that took place between the Qua plantation slaves and the Duke Town chiefs is recounted in missionary Anderson's letter, dated February 20, 1851, published in the U.P. *Missionary Record*, August, 1851, and reproduced in W. Marwick, op. cit., p. 250ff., also, F.O. 84/858, Beecroft to Palmerston, 4 March, 1851.

76   CALPROF 2/1, No. 6, (or F.O. 84/858), Palmerston to Beecroft, 24 June, 1851.

77   F.O. 84/858 (and CALPROF 2/1), Beecroft to Palmerston, No. 6, 21 February, 1851; W. Marwick, op. cit., p. 252. The agreement was witnessed by Commanders Strange of the vessel *Archer*, Bedinfield of the *Jackal*, and masters of the merchant ships *Celma*, *Ambrosine*.

I

Magistrate, Clifton, Abeona, Majestic and *Tapley*, on the one hand, and by King Archibong and his headmen, on the other.

78 CALPROF 4/1, Vol. 1, Masters and supercargoes of vessels lying in the Old Calabar River to Beecroft, 5 February, 1852.

79 W. Marwick, op. cit., p. 205; F.O. 84/886, Beecroft to Malmesbury, 30 June, 1852; and E. Herstlet, op. cit., Vol. 10, p. 13. 'Agreement of King Duke Ephraim Confirming Treaty with Old Calabar of 1841', 2 February, 1854.

80 H. M. Waddell, *Journals*, Vol. 7, entry for 4 December, 1849, p. 49. Waddell suggested that the two rival bells of Ekpe and the mission should not come into collision, that the school bell ringer should retire when he heard the Ekpe man's bell or drum and likewise that the Ekpe man should retire when he heard the school bell, and each keep to his own side. To this proposal, Eyo remained silent; ibid., p. 50.

81 H. M. Waddell, *Journals*, Vol. 7, entry for 6 December, 1849, p. 50.

82 Ibid.

83 Ibid., Vol. 10, entry for 28 August, 1859, p. 35.

84 Wrote Waddell: 'Not liking that style of remark I said that moderate counsels became us. We were not men of war but men of peace. All we wanted was that the old men of Old Town would keep their town quiet and not let the young men be guilty of excesses'; ibid., p. 36.

85 E. A. Ayandele, op. cit., p. 23.

86 Ibid.

87 H. M. Waddell, *Journals*, Vol. 10, entries for 7 January and 19 January, 1855, pp. 55 and 58 respectively.

88 Vide Waddell to Rev. A. Somerville, 22 January, 1855; H. M. Waddell, *Journals*, Vol. 10, pp. 61–63.

89 Vide Chapter 4 in this volume.

90 The memorial is reprinted in full in the U.P. *Missionary Record* for December, 1855. A summary of the memorial appears in W. Marwick, op. cit., pp. 305–08. The incident also received wide publicity in the Scottish newspapers of the time.

91 H. M. Waddell, *Journals*, Vol. 2, entry for 11 October, 1855, pp. 16–17.

92 CALPROF 2/1, Vol. 7, Clarendon to T. J. Hutchinson, 13 November, 1855; also H. M. Waddell, *Journals*, Vol. 2, entry for 21 January, 1856, p. 38.

93 For Waddell's ideas about the 'African environment', vide ibid., Vol. 2, entry for 1 May, 1856, p. 64.

94 The right of asylum claimed by the Mission House was described as 'dangerous' by the secretary to the Presbyterian Mission Committee in 1848:

> The principles involved in this seems to me a dangerous one, liable to be greatly misunderstood and abused. It is the principle which in the palmy days of popery made the clergy demand exemption from the operation of the Civil Power . . . Missionaries cannot interfere with the civil administration of a country any further than teaching what is right. Their office is instruction.

Somerville to H. Goldie, 20 November, 1848. U.P. Secretaries' *Letter Book*, Vol. 1, p. 211, cited in J. F. A. Ajayi, op. cit., p. 117. The secretary of the Foreign Mission Committee thought that it savoured of Roman Catholicism to claim any such right. Vide also H. M. Waddell, *Journals*, Vol. 7, entry for 4 December, 1849, p. 49.

95   W. Marwick, op. cit., p. 341.
96   Ibid., p. 346.
97   Rev. Anderson, Journal entry for 1 June, 1856, in U.P. *Missionary Record*, 1856, pp. 151–8, cited in J. F. A. Ajayi, op. cit., p. 120.
98   W. Marwick, op. cit., pp. 351–2. For a full narration of the negotiations vide H. M. Waddell, *Journals*, Vol. 2, entry for 14 June, 1856, pp. 74–75, and 17 June, 1856, pp. 77–78.
99   Ibid., Vol. 8, 10 September, 1850, p. 33.
100 Ibid., 26 September, 1850, p. 36.
101 Ibid., 3 October, 1850, p. 37.
102 W. Marwick, op. cit., p. 261.
103 H. M. Waddell, *Journals*, Vol. 2, entry for 28 April, 1856, pp. 61–62.
104 Vide CALPROF 4/1, Vol. 1, Liverpool African Association to Beecroft, 27 January, 1852; Masters and supercargoes in the Old Calabar River to Beecroft, ibid, 26 April, 1852.

IV

Economic Stress: the 1860s

The 1850s was a decade characterized by a buoyant economy as well as by a political mechanism able to redress shifts in the balance of economic and political power between European supercargoes and Efik traders. The volume of trade remained high despite appreciable fluctuations, the prices realized were favourable and there was sufficient oil to accommodate all traders. There was security for trade to develop and, despite the occasional incident when supercargoes seized Efik middlemen on charges of failing to honour trade agreements, a general acquiescence to Efik authority could be noted. The anti-slave trade treaties, for instance, confirmed the supremacy of Efik authority by referring disputes between Efik and European traders to Efik kings.

In the 1860s and 1870s the political situation underwent a dramatic transformation. The kings who succeeded the Great Duke Ephraim in Duke Town and King Eyo II in Creek Town were of lesser political genius and, as earlier writers have shown, there was a consolidation in the position of the supercargoes and the consul. The Efik kings were unable to circumvent the rash lawlessness of the supercargoes who deliberately used the trust system of trade in order to weaken the Efik political machinery and to strengthen their own position. This decline in Efik political leadership after about 1858 cannot be explained merely by reference to the want of political dynamism in the later kings nor can it be explained by showing that there was a consolidation in the position of the super-cargoes.

A crucial factor explaining why later kings were less able to use their positions to obtain favourable trading concessions from European traders, why supercargoes found it possible to extend their trading frontiers, and why the kings accepted commercial codes drawn up by supercargoes, seems to be the changes which occurred in the economy of Calabar in the 1860s and the 1870s.

The theory, in simple terms, is that the trade in oil in these two decades did not expand with sufficient rapidity to contain the increase in trade competition and as a consequence engendered an economic stress in Calabar. The premise on which this theory is based departs from the observations of earlier writers who claim that trade actually expanded until 1872. Professor Dike states that the sixties, far from being the era of retraction, saw the rapid expansion of trade (and empire) in Nigeria.[1] Gertzel has remarked that the sixties were boom years in the oil trade.[2] She placed the peak of the expansion in the Niger oil trade at about 1878.[3] This premise about expansion in trade was not only basic to her extensive treatment of the commercial organization on the Niger Coast but also led her to conclude that the major problems faced by European supercargoes were not economic but political and social. Even the British consuls of the period were writing about the prosperity of the trade along the coast.

The data available for the volume and value of trade at the Bights of Benin and Biafra in the 1860s and 1870s indicates that trade had not really expanded at any phenomenal rate compared with the boom conditions of the 1850s. There are only two good years, 1867–1868 and 1870–1871, as the following figures illustrate.[4]

FLUCTUATION OF TRADE AT THE BIGHTS OF BENIN AND BIAFRA, 1860s AND 1870s

	Increase(+)/*Decrease*(−) *in trade between years shown*	
Years	*Expressed in tons*	*Expressed in percentages*
1857–64	+4,408	+20·41
1864–66	−3,700	−14·23
1866–67	+1,900	+8·25
1867–68	+6,800	+28·10
1868–69	−7,500	−24·19
1869–70	−100	−0·43
1870–71	+5,100	+21·79

For the most part, British trade with the Niger Delta was included under the title 'western coast of Africa, not particularly designated'. This classification included other parts of the coast outside formal British jurisdiction in addition to the Bights. However, the bulk of the imports into Britain under this heading must have originated from the Delta. Also, existing statistics do not always take into account exports from the coast to France and Germany and the average prices quoted might disguise fluctuations likely to occur within an oil season. Even the figures available for oil imports into Britain from the 'Western coast of Africa, not particularly designated'[5] do not seem to indicate any substantial increase in the value of imports: (see overleaf).

Year	Value of imports (£)	Quantities (in cwt.)
1864	1,121,370	666,582
1865	1,450,409	798,724
1866	1,606,797	799,210
1867	1,568,194	812,080
1868	1,891,573	960,059
1869	1,583,701	814,520
1870	1,583,830	868,270
1871	1,820,698	1,047,882
1872	1,805,153	1,006,497
1873	1,713,829	1,017,947
1874	1,792,041	1,067,767
1875	1,508,299	904,562
1876	1,529,360	879,824
1877	1,598,166	897,264
1878	1,167,161	670,797
1879	1,450,000	

The prices paid for palm oil do not seem to have risen substantially in the 1860s and 1870s compared with the 1850s, as the following figures of selling price per ton in Liverpool bear out:[6]

1845–50	£32	1861			£47
1851	£29	1862			£43½–44
1853	£36	1863			£41
1857	£47	1864			£34
1858	£40	1865			£33–36
1859	£40	1872		Aug.	£35
1860	£46	1877		Feb.	£37–38

The figures cited above are not intended to prove that trade had in fact declined but merely to support the contention that even if it had increased it had not done so substantially, and that it was not in a position to contain the rapid increase in trade competition. Indeed, as will be seen later, there is also circumstantial evidence of an economic stress in the Bights in the 1860s and 1870s. The evidence includes over-extension by the trading companies, falling prices in England, rising prices in the Oil Rivers, lower profit margins, cut-throat competition for a non-expanding trade, determination to open new markets, tightening of credit, clashes of interests due to attempts at foreclosure, and similar trends. These developments are intimately related to the state of economic stress in the coast in the 1860s and 1870s. Hence, the major problems faced by both European and Efik traders were not merely political and social as Gertzel maintains, but also economic in nature. It is possible that the political and social relations between the Efik and European traders were largely determined by the stress and strain in the economy. The commercial treaties signed after 1858 transferred responsibility for the settlement of trade disputes from the jurisdiction of the kings to the supercargoes sitting in council with the kings. To give institutional expression to this new arrangement, courts of equity were created. The dissatisfaction that the equity court system engendered led to a series of unpleasant exchanges between Efik and European traders. Economic stress may be said to have in part led to political turbulence.

Increase in trade competition

It was the increase in trade competition after 1853 which was the genesis of the economic strain felt in the 1860s and 1870s. Two groups of traders, the Sierra Leoneans and the independent European traders, entered into the trade of the river in the early years of the 1850s. The former group had come to Calabar, Bonny and the other coastal states following the Jones Mission of 1853[7] while the latter were a group of self employed European merchants of small means who hoped to trade independently of the large trading factories. For convenience, both these new categories of African and European traders may be referred to as 'independent traders'.

What was it that enabled the independent traders to enter the oil trade hitherto monopolized by the well established Liverpool ring of large merchant companies? The answer seems to lie in the inauguration in 1853 by the African Steamship Company of regular steamship communication to the West coast of Africa.[8] Despite the probability that freight rates would have been higher on the first steamers, since steam was still not competitive with sail for bulk freight until the invention of the triple expansion steam engine in the 1880s, and despite too the inadequacy of cargo space since much coal had to be stored to meet the needs of inefficient boilers, the new means of transport introduced by the company initiated a revolution in West African trade. It provided passages when previously one could get them only with the greatest of difficulty; it opened up mail communication formerly non-existent; it speeded turnover in the sense that one could ship smaller consignments instead of a full vessel and therefore reduced the capital required to commence trading operations;[9] and generally the introduction of the steamship service afforded an opportunity for the small trader with humble financial resources to enter into the West African trade.

The Sierra Leonean traders were thus enabled to enter into the trade system and export their produce directly to England, thereby performing a function not dissimilar to that of the Efik middle-men.[10] Like the independent European traders who came out to the coast to trade with the Efik, the Sierra Leoneans were naturally advocates of the policy of economic liberalism and free trade. They stoutly challenged the monopoly thrown over the commerce of the river by the Liverpool ring of companies. These companies were Tobin and Horsfall, Hatton and Cookson, Stuarts, Harrisons, and Laughlands. They had been in the slave trade before they ventured into the oil trade. Although their monopoly came to be termed 'Liverpool monopoly', it was not strictly so. The monopoly spoken of was the trade control exercised or attempted by these firms and others, especially Glasgow firms, in the ring.[11] With two steamers operating between England and the African coast, the independent traders had by the 1870s secured nearly the whole of the carrying trade.[12]

The initial reaction of the Efik middlemen towards the entry of the independent traders into the trade system was not basically one of alarm. They saw in the Sierra Leoneans and the new group of European traders an opportunity to undermine or at least loosen the stranglehold upon them of the trust system of trade of the European supercargoes operating on behalf of the merchant com-panies. For instance, King Eyo refused to honour the trust pay-ment he had accepted from the supercargoes and instead sold his oil to the Sierra Leonean traders who subsequently sold it to the independent European traders. It is probable that the Efik kings profited from this pattern of transaction because the Sierra Leonean traders, by virtue of their lower capital costs, could pay a higher price for the oil than the supercargoes. But it must be stressed that the economic alliance between the Efik middlemen and the Sierra Leoneans was temporary. It was intended only to break the monopoly of the Liverpool traders by contracting trade arrange-ments outside existing agreements. There was no intention of allowing Sierra Leoneans a pre-eminent position in trade. The Efik middleman depended for his livelihood on his middleman position, and it was he who made possible the smooth conversion from slave to oil trade.[13] He was just as anxious to keep apart the Sierra Leonean traders and the interior producers of oil as he was to keep apart the coastal Europeans from the interior producers.

The supercargoes, feeling outrageously betrayed, struck out at the Sierra Leoneans whom they regarded as 'interlopers' since they bought from the Efik the oil for which the supercargoes had paid trust. In 1853, King Eyo began selling oil privately to a Sierra Leonean trader named Peter Nicoll,[14] a transaction which soon came to the notice of the enraged supercargoes. Matters came to a head on 1 November, 1855 when Captain Cuthbertson, a supercargo in the employ of Messrs. Wilson and Dawson of Liverpool, seized sixteen puncheons of palm oil belonging to Nicoll and a vessel, *Candance*, that was to have conveyed the oil to London. The explanation given by Cuthbertson was that he could not recover an outstanding debt owed him by Creek Town if Nicoll was not held hostage. Nicoll disavowed any association he had with Creek Town's debt, stated that he was a 'British subject' and had the same rights to trade in any part of the world as any British supercargo.[15] In appealing for redress from the acting consul, Lynslager, Nicoll pointed out that the seizure represented a breach of all the laws of commercial honour and honesty and a violation of his privileges as a British subject.[16] Cuthbertson and the other supercargoes, who were ruthlessly determined to deal firmly with the new competitors, claimed that they had been 'perfectly unable' to obtain their trust from the Efik. They argued that in disposing of his oil to others through Nicoll, Eyo had not only delayed the supply of oil to European vessels but had also shipped it in casks lent by supercargoes to the Efik for their own oil. Cuthbertson threatened, in the presence of the consul, 'to break Nicoll's head' if he was seen trading in Calabar any longer.[17] Another supercargo, Morgan, an agent for the house of Messrs. Stuart and Douglas of Liverpool, also claimed that King Eyo had failed to honour an arrangement made with him to bring out a small vessel, the *Mars*, laden with a cargo of salt and brass rods. The case of Eyo refusing the cargo of the *Mars* was perhaps an old importer's trick still widely used. If the price of the goods ordered suddenly fell in the market in which one wanted to sell, one would scrutinize the bill of lading and if there was any flaw in it, one refused to accept the goods.

It must be remembered that it was not always possible for the Efik middlemen to meet their trust obligations. An occasion could arise when the price of brass rods,[18] for example, suddenly fell and a commercial crisis developed. In the early years of the nineteenth century European traders found it advisable to take a certain proportion of their cargo in rods to allow for easy purchase in the interior markets.[19] Thus manillas, coppers and cowries were high in the European factory firms' exports to the coast. But in the second half of the century these were a much smaller item in consequence of a large variety of manufactures having taken their place.[20] This was a serious matter because Efik brokers or middlemen rarely offered trade goods to the oil producers in exchange for oil. The traders at Egbo Sharry, one of the principal oil markets in the early and mid-nineteenth century, only accepted copper rods in exchange for oil. This meant that the Efik were obliged to convert the goods that they received from the ships into copper rods at their own markets previous to going there. Consequently, it was not infrequent that Efik middlemen experienced a scarcity of rods, while there might have been a superfluity of them in the interior markets.

The supercargoes, whose only concern was that old debts be liquidated before fresh transactions with others were embarked upon, overlooked the difficulties experienced by the Efik in the interior markets. It was, for instance, never appreciated that the Efik middleman secured some benefit from the trust system only so long as he was the debtor, but as soon as he applied it to the producing peoples upriver he too suffered from precisely the same disadvantages that the supercargoes did, and that for this reason trust could not always be absolutely honoured even when the will to do so was never failing.[21]

The acting consul Lynslager, however, had more sympathy with the supercargoes whom he befriended than understanding of the realities of the economic system. He believed, with the supercargoes, that Creek Town chiefs were inclined to be insolent when asked for trust, fancying themselves to be safe from any hostile measures being taken against them by a man-of-war in consequence of their town being so high up the river.[22] He assembled King Eyo, the chiefs and traders to remonstrate with them on their conduct in obtaining trust. Eyo stated that he had supplied Nicoll with oil because he had received from him cloth, guns, brass rods and iron bars, as well as comey. There was thus no reason why Nicoll should not be entitled to his goods. The king added that October had been a dry season for oil and that he had not been in a position to liquidate all his debts but that the white men bothered him much and that he had 'no peace day or night'. The consul repeated the old arguments, that vessels awaiting trust were incurring heavy expenses, that they faced risk of ill-health, that Eyo had no right to ship oil to England till his trust had been liquidated and that the king had to protect the white men who paid the comey for that reason. He also warned Eyo that it might become necessary to make examples in Calabar of some debtors by taking them away to Fernando Po until their friends had paid the outstanding debts.[23]

In view of the acting consul's reaction Eyo had no alternative but to sign a document legalizing the detention of a Creek Town man for any other Creek Town man who was indebted. The new regulation was defended on the grounds that it was an old country custom, and that it was practised by Calabar people on their up-river neighbours. The traditional system of justice, it was contended, recognized the right of seizure of persons to be held as security for

the payment of debts of others.[24] King Eyo did not have the power
to 'blow Ekpe' on his friends and thus recover debts nor could
he give the acting consul any other mode of guarantee. By an
agreement signed on 17 October, the king promised to liquidate
all trust owed by him to the several supercargoes in the river in the
order of an agreed schedule of supercargoes.[25] Each of the vessels
were to receive in rotation the produce of one market, to consist
of fifty puncheons of 'good saleable' palm oil. In Duke Town,
where Duke Ephraim had refused to 'blow Ekpe' on bad debtors,
the king's attention was drawn to the fifteenth article of a commercial treaty signed in 1852. It was expressly stated in that article
that the house and property of any person who was unable to pay
his debts would be forfeited and sold, and the proceeds given
towards the liquidation of his debts. The king and his traders
promised to give the acting consul one further trial with their Ekpe,
and requested that he return in five months.[26]

The trust system of trade

The inability of the pioneer supercargoes to retain their monopolistic hold over the external trade of Calabar, their refusal to
recognize the independent position of either the African or the
new European small traders,[27] and the way in which the trust
system of trade, a central issue in the controversies of the period,
was used by the supercargoes to deliberately paralyse competitors
and tie the hands of the Efik middlemen illustrate the extent to
which supercargoes were prepared to go to stifle the competition.
Not only did they stand firmly against all competitors to meet the
rivalry, and in the process undermined their own position, but they
also resorted to all manner of ruthless price wars and indiscriminate
giving of trust.

Historians have hitherto pointed out the shortcomings or evils
of the trust system of trade. It is, however, necessary to draw a
distinction initially between the mode of operation of the system
as it was meant to be, and what it was reduced to after the 1850s
by those who operated it. To take the simple view that the system
was ipso facto evil is to ignore the extent to which the supercargoes
and the Efik middlemen were responsible for the failure of the
trust system. The system was faulty only to the extent that it tended
to make trade speculative and profits uncertain.[28] Beyond that,
the traders were to blame for what in fact happened. Initially, the
application of the trust system to the oil trade was vital given
Efik lack of capital. This method of advancing capital stayed on
and became a feature of the trade.[29]

During the days when competition increased in the river, the supercargoes used the trust system to wage a price war against other traders. They did this by lending out extensive credit in the hope that they might be able to wean the oil away from others. The abuse of the system was greater in Calabar than it was elsewhere on the coast.[30] Newcomers to the trade of Calabar in the mid-nineteenth century were staggered at the value of trust given. 'I have entrusted one man with goods, returns of which were worth £2,000 or £3,000', a trader stated, 'not one in ten however that asks for trust is worthy of credit to the amount of so many farthings.'[31] The general result was that more trust was given out than could possibly be honoured in good time. In 1856 a critical situation was fomented by the supercargoes. The latter had extended trust to the value of 9,030 tons of palm oil.[32] Since the average produce of the river between 1855 and 1856 was only 4,050 tons[33] and never at any time exceeded 5,000 tons a year,[34] this meant that the produce of the river had been purchased by the supercargoes for two and a half years in advance.[35] Consul Hutchinson stated that at this period the entire produce of three prospective years would have had to be absorbed to discharge the obligations of one.[36]

There can be little doubt that excessive trust payments were intended not only to complicate the operations of a trade system that was not sufficiently expanding but also to enable the supercargoes to entrench themselves in a formidable position vis-à-vis the Efik polity. They could not have overlooked the possibility that such excessive trust could not be kept by the African middlemen. On the other hand, it would have occurred to them that the trust system of trade, if perpetuated, provided them with the excuse and the occasion for the arbitrary arrest of chiefs and traders who failed to honour commercial agreements and to extract sureties from the chiefs for prompt payment. It was part of the calculated move to consolidate the political position of the supercargoes. Waddell relates how some of the Calabar traders were arrested on board the trading vessels: King Duke Ephraim was arrested for non-settlement of a debt, Young Eyo was arrested for a similar reason. Duke Ephraim, who owed a supercargo thirty-five puncheons of oil, was bound in chains on board the brig *May* till sureties were found for him.[37] In the long run, however, the policy was bound to be ruinous to the interests of the supercargoes; there is evidence of this being realized because attempts were made in the 1850s to control the situation after it had clearly got out of hand. The only way in which trust could have been stopped from being paid was by the European merchants arriving at an agreement between themselves that they would co-operate in no longer-paying trust. Such an understanding was not easy to reach. The competition had become so great that even if some supercargoes were willing and determined to refuse the advance of any more trust till all the outstanding ones had been fulfilled, there were always others who would secretly extend further credit to the middlemen.

Fraud and systematic violence characterized the strategy of the supercargoes in their bid to recover outstanding trust. Since Efik political authority was still supreme, the target of the supercargoes was the Sierra Leoneans. Attempts were made by supercargoes to undermine the confidence of the Efik middlemen in their Sierra Leonean partners. In 1856, Captain Edward Davies, a Liverpool supercargo of the vessel *Calabar*, seized the oil of a Sierra Leonean, Daniel Hedd, and refused to release it. Davies defended his action on the grounds that as Calabar was a 'trust river', all oil produced there belonged to the English ships.[38] Next, the supercargoes attempted to get the Efik kings to expel all Sierra Leoneans from trading in the river. Duke Ephraim of Duke Town was told that if the Efik rulers did not so comply with the advice, the Sierra Leonean men were sure to oust the rulers and take over the country.[39] The missionaries protested on behalf of the emigrants, and a near order by Ephraim to his countrymen to desist from association with Sierra Leoneans was averted by King Eyo.[40]

The Sierra Leoneans had reason to feel that their position in Calabar was an insecure one and they were deeply concerned over the strategy of the supercargoes. Although some had married into Calabar families and the children born on Efik land were regarded as sons and daughters of the soil,[41] other Sierra Leoneans had kept aloof from Efik society. The Efik had charged them with a haughty and arrogant pride and with taking away Efik women whose preference for marriage with the emigrants was related to their apparent wealth and social prominence. The Efik were envious of the economic and social position attained by the Sierra Leonean traders. And so it was that in June, 1856 nine Sierra Leoneans residing in Duke Town submitted to Consul Hutchinson a memorial stating that they lived in fear of being persecuted by the Efik chiefs at the instigation of certain British traders jealous of their entry into the oil markets. Hutchinson, unsure of the British policy towards the emigrants, transmitted the memorial to the Foreign Office and requested to be informed whether, if the liberated Africans were allowed to remain in Duke Town, they were to be subject to the existing laws of Calabar, or whether they were entitled to claim protection as British subjects. Hutchinson's request for instructions was calculated to make it difficult for the British government to deal with such an intricate point in any reasonable time. As later evidence uncovered, Hutchinson was on the side of the supercargoes.

Lack of controls over 'free' trade

A system of 'free' trade needed the exercise of certain controls in order to hold various competing traders together. Britain desired to avoid extensive political embarrassments with the Efik rulers. But she realized that since she espoused the principle of free trade, she would invariably have to support the rights of those who engaged in it. A law officer in the Foreign Office stated the position thus:

> . . . when they (liberated Africans) are attempting to do the very things which H.M's Government would be most desirous that they should do, viz. after receiving some education and embracing Christianity, returning to their native country and there embarking in that particular trade which of all others best promotes cultivation and commerce and most effectively checks S[lave] T[rade] they are met with jealous hostility of British Traders, and I hear thereby exposed to degradation and ill usage by the natives.
>
> The whole policy of H.M.G. in this matter (for which it has made and still makes great sacrifices) is thus effectually thwarted and defeated, and Africans tho' liberated from actual slavery, are prevented from returning to their native country with any security, or from engaging in the staple trade of West Africa, a state of things which H.M's Government cannot be expected to tolerate, especially formally brought under its notice, and going on as it were under the shadow of its Flag, a British man-of-war, a British Consul, missionaries, and merchants being on the spot.[42]

Hutchinson's instructions were to inform the Efik chiefs that the liberated Africans were entitled to the 'sympathy' and 'good offices' of the British government. The issue had received the attention of the Colonial Department many times, and it had been decided that, in the absence of any special legislation, the liberated Africans could not be considered as British subjects even in the Queen's Dominions. The law officer in the Foreign Office, working on the principles of British and International Law, submitted the opinion that those who voluntarily returned to and were resident in the territory of the African chiefs, whose subjects they were by birth, could not be treated as British subjects. But the law officer realized the difficulty of acting along such lines.[43] Hutchinson was further advised to propose to the chiefs the conclusion of a treaty recognizing the right of the Sierra Leoneans to British protection. The intention was to avoid an interruption of the friendly relations with the chiefs of the river as well as to satisfy the liberated Africans in their plea for security. However, Hutchinson's subsequent action was at variance with the spirit if not with the letter of the instructions he received from the Foreign Office. He warned the liberated Africans to be careful in their dealings with British supercargoes so as not to offend them, and to report any mischief to him for transmission to the Foreign Office. He also requested the Governor of Sierra Leone, Stephen Hill, not to freely permit anyone from Sierra Leone to reside within the consular areas;[44] this was agreed to by the Governor, who would henceforth issue certificates to intending emigrants, and the latter would not be allowed to land at Fernando Po except on production of these certificates.[45]

Hutchinson was not unaware of the extent to which the supercargoes were responsible for the worsening of Anglo-Efik commercial relations:

> The trading operations in the rivers of the Bight of Biafra, are not in anything like a condition that promises well for the commercial prosperity of such locality. It is my opinion that Europeans coming out, solely to barter legitimately for the country's products, ought not to interfere in matters of local government, local prejudices, or superstitions with the natives. The short interval that has elapsed (thirty-six years) between the slave trading of former times, and the legitimate commerce of our day, has not made the social and moral condition of the people to be changed *pari passu* with its progress. That is unfortunately overlooked by our commercial representatives, that men who before were liable to be seized, and sold any day in the markets as a puncheon of palm oil is disposed of now are becoming independent traders though not allowed to purchase their own freedom.[46]

Despite Hutchinson's knowledge of the liberties taken by the supercargoes to foment trade crises—a situation that would seem to have basically developed from the lack of any firm authority over the actions of the supercargoes—he was prepared to defend the supercargoes, if not overtly, at least by moral implication. Rather than exercising a stern check on his fellowmen, Hutchinson, at a conference of the Duke Town nobility held on board H.M.S. *Scourge* in June, 1856, made King Duke Ephraim agree that for the future,

> British subjects coming to, trading at, or residing within, the Calabar territory shall in no wise be maltreated without incurring the displeasure of Her Majesty's Government, and that, on a representation of any infraction of Article VI of the Treaty sanctioned by John Beecroft, Esquire, Her Britannic Majesty's Consul, on the 17th April, 1852,[47] and British subject making a complaint to Her

Britannic Majesty's Consul at Fernando Po, shall have a right to demand redress for such grievances.[48]

It should be added that Ephraim Duke, who had been asked to come on board the *Scourge* by some Kroo boys on behalf of the consul to meet the latter, had been forced to attend the meeting following 'a little war-like demonstration' by the supercargoes. It involved the pointing of the guns towards the town.[49]

The general effect of the terms of the treaty was to increase the confidence (and the indiscretions) of the supercargoes, as evidenced by a desperate plea made by Duke Ephraim to Hutchinson in August, 1856:

> I beg you to do something to stop the white men from going into the House of Calabar men and knocking them. You white men have fashion to bind men to keep the peace, so I beg you to do this, and not let palaver come up again.[50]

Ephraim had earlier been told of several attacks made on a lame Efik, Henshaw, by Cuthbertson, the ostensible cause of which (according to the missionaries) was Henshaw's disapproval of Cuthbertson keeping as his mistress a woman belonging to the Henshaw house.[51] The young men of Calabar took Cuthbertson to task for his brutality and summoned the consul. Hutchinson proceeded to fine Cuthbertson a nominal four puncheons of oil whilst the victim of the attack, Henshaw, was punished with a fine of twenty puncheons of oil, with the additional provision that his Ekpe titles be stripped from him.

Situations such as that described above, if allowed to persist, threatened to draw Britain into the fray of river politics. This was realized by Clarendon, head of the Foreign Office at this time, who noted that there was no special mechanism for making supercargoes amenable to justice in England through the intervention of the Foreign Office.[52] Neither the British government nor her consul at Fernando Po possessed any legal powers to oblige the British supercargoes stationed in the rivers to adopt, or to obey, any particular code of trading regulation. Lord Clarendon was convinced, as Hutchinson was not, that the African small trader must be given a fair chance to compete with others; but he left it to the consul's discretion to bring this about. He requested Hutchinson to inform the supercargoes that:

> If in order to recover debts due by the natives to them, they choose to have recourse to unjust, violent, and high handed measures, such as detaining one man on board ship as hostage for another, or seizing palm oil, the property of one man in payment of a debt, due by another, the British Consul at Fernando Po must leave the

supercargoes to themselves, and abandon as useless all attempts to arbitrate between them and the Native chiefs.[53]

Hutchinson said he felt the grievances of African small traders were of 'some importance',[54] both on commercial grounds, viz. the encouragement of an independent class of traders, and also with a view to the final extinction of the slave trade. His primary motive was to make it appear to the Foreign Office that he had to be clothed with additional powers if he was to be able to deal with recalcitrant supercargoes, and what he had in mind was 'magisterial powers'.

Fortification of the European position
Part of the strength of the Efik middlemen was their ability to impose an embargo on the trade with the supercargoes. The supercargoes contrived to prevent the effectiveness of this course of action and even more importantly to fortify their own position by drafting in 1856 a set of by-laws 'for the better regulation of trading matters between the parties subscribing to it'.[55] At a meeting of the supercargoes and Efik traders called on board H.M.S. *Myrmidon* it was resolved to create a 'court of equity' to keep in their integrity the by-laws and regulations made with regard to trade. The supercargoes counted upon the support of the consul, Hutchinson, who promptly sanctioned the resolutions of the meeting, even before he had sought the advice of Lord Clarendon.

A few illustrations, derived from the provisions of the agreement of September 19, will reveal that the rules, far from checking the excesses of both Efik and European traders, sought to fortify the position of the European against that of the African trader. Article one, which created the court of equity, did not confer voting rights on all the African members of the court but only on the two kings. Since the European members of the court had the privilege of being voting members, and constituted half the membership of the court, and since majority votes carried any particular motion, and since the chairman (who was always a European) had two votes, the European supercargoes virtually had their way. The fifth article stated that in the case of default in debt payments the supercargoes should refuse as a body to take any oil from the debtors until the ship first ready to go out was settled with; and that each supercargo should bind himself to intimate to the chairman of the court if any oil was being offered. All cases of appeal against the decisions of the court were to be referred to the consul. Article nine stated that in the event of any African trader attempting to evade the penalty of the court, by

K

non-appearance or otherwise, notice of such a defaulter would be sent to all the traders and supercargoes in the river. The supercargoes were bound, under penalty of a hundred crews of good palm oil, to forbid such a defaulter from coming to their ships for trade or on any other pretext. Article ten declared that if an Efik refused to pay a fine that was imposed by the court, he would be stopped from going on board ships in the river. But a supercargo refusing to pay up a fine was only to be deprived of the privileges of the equity court. By article seven, fines collected by the court were to be applied to the expenses of the erection and maintenance of the court house. Fines of palm oil were to be handed over to the ship next in rotation for going out, the supercargo paying the worth thereof in copper to the chairman who could not be at any time in the position of getting the oil from his own ship.

Article eleven stipulated that if, after the payment of comey for the privilege of trading, a supercargo could prove that the trade of his ship had been stopped 'either directly or indirectly', upon any pretext whatever, the kings would be held responsible for such stoppage, and would have to pay one puncheon of saleable palm oil per day for each hundred tons registered to the ship, as compensation for the loss incurred. The oil was to be paid within seven days after such stoppage, and would continue to be paid as long as the trade of any such ship was stopped. Persons who attempted trading without paying comey were liable to have their oil seized as smuggled produce, and delivered to the supercargo next in rotation to leave the river. That this was a deliberate measure to strangle the small trader there can be little doubt.

Article thirteen permitted supercargoes to commence trading even if their comey was not accepted by the Efik kings; such comey could be paid in cargo by the ship when subsequently demanded. Article seventeen tightened the payment of goods by requiring that in the event of the kings or any other traders making an agreement to take goods from a ship at a certain rate, all such agreements would be perfectly binding; in case the goods agreed upon were not paid for within the time specified, such goods would be forfeited and the oil considered due, as though the goods had actually been paid. Oil not supplied during the ship's stay in the river would be deducted from the comey of the ship on a future voyage, or from that of any other ship in the same employ. In the event of an Efik trader failing to pay his debt in the time awarded by the court of equity, article eighteen required that the king deliver the trader 'as a prisoner' until such time that his debts were paid to the supercargo concerned.

Article twenty stipulated that for the future all trust was to be given out in valid bills. Article twenty-two stated that any super-cargoes aiding a trader who had not met a previous commitment of trust would be denied the aid of the equity court in recovering his debts. The next article stipulated that in the event of the death of an Efik trader owing debts to supercargoes, if his successor be not of age or otherwise fit, an order from the court would be suffi-cient to empower the king and chiefs to take charge of the property, and be responsible for settling the late trader's debts. Article twenty-four stated that in the case of a Calabar trader being absent from a court hearing of his case, the court would order the king and chiefs to send for him, and that eight days would be allowed for his appearance, after which the king and chiefs would be fined twenty pieces of cloth for every seven days until the absentee was produced before the court. The eight days' grace might have been the normal time spent by a trader up the river.

The regulations were clearly designed to secure the observance by the Efik of a set of laws which guaranteed ideal trade con-ditions for the supercargoes. Having sanctioned these regulations, Hutchinson approached King Duke Ephraim and successfully negotiated with him for the making over to the consul of a piece of ground in Duke Town on which the proposed court house was to be built. The court, it was written into the agreement, would 'make stronger the ties of friendship and trade transactions between the (Europeans) and the natives of Old Calabar'. The gift was declared to have been made by the king's own free will 'without any offer of reward, purchase, bribe or because of any threat'.[56] It is not clear why the Efik traders accepted the stringent rules dicta-ted by the supercargoes. Perhaps they had lost their bargaining position as a result of the economic stress that confronted them. Or perhaps article twelve was attractive to the Efik rulers; this article provided that no man would be recognized a legitimate trader in the country unless he paid, through the court, a comey of 20,000 coppers per annum for the privileges of purchasing and shipping oil; it is probably that the Efik rulers believed this provision would increase their revenue.

Lord Clarendon was nervous about the code of by-laws that had been sanctioned by the consul. The British government was studying the matter of consular magisterial authority and did not desire to agree to the code of by-laws because it did not want to assert to any partial trading regulation that might later lead to embarrassing situations. The Foreign Office had several objections to the code of by-laws. In the first place, viewed as a whole, it was a fraud to favour and protect the interest of supercargoes at the expense of all others—whether Efik, British subjects or liberated

Africans. Sufficient protection was not provided for the Efik against the supercargoes; neither was there sufficient proof to be found in the code for compelling supercargoes to pay their debts to the Efik, or for punishing a supercargo for fraudulent or improper conduct towards the Efik. In view of the habitually harsh and unjust treatment of the Efik, it was manifest that some provisions for their protection were urgently requisite. Secondly, there was no provision for the prevention by punishment of fraud or wrongs committed by a supercargo against the non-Efik, such as liberated Africans, or non-British European traders.

Also considered altogether unjustifiable and likely to lead to serious abuses and crimes was the eighteenth article, which declared that any Calabar trader who might fail to pay his debts to a supercargo was liable to be detained as a prisoner on board the ships until his debts were paid. The fact that the king and chiefs of Calabar were consenting parties to that article did not alter its 'very objectionable character' as it was not calculated to diminish the evils to which it might give rise. Clarendon regretted that such a law should have received Hutchinson's sanction, and should have been enacted at a meeting held on board one of Her Majesty's ships.[57]

Some of Hutchinson's verdicts on disputes had been declared by Clarendon to be unsatisfactory. In the case of a Sierra Leonean man, Daniel Hedd, from whom a supercargo, Captain Davies, had seized with impunity six puncheons of oil, Lord Clarendon stated that the consul's statement, namely that Daniel Hedd's oil was liable to seizure because he had not paid his comey, was against his own remarks on the subject. Hutchinson had effected the twelfth article of the regulations, which had forbidden the trade in palm oil to all who did not pay a sum of twenty thousand coppers for that privilege. It would appear that the object of this article was to prevent certain Sierra Leonean men, resident on the mission grounds, from shipping oil to England before they had settled with the supercargoes. In this particular incident, the law had not even been in existence when the disputed oil had been seized; nor had Davies produced any evidence in proof of his claim that Hedd was not the rightful owner of the oil.[58]

Lord Clarendon spoke of the introduction of the new comey principle as open to grave objections, and the season assigned by Hutchinson for its adoption in the new code as unsatisfactory. While such a regulation may be very beneficial to Calabar chiefs and supercargoes, it was not just as it affected other persons, especially Sierra Leoneans. If the export of palm oil had been hitherto free from all tax or restriction, argued Clarendon, there was no reason why it should be burdened or be made a monopoly.

In October, 1856, the Foreign Office drew up a memorandum as to the mode of investing the British consul with magisterial powers. The preamble explained that it was done as a result of the attention of the Foreign Office being called to the difficulties of the consul in guarding the commercial intercourse between British subjects and African chiefs against any disputes and misunderstandings. The proposed measures were to place the important trade on a more secure footing. Lord Clarendon outlined two ways of ensuring the latter.

The first was for the consuls to draw up rules for the regulation of trade which the chiefs would promulgate, enforce and should there be any infringers, punish either by fine, suspension of trade, or expulsion. The memorandum observed:

> It is to be borne in mind that, without the active co-operation of these chiefs it will be difficult, if not impossible, to exercise any real control either over the British captains and traders, or over the natives connected with them; and also that this system is applicable to places where, from particular circumstances, it might be impracticable to establish a Consular Court.[59]

The second was for the Queen, by Order in Council, to exercise whatever power or jurisdiction she actually had, or might acquire over British subjects in the territories or waters of the African chiefs, as was done in the Ottoman dominions, China and Siam, and accordingly invest British consuls in Africa with magisterial powers. Such powers would include a certain control over the supercargoes engaged in trade with Africans within the consular jurisdiction. The second course was to be followed if the first failed, and a district was to be selected for trying out the above-mentioned scheme.

Clearly, Hutchinson had no great love for the liberated Africans engaged in trade. They threatened to complain to Clarendon about Hutchinson's high-handed dealings with them and 'your [Hutchinson's] very disgraceful conduct in the administration of the office you hold'.[60] They listed three instances of this 'disgraceful conduct': his threats to shoot down 'like a crow' a Sierra Leonean, Thomas Williams; his instigation to Governor Lynslager of Fernando Po to declare war on the inhabitants; and his refusal to recognize them either as British or Spanish subjects of the island.[61]

Towards the end of 1857, when the question of comey payments was raised by the supercargoes, Hutchinson supported the latter in their bid to change the proportion paid to Creek Town. In 1852, it had been decided that Eyo II was to receive two-thirds of the comey paid by British supercargoes to the Efik kings, while King Ephraim Duke would receive one-third.[62]

The payment of comey carried a direct political significance. Its amount was related to the volume of trade done with the town,[63] and since wealth was an important element in the political process, each town sought to gain as much of it as possible. Supercargoes who paid the comey used it as a political weapon to support those houses which did most trade with them. Following Eyo's private trading methods, the supercargoes decided to revise the amount of comey paid to him. In 1857 an agreement was arrived at between the Duke Town traders and the supercargoes to reduce the comey hitherto paid to King Eyo from two-thirds to one half. King Eyo and the Creek Town chiefs were absent from this meeting, which also decided that if King Eyo did not acquiesce in the arrangement reducing the amount of comey to be paid to him, the payment of all comey would be suspended until the consul's next visit to the river.

Clarendon refused to approve the agreement until he had heard what the Creek Town chiefs had to say on the matter as it occurred to him that if the proposed changes were resisted by King Eyo and his chiefs it was likely to produce an interruption in the trade of the river and injure British interests. Hutchinson, who had gladly sanctioned the arrangement, defended it on the grounds that he was 'doing only what conduced to British interest'. Comey was British goods paid for protection of British property, he argued, and King Eyo had set the example to others of commercial speculation to his own advantage before discharging his debts. A precedent of this nature, argued Hutchinson, was likely to result in an enormous loss of British property.[64]

Moreover, he added, the trading peoples of Duke Town were in the proportion of twenty to one compared with Creek Town, and they had many a time complained to him of the inequitable division of comey. No rent was paid, alleged the consul, on the cask houses at Creek Town beach; palavers often arose in the interior of Creek Town and traders had to pay to settle the palavers while also paying comey. King Eyo invited the consul to come to Duke Town palaver house to discuss the subject of comey. Hutchinson refused to do so, and went ahead with the arrangements for comey payment. He also told the kings of both towns that although comey was a matter best arranged between them, as Duke Town traders furnished the ships with three-quarters of the oil brought out of the river, it seemed to him at least an 'act of common justice' that the protest of King Duke against his receiving only one third of the comey should receive 'very serious consideration'.[65] The trade figures of the time could not be ascertained. But the palaver over comey sharing dragged on for a decade. The British government's view that all the interested parties must agree to any decision made was repeated time and again.[66]

That Hutchinson's policies were not guided by any altruistic motives was made manifestly plain following the enquiries into the '*Olinda* incident' in Calabar in 1857. This incident is described as the biggest effort ever made by the African community to break the Liverpool monopoly.[67] It concerned the proceedings of King Eyo who shipped oil on his own account in the brig *Olinda* to England, before he had liquidated a debt of four hundred tons of oil (worth £18,000) owing to the supercargoes in the river. Hutchinson, determined to see that Eyo did not trifle with British capital,[68] summoned him on board H.M.S. *Firefly*, and intimidated him into signing an agreement not to ship oil in the *Olinda* till all his debts to the Liverpool firm of Cuthbertson were cleared. Hutchinson's action could hardly be said to be in accord with his admission later, which could not have escaped him in 1857, that the existence of credit was utterly subversive to all principles of commercial morality.[69] It should also be remembered that the British government made it abundantly clear to the consul that the system of inordinate credits was one which she did not condone and that she was anxious for the discontinuance of the system and the substitution of an open and healthy trade in the African rivers. The British government was categorical that the parties least entitled to official support in their transactions with the Calabar chiefs were those which perpetuated a species of trading 'so opposed to sound policy and so prejudicial to the extension of commerce on the African coasts.'[70]

The British government's enquiries three years later into the entire question of trust and monopoly on the African coast, which the *Olinda* incident occasioned, brought to light highly revealing evidence of the ulterior motives which had guided Hutchinson's actions. It was proved that Hutchinson was a former employee of a large merchant company, Hearn and Cuthbertson, and that it was on their behalf that he had interfered in trade.[71] The most damaging evidence which exposed him as 'a very imperfectly qualified individual' was, however, that the consul had received bribes and had a vested interest in the trade. King Eyo complained of Hutchinson's conduct towards him on matters connected with trade in the river. Hutchinson replied that, except for the signature of Eyo on the letter, the whole tenor of Eyo's argument as well as its composition was believed to be that of Lewis, the agent for *Olinda* who had since his trip to Calabar been a resident in the king's house.[72] The *Olinda* affair dragged on for some time and Hutchinson was eventually found guilty as charged and replaced in 1861 by Burton. Dike sees the importance of the incident as showing the disparity between the views of the consul and those of the Foreign Office,[73] but the disparity had become clear for some time before April, 1857. The incident is also significant in that it raised the question of how much discretion the consuls, as 'men-on-the-spot', had been allowed in sorting out the problems of the coast.

Strained relationships

One of the factors that affected economic circumstances in Calabar in the late 1850s was the opening of Lagos to British trade after the bombardment of 1851. Western Nigeria soon became a substantial producer of oil in competition with Calabar for the English market. The supercargoes began to express doubts regarding the future security of the trade, and in particular about the collection of outstanding debts. After 1858, when trade failed to expand in proportion to the growth in number of traders, the attitude of the supercargoes towards the regulation of society by Efik or English laws was even more disconcerting than it had been before. The supercargoes wanted to be free to choose under what laws they were to be judged or to judge others by, as circumstances warranted.

While the consul had made it clear that Ekpe authority should not be invoked upon supercargoes who were British subjects and therefore outside the jurisdiction of Efik laws, the supercargoes felt free to resort to Ekpe laws for the capture and detention on board British vessels of Efik men who owed them debts. Yet the supercargoes insisted that the employment of Ekpe by the Efik to stop trade with the Europeans was directly contrary to article nine of the treaty ratified between Beecroft and Calabar authorities on 17 April, 1852. When in May, 1858 Ekpe was 'blown' by Kings Eyo and Duke Ephraim on Captain Cuthbertson of *Soodianah*, Consul Hutchinson felt obliged to inform the captain that his action in taking a man prisoner according to Ekpe fashion, and the practice of appealing to Ekpe law for the payment of their debts, would render him amenable to the provisions of Ekpe statutes. His reasoning was:

> Because if they appeal to Egbo law in one matter, they should not in common justice, honesty and straight-forwardness of dealing repudiate it in another.[74]

But the supercargoes did not make any fine distinctions. They demanded to know why Ekpe had been 'blown' on Cuthbertson, as it was at variance with previous treaties on the subject, and they were aware that the penalty for the offence was nine-and-a-half puncheons of palm oil per day for every day of such stoppage. They threatened to send a boat to the consul[75] and hold King Eyo responsible for all detention caused to that ship.[76] The consul said that he had no jurisdiction in such palavers.[77]

In May, 1858 the British supercargoes and the Efik traders signed an agreement on board H.M.S. *Pluto* at Duke Town. They agreed firstly that King Eyo guarantee the payment of ten puncheons of palm oil for any assault committed by an Efik trader on a British subject; the British supercargoes also agreed to a vice-versa provision; this was to prevent the recurrence of future complaints of assaults between the contracting parties; secondly, to prevent any collision of misunderstanding between the British supercargoes going ashore to demand their debts at Creek Town and the Efik traders, it was agreed that until all the old debts were paid King Eyo would guarantee (on the visit of any supercargo to his town) to have all the debtors called together at his house, and to use his influence as well as authority to oblige them to pay their debts.[78] This agreement, it was hoped, would obviate recurrence of past proceedings.

The years after 1858 also marked a breakdown in the relations between supercargoes and missionaries because the latter sided with the Efik rulers in questioning the practice of supercargoes habitually seizing defaulters. The missionaries also gave protection to those defaulters who fled to the mission house in order to avoid seizure by the supercargoes. In 1858, one Egbo Bassey was detained by Captain Baak on board a Dutch vessel, *Endragt*, for a debt of two puncheons of oil and a trade cask due for about three years.[79] Egbo Bassey, who had been extended British protection by Consul Beecroft, fled from the *Endragt* to the mission house to seek protection from further arrests. Hutchinson, while still the consul, stated that the protection given to the fugituve by Rev. Baillie of the Duke Town mission house established a precedent likely to hinder the collection of the large amount of outstanding debts.

The supercargoes could never tolerate missionary endeavours to prevent the seizure of persons entitled to British protection. To them, such policies amounted to an interference with their trade.[80] Another supercargo, Hearn, actually went to the lengths in 1858 of asking if anyone had appointed the chief missionary, Rev. Waddell, a 'British vice-consul'. He warned Waddell that he would hold him responsible for any loss caused to supercargoes by missionaries who tried to usurp authority and took power out of the hands of British merchants during the consul's absence from the river. Waddell was accused of preventing the traders from collecting their debts, affording sanctuary to debtors in spite of the king of the country, and of telling King Eyo not to fear anything that the traders had to say.[81] The supercargoes also wrote to the consul that Waddell would not deliver up Egbo Bassey to the six British supercargoes and a Dutch trader, and that they could expect no redress from any quarter for their grievance. They threatened to send word to their employees to sue the mission party for any loss the traders incurred. Added the supercargoes:

> The Mission Houses are the resort of every low and bad character in the place—as they have done no good here of any king, they must make a show of congregation. The object of this attack is looked upon by all, as a conspiracy to try and throw off their debts.[82]

Hutchinson reasoned with the traders against the missionaries:

> . . . I trace the generation of the present spirit manifested by the supercargoes towards the missionaries, chiefly to the facts that Sierra Leone Negroes coming to Old Calabar and settling there—chiefly on the mission grounds—are assisting the natives in shipping oil to England before they have paid their debts to the supercargoes. As I believe the Liverpool Merchants give the supercargoes instructions to recover these oil debts by whatever means they can, the practice which has existed out here for a very long time of British traders taking the law into their own hands, no doubt influences these men still to persist in the custom of by-gone times. This is to adopt the country laws for enforcing the payment of their debts—that of Egbo especially—one provisions of which gives the power of 'chopping' oil or seizing and imprisoning the person to enforce the payment of debts claimed.[83]

The Court of Equity: a movement away from tradition
    The fact that supercargoes felt at liberty to seize indebted middlemen and Efik traders in retaliation did not mean that the Efik kings had lost control over their own traders; they still retained that authority but it now became increasingly difficult to contain supercargoes within bounds. Law and order, so effectively maintained by the Efik kings in the first forty years of the nineteenth century, had progressively become a more complicated matter and the security needed for trade to develop was threatened by disputes within the trade system.[84]
    The court of equity formed in 1856 had transferred the responsibility for the settlement of trade disputes from the African chiefs

to the supercargoes acting in conjunction with the kings, in the court of equity.[85] But the court functioned only in the records of the British Consul. The establishment of the court could there-fore be related to the political and economic turbulence engendered by the commercial malpractices of the supercargoes and Efik middlemen. It represented a radical movement away from tradition. In earlier days, the Efik king was usually the one who integrated and co-ordinated relations between the European and African traders. He was the supreme political authority and maintained the peace of the river. But by the end of the first half of the nineteenth century, the economic strain experienced by Calabar altered the pattern of inter-state relations. Henceforth, the external policies of the state were no longer the preserve of the Efik kings but that of a tribunal, consisting of both Efik kings and European traders. This tribunal or court signified a change from the personal relationship of the kings with the European supercargoes to an institutionalized relationship. It did not mean that European traders refused to accept the political authority of the kings, but that this was largely confined to domestic matters. Supercargoes could call upon the king as the head, or at least as an important member of Ekpe, to mobilize the society to collect their debts.[86]

While supercargoes formed their court of equity, the British government, yielding to the persistent demands of the consuls, drafted a lengthy Order in Council for the government of British subjects within the jurisdiction of the consuls. The order provided also for the protection of Kroomen and others serving on British vessels.

In January, 1860, an agreement signed between Hutchinson and Eyo Honesty III on board the *Spitfire*,[87] declared that the interests of all British subjects coming to, or residing in the territories of Eyo Honesty were to be placed under the regulation and control of the consul at Fernando Po. The consul was also to give effect to all rules and regulations that were or might be enacted by Her Majesty in Council or by any authorized British officer, as regards the conduct of their trade and the prevention of violation of laws.[88] A similar agreement was signed with a chief of Duke Town, John Archibong, in May, 1860.[89]

By 1862 it was clear that the court of equity had failed in its task of establishing fair and equitable trading conditions. Nor was it surprising, since the regulations were designed to benefit only one of the parties to the arrangements. Supercargoes, Sierra Leoneans and Efik traders hurled accusations at each other. On 5 May, 1862, a meeting of the white traders was called to consider the re-establishment of a court of equity based on the articles of previous

treaties concluded with the late Governor Beecroft and Consul
Hutchinson in 1856.[90] The real reason for this was that the consul
at Fernando Po could not visit the rivers frequently without the
service of a gunboat. There were also other limitations in consular
administration which had to be overcome if the consul was to
administer more effectively.

The court was resurrected at a meeting on board H.M.S. *Griffon*.
The Duke Town king, Archibong, continually refused to assent
to the agreement reviving the court. Indeed, he had to be forced
to attend the meeting.[91] From the complaints forwarded by the
supercargoes to Burton,[92] the new consul, it might be deduced that
the Duke Town people expected to lose from the new agreement.
It prevented them from adjusting the price of oil according to the
state of the oil markets. It took away the right of Efik middlemen
to refuse to sell oil below a certain price, or in smaller quantities
than the usual trade casks or puncheons. It robbed them of the
right to insist on local labour being used to erect the cask houses
and trade establishments of European traders. These reasons probably motivated Archibong's refusal to sign the treaties. In spite of
the king's pretence to have been taken ill and being therefore
unable to attend a meeting, he was forced to sign an agreement on
7 May, sanctioning the re-convening of the court.[93]

Although King Archibong had signed the agreement, he was
still determined to resist its enforcement. On 8 May, Consul Burton,
accompanied by supercargoes, proceeded to the Cross River to
inspect the several markets there. On 9 May, his squadron arrived
at Itu, an important oil market town forty miles from Duke Town.
Here the squadron was repulsed by some sixty slaves of the Duke
Town people who pointed their muskets and ordered it to retire.
King Archibong was made to apologize for the humiliation and
to produce the ringleaders. The king warned all the people to keep
out of his town ('the very doors and windows were removed'), and
armed men filled the town to resist the supercargoes' attempts to
burn it. The court of equity resolved to move the shipping to
Parrot Island,[94] and to hold Iron Bar, a highly influential man
of considerable power in Duke Town, as hostage while the Europeans bargained with the Efik chiefs. However, it is probable that
the shipping was moved to Parrot Island for fear that yellow fever
might sweep Duke Town about that time. The island, some miles
down the river, was always considered a safer and healthier place
for shipping during the yellow fever season.

However, in spite of the unsuccessful resistance against the
new agreement, King Archibong managed to hold his fort for a
while. He was, for example, able to implement the stipulation that

he reserved the right to nominate workers to construct the cask houses, and sanction the building ashore of houses of European agents.[95] The supercargoes complained that they could never obtain redress for their grievances from King Archibong or King John, the latter of whom 'blew Ekpe' on one Roy's boat when he attempted to give up the custom of providing breakfasts on the arrival of a ship.

But the greatly increased consolidation of the European traders made the Efik political and economic position difficult. The reestablishment of the court of equity witnessed a revival of the old problems. The court levied fines on Efik traders. On one occasion, in December, 1867, the Duke Town chiefs, having no money to pay their fines, promised in a note to pay the chairman of the court of equity or the consul twenty puncheons of 'good' palm oil before a specified date, failing which they bound themselves to pay thirty puncheons at a later date.[96] The fine had been imposed on King Archibong for sacrificing two of seven women, the sole survivors of a village which had been attacked and whose inhabitants had been killed by the king's orders.[97] It is not clear from the records what exactly the court of equity had to do with King Archibong's wars with other villages.

Archibong found it extremely difficult to contain the excesses of his own men who either committed armed robberies or engaged in assaults on the cask houses of European traders thus violating acticles nineteen and twenty-three of the code of trade regulations of 1862. For example, in July, 1868 at Duke Town, about five hundred Calabar armed men and slaves burgled the cask house of the supercargo Captain Thomas and stole about a hundred puncheons of palm oil.[98] The European traders wrote to John Holt, then acting consul, to procure the assistance of a gunboat and proceed to Calabar. They wished steps be taken to punish the offenders and prevent the recurrence of such incidents.[99] A few months later, Captain Thomas's cask house was again broken into by one of King Archibong II's men.

Whether these incidents were purely retaliatory or wilfully undertaken, there is no doubt that they provoked the anger of the supercargoes. They also became the excuse for the supercargoes to push through the courts of equity fresh regulations for the conduct of the trade. A meeting of the court called on 23 February, 1869 on board H.M.S. *Speedwell*, and attended by the supercargoes and the Efik kings, discussed the above-mentioned incidents and fined Archibong ten puncheons of oil on the grounds that the king was responsible for the safety of all British property within his jurisdiction.[100] Also, the kings of Duke Town and Creek Town were to prohibit any of their subjects visiting the cask houses of the European traders on any pretext whatever. They were held responsible for all thefts committed by Calabar men if proved before the court of equity, or losses caused by the inhabitants of their respective towns.[101] A crucial clause, article XXIII, obtained the pledge of the kings and chiefs that no British subject would be detained on shore or maltreated in any way or under any pretence. If the Efik authorities did so, they would become the 'declared enemies' of Great Britain; the men-of-war would hasten to the Calabar River to protect British subjects.[102]

Of greater significance was the decision of the court to ratify the agreement of 7 May, 1862 with a view to cancelling certain articles, namely articles IV, VI, XIV, XV, XVI, XX and XXI. Some of these articles had been deliberately written into the agreement in order to check excesses. For example articles XV and XVI had sought the abolition of the trust system of trade, and by declaring them to be obsolete on the grounds that they were constantly violated by Europeans who were prepared to extend credit to the African traders, an important legal safeguard was being removed. The British government, having taken the position that it could not lend any encouragement to a revival of the system of trust, requested that the articles be retained.[103]

It seems unfair to accuse Archibong entirely for the lawlessness of the river. Apart from the fact that supercargoes were guilty of engendering many of the disputes, no real opportunity was ever afforded to the Efik rulers to settle the trade palavers. As Archibong stated, in replying to the demands of supercargoes to hand over one David King to the authorities of the hulk *Winefred* for trial on charges of theft and assault in Captain Thomas's cask house, the king was never given a chance to rectify the situation by the administration of Efik justice. Complaints generally were not made to the king; only demands were made by the traders to produce the culprits. It was not that Archibong was reluctant to bring the juveniles to justice; he was never allowed time to do precisely that. When the king insisted on looking into the matter himself, and refused to hand over persons arbitrarily to the supercargoes as in the case of David King, the supercargoes promptly complained of their inability to 'get satisfaction' from the king and forthwith appealed to the consul for assistance.[104] It would sound absurd, therefore, for the traders to hold the king responsible for the safety and protection of all British property within his jurisdiction[105] without at the same time allowing him the necessary leave to punish those who contravened the regulations.

Changes in the trade pattern

The price paid for palm oil per ton in England in the 1860s was generally above £40 between 1860–1863 and less than that figure after 1863,[106] and indeed, except for 1861 when the price per ton was £47, the general trend was a fall in the price for oil. In April, 1862 the supercargoes exerted pressure on the Efik middlemen to reduce palm oil prices in Calabar on the argument that the English market prices were falling. The Efik kings were not willing to entertain any such pleas. Both Archibong II and John Eyo (or Tom Eyo) of Creek Town suspended the trade of the river and permitted no oil to be sold to any ship at the reduced prices that were being offered.[107] Archibong and Eyo also enforced their decree that oil should not be sold in quantities smaller than trade casks or puncheons. When the supercargoes protested at this move, Archibong coldly replied that as he was king he would make any law he thought fit. With this order Archibong dealt with both the supercargoes and the petty traders who were unable to command the necessary means to engage in wholesale trade.

Another consequence of falling prices in England was a reduction in the amount of credit in the hands of European firms and hence the amount of credit that could be issued to Efik middlemen. This situation gave rise to a new development in Calabar, namely the growth of an Efik capitalist group. One reason why such a group had been slow to develop was that for a long time the capital which financed the oil trade came primarily from foreigners. Without necessarily taking a simple view of the role of metallic currency in relation to credit, it might be stated that coinage was a recent innovation and the storage of capital in liquid money a new concept because capital in the form of slaves did not lend itself to investment in the same manner as metallic currency. It is significant to note that ex-slaves were also prominent capitalist traders at this time. Notable among them was Black Davies who owned a number of men on the plantations[108] and who on his death on 25 January, 1874 had piles of European goods buried with him. Another ex-slave who had made good was Yellow Duke, a former slave of Ekpe Offiong[109] who traded in palm produce as far as the basin of the Cross River and the Cameroons in fleets of hundreds of canoes.[110] He was described in consular reports as one of the most dangerous men in the river because he was a favourite and a creditor of King Archibong,[111] and a member of the cabinets of two kings, Archibong II and King Duke.[112]

The Henshaw family also made a spectacular effort during the period to pool their resources and set up a trading concern, called the Henshaw Brothers' Company. The company owed its origin to the decline in credit from European firms, but the venture was short-lived. The reason for the short span of the company's life is difficult to ascertain, but though of brief duration, it was nevertheless significant in that it represented the emergence of an organized embryonic Efik capitalist group.

An important change in the trade pattern during this period was the establishment of fixed European premises ashore in place of the system of hulks, and the giving of company names to businesses formerly conducted by individuals who had sold their assets to those companies. Thus, in 1864 the West African Company with a subscribed capital of £100,000 was established; in 1868 the Miller Brothers founded a firm; and in November, 1879 the United Africa Company followed suit. In all, in 1866 there were 17 firms trading in the rivers of the Bight of Biafra. In 1872 the number of Liverpool, Bristol and Glasgow houses was 24, and there was a Dutch and a German firm. These 26 palm oil trading houses had 55 trading establishments in 7 rivers, and employed 207 white agents, clerks and mates, 419 African coopers, carpenters, cooks and stewards from all over West Africa, and 2,000 Kroomen from Cape Palmas and other parts of the Kroo coast.[113] It must be borne in mind, however, that in many cases, since statistics of trade are either absent, unreliable or misleading, the records have to be accepted with reservations.

There were also private individuals who bought up sheds and commercial houses on the shore. One of the first of these was Captain James Walker, who in December, 1869 approached Willie II, King of Old Town, and in return for six hundred coppers, obtained the lease of a parcel of land 'forever'.[114] Walker or his heirs were to pay the usual comey for cask houses and employ Old Town men to work on their premises. The factory established was known as Hope Factory.

The Hope Factory, it is significant to note, seemed determined to move into a half-way position between the supercargoes and Efik houses. Walker was selling to European shippers and buying from Efik traders. He was in effect doing what the Sierra Leoneans were doing. This was a most important development in the whole trading mechanism. By employing Old Town men Walker was, as it were, beginning in a new 'house'. Unfortunately, paucity of both documentary and oral evidence prevents us from carrying the story further.

The lease covering a factory established ashore in 1874, cost 1 hogshead of rum, 300 kroos of salt and 500 ships' coppers. The trading stores, or factories as they were called, of the European firms were open at six and closed at ten or eleven in the morning for breakfast, after which they opened in the afternoons until five in the evening. They received payment in cowries, guns, and cloth, etc., in exchange for palm oil, kernels and other produce delivered to the firms.[115]

The question is not one of why new firms should be established at a time when the trade was not expanding because it was not altogether 'new', but why the European traders decided to abandon Fernando Po for the rivers or the coast. The reason appears to be the fact that the economic position of Calabar had been brightened by the export through it of Cameroonian produce. The Cameroon River had for some years been the most disorderly of all the palm oil ports. Consequently, much of the produce which had hitherto been exported through the Cameroons now passed through Calabar. There was a noticeable increase in the activities of Efik middlemen in the Rio del Rey country between Calabar and the Cameroons. Oil was beginning to be exported direct to England from Calabar rather than through Fernando Po with the result that the number of ships that called at the island decreased. This switch from Fernando Po to the Calabar waterfront and the extension of the area of Efik trading to the Rio del Rey was of great importance as it modified the trade pattern. Perhaps the rise of Duke Town was connected with the development of the Rio del Rey trade.

This was perhaps also the reason why Britain decided in 1872[116] to transfer the site of the British consulate from Fernando Po, which had declined considerably from its earlier position as a centre for the oil trade[117] since its occupation in the 1830s. The transfer followed the demand of English traders in the Niger Delta that the Delta was a suitable base from which oil might be exported[118] to Calabar.

A second factor that probably encouraged the establishment ashore of trading houses was the trade in palm kernels which was being developed in response to the needs of the margarine industry in England and Germany. The first export of palm kernels from Calabar, albeit in small quantities, was said to have been in 1869.[119] This does not mean that kernels were till that date considered waste. Indeed what did happen was that oil producers threw away kernels after separating the oil from the fibres round the nut (the pericarp) in spite of the knowledge that it contained a valuable oil.[120] The reason for this deliberate action was one of price. The price paid for the nut prior to 1869 was never high enough to induce the Africans to carry the nuts in unbroken form in canoes to the coast. In England, too, there were complaints that the pressing machines were not suitable for the different shapes and sizes of the nuts.

L

At length, when prices for kernels were pushed up, the Africans undertook to crack the nuts by traditional methods and sold the kernels. It was principally a wet season occupation and chiefly that of the women. It is said that in 1869 a trader visited several oil producing villages and urged the people to begin nut cracking. In that year alone, at Calabar, a thousand tons of kernel were bought at two shillings a bushel. By 1871, upwards of two thousand tons were being bought yearly at eight shillings per bushel.[121]

It is possible that the two factors mentioned above, namely the expansion of the trade area of Calabar and the development of the trade in palm kernel, motivated the Company of African Merchants to speak of the great promise of trade in the river. It was believed that the resources in West Africa were inexhaustible and of the most varied character and that Africans were most anxious to carry on trading operations with the English nation. In effect, too, the Company of African Merchants was not just a West African trading company; it was a body backed heavily by missionaries and was bound to issue a glowing account of West African trading prospects.

Trade, however, did not improve vastly and the increase in the scale of trading companies verged on the uneconomic. Cut-throat competition became the order of the day and its natural corollary was losses in trade. The price paid for oil in the rivers rose to twice or even thrice its former figure. One firm reported a loss of £20,000 from the 1871 trade.[122]

The reason for the sharp rise of oil prices in the rivers is not difficult to determine. The country markets had been flooded with European trade goods that were given out freely to all and sundry. These goods were sold in the markets for less than cost, with the result that certain goods were cheaper in the Calabar markets than on board the hulks. Every steamer that arrived brought in additional cargo and 'spoilt' the markets, to the detriment of both African and European traders. In a single river in 1869, upwards of £40,000 worth of goods was declared on trust to African brokers. Another agent declared that when he gave seven hundred puncheons on trust he lost two hundred. It was more than a matter of bad debts. It tended to lower the value of European trade goods, and thereby raised that of oil which had to be paid for in trade goods. Brokers had to pay more and they often charged this to the debit of the European traders. It led to lawlessness since African and European traders took the law into their own hands in order to settle disputes in their favour. As Livingstone put it, 'Loud is the call for the immediate presence of the consul in a man-of-war to punish the lawlessness of the black goose, but not the lawlessness of the white gander'.[123]

Livingstone observed that if the firms that groaned over a yearly loss would retire from the trade, their departure would be twice blest; they would save their thousands, and those that remained might be enabled to make a fair profit.[124] But this was not the case. A trader like J. B. Walker was writing in 1877 that besides palm produce, ebony, ivory and barwood inter alia, other items of export, india-rubber, shea butter, and even gold in the mountainous districts, might be successfully exploited in the interior country.[125]

The European trading corporations persisted in their belief that trade might improve if fresh markets were opened up for that purpose. They insisted that the British government should undertake schemes to this effect and ensure peaceful trading up the Cross River. What the traders overlooked, or were ignorant of, was the fact that Britain did not have jurisdiction over some of these areas. For instance, Charles Horsfall and Sons, who were interested in the rivers Andony and Coupatana, between Bonny and Calabar, were informed by the British government that Britain had no jurisdiction over those areas.[126] This being the case, a resolution was adopted in May, 1870 by the Liverpool African Association that in view of the extension of the oil trade between Britain and the West coast of Africa it was desirable for Britain to open up fresh rivers. The government was requested to order a survey of the rivers betwen Bonny and Old Calabar and to extend British protection to British subjects trading therein.[127]

It is quite clear from the above that there was a serious economic stress developing in the river and that European capital in the oil rivers during this period could hardly have been engaged in a more 'bootless' enterprise. The competition among European firms was fatal to their profits. It led one or two of the old wealthy firms to intensify their efforts to crush the new European traders of limited capital, but the chief sufferers of the cut-throat competition were the wealthy firms themselves who had more expensive establishments than the other firms or independent traders. It has been stated above that firms were losing on their trade while their excessive trust payments ruined the internal Calabar markets. And yet European firms in Calabar would not give up their trust system of trade. Instead, they resorted to other fruitless methods to lower the prices in the river. They stopped trade in one of the rivers for three months. As Livingstone aptly remarked, it was a sad sight in a sickly river to see a few melancholy whites doing nothing except, perhaps, struggling for existence with fever.[128]

Up to a point, disunity between supercargoes benefited the Efik middlemen. The African traders were more able to join together to achieve their ends than were the Europeans. They frustrated the European merchants who were on the coast seeking quick returns and large profits by giving out small consignments of goods. They obtained for themselves a large margin of profits on the capital they received, since they sold their oil to those who paid higher prices. With the revenue from trade they owned fleets of canoes. They were able also to prevent the movement of supercargoes into the interior markets by retaining a commercial organization in which the Efik middlemen alone supplied oil to all traders at the coast. Above all they raised the price of oil. It was done by an understanding reached amongst Efik middlemen to keep the ships a certain length of time in the river in order to force the super-cargoes to pay the higher prices.[129]

They often discovered that when they were just on the point of yielding to an embargo placed on them by European traders, one of the European agents would come in and resume trade at the ruinous prices. The others would soon follow, and the Efik middle-men triumphed. But as prices in the river remained high, the exports were not likely to be augmented. The attempts made by European agents to find new markets, if they succeeded at all, only diverted a little of the trade from the nearest large river, irritated its chief and endangered the peace of the river.

An African embargo was likely, however, to be more effective. As stated earlier one of the pernicious effects of the trust system of trade was that it produced a glut of English goods in the country fairs and consequently the value of trust goods fell. Since the depreciation of the goods forced the principal oil middlemen or brokers to pay higher prices for oil their reaction was to shut trade goods out of the markets until prices rose. As the kernel trade was entirely in the hands of poor people, who had neither capital nor credit to become oil brokers, the richer brokers were determined to stop the kernel trade. The trade, so valued by the poor, was hence crushed for the benefit of the few capitalists.

The chiefs stated that their reason for terminating the trade in kernel was their fear that Europeans might prefer the new com-modity to oil, with the result that the oil trade might decline.[130] But the kernel trade could hardly have injured the oil trade. It is not possible that the women who did most of the work on it would throw away oil worth twice as much as kernels in order to get kernels only when they could have both. The placing of an em-bargo on the export of kernels by the coastal Efik was a device to push up the price of kernels, a contrivance hardly known to the unsuspecting interior producers.[131]

The British power position

The supercargoes' insistence upon the necessity of investing the consul with 'more absolute power' than he had hitherto enjoyed[132] was not for the purpose of settling petty disputes between African traders which they claimed hampered trade, but for strengthening the position of the Europeans vis-à-vis the Efik middlemen. Many of the fears expressed by the supercargoes were imaginary and they were often exaggerated in order to convince the home government of the strength of their case. For example, they alleged that as matters stood African traders were perfectly aware that many months had to elapse before any punishment could be inflicted on them for infringement of treaties. Fears were expressed that the immediate connection which existed between Calabar and the Bonny river rendered it possible for the Efik any day to identify themselves with the war being carried on in Opobo. Also, that in view of the large interests held by British merchants in Calabar, any 'aggression' on British capital had to be promptly checked before an open war was declared. Such fears were at best remote; it ought not to be forgotten that the supercargoes were themselves provocative in their conduct. And the British government was clear on this when it replied:

> Putting aside, as not necessary to be now discussed, the Question of the Right of the British Government to interfere forcibly to prevent the Wars between Native chiefs on the ground that they are detrimental to British trade, Her Majesty's Government cannot close her eyes to the fact that the native animosities have in too many instances been promoted by the Europeans, who under the stimulus of competition between themselves, hoped to reap from them some material benefit of the trade of the particular firms of which they were the Representatives, and that moreover in the ordinary course of trade with muskets, and gun powder which were eagerly bought by the Natives as furnishing them with weapons with which to carry on the wars so justly characterized as detrimental to trade.[133]

The courts of equity had never functioned in the manner the British government had intended, that is, they seldom resolved trade disputes in a way acceptable to all traders, both European and African. In fact, the government began to question the legal competency of the courts. The law officers of the British Crown advised Lord Granville, then Foreign Secretary, that the judgements of these courts were not entitled to the same respect in law as the judgements of regularly constituted tribunals of 'recognized and civilized' communities. It was suggested that steps should be taken to encourage and improve them, and possibly even to replace them by legislation on some more recognized footing. Besides, there were legal difficulties with regard to the compositions of the courts, since they were composed of non-British ('foreign') members, in addition to British agents, and it was difficult for the Queen to confer powers on foreigners.[134]

It does appear that Granville had these legal technicalities in mind when he decided to exercise the Foreign Jurisdiction Act of 1871 and set up consular courts and reorganize the courts of equity. He saw the solution in terms of investing the consul superintending the courts with magisterial powers and jurisdiction over British subjects in the consular district within the framework of the Foreign Jurisdiction Act. He did not anticipate that any difficulties would be raised by the chiefs to the exercise of such jurisdiction.[135] On 21 February, 1872 a lengthy Order in Council relating to the power and jurisdiction of Her Majesty on the West Coast of Africa (Old Calabar, Bonny, Cameroons, New Calabar, Brass River, Opobo River, Benin River) was published.[136] Rules and regulations were subsequently framed by Livingstone under this order in April, 1872.[137] The rules for civil and criminal justice were chiefly taken from the rules of the Zanzibar consular courts, with such alterations as the different circumstances seemed to require. Though the document outlined the nature of the relations between the British government and British subjects on the Bight, it remained vague about the position of Africans and of liberated Africans should they refuse to accept the decisions of the courts of equity.

The general effect of the Order in Council was to entrust the consul with greater discretionary powers than he had had previously. It also aimed at a reduction of the area in which conflicts between European and African traders could occur. The preamble laid down that firstly British traders in any of the territories situated upon the rivers were not permitted to take the law into their own hands, or to seize and put under restraint persons or property of any of the African chiefs under any pretence whatever. It also hoped that this stipulation would remove the main prop of the trust system (which led traders into lawless acts) by prohibiting the seizure of persons and property of African traders. Consuls were given the power to fine up to £200, imprison up to twenty-one days, or banish British subjects for up to twelve months if violation of the provisions of treaties and conventions could be proved.

Secondly, the rules provided for the observances of treaty stipulations with regard to comey. In the Calabar river, the comey, fixed at half a crown a ton on the oil shipped by steamer, was to be paid directly after each steamer left. The chief in this and other rivers generally took the traders' word for the amount they shipped. As each trader received from the captain of the steamer duplicate bills of lading, these might be accepted as vouchers when disputes arose over the amount of comey due. The consul was empowered to carry into effect and enforce the observance of the stipulations of all treaties and conventions between the British and the coastal chiefs. But the local regulation made by the consul had to be approved by the Foreign Office.

The Order also re-organized the courts of equity. Rule four made the court an assessor to assist the consul in deciding sentences to be passed on defaulting British subjects. All cases of litigation of a civil nature arising between British subjects were to be heard by the court of equity, which then submitted its decision to the consul for final sanction. Rule five conferred upon the court, subject to approcal and guidance of the consuls, limited powers to settle trade disputes between British subjects and Africans. But the court had jurisdiction over such matters only after the parties to be tried had consented to abide by its decision. So far as it went, rule thirteen laid down that British subjects in the Bights were liable to punishment for breach of treaties or agreements concluded between the British government and the chiefs, or for offences against the Order of February, 1872.

But the Order in Council remained notoriously unclear on certain crucial questions. For example, what would happen if either Africans or British subjects refused to accept the authority of the courts of equity? Could the consul continue to dethrone legitimate African kings as in former times? How could the Foreign Office treat the recurrence of such rash actions?

Conclusion

Though several interlacing themes have been linked together in this story of the economic stress experienced by Calabar, it can nevertheless be seen that a close relationship existed between identifiable movements in the economy and the lawless conduct of the supercargoes. The periods of greatest economic stress were coincidental with periods of intensive efforts by supercargoes to bring commercial and political pressures to bear upon Efik kings. It is not unreasonable to say of the supercargoes that they perpetuated the economic strain by their practice of cut-throat competition, unjudicious over-extension of firms and their indiscriminate advance of trade credit. Perhaps greatly reduced profit margins were preferred to no profits at all even if that spelt bad economics.

In spite of economic reversals, however, the European traders scored political gains. Through their fairly solid combination of commercial interests, the Europeans transformed the court of equity into a European dominated council. Though it operated on the principle of associating Efik leaders with European traders in the adjustment of trade claims, the Efik kings were powerless in the face of organized pressure by the predominantly European membership. Though it was never intended that the court supersede the Efik government in affairs of a strictly domestic nature, it nevertheless threatened the extinction of the palmy days of the Efik kings. The events of this period clearly indicated that even before the actual European scramble for Africa, the British had already entrenched their position on the southern Nigerian coast. It is vital to note this point because it helps to explain the ease with which British consuls secured the treaties of 1884 which provided the basis for the Protectorate government.

REFERENCES

1 K. O. Dike, *Trade and Politics* et seq., p. 168.
2 C. Gertzel, 'John Holt: A British Merchant in West Africa in the Era of Imperialism'. Unpublished Ph.D. thesis, Oxford, 1959, p. 79.
3 C. Gertzel, 'Commercial Organization on the Niger Coast, 1852–1891', a paper delivered at a Leverhulme Inter-Collegiate History Conference held at the University College of Rhodesia and Nayasaland, September, 1960, and published in the conference report entitled *Historians in Tropical Africa*, (Salisbury, 1962), p. 289.
4 For trade statistics, see also Appendix D.
5 The figures are compiled from Tables 15 and 16 in the *Statistical Abstract for United Kingdom*, 1864–1878, (London, 1879); from *Parl. Pap.*, 1886, Vol. 68, Statistical Abstract for the United Kingdom, 1871–1885 (Customs 4, ledgers of imports into United Kingdom); and from C. Gertzel, 'John Holt', et seq., p. 614.
6 Source: C. Gertzel, 'John Holt', et seq., pp. 615–6 who cites the John Holt papers.
7 Rev. E. Jones, 'Journal of a voyage from Sierra Leone to Fernando Po in 1853', (C.M.S. West African Mission), op. cit.
8 *Parl. Pap.*, 1852, Vol. 49 (284), 'Correspondence Relating to Conveyance of Her Majesty's Mails to West Coast of Africa'. Vide also N. H. Stilliard, op. cit., Chapter 5.
9 Capital in the form of trade goods essential to West African trade was also provided on credit by European commission houses who in turn sold the produce of the independent traders. These houses therefore took commission in both cases.
10 McPhee calls the independent African traders 'economic middlemen' as opposed to the chiefs who are called 'semi-political middlemen'. Those who went upriver with trust are called 'credit middlemen'. Vide A. McPhee, *The Economic Revolution in British West Africa*, p. 99. Also, W. F. Hutchinson, 'Commerce, Money and Currency in West Africa', *West Africa*, (1919–20), p. 1152.
11 Vide C. Gertzel, 'John Holt', et seq., p. 62.
12 Report by Consul Livingstone on 'Trade and Commerce of Old Calabar for the year 1872', in *Reports from Her Majesty's Consuls on the Manufactures, Commerce & c. of their Consular Districts*, No. 4, C–828, August, 1872, London, 1873, p. 694.

13 *Parl. Pap.*, 1865, V. Select Committee on West Africa, 1865; evidence of Captain R. F. Burton, question 2156, p. 90. For the view that in the period of transition from slave to oil export the role of middlemen could not have been done without, vide A. A. Cowan, 'Early Trading Conditions in the Bight of Biafra', Part 2, *J. A. S.*, January, 1936, Vol. 34, No. 138, p. 56.

14 Peter Nicoll was a Calabar man captured from his home town, Egbo Sharry, and sold to a slave ship. He was saved by a British cruiser which intercepted the vessel, and was taken to Sierra Leone. He then returned to Calabar as a merchant and a respected member and leader in the Wesleyan Church. He spent two years in Calabar and when he could no longer bear the maltreatment of the supercargoes returned to Freetown. When he died in 1880, he left a legacy of £50 to the Calabar mission. For a description of his life and work vide Anderson's annual report for 1880 in W. Marwick, op. cit., pp. 572–3; and C. Fyfe, 'Peter Nicoll—Old Calabar and Freetown', *J.H.S.N.*, Vol. 2, No. 1, December, 1960, pp. 105–114.

15 CALPROF 4/3, Vol. 1, Peter Nicoll to Captain Cuthbertson, 31 October, 1855.

16 CALPROF 4/1, Vol. 2, Nicoll to Lynslager, 2 November, 1855.

17 F.O. 84/1001, No. 23, Hutchinson to Clarendon, 12 March, 1856.

18 Livingstone's trade report for 1872 states that copper wires and brass rods, three feet in length and bent double, were the currency of the Calabar markets; 'Report by Consul Livingstone on the Trade and Commerce of Old Calabar', op. cit., p. 693.

19 Vide Bold, op. cit., p. 78.

20 K. O. Dike, *Trade and Politics* et seq., p. 105, for a list of trade goods at the beginning of the nineteenth century, and K. Davies, *The Royal African Company*, for development of trade goods and African currencies in the slave trade period; also vide J. Smith, *Trade and Travels* et seq., Chapter 19, and T. J. Hutchinson, *Impressions* et seq., p. 252. For a discussion on currency problems see G. I. Jones, 'Native and Trade Currencies in Southern Nigeria in the Eighteenth and Nineteenth Centuries', *Africa*, Vol. 28, No. 1, January, 1956. Jones distinguishes by the end of the eighteenth century between 'Native' and 'Trade' currencies: 'native currency' was 'that used by the people of the country in their internal market transactions'; 'trade currency' was 'that used in commercial transactions between foreign (European) and native (African) traders'. In some cases, however, these currencies were fused. The John Holt Papers, writes Gertzel, contain evidence that this distinction was still valid even in the 1880s. Vide C. Gertzel, 'John Holt' et seq., pp. 47–48.

21 N. H. Stilliard, op. cit., p. 107.

22 CALPROF 2/1, Vol. 7, and F.O. 84/975, 'Journal of Proceedings of Acting Consul Lynslager in the River Old Calabar', entry for 11 October, 1855. Vide also other entries, ibid., 10 October–19 October, 1855.

23 CALPROF 2/1, Vol. 7, 'Journal of Proceedings of . . . Lynslager', op. cit., entry for 11 October, 1855.

24 Hertslet, op. cit., Vol. 10, p. 29; (CALPROF 5/7, Vol. 1, Lynslager to F.O., 17 October, 1855, incl. 7. Vide H. M. Waddell, *Journals*, Vol. 2, entry for 21 September, 1855, p. 9.

25 The order of ships was *Sarah*, Capt. Crampton, supercargo; *En-*

draght, Capt. Baak, supercargo; *Lady Head*, Capt. Morgan, supercargo; *Calabar*, Capt. Davies, *Thornhill*, Capt. Davies, supercargoes;
Africa, Capt. Cuthbertson, supercargo; *Mars*, Capt. Morgan, supercargo; *Ellen Stuart*, Capt. Morgan, supercargo; *Hantz*, Capt. Straw,
supercargo. Vide E. Hertslet, op. cit., Vol. 10, pp. 28–29.

26 CALPROF 2/1, Vol. 7, 'Journal of Proceedings . . . of Lynslager',
op. cit., entry for 19 October, 1855; and CALPROF 5/7, Vol. 1,
Lynslager to F.O. 19 October, 1855, incl. 8.

27 W. N. M. Geary, op. cit., p. 84.

28 J. Whitford, op. cit., p. 303. Whitford was a trader in that part of
Africa between 1853 and 1875.

29 N. H. Stilliard, op. cit., pp. 101–102.

30 Vide G. I. Jones, *Trading States* et seq., p. 96 and J. Adams, *Sketches*
et seq., p. 112.

31 J. Smith, op. cit., p. 187.

32 The figures relating to the quantities of palm oil on trust to the
ships are enormous. Vide the table reproduced by K. O. Dike, op.
cit., p. 119, where it is shown that 9,030 tons of palm oil were given
on trust to 10 ships. If the price of oil is estimated at £40 per ton,
then the total trust given out was worth about £360,000. It must be
remembered that this was an estimate of good and bad debts given
out over a considerable period, and lumped together by the European
traders for the sake of their argument.

33 F.O. 2/16, Hutchinson to F.O., No. 69, 20 June, 1856, incl. 1, 'General Report on the Bight of Biafra' by Hutchinson. The report gives
the following table of returns of palm oil from those places engaged
in the trade:

| DATE | | NAME OF RIVER | AMOUNT |
From	To		IN TONS
1855	1856		
Jan. 1	Jan. 1	Brass	2,280
1854	1855		
July 1	July 1	New Calabar and Bonny Rivers. They have been placed together because they have a common embouchure and trade was carried on in both by the same agent.	16,124
1855	1856		
Jan. 1	Jan. 1	Old Calabar	4,090
1855	1856		
Jan. 1	Jan. 1	Bimbia	96
Do.	Do.	Cameroons	2,110
Do.	Do.	Fernando Po	360
			25,060

34 CALPROF 2/1, Vol. 7, 'Journal of Proceedings . . . of Lynslager',
op. cit., October, 1855.

35 F.O. 84/1001, No. 126, Davies to Hutchinson, 17 June, 1856, encl. 4.

36 See T. J. Hutchinson, *Wanderings* et seq., p. 190, where the author
quotes a letter dated 28 May, 1857, from the Office of the Com-

missioner of the Privy Council for Trade to the secretary, Association of Merchants Trading to West Africa.

37 Vide H. M. Waddell, *Twenty-Nine Years* et seq., p. 274.

38 F.O. 84/1001, No. 26, Davies to Hutchinson, 13 October, 1856, encl. 4.

39 Ibid., No. 126, Anderson to Hutchinson, 17 June, 1856, encl. 2.

40 Ibid., No. 71, Hutchinson to Clarendon, 24 June, 1856.

41 The children bore Efik nationality and took Efik names (generally those of the chiefs or wives of chiefs who gave them protection).

42 C.O. 147/10, encl. in F.O. to C.O., 7 December, 1865, J. D. Harding (Law Officer) to Earl of Clarendon, 25 September, 1856. The Colonial Office was not informed of the state of the discussion till 1865. Vide C. W. Newbury, *British Policy towards West Africa*, pp. 566–67.

43 CALPROF 2/1, Vol. 8, Clarendon to Hutchinson, 19 October, 1856.

44 F.O. 2/19, Hutchinson to Stephen I. Hill (Governor of Sierra Leone), 26 November, 1856.

45 F.O. 2/19, No. 7, Stephen Hill to Hutchinson, 12 January, 1857.

46 F.O. 2/16, Hutchinson to F.O., No. 69, 20 June, 1856, incl. 1, 'General Report on the Bight of Biafra', op. cit.

47 The date of this treaty as it appears in E. Hertslet is queried. It is believed that the treaty referred to is the one signed on 8 August, 1857; vide E. Hertslet, op. cit., Vol. 9, p. 26.

48 E. Hertslet, op. cit., Vol. 10, p. 685. The treaty was approved in Clarendon to Hutchinson, 13 August, 1956; CALPROF 2/1, Vol. 8

49 W. Marwick, op. cit., p. 353.

50 F.O. 84/1001, No. 115, Duke Ephraim to Hutchinson, 15 September, 1856, encl. 8.

51 Ibid., Missionaries to Hutchinson, 27 August, 1856, encl. 6. In a letter despatched by them, the missionaries pointed out to the European authorities that European traders believed they had 'a licence to perpetrate any outrage they choose on the natives of Old Calabar'. Vide also ibid., Hutchinson to Clarendon, 23 September, 1856.

52 CALPROF 2/1, Vol. 8, Clarendon to Hutchinson, 21 May, 1856. This despatch that sounded the warning was in approval of Hutchinson's successful exertion in getting Cuthbertson to pay compensation to Nicoll for the oil seized.

53 Ibid.

54 Hutchinson, *Wanderings* et seq., pp. 189–95.

55 For the agreement vide E. Hertslet, op. cit., Vol. 10, pp. 686–90, 'Agreement between British supercargoes and Native traders of Old Calabar', 19 September, 1856. The agreement was signed by the consul, six supercargoes, King Eyo Honesty, King Duke Ephraim, and seven other chiefs; it was witnessed by H. J. De Robeck, Lieutenant commanding HMS *Myrmidon*, and the second master.

56 E. Hertslet, op. cit., Vol. 10, p. 690, 'Grant of land for erection of a court house at Duke Town, Old Calabar', dated 20 September, 1856.

57 CALPROF 2/1, Vol. 8, No. 34, Clarendon to Hutchinson, 20 December, 1856.

58 Ibid., No. 35, Clarendon to Hutchinson, 20 December, 1856.

59 Ibid., No. 34, 'Memorandum as to the mode of investing British consuls on the west coast of Africa with magisterial powers'. F.O., 17 October, 1856.

60 F.O. 2/19, No. 20, encl. 2, liberated Africans of Clarence, (Fernando Po) to Hutchinson, 9 March, 1857. Vide also encl. 3, a statement by

the vice consul of Fernando Po, dated 10 March, 1857, about the rebellious mood of the inhabitants who defied the government and made it necessary to call in the aid of the crews of merchant vessels in the harbour.

61 The position taken by Fernando Po, even in May, 1857, was that although the liberated Africans were not to be regarded as British subjects, the British Government could not cease to feel 'the liveliest interest' in them; CALPROF 2/1, Vol. 9, F.O. to Hutchinson, 21 May, 1857. But in August, 1857, the Foreign Office, dealing with the question of the legality of marriage of liberated Africans at Fernando Po, described the entitlement of the latter to treatment as British subjects. The position of the government was vague; vide CALPROF 2/1, Vol. 9, F.O. to Hutchinson, 4 August, 1857.

62 G. I. Jones, 'Political Organization', op. cit., p. 131; vide also F.O. 2/16, No. 69, Hutchinson's Trade Report, 20 June, 1856, incl. 1.

63 Vide G. I. Jones, *Trading States* et seq., p. 95.

64 F.O. 84/1061, No. 6, Hutchinson to F.O., 28 January, 1958.

65 CALPROF 2/1, Vol. 2, Russell to Hutchinson, 23 March, 1860; and CALPROF 2/1, Vol. 22, F.O. to Livingstone, 24 January, 1870.

66 K. O. Dike, *Trade and Politics* et seq., p. 122.

67 F.O. 84/1030, No. 23, Hutchinson to Clarendon, 29 April, 1857.

68 This was repeated in Clarendon to Hutchinson, 21 December, 1857; CALPROF 2/1, Vol. 9.

69 B.T. 2208; General Dept. No. 1794 (encl.), Schwerzensky to Clarendon, 2 November, 1857, cited in Dike, *Trade and Politics* et seq., p. 123, n.1. Waddell noted that Hutchinson 'had formerly been a surgeon in the Calabar River, and had not inspired all who knew him with a conviction of the super-eminent abilities for such a sphere of duty; we were prepared to receive him as an old acquaintance, without expecting too much from him'. H. M. Waddell, *Twenty-Nine Years* et seq., p. 577.

70 A view repeated in Hutchinson to F.O., 28 January, 1858; F.O. 84/ 1061, No. 6.

71 F.O. 84/1061, No. 12, Hutchinson to Clarendon, 22 February, 1858.

72 K.O. *Trade and Politics* et seq., p. 123.

73 D.O. 84/1061, Hutchinson to Rev. Baille (of Duke Town mission house), 10 February, 1858, in Hutchinson to F.O., No. 13, 22 February, 1858.

74 F.O. 84/1061, No. 26, Hutchinson to Earl of Malmesbury, 25 May, 1858, encl. 2, Supercargoes to Eyo Honesty and gentlemen of Creek Town, 15 February, 1858.

75 Ibid.

76 F.O. 84/1061, No. 25, Hutchinson to F.O., 25 May, 1858.

77 F.O. 84/1061, No. 33, Hutchinson to Malmesbury, 12 June, 1858, encl. 1 for the agreement dated 12 May, 1858. This agreement does not appear in E. Hertslet, op. cit.

78 J. Smith, op. cit., Chapter 19, describes the measures that supercargoes might take to recover their debts.

79 F.O. 84/1061, No. 13, Baille to Hutchinson, 1 February, 1858, in Hutchinson to F.O., 22 February, 1858.

80 Ibid., Hearn to consul, 3 March, 1858.

81 Ibid., Hutchinson to F.O., 22 February, 1858, encl. 2, in supercargoes to consul, 3 March, 1858.

82 Ibid., No. 22, Hutchinson to Malmesbury, 25 May, 1858, and encl. British consular records of this period are full of complaints and counter complaints between supercargoes, chiefs and the missionaries. Vide, for example, F.O. 84/1061, No. 13, Hutchinson to F.O., 22 February, 1858, encls. 3 and 10; F.O. 84/1061, Bassey Henshaw Duke to Hutchinson, 25 March, 1858, and its encl.; F.O. 84/1066, No. 24, Hutchinson to Malmesbury, 25 May, 1858, and its encl. especially encl. 6, Hutchinson to F.O., 25 May, 1858.

    Hutchinson's reference to the practice by supercargoes of taking the law into their own hands as of 'long standing' would seem to suggest that Europeans had begun to dominate Efik society forcibly earlier than 1858; but as shown in the previous chapter it was not as serious as the position in 1858.

83 F.O. 84/1061, No. 26, Hutchinson to Malmesbury, 25 May, 1858, and incl.

84 C. Gertzel, 'John Holt' et seq., p. 76.

85 Holman, op. cit., pp. 392–93.

86 CALPROF 2/1, Vol. 10, F.O. to Hutchinson, 4 September, 1858. For copy of the Order in Council of 1858, vide F.O. 84/1061, F.O. to Hutchinson, 4 September, 1858, encl. 1.

87 E. Hertslet, op. cit., Vol. 14, p. 966, 'Agreement with the Third Chief of Creek Town, Old Calabar, relative to the appointment of a British Consul to reside at Fernando Po', 16 January, 1860.

88 Ibid., Vol. 14, 'Agreement with Chief of Duke Town, John Archibong, dated 3 May, 1860', pp. 966–96.

89 Ibid., Vol. 10, p. 686.

90 F.O. 84/1176, No. 16, Burton to Russell, 22 May, 1862. Consul Burton spoke of 'murders', 'torturings' and 'crimes' in Duke Town, and even called the town an African Sodom and Gomorrah. King Archibong sent excuses that he was sick and could not attend the meetings. But the medical officers of the ships *Griffon* and *Gressy* reported him well enough to attend the meetings. Added Burton, 'The only result was an insolent and taunting refusal on the part of the King to offer his signature. His reason, taken down in writing by Dr. Adams, proved to be signatory, the chief objections raised being against the abolition of compulsory breakfasts, and points already determined by treaty'. Approval to the despatch stating above was given in F.O. 84/1176, F.O. to Burton, 23 September, 1862.

91 F.O. 84/1176, No. 16, Burton to Russell, 22 May, 1862, encl. 2, supercargoes to Burton, 28 April, 1862.

92 Ibid., Burton to Russell, 22 May, 1862.

93 Ibid.

94 *Parl. Pap.*, 1964, Vol. 41 (581), 'Prospectus of Company of African Merchants Ltd.'. Also C. Gertzel, 'John Holt' et seq., p. 79.

95 E. Hertslet, op. cit., Vol. 13, p. 21, 'Agreement with Old Calabar. Fine for Violation of Treaty Duke Town, December 7, 1867'. The fine was paid and the oil sold by public auction; F.O. 84/1290, No. 6, Livingstone to F.O., 24 February, 1868.

96 F.O. 84/1290, No. 5, Stanley to Livingstone, 14 February, 1868. Also in CALPROF 2/1, Vol. 20.

97 CALPROF 4/1, Vol. 2, European traders to John Holt, 1 August, 1868, encl. 1, J. Thomas to European traders, Old Calabar, 27 July, 1868. Thomas had threatened Archibong II with calling the consul

if he did not pay up the ten puncheons of oil; encl. 2, Thomas to
King Archibong II, 27 July, 1868. A meeting was held between the
king and the traders on board *Araminta*, and it was decided to hand
the case over to the consul; encl. 4, European traders to King Archibong, 28 July, 1868.

98   CALPROF 4/1, Vol. 2, European traders to Holt, 1 August, 1868.

99   F.O. 84/1308, No. 8, F. Wilson, (acting consul) to F.O., 23 February,
1869, and incl.; CALPROF 4/1, Vol. 2, King Archibong II to Wilson,
15 May, 1869, in which the king requested casks to pay the fine; the
court agreed to do so; CALPROF 3/1, Chairman, court of equity, to
Wilson, 15 May, 1869.

100   F.O. 84/1308, No. 8, Wilson to F.O. 23 February, 1869, encl. 3,
'Agreement between the Supercargoes and the Native Traders of Old
Calabar'.

101   CALPROF 2/1, Vol. 12 and F.O. 84/1308, No. 5, Clarendon to
Frank Wilson, 7 May, 1869.

102   CALPROF 4/1, Vol. 2, European traders to John Holt (acting consul), 1 August, 1868. See encl. 3, King Archibong to traders, 27 July,
1868, and encl. 4, European traders to King Archibong, 28 July, 1868.
These despatches explain how Captain Thomas's cask house was
captured by some four or five hundred men under the command of
David King. King was fined 10 puncheons of palm oil: CALPROF
2/1, Vol. 21, F.O. to Livingstone, 10 November, 1869.

103   CALPROF 3/3, copy of minutes of meeting held on board the hulk
Athelstan, Old Calabar, 5 June, 1871, 9.30 a.m.–8 p.m.

104   F.O. 84/1308, No. 8, F. Wilson to F.O., 23 February, 1869. It reiterated the clause providing for the king's responsibility which formed
part of a treaty signed on 7 May, 1862, following its ratification at
a meeting on board HMS *Speedwell* on 5 February, 1869.

105   E. E. Offiong private papers; Agreement Book 'A', 'Certified copy of
title to Ground at Hope Factory granted to Captain J. B. Walker
by Willy II, King of Old Town, 31 December, 1869, p. 30.

106   R. J. Gavin, op. cit., and the London *Economist* of 11 March, 1965.

107   F.O. 84/1176, encl. 2, Supercargoes to Burton, 28 April, 1862, in
Burton to Russell, No. 16, 22 May, 1862.

108   Harry H. Johnston, *The Story of My Life*, pp. 186–187.

109   Chief Umo E. E. Adam, interview, 23 November, 1865; Chief Thomas
A. Effiom, interview, 7 December, 1965.

110   F.O. 84/1176, No. 16, Burton to Earl Russell, 22 May, 1862.

111   Chief Ene Ndem Ephraim Duke, interview, 23 November, 1965.

112   F.O. 84/1176, encl. 2, Supercargoes to Burton, 28 April, 1862, in
Burton to Russell, No. 16, 22 May, 1862.

113   F.O. 84/1343, Consul Livingstone to F.O., 8 December, 1871, and
Parl. Pap., 1884–5, 55, Board of Trade to F.O., 5 November, 1884.

114   J. Whitford, op. cit., p. 91.

115   CALPROF 4/3, Vol. 1, Charles Horsfall & Sons to Clarendon, 29
December, 1869.

116   C. Gertzel, 'John Holt' et seq., p. 105. Said Livingstone in his trade
report of 1872: 'The Fernando Po oil crop never exceeds—seldom
equals—400 tons a year. A trustworthy observer who trades in various
parts of that island states that, from the number of oil palms he has
seen, at least 400 tons might easily be obtained. But the 25,000
aborigines, or Bubees, do not choose to work beyond 400 tons. Their

wants are few . . . If traders could create new wants, trade might
increase; but where is the genius who can create a new want for
Bube'; Livingstone's Trade Report, op. cit., p. 695.

117 K. O. Dike, *Trade and Politics* et seq.
118 F.O. 84/1221, Burton to F.O., 15 April, 1864.
119 The method of cracking the kernel by hand was often tedious, slow
     and uneconomical. But it was almost the twentieth century before
     a more satisfactory machinery was set up for the efficient treatment
     of the palm fruits; for details of the manual method of separating the
     pericarp from the kernel, vide N. H. Stilliard, op. cit., p. 112, who
     cites W. L. Carpenter, 'Manufacture of Soap and Candles' (London,
     1895), pp. 32ff. For attempts to introduce the mechanization process,
     vide H. M. Stilliard, op. cit., pp. 159ff.
120 Livingstone's Trade Report, 1872 et seq., p. 696.
121 Ibid., p. 695.
122 Ibid., p. 694.
123 Ibid., p. 695.
124 J. B. Walker, 'Notes on the Politics, Religion and Commerce of Old
     Calabar', *Journal of the Anthropological Institute of Great Britain
     and Ireland*, Vol. 6, (London, 1877), p. 124.
125 F.O. 84/1343, Hopkins to F.O., 28 January, 1871.
126 CALPROF 2/1, Vol. 22, F.O. to Livingstone, 24 January, 1870, and
     CALPROF 2/1, Vol. 22, Secretary, Liverpool African Association
     to Clarendon, 30 May, 1870.
127 Vide 'Report of Livingstone, 1872' et seq., pp. 693–4.
128 N. H. Stilliard, op. cit., pp. 106–107; vide also *Parl. Pap.*, 1842, 11,
     question 4298.
129 N. H. Stilliard, op. cit., p. 158.
130 Livingstone's Trade Report, 1872 et seq., p. 679.
131 CALPROF 4/1, Vol. 2, W. J. Thomson (agent for Messrs. Charles
     Horsfall & Sons and chairman of court of equity) to David Hopkins
     (acting consul), 25 July, 1871.
132 CALPROF 2/1, Vol. 25, Granville to Hopkins, 25 September, 1871.
133 CALPROF 2/1, Vol. 22, F.O. to Livingstone, 4 August, 1870, and its
     eight encl. on the legal competency of the court of equity on the
     West coast of Africa.
134 E. Hertslet, op. cit., Vol. 13, pp. 50–62, 'British Order in Council',
     dated 21 February, 1872.
135 F.O. 84/1343, C. Vivian to Consul Livingstone, 9 November, 1871.
136 E. Hertslet, op. cit., Vol. 13, 'Rules and Regulations framed under
     Her Majesty's Order in Council of the 21st day of February, 1872 by
     Her Majesty's Consul at Old Calabar, April 29, 1872', pp. 63–68.
     Appears also in F.O. 84/1356 and in C.O. 147/31.
137 Vide 'Rule and Regulation framed . . . by . . . Consul at Old Calabar
     29 April, 1872, op. cit. Vide also F.O. 84/1356, Livingstone to Earl
     Granville, 29 April, 1872, which explains and transmits the consular
     court regulations.

V

Lineage Rivalries:
the 1870s & 1880s

The economic circumstances of Calabar between the late 1850s and the early 1870s resulted in more than just a crisis in the relations between British commercial interests and the Efik middlemen kings. They also had a significant effect on the internal distribution of political power between the various Calabar towns, and within the towns between the principal lineages.

The present chapter attempts to examine the story of conflict and segmentation in the political evolution of the Calabar towns. Such conflict and segmentation was probably less noticeable in Creek Town (even granting that the Eyo house had to contend with the Ambo and Ibitam) where politics were less turbulent than Duke Town. It is in the latter town that one can clearly identify a re-markable movement by the hitherto unprivileged houses or lineages to re-assert their traditional rights to political office. In the story of these events that occurred in the last quarter of the nineteenth century two major features must be noted: the first is an intense hostility between the Henshaws and the Dukes which resulted in the Henshaws declaring a secessionist movement, and the second is the continuation of lineage tensions within the Duke house which led to the ultimate segmentation of that house.

Economy and Politics in Duke Town
The balance of economic power in the Calabar towns during the greater part of the nineteenth century was largely in the favour of Duke Town. Though Creek Town, during the reign of King Eyo II, had built up its trade, obtained two-thirds of the comey paid to Calabar by the supercargoes and successfully defied the economic strength of Duke Town, her fortunes did not last for long. In 1858 there was the specific effects of a fire accident which destroyed Eyo's property.[1] King Eyo died at the time of the calamity and the loss told severely on his son, later Eyo III, who had to make good his father's liabilities to the European traders.

Besides the misfortunes of Creek Town, other factors explain

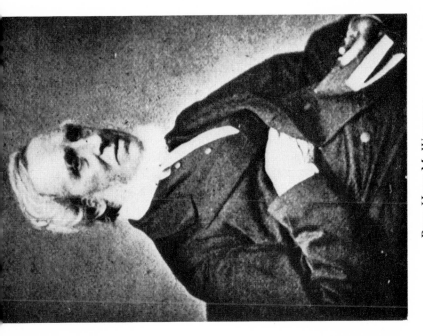

Rev. Hope M. Waddell

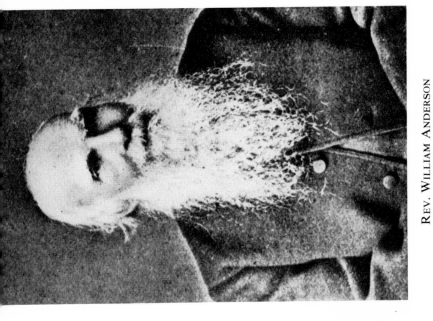

Rev. William Anderson

A TRADING VESSEL MOORED AT DUKE TOWN

REV. H. GOLDIE WITH GREEK TOWN TEACHERS

why Duke Town became the major trade emporium in Calabar. A plausible factor in this respect is the more convenient location of Duke Town with regard to European shipping. Duke Town was situated down the estuary eight miles lower than Creek Town, at a point where the river was about nineteen feet deep thus ensuring a good holding bottom. Here a convenient anchorage was available for vessels of up to 10,000 tons. A draught map of Calabar waters[2] seems to indicate that vessels drawing more than a certain draught were not able to ascend up the river and sail into the narrow creeks leading to Creek Town. It must be remembered that there was a revolution in the construction of steam vessels in the middle years of the nineteenth century which brought about the manufacture of larger and more efficient iron ships, and the draught of these vessels continually grew. It would thus appear that the more convenient anchorage was at Duke Town. Further, the rise and fall of the water between the spring and neap tides in the creeks were natural difficulties in the passage to Creek Town. Traders, therefore, preferred to anchor at Duke Town and visit Creek Town in an oared gig.[3]

Secondly, the oil trade was greatest at Duke Town. As early as 1823 the trader Captain John Adams was writing that the town off which the ships anchored in the Old Calabar river was Duke Town, five miles from the sea.[4] By 1858 Duke Town traders were reported to have furnished to the ships three-fourths of the oil brought down the river. In 1877 another trader wrote that the anchorage chosen for trading hulks extended from abreast the mission station on the hill, below Duke Town, to three miles up the river, below Old Town.[5] It must here be borne in mind that the agricultural plantations of Akpabuyo and Odukpani lay in the immediate hinterland of Duke Town; the houses in Duke Town produced between them a far larger share of the export commodities than Creek Town was able to do. Thus canoes flocked to Duke Town from distant villages bringing palm oil and kernels for trade.[6] There could not have been much difficulty in shipping out slaves in canoes and getting them to climb manacled into a ship. It was much harder work paddling out inanimate casks of palm oil and manhandling them on to the deck of a ship. It is not known whether the rents paid for the grounds on which cask houses stood were cheaper in Duke Town than they were in Creek Town. If this were so, it might constitute a further reason why traders preferred Duke Town to any other town.

It seems reasonably clear that the leadership did not have sufficient resources with which to build an effective power structure directly through the enlargement of the king's house. Economic

M

issues altered the pattern of political relations between the several lineages of the town. The spirit of clannishness and of affectionate attachment to tradition and genealogical inter-relationships was denuded by the economic difficulties posed by a non-expanding trade. Bickering and internal feuds between kin groups became rife. Since several houses contributed to the wealth of Duke Town, the result was that the chief house, Duke house, had to meet the increasing demands of the other houses for a larger share of the wealth accruing from trade. The smaller houses (or lineages) challenged the pretensions of the larger houses. Since European traders preferred to conduct their trade with an individual African middleman whom they appointed from a particular lineage group, other lineages not so favoured resented the practice of having to negotiate trade arrangements with that individual. These lineages naturally nurtured their own economic and political aspirations. Lineage rivalries thus led to an over indulgence in domestic politics in Duke Town, and more particularly in the Duke house.

In 1858 there occurred one of these recurrent lineage disputes. In August of that year King Duke Ephraim of the Duke lineage died, and three lineages—the Duke, the Eyamba and the Archibong —contested the succession. The Archibong lineage successfully produced the successor to the late king, the explanation for which is probably related to the fact that John Archibong had been a de facto ruler of Duke Town while the weak Duke Ephraim had been a nominal de jure king. The election to kingship of John Archibong in March, 1859, and his coronation in August of that year, received the genuine approval of the Duke Town populace and the European traders. No foreign influence was used by super-cargoes with the people in Archibong's favour—as Rev. Anderson remarked, Archibong did not hold his appointment by virtue of a foreign magistrate. Nevertheless, the actual coronation was presided over by a European supercargo, Thomas Hogan; flags were waved and firearms of various sorts were discharged nearly all day in celebration of the event.[7]

Archibong was nevertheless sensitive to the fact that he needed to consolidate his position with the European traders and missionaries if he were to contain the rivalries between the several lineages of his town. He secured the friendship of the missionaries by declaring publicly his disbelief in Idiong and other Efik ritual beliefs, and upheld the words of the missionaries as the only true ones.[8] He also agreed without hesitation to the suggestion of Rev. Anderson, at 2 p.m. on the day of his coronation, to prevent the Sabbath market from being any longer held within the town limits. But he was careful enough to ward off the further request of the mission-

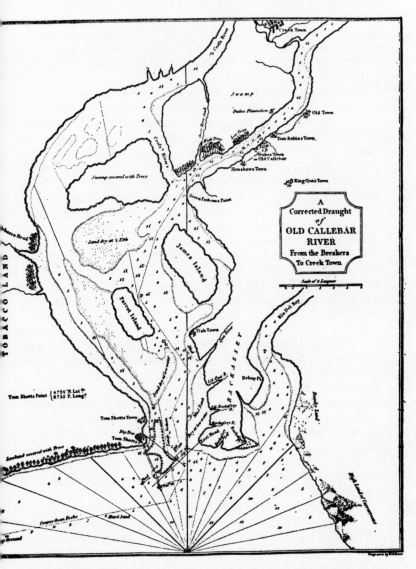

Source: E. Bold, *The Merchants and Mariners African Guide* (1819)

aries that he prevent the holding of Sabbath markets on the Qua frontier outside the town.[9] Though Archibong pleaded that he had no authority to fulfil this wish of the missionaries, it is easy to see what the actual reason was. It would have meant interference with market revenue if the market went out of his jurisdiction.

Next, he set about fortifying his position in Calabar by gaining the goodwill of the British government. What provoked Archibong's concern in this regard was the action of the British consul, Hutchinson, who refused to give his assent to the coronation until Archibong gave certain assurances regarding the trade of the river. Archibong had, it appears, refused to send a pilot to navigate into the river the vessel *Clan George*, belonging to Messrs. Jyson and Richmond of Liverpool, or to build a roof over it, or allow any trade with it. It is easy to understand what the consequences of non-recognition by the British government would be: the payment of comey might be indefinitely suspended. On the day of his coronation, 9 August, Archibong II wrote to Lord Russell, the new Foreign Secretary, of his desire to be on friendly terms with the British government, and sought to gain the approval of the British crown for his title. The letter was supported by the signatures of the supercargoes, agents of European trading houses, leading Efik gentlemen from the Duke, the Archibong and Henshaw families, and influential ex-slaves such as Yellow Duke and Iron Bar.[10] Archibong won, for Lord Russell instructed Hutchinson to reverse the consul's decision to withhold the recognition of Archibong made when Malmesbury was Foreign Secretary, and authorized him to recognize Archibong as king after he had promised peaceful conditions for the trade of the river. What was represented by the consul as misconduct on the part of the king was repudiated by Russell as action that was provoked by the arbitrary and illegal conduct of the British supercargoes themselves. The reference is to a certain rash action in 1859 of Michael Hearn, a supercargo in the employ of Messrs. Jyson and Richmond.[11]

Within Calabar itself, Archibong tried to reinforce his position as king by cultivating close relations with the powerful band of 'Bloodmen' in the plantations. This was a clever diplomatic move since Archibong, unlike earlier kings, had not borrowed the Ekpe title of eyamba from the Eyamba family. The Bloodmen order was a decisive political and social force in Calabar society and although it took advantage of the alliance with Archibong to come to the town, it made good sense for Archibong to court and retain the friendship of that order. The European traders were always nervous about the intentions of the 'crowds of armed men' whose entry into the towns had been prohibited by the treaty of February, 1851. They threatened a trade boycott if Archibong did not immediately order the Bloodmen to the plantations. Archibong protested that the men from the plantations had come only to wish him a speedy recovery from his illness and promised to send them back the following day.[12] This was the last appearance in Duke Town of Bloodmen. When Archibong II died in 1872 there were no 'untoward' incidents. The last appearance of Bloodmen in Creek Town was in 1861 on the death of King Eyo III.

In collaboration with King Eyo VI, Archibong also made a significant attempt to bring the Okoyong people under his control. The people of this town had successfully defied the authority and commercial ambitions of the Efik. Lying between the two main tributaries of the river, immediately behind the farm districts of Creek Town and Ikoneto, Okoyong was in the possession of a people from beyond the Qua River. The 'war' (as it was called) between Calabar and Okoyong began as a struggle between Ikoneto (an Efik town) and Okoyong and developed into a larger affair in September, 1868.

The war is said to have originated over the unsettled question of the boundary between the two areas. This is the interpretation attached to the cause of the war by those who were interviewed in Calabar.[13] A quarrel at the Ikoneto market between the Ikoneto and the Okoyong people[14] provided the occasion for the commencement of hostilities. The Okoyong were not Efik, but belonged to the group of the Ododop-speaking people who lived about sixteen miles north of Creek Town. The Okoyong claimed that it was they who had given the Ikoneto the land on which the latter built their town. For this reason they reserved the right to demarcate the boundary. The Ikoneto refused to acknowledge this claim by denying that they had received the land from an outside party. Since it appeared to both parties that only a war would solve the problem and bring to an end the frequent charges of trespass that each hurled at the other, they marched to war.

The war was fought in two stages,[15] Calabar entering into it only in the second stage. In the first phase, the head of the Okoyong, Chief Anko, was engaged in keeping the fighting beyond Okoyong. The fear was that if the Ikoneto came within close enough range of their town, the Okoyong would find their town reduced to ashes. But the Ikoneto, who knew the country and its terrain much better than the Okoyong, inflicted heavy casualties on the latter. They were about to take the town when the Okoyong chief despatched his son with a message of surrender to the chief of the Ikoneto, Chief Eniang Offiong. At the appearance of the son, carrying around his neck the traditional symbol of defeat (the fruit mfang),[16] the skirmish ceased. It was at this stage of the war that the Calabar towns jointly intervened to support the Ikoneto against Okoyong. The victory had been almost won by the Ikoneto alone. Nevertheless, the Calabar towns, with Odut and Uwet acting as auxiliaries, helped Ikonteo to carry the war into Okoyong territory and succeeded in destroying Okoyong completely.

The success of Calabar in bringing Okoyong within its control, it might be added, belonged less to Archibong's Duke Town than it did to Eyo's Creek Town. Before full victory was won, the Duke Town warriors left the battlefront for Calabar. The reason for this retreat is not certain,[17] but it is plausible firstly that Duke Town's entry at a later stage in the war may not have been well received by the Ikoneto; secondly, Duke Town had already realized its aim of punishing and obtaining the surrender of Okoyong. Thirdly, they had had the worst part of the war, since they were unfamiliar with the terrain on which they fought, and a retreat saved many lives. Rev. Anderson recorded, for instance, that Duke Town had lost about twenty men in various engagements. Creek Town, which lay next to Ikoneto, was more anxious for an Ikoneto victory and was left to fight the last few days of the battle without Duke Town's aid. It cut its way up to the Okoyong position and eventually obtained the surrender of Okoyong which had, as noted above, previously submitted to Duke Town forces. Creek Town's losses, numbering about a hundred men,[18] were far heavier than those of Duke Town. The entire war, which lasted nearly a month, claimed several Calabar lives. Odut, one of the auxiliaries of Calabar in the battle, was entrusted with the drawing up of the treaty of peace.[19]

The significance of the war was that King Archibong used it to extend his authority to include Okoyong once the dispute between Okoyong and Ikoneto had weakened the former.

Archibong II had so securely consolidated his position in Duke Town that he reigned for thirteen years, perhaps the longest single reign of a king for many decades of Calabar history. He had also entrenched the position of the Archibong lineage in the town so that when he died on 26 August, 1872,[20] the kingship was retained by the lineage. His successor, Edem Archibong, who had already been functioning as a regent and executing the office of king for some time before his coronation as King Archibong III, was a brother of Archibong I and II. The retention of the office of king in the Archibong lineage is all the more remarkable in that Archibong III suffered from blindness (since 1870), and on account of this physical infirmity had scarcely left his house even on state matters.[21] In order to execute the affairs of state he had to in-augurate a system by which he had a representative, Prince Eyamba,[22] to assist him.

The shortcomings of the system were exaggerated by the super-cargoes who frowned at the fact that the representative was inter-dicted from assenting to any measures that might be resolved upon until he had communicated with the king and chief in council. The supercargoes tended to tire of the non-autocratic nature of Calabar kingship. It had always been a tradition that full and final authority scarcely rested with the kings who had to accept the advice of their chiefs or cabinets. The official records abound in instances where Efik kings told supercargoes or consuls that they were unable to reply to correspondence addressed to them until they had first con-sulted the chiefs.[23]

To this extent, Archibong III was no different from the earlier kings of Calabar. Where the point of departure from tradition occurred was in Archibong's inability to be physically present at meetings with the extra-territorial agents. He was constrained to send out men to conduct, on his behalf, negotiations with the consul or members of the court of equity. It was not always a satisfactory state of affairs. The European supercargoes felt it beneath their dignity to negotiate with a mere representative of the king. Neither did they want to humble themselves by holding audiences with the king in his 'Imperial Palace'. The consul had more sympathy with Archibong III: 'it does appear somewhat un-reasonable to compel a blind man who has not left his own premises for the last four years, to venture on the water'.[24]

The immediate social and political problem faced by Archibong III was to arrest the centrifugal forces within his state. The Sierra Leoneans and the 'Accra men', who styled themselves 'British Africans' and held 'free papers' issued by the consul, began a movement to rid themselves of control by the king. They con-tinually petitioned the consul about ill treatment received at the hands of both the king and his representative, Prince Eyamba. In 1876, the Sierra Leoneans complained of the 'daily cruelties' of Prince Eyamba who, they alleged, enslaved as he wished and inflicted punishments without regard for the consul. They cited the instance of one Sierra Leonean, James Croker, whom Eyamba flogged and kept in chains for twenty-four days.[25]

Whatever the status claimed by the complainants, it would have been disastrous for Archibong if he took a lenient attitude towards the 'British Africans'. Archibong firmly advised the court of equity that he would not have African-born British subjects in his town who did not abide by the law of his country. Those who chose not to submit themselves to his laws should leave his country or abide in one of the hulks.[26]

The supercargoes, who had little love for the Sierra Leoneans, agreed that if African-born British subjects committed an offence, the king ought to have the power to punish them. One of them even ventured to state that he thought a king had a right to make the hulks in Duke Town abide by his law in regard to the above. This was somewhat hypocritical, since the supercargoes had never considered themselves subject to Efik law.

In addition to the aversion of African-born British subjects to Archibong's rule, there was also the challenge from holders of 'free papers' with which to contend. The 'free papers' had been given to ex-slaves as a protective measure against seizure of their persons. Rev. Anderson has pointed out that the first free papers, and probably the later ones too, were approved by the Foreign Office and were published in the British *Parliamentary Blue Books* from 1856 or 1857. It is easy to understand Archibong's concern over the distribution of these 'free papers'. Those who were in possession of them considered themselves British subjects, and had gone off to occupy the hill close to the mission premises. The holders of such papers did not consider themselves subject to either British or Calabar laws, and set themselves up as a people without a government.

The king was fearful of rapidly losing the allegiance of several of his subjects. He desired that those of his subjects who were not redeemed by the mission, with money, should leave Duke Town entirely unless they consented to sign a document recognizing him as their king and agreeing to abide by his laws. If the king had not done this, he would have continued to lose the obedience of those who possessed 'free papers' and his authority over his people would pari passu have been diminished and his country ruined.[27]

Archibong made a test case with one of the holders of the free papers. He claimed that one Egbo Bassey, who had held free papers for nine years and had presumably been under British protection for twenty-four years,[28] was a slave belonging to him. This involved him in a bitter conflict with the consul and the missionaries, particularly Rev. W. Anderson. To the missionaries and the consul, Egbo Bassey typified those slaves who had improved their inferior social status, bought their freedom, and were engaged in an honest living. Egbo Bassey complained to Anderson about Archibong's 'molestation', and 'rapacity'.[29] The claim occasioned a tremendous number of letters being exchanged on the subject between the missionaries, the consul and King Archibong.[30]

It appears that the controversy began when Fanny, the wife of Egbo Bassey, who had been for several months at Fernando Po, was invited by Mrs. Anderson to Calabar for a few weeks to recuperate from an illness. Archibong III objected to her visit on the grounds that he wanted to exclude from his country those who, on account of their acquired 'free' status, did not want to be subject to his rule. He added that he had the right to exclude from his dominion anyone he so pleased, and issued the warning that no European had any right to make any of his subjects equal to the king. He wanted no foreign interference in the matter of Egbo Bassey.[31] Anderson retorted that Fanny had been a friend of theirs for more than twenty years; he did not see why Europeans should in any way be hindered in bringing their friends over to visit them. Egbo Bassey had been asked to leave Duke Town, added the Rev. Anderson, because he held free papers from the consul.

The political and social upheavals that no doubt would be caused by those who lived in the town and paid no heed to the king would have significant implications for stability and maintenance of law and order. No state could afford to ignore the potential threat of a group of people within it who considered themselves immune to the laws of the state. Archibong was as determined to resist growing missionary and consular inroads into his legitimate rights as the missionaries were in enforcing the provisions of the free papers and resisting Archibong's alleged disrespect for the redeemed slaves.

Clearly in exceptional circumstances exceptional measures were necessary.[32] The danger of the political authority of Archibong being undermined by other fellow Africans was not to be minimized. The traditional lineage rivalries assumed a new turn for the Henshaws who had their own quarrel with the Dukes and who were now prepared to use other means to settle their scores with their rivals. And so in 1875 Henshaw Town decided to offer refuge to those who held free papers in Duke Town.

Rivalry between the Henshaws and Dukes

Thus in addition to the disarray in Duke Town and the judicial, political and economic undermining of the state by foreign agencies, all of which seriously weakened the political system, must be noted the factor of internal disunity. Conflict between Duke Town and some of the other wards, particularly Henshaw Town, was easily evoked during the period of economic strain in the river. It was then that the old traditions which gave expression to the primary social sense of belonging together wore thin. Each lineage was interested in gaining a larger share of the trade of the river. The lineage which supplied the king of the town, and conducted the commercial intercourse of all lineages within the town in its external relations with European supercargoes, found its traditional rights to authority seriously challenged. The arguments of the other lineages were directed at gaining direct access to the European trading vessels or to reducing the dominant position claimed by the privileged lineage.

In 1875 Henshaw Town revolted against Duke Town in a bid to modify the traditional political and economic relations between them. Duke Town was hostile to any move made by other lineages to undermine its trade by entering into bilateral relationships with foreign firms. The Henshaws had entered into contracts with trading agents and others in the river to build beach houses and roof the hulks with mats. In March of that year the Henshaws contracted with one Gilbertson, the agent of Messrs. Taylor Laughland and Company, to roof his hulk *Realm*. The Henshaws had procured about four thousand mats, when King Archibong wrote to inform Gilbertson that he would not allow the Henshaws to execute the work. Archibong took the contract from Henshaws and gave it to one Egbo Young Hogan of Duke Town. Since roofing hulks was apparently a profitable line of business in Calabar and imports of mats a considerable item of trade, it is easy to understand the frustration of Henshaw Town.

In that year, too, Archibong had stopped the trade in Calabar by 'blowing' Ekpe. A few months later the trade was reopened, but before three months had passed the Henshaws were interdicted from the trade. Duke Town imposed a monopoly over the trade in salt, which commodity the Henshaws took to the markets for sale. The salt had been purchased by the Henshaws with the trust given them by European traders; salt, which the Henshaws had already put for sale on the markets, was also declared by Ekpe law to be forbidden for sale; salt bought a day earlier to the Ekpe law was not to be sent to the market. The result of the embargo placed by Duke Town on the export of salt was that the commodity purchased on trust from the markets was left to pile up in Henshaw Town. Archibong tried to hoodwink the Henshaws by informing them that it was not he, but the young men of his town, who had interdicted the trade.[33] It is however unlikely that King Archibong III, who had bought the Ekpe title of Eyamba (he was Eyamba VIII), would not have known what the young men were doing. It was then that Henshaw Town, which Duke Town had always considered to be part of it, decided upon secession from Duke Town.

The secession of Henshaw Town from Duke Town raises certain

fundamental questions about the dynamics of the relations between the two towns, and the implications of the secession for the constitution of the Efik towns, since the towns were nodal points of a widespread trading system. In the same way that historical evidence may be twisted to suit one's case better, the Dukes and the Henshaws studied the dynamics of their relationship by interpreting Efik traditional history in such a manner that it seemed to favour their separate cases.

The fundamental basis of Henshaw Town's case remained the same in both the struggle against the salt monopoly and in the independence issue. In order to be able to grasp fully the essence of Henshaw Town's arguments, which rested on tradition and history, it is necessary to examine closely the genealogical relationship of the Henshaws and the Dukes.

(In the tables the names of families have been underlined.)

TABLE 1

The genealogy of the Effiom Ekpo group

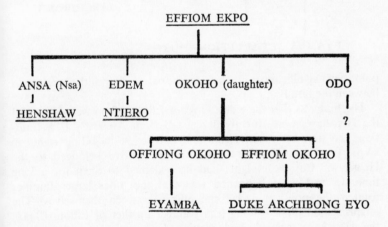

It would be clear from this simplified genealogical chart of the Efik that the Henshaws were descended from the first stock (Nsa) of Effiom Ekpo, one of the two legendary fathers of the Efik. The Duke Town people are said to have descended from Okoho Effiom, the daughter of Effiom Ekpo, thus: (see Table 2 overleaf).

The fact that the Henshaws were descended from Ansa and that the Dukes were descended from Okoho Effiom had two major

TABLE 2

The genealogy of the Okoho Effiom group

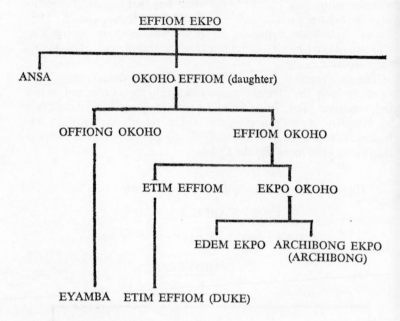

points of significance in the traditional socio-political relations between the families.

The first was that the eldest child of Effiom Ekpo was Ansa, and the Henshaws were directly descended from Ansa. By Efik tradition, the first born had rights and privileges, including rights in Ekpe, over all the others and this prerogative belonged to the Henshaws. But these rights had been denied to them for a long time. Instead what happened was that the other larger families rotated the political and Ekpe offices between themselves. The offspring of Effiom Effiong (the younger brother of Effiom Ekpo), the Henshaws argued, had continued to make the kings from amongst their numbers. Unfortunately for the Henshaws, the family of Okoho Effiom grew at a more rapid rate than the Henshaws, with the result that the Duke family far outnumbered that of the Henshaw. The Henshaws represented their struggle as one against the illegitimately assumed leadership and oppression of an upstart people. They hastened to point out for instance that the very first two kings of Duke Town, Nsa Effiom and Ekpo Ansa, were both from the Henshaw family.

The second point of significance revealed by the genealogy of the Efik is that the Dukes descended from a daughter (Okoho), and not from a son of Effiom Ekpo. Though Efik women today are noted for their emancipation and rights to franchise, in the tradition of the old days they could exert no superiority over a man in matters of state. Hence, the Henshaws were not willing to accept the position of the Dukes.

The Dukes proved equal to the Henshaws in recalling their early history. Though they were not descended from the eldest stock of Effiom Ekpo, explained the Dukes, they were nevertheless the founders of Duke Town. It was Effiom Okoho who founded Duke Town, and as such the Duke family who descended from Okoho had rights over the land, including rights to the land on which Henshaw Town stood. The Henshaws had migrated to Duke Town only after the Dukes had settled on that site. Therefore, as the Henshaws were subject to Duke Town they had, in the customary manner, to trade their produce to European agents through Duke Town. They were expected to and had to pay the necessary tribute to the king of Duke Town.

It was shown in the introductory chapter that lineage rivalries were an important characteristic of the political history of Calabar. When the Duke lineage grew in its numerical strength, and multiplied its wealth through the favour of European supercargoes, the Henshaws moved away from Duke Town proper into the outskirts and lived physically separate from it. But the Ekpe institution still bound them to the larger Efik community so that their relations with the Duke lineage were determined by that factor alone. In 1871 this binding social sense had somewhat reduced when Duke Town excluded Henshaw Town from the Ekpe shed in their town. The reduction of the political system to one of narrowness and rigidity, and the repression of the individuality of the lineages, removed the last vestiges of an affectionate attachment to tradition and gave rise to a sense of alienation.

Henshaw Town proposed to move ahead of tradition. In the early 1870s they produced a breed of efficient and forward looking men who resolved to rebuild their old town. They sponsored in 1871 a movement, called the Young Calabar movement, which drew up a programme for the restoration of their old town. They desired to have a king over them as other Calabar towns did, so that they could have their own laws and constitution for the government of their town, independent of Duke Town. Also, the Henshaws wrote down that one of their aims was to advance 'the cause of civilization and Christianity' among their people.

In fact, the Young Calabar movement was designed as a force

to eradicate the old religion, superstitions, and traditional customs of the Efik and to accept en masse Christianity and the adoption of western customs and clothing. Whether this was an attempt to court the support of the missionaries and Hopkins, the pro-mission- ary, intensely Christian acting Consul of the time who preached at Calabar and Fernando Po and opened meetings of consular courts with prayers, remains uncertain. It is not improbable that the Hen- shaws knew that support for the independence project would depend on meeting the demands made by the missionaries. Never- theless, superficially at least, the movement espoused a social and religious revolution.

The principal men wrote to Hopkins on 16 February, 1871, ask- ing him to favour them with any encouragement he could in their desired project. The letter which contained this request was also signed by the missionaries (William Anderson, Hugh Goldie and Samuel Edgerley) and by some of the influential supercargoes (George Watts and J. B. Walker, among others).[34] On the following day a conference was held between the young men of Henshaw Town and Hopkins.[35] The acting consul felt that the Young Cala- bar movement should receive every encouragement so long as it did not rebel against King Archibong.[36] Archibong himself sanctioned the rebuilding of the town.

But when he realized the more radical intentions of the Hen- shaws, namely to create their own king, Archibong expressed annoyance. On 11 March he spoke to Anderson about the pre- sumption of the Henshaw Town 'boys' wishing for their own king, and promised he 'no will for that'.[37] Archibong no doubt astutely saw through the political and economic motives underlying the manifestly social programme of the Young Calabar movement. If the Henshaws had their own king and if Duke Town recognized a second king in the town the consequences could be enormous. Principally, there was the strong possibility that the Henshaw king would be entitled to a share of the comey paid to the town by the European supercargoes. Duke Town would have to split the comey between two kings. The Henshaws would no longer trade through the king of Duke Town but through their own king. Henshaw Town would be able to consolidate its economic and political power and eventually aspire to exert a monopolistic hold over the trade of the interior.

The missionaries, flattered by the social reforms that the move- ment envisaged, threw their support in with the Henshaws. They had always derided the indifference of the Duke Town people to- wards missionary work, and had almost nothing but praise for the Henshaws. The latter had continuously renewed their earnest appeal

for more teachers, expressed their willingness to build school houses,
and attended church services regularly.[38] In fact, Anderson noted
that more young men came to church from the small village of
Henshaw Town (the population of which was between three and
four hundred)[39] than from the larger town of Duke Town (whose
population was about 6,000). The average attendance at the Duke
Town church was in the neighbourhood of 800–850.[40] Though
none of the Henshaws who came to church were church members,
they were better dressed and used books better than the Duke
Town people. However, Anderson estimated that half the Sabbath
congregation of the Duke Town Church came from Henshaw
Town.[41] It was partly to bring them fully into the Christian fold,
and to free them from the 'grasp of Duke Town heathenism', that
the missionaries gave moral support to the struggle of Henshaw
Town.

But the Henshaws moved too far ahead of tradition. Unable to
obtain any better explanation or reparation for the embargo on
the salt trade placed on them, the Henshaws took the offensive
and laid hold of a Duke Town chief, Prince Duke (Orok Edem),
who was then visiting a friend in the neighbourhood of Henshaw
Town. The captive was put in chains and handled roughly.[42] In
about half an hour hundreds of armed men from Duke Town
rushed up the hill, while about forty or fifty came to meet them
from Henshaw Town. The explosive situation was only contained
by the timely interference of the missionaries, especially Anderson.
He drew a line across the road with his staff, and proclaimed that
whoever crossed that line would involve himself in war with the
white men. The missionaries were soon relieved from their position
by an Ekpe drum, sent by King Eyo, which forbade all firing of
guns and ordered a cease fire.

Secession of Henshaws from Duke Town

During the next few weeks of negotiations, the Henshaws pressed
on with their claim for independence from Duke Town. The missionaries warned the Henshaws that their cause would be damaged
by precipitate action, and consequently advised them

> to go on quietly building their town, drawing to it a large popula-
> tion, clearing off all debts to the shipping; increasing their trade,
> etc., till they should be able to command the respect of all neigh-
> bours and rivals before they considered any change in their political
> situation.[43]

But Henshaw Town turned a deaf ear to the well meant advice
and was determined to proceed with the programme of the Young

Calabar. They procured a sort of crown from a Dutch supercargo. The man chosen to be honoured as king was James Henshaw (Ekeng Ita) who had descended from the eldest son, Effiom Ansa, of Ansa (Henshaw Ansa Effiom). James Henshaw assumed the title of Henshaw III. His assistant was one Joseph Henshaw,[44] a man who was destined to play an important part in the economic development of the Henshaws.

TABLE 3

The genealogy of James Henshaw

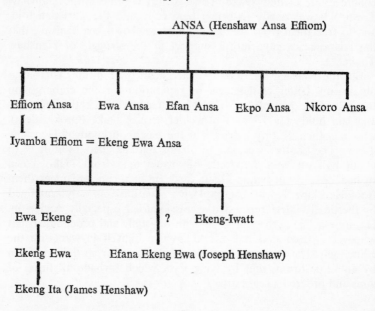

Iyamba Effiom was a daughter of Effiom Ansa (the spelling 'Iyamba' is the female version of the masculine name 'Eyamba') and she married, according to Efik sources, Ekeng Ewa Ansa. It was to this marriage that both Henshaw III and Joseph Henshaw traced their origin.[45]

The coronation of Henshaw III was a rash step. The grandees of Duke Town who were determined that there could be no two persons in Duke Town who bore the title 'king' were annoyed with the Henshaws. The Duke Town chiefs were willing to go so far as recognizing James Henshaw as a 'headman' of Henshaw Town as this was in accordance with the fashion in most Efik towns without kings. But Henshaw Town went ahead with their own plans

(by courtesy of Chief L. A. Esien Offiong)

CHIEF ESIEN ETIM OFFIONG III

KING EYO HONESTY II

MARY SLESSOR

and in August, 1875 erected a barricade on the mission hill. The European traders at a meeting on board *Dawstone* on 29 August deplored the construction of such a barricade and when Henshaw Town refused to remove it[46] they summoned the consul 'with all speed' in a gunboat. The supercargoes complained that the inviolability of the cask houses had been utterly disregarded.[47]

The battle broke out on September 7. It followed the diplomatic manoeuvre of Archibong III who enlisted the white traders and the whole Ekpe fraternity on the side of Duke Town against Henshaw Town. Archibong compelled the Henshaws to surrender the crown and the regal title of 'king' to Duke Town. A heavy fine was levied by Ekpe on Henshaw Town for a breach of Ekpe law.[48] But the release of Prince Duke, who was held captive by Henshaw Town, had to be secured.[49] Duke Town was anxious to reciprocate this harsh treatment by detaining Henshaw III, and issued orders for his surrender into the hands of Duke Town.

It was Duke Town which opened the battle by pitching billets of wood, spiked at each end, among the Henshaw Town people. The casualties on either side were not exceedingly great. Anderson estimated that 'there were killed, of Duke Town eight or ten; and of Henshaw Town, fourteen or sixteen; wounded of Duke Town, about twenty; of Henshaw Town, about twenty-five'.[50] The firing lasted the whole day. Henshaw III escaped to one of the hulks to meet the court of equity. Harry Hartje of the court met Henshaw III on the hulk and agreed to settle the matter temporarily. It was decided that James Henshaw would be handed over to King Archibong, and that Henshaw Town people would be given six hours of grace in which to escape with the most valuable portions of their property. The Henshaws were harboured on the beach of the European trader, J. B. Walker.[51] At noon on the following day, when Henshaw Town was vacated, the Duke Town hordes poured in, removed any remaining valuables in the houses, and set fire to the town.

Towards the end of the month the consul, Hartley, arrived to make the peace between Duke and Henshaw Towns. One of the questions which had to be faced was whether the uprising of Henshaw Town constituted an act of rebellion against Duke Town. The Rev. Anderson did not believe that this was so. In the twenty-seven years that he had been in Calabar, the Henshaw Town people had always been treated by the Duke Town people as a separate community. He stated that he was present at the coronation of King Archibong II, and was responsible for drawing up the papers concerned therewith. One of the documents consisted of a declaration of allegiance signed by all the headmen of Duke Town, but not one person belonging to Henshaw Town had been required to sign the declaration. Added Anderson:

> Look at your Vols. of Treaties—I don't think you find a Henshaw Town man's name attached to one. The last treaty I saw made was that with A. G. Hopkins about Twin Murder. All Duke To. gentlemen and all Henshaw To. gentlemen were present when it was made and I observed that king A. called some of the lower class of freemen of D. To. to sign the treaty—but he did not call a single person belonging to Henshaw To. to do so—which I considered as one proof among many that Duke To. people considered Henshaw To. people—as a separate community—and not as a part and parcel of themselves.[52]

It is difficult to be legalistic about Anderson's view that Henshaw Town owed no allegiance to Duke Town as the internal evidence offers little clarification of the confused state of relations between Henshaw Town and Duke Town. However it may be said of Henshaw Town that it began the train of events by seizing a Duke Town chief, that it acted under a strange compulsion in the matter, and that Duke Town was in the earlier stages remarkably forbearing. As for the future, Anderson felt that if all the Henshaw Town freemen wanted to subscribe to a document owing allegiance to Duke Town, and petitioned for the restoration of the land, or at least permission to rebuild their town, the consul might be able to prevail on Duke Town to let matters rest. On the other hand if Henshaw Town was not willing to do so, the Duke Town people could not be blamed for rendering the former incapacitated for war for a generation or two to come. They should, in the latter case, move to some other site so that it would free the Europeans 'from the burden of supporting a whole community'.

The agreements of 1875 and 1878

It cannot be maintained that the terms of the agreement[53] of September, 1875, which concluded the battle between the two towns, were entirely satisfactory to Henshaw Town. The first clause of the agreement, for instance, stipulated that the Henshaw Town people could return to their town on swearing allegiance to King Archibong III and his heirs. But if we view the struggle between the two as the struggle of a small but growing family or lineage to displace the pretensions of a larger and wealthier family or lineage, then certainly the agreement can be criticized for having prevented the natural development of Henshaw Town by securing the subservience of that town to Duke Town. It is clear that Henshaw Town believed that the old relations between it and Duke Town had become obsolete, and that the tradition inherited from a common past was not alone sufficient to ensure the prosperity of its people. Fierce pride and refusal to be dominated by another lineage, coupled with a desire for political and economic enfranchisement, were buttressed by the fear that the traditional political system had failed to secure the social ends of the people for whom it was devised. The Henshaws, who had moved away from Duke Town, had come to prize their reputation and separation as something with which their own lives were bound. Economic gains could only be attained through political isolation. Putative or real blood bonds, which characterized the social system, had no longer the same psychological support of the Henshaws. A new social system had to be devised in which each lineage not only contributed its own share to the trade, but also received in return satisfactory gains from it. The competitive struggle for trade sharpened the sense of lineage.

In addition to economic disharmonies that had broken down the system of power and authority, Henshaw Town had suffered a shattering experience in the battle. When it was called upon to make debt payments to Duke Town over a period of four years, Henshaw Town was certain to resent any such payment on the grounds that the custom of Calabar was specific that no such demand for debts could be made by either of the towns which had engaged in war between themselves.[54]

The peace could not last for long. Duke Town held itself aloof from Henshaw Town and refused to meet with it on matters decreed by Ekpe. The Henshaws claimed that they had signed the treaty on the understanding that by acting under its tenor all disagreements were ended, and that they would have nothing more to do than to pursue their legitimate trade in peace and quiet. Unfortunately, however, there were persistent acts of alleged provocation by the Duke Town people who accused the Henshaws of poisoning some of their chiefs. In November, 1875 the Henshaw chiefs despatched a representative, Joseph Henshaw, to meet the acting consul, H. C. Tait, in Fernando Po. While Joseph Henshaw was away on his errand, it was rumoured that the Bonny people were coming to invade Calabar for the purpose of war. The Duke Town men sent their warriors to lie in ambush all round Henshaw Town, under the suspicion that it was the Henshaws who had invited the Bonny men to avenge Henshaw Town's defeat.

In February, 1876, James Henshaw and six other chiefs petitioned the British government about the heavy oppression they suffered under Duke Town administration.[55] They listed the grievances mentioned above, and begged for an independent inquiry into the issue. But the odd thing was that a few days after the petition had been sent, another letter was addressed to the Foreign Office stating that they wished to withdraw their earlier petition as they had by 'friendly conversation' with Duke Town resolved all their points of difference.[56] It had also been agreed that Henshaw was no longer to use the style of address, 'Henshaw III'.[57] That this understanding reached privately between the two towns did not stand the test of time is apparent from the fact that on 30 December, 1877 the Henshaws sent a long memorial to Lord Derby, then British Secretary for Foreign Affairs. It was followed later by a statement, dated 20 August, 1878, in which twelve Henshaw chiefs gave further evidence of their pathetic lot under the Duke Town chiefs.[58]

The memorials were clearly asking Lord Derby to persuade the Admiralty to assist Henshaw Town people move away from their location to either Rio del Rey or the Qua Ibo River, and to place the Henshaws under the protection of the British Crown. The natural growth of Henshaw Town had been considerably stifled by many obstacles thrown in its way by Duke Town; property had been lost, trade hindered and life threatened. In these circumstances Henshaw Town was convinced that it could no longer live peaceably with Duke Town.

On 6 September, 1878 yet another agreement was signed between Henshaw Town and Duke Town, through the assistance of Consul David Hopkins.[59] The agreement, consisting of fifteen articles, related chiefly to such matters as twin children and their mothers, human sacrifices, the esere bean, the stripping of women and such other provisions, which put a political seal on the social reform which had been carried mainly by the moral influence of the missionaries and European residents.[60] Also, a subsidiary 'Rules and Regulations for the Management of Henshaw Town' was drawn up and approved by the consul on the same day. It provided for making Henshaw Town a Christian community. The constitution by which the town was to be administered henceforth stated that every inhabitant of the town must observe the Sabbath strictly by doing no work at all. Anyone breaking this regulation would be fined twelve brass rods for the first offence. Article five of the constitution stated:

> There shall be no worshipping of rituals or sacrifices made to supposed Gods, nor Devil making [connected with burial] or making offerings to the spirit of deceased persons.[61]

The first offences carried a punishment of between a hundred and twenty to three hundred brass rods. So severe were these rules that, for instance, 'no unseemly noises such as firing of guns or cannons' were permitted.

On the more immediate issue of political matters, the agreement stated that there should be 'but one king in Old Calabar'. 'Old Calabar' here, it would seem, meant Duke Town (the two names are sometimes erroneously used interchangeably in some consular correspondence). The head chief of Henshaw Town was to be called Chief Henshaw, and he would rule his town in accordance with the rules arranged for the same by the consul. King Archibong and his chiefs bound themselves not to interfere in any way with Chief Henshaw and his people either in Henshaw Town, the markets or the plantations. Similarly, Chief Henshaw bound himself to obey all the lawful orders of King Archibong, provided always that he was not called upon to do or suffer to be done any act which was un-Christian. To keep the two heads of the town in lasting friendship and to give expression to the close family ties of the Dukes and Henshaws, it was agreed that Chief Henshaw should have a place at all times in the Duke Town council, whether the subjects to be discussed were trade matters or issues connected with the general welfare of the country.

Other articles of the treaty were taken up by provisions intended to open up the trade of Calabar more freely to others, especially Qua Town, which, though the original owners of the soil on which Duke Town stood, nevertheless had hitherto been denied free access to external trade. In return for these privileges, the king and people of Qua Town were to assist the missionaries to establish schools and send their children there for instruction; they were also to abstain from work on the Sabbath.[62] It was agreed that the people of Qua Town were at liberty to buy, sell, visit and trade with any European house in the river or on the beach in all articles of produce, such as palm oil, kernel, ebony, yams, goats, fowls, eggs, corns, cassava, or fruits. It became unlawful for any person to induce the Europeans by threats or bribes to pass their produce through brokers' hands if the Qua did not wish to transact through middlemen. The Qua were granted a certain part of the river frontage near Old Town beach to embark or disembark their properties. Both of these actions must have greatly weakened Duke Town commercially.

The provisions were probably inserted into the treaty in order to ensure that no town, owing to its dominance, interfered with the trade of the others. Duke Town had on an earlier occasion 'blown Ekpe' to the effect that no man could buy oil in the markets in barrels and hogsheads but only in puncheons; also that no man could buy palm kernels in the markets.[63] Under the new regulations, all traders were permitted to buy in large or small quantities as suited them, whether these were puncheons, hogsheads, barrels or any lesser measure. Brass rods could be sold to the traders in any numbers the traders chose to receive them.

It was lawful for all the kings and chiefs of the towns to form among themselves a Court of Commerce where they could arrange the prices that were to be paid in the markets. Fines for breach of the commercial code were made less excessive so as not to press unduly on the poor traders. The kings and chiefs of Calabar proper could close any of the markets, without first informing the court of equity, provided they could show sufficient reasons for so doing as would justify it in recommending the consul to give his permission for the same. Kings were not to wage war amongst themselves or on others, without first informing the consul, giving him the reasons for the intention of so doing, and showing him the receipts of all debts paid. Canoes lying at any European beach or alongside the hulks, whether loaded or otherwise, were placed under the protection of Europeans residing on the beach or on the hulk. They could not be seized by any person whatsoever either by Ekpe law or otherwise. Europeans could build dwelling houses on the beach, but they were not to encroach on the brow of the hill. Comey on palm kernels and ebony was fixed at five coppers a ton, and on oil as before arranged, namely ten coppers a ton.

The expansion of Henshaw Town's economic activities

The end of the war left Henshaw Town in a shambles. The economy had been ruined after the pillage and plunder, and the effort to revive it after 1875 had met with the jealous hostility of Duke Town. There were very few goods on hand with which to resume trade. It was at this critical moment in its political and economic history that Henshaw Town began to look farther afield, to the Qua Ibo region, to put the pieces together and begin anew.

The architect of this vision and enterprise was Joseph Henshaw, who reputedly was the first to introduce cocoa into Calabar. He also initiated the beginnings of trade connections with Qua Ibo.[64] It was while Joseph Henshaw was at Fernando Po, informing the consul about the Henshaw–Duke Town war, that he was shown around the cocoa plantations there. He bought some cocoa seeds from the farmers, and brought them to Calabar in the hope of commencing a profitable trade in cocoa. On his return to Calabar, in 1879, he bought up some land at Oron on the left bank of the Cross River estuary, from Chief Ating Edem Umo of Equita.[65] He then began a plantation there growing cocoa among other crops. He dealt in the sale of palm oil and kernel, and developed the cocoa industry, which at this point in time was a profitable one. Traders and farmers from the plantations of Calabar, namely

Odukpani and Akpabuyo, bought seeds from him and planted them. Thus cocoa was introduced to Calabar and its environs by the enterprise and keen commercial acumen of Joseph Henshaw.

Soon after he had founded the port of Idua Oron, he opened up Ibeno and Eket to trade and collaborated with a European merchant, George Watts, to develop the trade of the Qua Ibo River. Qua Ibo was inhabited by Ibuno, Eket, Ibibio and Obium peoples, whose root language was Ibibio. The area was one of the most thickly populated districts on the coast.[66] A representative, William of Ibeno, was despatched to visit the land and report on its trade prospects.

The collaboration between Henshaw and Watts was a convenient one. Watts was a poorly educated but tough and independent trader who had been reduced to a state of financial insolvency. He had been one of the less fortunate ones in the stiff competition between the trading firms in Calabar so that his firm, Irvine and Woodward, never made much of a success in its trading venture. In the first place Watts had extended credit too generously and allowed his resources to be drained away rapidly. Secondly, the battle between Henshaw Town and Duke Town in 1875 had seriously affected Watts because the bulk of his trade had been with Henshaw Town. In October, 1877 the firm Irvine and Company and John Holt agreed to advance Watts capital at five percent interest to keep him going. The Company, however, was so greatly in debt that Watts had to rely almost entirely on Holt for financial assistance.[67] It was in order to break the monopoly of the factory firms' control, which acted as an obstacle to his plans for expansion, that he concluded the alliance with Henshaw to exploit new areas of trade.

Henshaw could not have organized the trade without the assistance of Watts. Henshaw needed a supercargo to buy his produce and since Watts was willing to establish a factory and buy the produce of Henshaw,[68] the latter saw a brilliant opportunity to commence trade in that district. After all, Idua Oron lay outside the mainstream of Calabar activity.[69] Here, a new trading centre could be built to establish contact with the Ibibio people who lived inland behind the western bank of the estuary. There was also a fairly easy route overland into the Qua Ibo district, which was not one of the usual Calabar markets.[70] This hitherto underdeveloped river,[71] outside the pale of Calabar authority and therefore free of Duke Town's incursion, was the ideal trading post.

The arrangement was that should new firms wish to come in for trading purposes, of each sum paid for the privilege, Henshaw would have two-thirds of the profits since he had discovered the place and Watts would receive one-third.

The venture began at Ibeno and then expanded towards Eket, where a factory was opened, and finally Okatt. But there was one major problem that had to be overcome. Across the river mouth of Qua Ibo there was a deep bar which prevented easy access to the sea. There was consequently no harbour at the mouth of the river. Watts and Holt decided that the best policy was to work Qua Ibo as a branch station from Calabar. In 1880 both Watts and Henshaw visited Qua Ibo and subsequently established a factory with a European agent at the mouth of the river. Holt sent out a large quantity of trade goods. Watts went up Qua Ibo in search of cheaper produce and concluded agreements with the chiefs he met. On 7 February, 1881 they handed over to him trading rights in their rivers and ceded to him land on which he might build factories. He also obtained the right to collect customs duties on the rivers on behalf of the chiefs of the region. Henshaw did not meet with the jealousy of Archibong. This might be attributed either to the fact that the opening of new produce markets and the tapping of the country behind Qua Ibo for produce did not challenge the trade of Duke Town, or that Archibong was too tired or unable to wage any more wars with the Henshaws.

The opposition was largely from King Ja Ja of Opobo who claimed sovereignty over the Qua Ibo River, and, therefore, full control of its trade. Certainly Ja Ja had driven off other trading ventures in Qua Ibo. Messrs. Miller Brothers were forced to withdraw their agency on the Qua Ibo River in 1873 owing to threats from Ja Ja, and another trader, M'Eachan, had to retire for a similar reason.[72] Ja Ja was prepared to drive away the Calabar traders in the same way. At daylight on 11 April, 1881, some fifty of his canoes, flying the British flag and armed with breech-loading cannons and rifles, entered the Qua Ibo River, bombarded seven villages, and burnt five of them, namely, Ibot Etu, Ikot Itak, Eboti-yan, Obarekan and Mkpanek.[73] They also broke into Watts's factory and destroyed or carried off a great part of his goods. Over a hundred prisoners, chiefly women and children, were seized and taken away to Opobo, where they were allegedly slain. It has also been said that some of Ja Ja's young sons cut off the heads of Qua Ibo children in order to earn the right to wear the eagle plume.[74]

On 8 June, 1881 Ja Ja formally proclaimed himself king of the Qua Ibo.[75] He brushed aside Consul Hewett's warnings that Ja Ja's country did not extend up to Qua Ibo which was placed under British protection, thus, 'My first and last words are that the country [Qua Ibo] belongs to me and I do not want white traders

. . . there'.[76] In February, 1882 John Holt appealed to the Foreign Office to protect Watts and annex to Britain the entire coast from Lagos to Cameroons in the interest of commerce.[77] In 1883 Hewett was asked to conduct enquiries into the conduct of Ja Ja's people in that river, especially in regard to trade.

It had become well known that after his recognition as king of the new state of Opobo in 1873, Ja Ja had undertaken the consolidation of the port of Opobo and built up his plantation settlements in the neighbourhood. His commercial expansion radiated northward to the oil markets of Ohambele in Ndoki land, north eastwards to the creeks which discharged into the Opobo River where Essene (or Asien) was situated, and eastwards to Qua Ibo River.[78] From such strategic locations spread out the ramifications of Ja Ja's trading empire. He paid no heed to the repeated threats of Consul Hewett. Instead he tried to induce the Qua Ibo not to sell oil to European merchants who came there to trade, nor even to feed them, in the hope that this would starve them out.

One of the findings of Hewett in 1883 was that Ja Ja did not have the means to develop the resources of the country. From the time when Messrs. Millers' Factory was closed in 1873 till March, 1881—a period of eight years—no oil had been sold by the Qua Ibo. Ja Ja had been sending his canoes there only for manillas, which were not a product of the country. If Ja Ja had desired to encourage the oil trade in Qua Ibo, he would have done so before Watts came to it. It is true that Ja Ja tried to dissuade the people from selling their oil to Watts by offering the Qua Ibo twenty to thirty percent more for their oil than he himself could sell it for at Opobo. He hoped by this that Watts would find himself left high and dry by the price. But this encouragement to the Qua Ibo oil trade was restricted to the purchase of a very small quantity. Ja Ja wanted to close the river against all trade, since he feared that keeping it open would affect his market at Essene which he used to monopolize the interior markets. Even the Qua Ibo people were opposed to him. Hewett concluded that even a heavy fine on Ja Ja 'would not be a sufficient atonement for his criminal behaviour', which included, besides the ill treatment of the Qua Ibo, the expeditions of 1877 (known as the Ikot Udo Obong war) against the Anang and Ibuno peoples, and those of 1879 and 1881 against the Qua Ibo.[79]

Joseph Henshaw apparently lived in Qua Ibo till 1884 when he died.[80] The Young Calabar spirit which he symbolized, in checking Ja Ja's commercial expansion on the Qua Ibo, had suffered a serious reversal in the 1880s. In February, 1885, upon the request of Watts, the British Government reiterated its stand that the sovereignty over Qua Ibo belonged to the British, and that if Ja Ja molested independent European traders there he would be punished with a heavy fine.[81]

In 1887 H. H. Johnston, acting consul, made a visit to Essene market in Qua country. He reported that matters looked bright for British trade, that the Qua Ibo had plucked up courage to brave Ja Ja's anger, and that they had given white men a fine site of ground on which two factories were already half built. Ja Ja's emissaries had, reported Johnston, visited the place and had threatened to pull down the European factories and deliver Essene to Ja Ja as a punishment. Johnston had allayed these fears.

It is clear from Johnston's description of Essene country why Ja Ja held so tenaciously to it. The district was a very large one stretching nearly all the way from the Opobo to the Cross River, and included the basin of the Qua Ibo stream. Large and navigable streams penetrated its very centre. The inhabitants were industrious and unwarlike. The country was admirably cultivated and was superior in agriculture to any of the surrounding districts. The people kept large herds of cattle, sheep and goats; meat and vegetables were abundant and cheap. Such an area was a prize that could not be surrendered. The British government was determined to support the commercial interests of British firms in Qua Ibo against those of a 'passing, nevertheless, overbearing ex-slave whom adventitious circumstances have surrounded with a prestige and importance he does not merit'.[82] In 1885 Britain annexed to the Crown all the area along the coast.

Struggle of Henshaw lineage for rights to the Duke Town throne

The success of Joseph Henshaw, in warding off the restrictions of Duke Town on the commercial activities of the Henshaws, gave fresh impetus to the other lineages which did not dominate the Efik middlemen system to liberate themselves. The opportunity came with the death of the reigning king, Archibong III, on the night of Monday, 5 May, 1879. Although he had been de facto king for seven years since the death of Archibong II on 26 August, 1872, he died eight months after his coronation as king.

As in the Delta states, the death of the king was always the most suitable opportunity for giving vent to discontent. Duke Town had a regency to fill the political vacuum created by the death of the late king. The chiefs took advantage of the interregnum to put up candidates from their own lineages for the kingship. The acting consul, Easton, who went to Calabar in 1880 to elect a king, described the political situation then prevailing as one of 'anarchy and disorder'.[83]

Easton must have believed, when he chose on 17 April and crowned under his auspices Prince Duke as King Duke Ephraim Eyamba IX (Orok Edem), that he had settled the issue. Easton was in no doubt that Prince Duke was the best choice, and since 'trade was going on briskly' and everybody anticipated a good oil season that year,[84] no trouble would arise from the appointment. The missionaries were equally happy with the choice and expected great things from the new king. But resentment apparently smouldered among the other chiefs as the political affairs of Duke Town were far from being settled. The resentment against the king became more apparent a few months after the coronation. The records are silent about the exact nature and substance of the grievances of the other Efik chiefs, beyond the fact that Easton had ignored the custom of the country, both as regards the period of interregnum and the mode of proceeding for the election of a new ruler.[85] Clearly the other lineages were no longer going to have a king imposed upon them. It is possible to infer from a letter of Anderson's that the Eyamba family had refused to take instructions from the acting king, but the other parties in opposition are difficult to identify.[86] It is also instructive to note that after the death of King Duke IX, the Eyambas did not give away their Ekpe title to any other king. One hypothesis is that as King Duke IX had purchased the Ekpe title of eyamba from the Eyambas, the latter felt that Duke, who had become Eyamba IX, should respect the Eyamba family.

The missionaries avoided all appearances of partisanship toward any of the disaffected parties in the dispute. The Foreign Office, embarrassed by Easton's handling of the election of the king, wrote to the new consul, Hewett, to disavow the act of Easton and allow the chiefs to elect a king in accordance with the usages of the country. The only proviso, a 'face-saver', the Foreign Office wished to put to the consul was that 'in adopting this course, however, your consul's language must be so framed as to avoid lowering the authority of acting consuls in the estimation of the natives'.[87] Hewett was to explain that the Queen, finding that the proper formalities had not been complied with, had declared the throne of Calabar still vacant. The chiefs were to assemble and duly elect a king whom the Queen might be able to recognize. Hewett, as instructed, quashed Easton's 'tomfoolery' at the former coronation, but deferred the crowning of a king by popular choice.[88] It does appear from later correspondence, however, that Hewett restored King Duke IX to the throne.

But the reign was a melancholy period in Calabar history with several complaints being lodged against King Duke's administration.[89] In August, 1883 the Henshaws petitioned to the consul that they were being distrusted by the Duke Town people because they had never attended the meetings of Duke Town and were not present at the coronation of King Duke IX.[90]

Duke Town continued to experience political turmoil. On 1 January, 1885 civil war broke out between the Archibong and Duke families. It was widely feared that this war, which began on the farms, might be carried into the town. In fact, Prince Eyamba V of Eyamba Town wrote to James Eunro, the chairman of the court of equity, to send one or two members of the court to accompany him to settle the trouble before it was too late.[91] The leader of the Archibong faction was Archibong Edem (the son of the former King Archibong III), a man said to be of a singularly war-like temperament. The hostilities were begun with Archibong Edem's boys firing the first gun. Since this was acknowledged by Archibong himself, Consul Hewett fined him two puncheons of oil. It was also decided that should the public peace be again disturbed, the guilty party would be subject to a fine of fifty puncheons of oil for the payment of which the town would be held responsible.[92] James Eyamba was fined two boxes of rods for failing to attend a meeting summoned by the consul.

Matters, however, were far from being settled. Archibong complained that prisoners taken by the Dukes had not been returned to him. Instead he was told either to face war or relinquish the land on which he dwelled. Since he could not declare war, Archibong agreed to leave the land and he settled down at a place which came to be called Archibong Town (Obufa Obio).[93] The land vacated was later burned by the Dukes,[94] who also shot one of the Archibong men in the plantation.[95]

Segmentation of the Duke house

The protest of Archibong against the pretensions of King Duke IX and his house was to result in an important development, namely, the segmentation of the Duke house. It should be noted that in Calabar only the Duke house segmented into its component lineages—namely Archibong, Eyamba and Etim Effiom. The last two lineages mentioned broke off from the Duke house early in the twentieth century, and left that house more or less synonymous with the original Effiom Okoho family. The Archibong, Eyamba, and Etim Effiom lineages, which broke away and founded their own houses, nevertheless continued to live in Duke Town but as independent units.[96] Each of the families which set up their own houses were outside the pale of Duke house control. In part, this was possible because the party which wielded effective authority was no longer King Duke[97] but the British government.

The segmentation of the Duke house raises once again the issue of the centrifugal forces within the lineage structure of Duke Town society. These forces were primarily the constant friction and tension in the Duke houses. Segmentation was a response to these centrifugal forces. Most of the disputes and tension arose as a result of the claims of the Effiom Okoho family (of the Duke house) which pretended to the throne of Duke Town. The other houses were resentful of the claim of this family to political power. But once the Archibongs successfully wrested the throne from the Effiom Okoho group, the smaller families too wanted a share of the political office and they broke off from the Duke house to found their own. As political leadership declined in the Duke house, and as power vacuums were created on the death of kings, the other families found these opportune moments to break away and look for wealth and power for themselves.

It is important to note the difference in the causes and effects of segmentation between the houses in the Delta states and those in Calabar. It is a well-known fact that in Bonny and in Kalabari, the oil trade seemed to create amalgamation in the form of 'canoe house groups' which got larger and larger and eliminated the smaller houses from the scene. The best example of this process, described by G. I. Jones as 'overall political accretion', is the political machine built up by Amakiri in Kalabari.[98] This machine was based originally on the Endeme ward, which succeeded not only in breaking up and absorbing the other Kalabari wards but also in completely destroying the previous internal structure of the ward itself. The houses into which the ward was segmented were established by King Amakiri's expanded household. A similar process is described by Jones for the expansion of the political machine of King Pepple; by the nineteenth century all the powerful houses (opuwari), were derived from King Pepple's original house.

In the Bonny and Kalabari states, segmentation was encouraged and carried out by the house chiefs and lesser leaders in combination, and as a reward for those subordinate leaders who had been most successful in advancing the main house's fortunes and their own. Segmentation of this nature made the Delta houses stronger and administratively more efficient. The head of the canoe house group and his lieutenants, freed as they were from political tensions (which were largely resolved) within the group, were able to expend their joint energies in political and economic competition with other house groups. Since the smaller houses could be depended upon to support the main houses in times of war or in need it made the original houses more powerful.

The same process does not seem to have taken place in Calabar.

There, lineage segmentation appeared to have taken place in order to sever connections with the original houses and thereby to relieve political tension; it was not necessarily done as a reward for efficient leadership. Men of noble birth who were able to gain the support of a sufficient number of followers grouped themselves and formed a new ward. This pattern of lineage segmentation at the ward level amounted virtually to a peaceful form of fission since the new ward was politically independent of its parent house. It was quite unlike the canoe house group where a newly segmented canoe house remained politically an integral part of the house group and actively involved in the group's struggle for political dominance.

The causes for these differences in the political development of the coastal states are more difficult to analyse. The most plausible one appears to be that which explains the political development of the Delta houses in terms of a natural increase in the descendants of the founder of a lineage. The segmentary process followed lines of cleavage laid down in the household by the original founder.

In Calabar, on the other hand, lineage segmentation was not the result of a normal expansion of the lineages but mainly the result of a process referred to as 'population drift'. In Chapter One, where the dynamics of this process were examined, it was stated that 'population drift' operated at two structural levels: at the higher level the drift was from the less dominant to the more dominant wards; at the lower level it was within a ward, from a less dominant to a more dominant section. The genealogy of the Duke house shows clearly a continuous division into dual segments of the dominant ward of the Effiom Ekpo group (see Appendix A). One of these new segments continued its existence as a new ward, while the other developed by division into more wards. The office of king remained within the Okoho group, and rotated between the chiefs of its four wards. These wards considered themselves as being of equivalent political status.

The effects of the differences in the process of segmentation between the Delta and the Calabar houses can be seen more clearly. The political evolution of Calabar differed remarkably from that of the Delta states in that politics in Calabar remained far more stable than they did in the Delta. Calabar experienced little of the violent faction struggles that were characteristic of the political history of the Delta. The houses of each of the leaders in the Delta states had so expanded into groups of canoe houses by the process described above that they began to compete against each other for control of the kingship. In Bonny, the Manilla Pepple and Anna Pepple houses had become so large that, on the death of King

Opobo, they were able to split the Pepple political machine into the rival groups which eventually divided Bonny between them. In Kalabari, the Barboy and the Amakiri groups divided the community during the nineteenth century.

In Calabar there were lineage rivalries as shown in this chapter, but these rivalries had not the same effect on the final distribution of power in the state as they had in the Delta states. In Calabar the checks and restraints on the development of political leadership were much stronger. One ward remained dominant, but its continuous expansion was checked by segmentation or fission within it as soon as it had expanded to a certain size. This meant that since the expansion of the dominant ward was temporarily halted, the balance between the wards was temporarily restored by the creation of a new ward from the excess of population in the dominant ward.[99]

The power structure or alliance built by the Efik leaders did not unduly disrupt the social life of the majority of the people since the Efik system of marriage acted as a stabilizing force. Since cousins of any sort could marry each other,[100] the noble families were a closely intermarried group of kinsfolk. Thus, while political differences divided the interests of houses, and the struggle between the bigger and small houses continued until the twentieth century, the system of marriage preserved the genealogical relationship of the houses. There was no change made to the segmentary structure of the town, and the traditional religious cults were never involved in political rivalries. Succession disputes were referred to consuls in the case of Duke Town, or resolved within the traditional framework of government, as in the case of Creek Town, so that the endangering of stability that these might normally give rise to was overcome. Unlike Bonny and Kalabari, political rivalry did not crystallize into permanent political associations of houses, each courting the favour of the European community. The struggle to establish separate political entities, which led Henshaw Town to war with Duke Town, and which later in the period led to the segmentation of the Duke house, did not upset law and order. The Bloodmen intervened in the politics of the town only when their interests were endangered. These struggles for power were often, though not always, kept beneath the surface.

Political position in Creek Town

What was the political position in Creek Town during these years of upheaval in Duke Town? It is remarkable that except in 1874, when the Ambo seriously challenged the Eyo over the election to the kingship of the town of Eyo VII, there were very few of the characteristic political disturbances of Duke Town. There are two reasons explaining the relative quiet of Creek Town politics.

The first of these relates to the way in which the Eyo house was constituted. The Efik recognized two principal Eyo houses—that established by Eyo I (Eyo Nsa) and that by his brother, Ekpenyong Nsa. But below these houses there were a number of sub-houses, the chief of them being Eno, Otudor, Ukpabio, Essien Ekpe and Eyo Nkune. Each of these sub-houses had their own heads or obongs. But there was a neat arrangement which decreed that the sub-houses had no right to produce the candidate for the 'obong-ship' from amongst their several obongs. It appears that the king could come only from the Eyo Nsa or Ekpenyong Nsa houses.

It is difficult, owing to the diversity of opinion regarding the genealogical descent of Eyo VII, to state whether the Ekpenyong Nsa house produced any of the kings of Creek Town, but it is commonly accepted as a historical certainty that Eyo II, III, IV, V, and VI were descended from Eyo Ansa. One version states that Eyo VII (Ansa Okoho) was descended from Ekpenyong Nsa, but he was declared king because none of Eyo's sons was wealthy enough to compete with Ansa Okoho for the title of Eyo VII.[101] The other version has it that, in the controversy precipitated by the death of Eyo VI, the Ekpenyong Nsa group laid claim to the

TABLE 4

The genealogy of the Eyo family

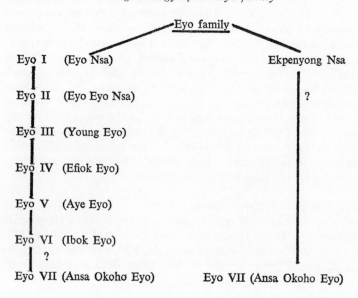

throne by producing as their candidate one Ekpenyong Esim. But this candidate lost to Ansa Okoho, who was crowned Eyo VII. Ansa Okoho was descended from Eyo Nsa.[102] Most of the kings were sustained by foreign power. In order to restrain the other sub-houses from feeling that they had no role in the political process of the Eyo house, the latter had devised a way in which the others could be brought within the political framework of the house.

A distinction was drawn between the king of Creek Town produced by one of the two Eyo families, and the head of the Eyo house. The two positions were not synonymous so that the king of Creek Town, though from the Eyo house, was not necessarily also the head of that house, and therefore not necessarily, either, the traditional ruler of the Eyo family. The only example of a house which adopted this system in Duke Town was the Tete house founded by Effiom Ededem.[103]

A few examples will illustrate this development in the political evolution of Creek Town. Whereas Eyo II had restored the broken fortunes of his father's house and was elected king of his town, he was not the traditional ruler of the house he inherited. The latter position went to his eldest brother who was the embodiment of their dead father. He was, that is, the patriarch and etenyin of the children of Eyo Nsa (Eyo I) and their respective households. When Eyo III succeeded to the throne as the king chosen by the European traders, Efiok Eyo (Father Tom) continued in his position as patriarch of the family.[104] However, there was a temporary break in the system when Eyo III died in May, 1861. Four people were killed on the charge of having compassed the king's death by ifot, two of them being members of the Eyo family. The uncle of the king, Egbo Eyo, and a sister of the king, Inyang, were victims of the malice of the Bloodmen as well as the elder sister, Ansa.[105] Apart from this incident the pattern described above continued. Efiok Eyo, who had been head of the family, became Eyo IV, and on his death in June, 1871, Aye Eyo Nsa (the fourth child of Eyo Nsa) became Eyo V. On the latter's death the sixth son of Eyo Nsa namely Ibok Eyo Nsa became Eyo VI. He was the last of the surviving male children of Eyo Nsa. After him the succession descended to the third generation of the Eyos.

The second factor which explains the comparative peace in Creek Town politics is the connection that most of the kings traced genealogically to the Ambo family. The Ambos considered themselves the royal family of Creek Town and conferred recognition only on those kings who were able to trace matrilineal connections with them. Thus they accepted as kings of Creek Town Eyo II,

Eyo III, Eyo VII and Eyo IX since each of them had matrilineal connections with the Atai who were founders of Otung and Mbarakom (Cobham) families.[106] In all the other cases, except for the trouble stirred up in 1874, there were no disputes when Eyo IV, V, VI and VIII were made kings. This was because the kings failed to make their influence felt and ruled only for short periods of time,[107] and they were not accepted or recognized as kings by the Ambo. Instead, they were looked upon by the Ambo as regents or caretakers (or mkpene obio) of the town.

That the Ambo have always reserved for themselves the right to confer recognition on the Eyo kings if the latter were able to trace the necessary genealogical relations to them did not mean they subjected themselves to the rule of the Eyo kings. In fact, if anything, they were not on the best of terms with the Eyos who dominated Creek Town by virtue of their numerical superiority. The Ambo position became clear in 1874. The Ambo, who had recognized Eyo VII (Ansa Okoho or Henshaw Tom Forster) as king of Creek Town in February, 1874,[108] refused to surrender themselves to his rule. They declared that they had lived with many Eyo kings but had not been ruled by them and were not subjects of Eyo. There was, therefore, no reason why the Eyo should at this point of time rule them.[109] The records are silent as to what transpired next, but it is possible that since King Eyo VII had the support of the supercargoes there could not have been any major impediments to his continuing to reign. Moreover, the economic position of Creek Town had by this time been reduced greatly. Consul Hopkins said, for instance, that the 'crippled state of his [Eyo VII's] country' did not allow the consul to fine the town for a case of twin murder.[110]

It was while these developments were taking place in the internal political structure of Calabar that plans were afoot elsewhere to impose a different political system upon it by the creation of a British Protectorate in the Oil Rivers. The colonial period, to which we must now turn, opened a new chapter in the history of Calabar.

REFERENCES

1   H. Goldie and J. T. Dean, op. cit., p. 202.
2   Vide map showing the draught of the Calabar river on p. 161, from Bold, op. cit., facing p. 73.
3   J. Whitford, *Trading Life in Western and Central Africa*, p. 297.
4   J. Adams, *Remarks* et seq., p. 143.
5   J. Whitford, op. cit., p. 292. J. B. Walker, another of Calabar's important European traders, wrote in 1872 of Duke Town as the chief town of the Calabar people; J. B. Walker 'Note on the Old Calabar and Cross River', *P.R.G.S.*, Vol. 16, (London, 1872), p. 136.

6   J. Whitford, op. cit., p. 293.

7   For a description of the coronation see W. Marwick, op. cit., pp. 677–79. An interesting letter entitled, 'A Coronation without a Crown', containing the address delivered by Rev. Anderson on the occasion, appeared in the *Juvenile Missionary Magazine*, November, 1859.

8   Anderson's journal entry for 15 September, 1864 in W. Marwick, op. cit., p. 408.

9   Anderson's letter dated 30 August, 1859 in W. Marwick, op. cit., pp. 376–77.

10 CALPROF 4/3, Vol. 1, King Archibong II to Lord J. Russell, 9 August, 1859.

11 CALPROF 2/1, Vol. 2, Russell to Hutchinson, 24 March, 1860.

12 CALPROF 3/3, Minute of meeting held on board the hulk *Athelstan.* Old Calabar, 5 June, 1871, 9.30 a.m.–8 p.m. Vide also CALPROF 3/2, King Archibong to chairman and members, court of equity, 5 June, 1871.

13 Chiefly, interviews with Chief Etim Ekpenyong, 3 December and 9 December, 1965. The boundary is not clear even to this day and is a subject of occasional litigation.

14 H. Goldie and J. T. Dean, op. cit., p. 225.

15 Chief Etim Ekpenyong, interviews, 1 December and 3 December, 1965.

16 This fruit is of a species of amomum and looks like a ginger fruit. It is known in trade as Guinea grains. It is held to symbolize the poverty of the defeated who had been reduced to subsist on that fruit; H. Goldie and J. T. Dean, op. cit., p. 228.

17 Vide H. Goldie and J. T. Dean, op. cit., p. 227; Anderson's journal entry for 3 October, 1868 in W. Marwick, op. cit., p. 434. Relations between the Ikoneto Chief and King Eyo VI were cordial. It was King Eyo who had sanctioned missionary penetration to Ikoneto in 1856; H. Goldie and J. T. Dean, op. cit., p. 255.

18 H. Goldie and J. T. Dean, op. cit., p. 228.

19 H. Goldie, *Memoir of King Eyo VII* et seq., p. 23.

20 Anderson's letter of 28 August, 1872, states that Archibong died on the evening of Monday, 26 August, 1872. This is the official date but, added Anderson, many alleged that the king had died the previous day. Vide W. Marwick, op. cit., pp. 504–05.

21 Anderson's annual report for 1875 published in the U.P. *Missionary Record*, June, 1876; W. Marwick, op. cit., p. 543. Also, CALPROF 3/2, Archibong to court of equity, 8 May, 1874.

22 CALPROF 4/1, Vol. 4, Anderson to George Hartley, 8 October, 1875.

23 Vide, for example, CALPROF 3/2, Edem Archibong to court of equity, 1 May, 1874.

24 CALPROF 3/2, G. Hartley to chairman, court of equity, 29 May, 1874.

25 CALPROF 4/1, Vol. 5, W. Hewett (Commodore of *Active Quettal*) to McKellar (acting consul, Bonny) 13 September, 1876, and encl. James Africans Croker to William Hewett, 20 July, 1876.

26 CALPROF 3/2, Archibong III to court of equity, 10 October, 1876; vide also CALPROF 4/1, Vol. 4, Archibong III to Hartley, 8 October, 1875.

27 CALPROF 4/1, Vol. 4, Archibong III to George Hartley, 4 October, 1875.

28 CALPROF 4/1, Vol. 3, Anderson to Consul Livingstone, 8 August, 1873, and encl. Consul Livingstone to King Edem Archibong, 8 August, 1873. Egbo Bassey had been taken under British protection by Commander Selwyn of H.M.S. *Teaser* in about May, 1849; CALPROF 4/1, Vol. 4, Anderson to George Hartley, 25 September, 1875.

29 CALPROF 4/1, Vol. 3, Anderson to Livingstone, 8 August, 1873, encl. Egbo Bassey to Hartley, 17 June, 1874.

30 For a full story of Egbo Bassey, vide CALPROF 4/1, Vol. 4, Anderson to Hartley, 8 October and 12 October, 1875.

31 CALPROF 5/8, Vol. 1, statement by Anderson, June/July, 1875, and its several encl.

32 CALPROF 3/2, Archibong to court of equity, 1 July, 1875.

33 CALPROF 4/1, Vol. 6, statement of Henshaw Town, with reference to their Memorial to Lord Derby, 20 August, 1878, para. 10 and 11. The memorial was sent through a London trading house, George Offor and Company, which acted as the agents of Henshaw Town.

34 CALPROF 4/1, Vol. 2, Principal Men of Henshaw Town to Captain Hopkins, 16 February, 1871.

35 W. Marwick, op. cit., p. 481.

36 Vide also F.O. 84/1377, Livingstone to Granville, 7 January, 1873.

37 W. Marwick, op. cit., p. 482–83.

38 W. Marwick, op. cit., p. 503.

39 Anderson gives the population of Henshaw Town variously as 300–400; ibid., p. 503 and as 500; ibid., p. 518.

40 Ibid., pp. 570, 592.

41 Ibid., pp. 484, 518.

42 Orok Edem was captured on 10 August, 1875, and kept as a prisoner for three weeks; ibid., p. 535.

43 Ibid., p. 508.

44 Henshaw III's grandfather and James Henshaw's father were brothers. Refer to Table 3 in this chapter.

45 Chief Michael Henshaw, interview, 18 November, 1966.

46 CALPROF 3/1, Chairman, court of equity (J. B. Walker) to Hartley (consul), 31 August, 1875. F.O. 84/1455, No. 11, A. McKellar to F.O., 29 February, 1875, encl. 4, J. B. Walker to chief of Henshaw Town, 29 August, 1875.

47 CALPROF 3/1, Chairman, court of equity (John MacArthur) to Hartley, 8 September, 1875.

47 The indemnity to be paid, according to one informant, was in the region of £700; Michael Henshaw, interview, 18 November, 1865. Most other sources are agreed, however, that the fine was heavy enough to cripple the resources of Henshaw Town and its energies for years to come; vide W. Marwick, op. cit., p. 508.

49 Various attempts had been made by the European traders to secure the release of Prince Duke. Vide F.O. 84/1455, No. 11, W. A. McKelean (acting consul, Bonny) to F.O., 29 February, 1876, encl. 3, Henshaw III to court of equity, 26 August, 1875, and encl. 4, J. B. Walker (chairman, court of equity) to Henshaw Town, 28 August, 1875.

50 Anderson to Rev. John Law and others, 14 September, 1875; W. Marwick, op. cit., pp. 536–37.

51 CALPROF 4/1, Vol. 6, Statement to Henshaw Town, with reference to the Memorial of Lord Derby, 20 August, 1878, para. 14.

52 CALPROF 4/1, Vol. 4, W. Anderson to Hartley (private), 23 September, 1875.

53 For details of the agreement vide F.O. 84/1455, 'Agreement Between the King and Chiefs of Duke Town and the Chiefs of Henshaw Town with George Hartley, Esq., Her Britannic Majesty's Representative for the Bights of Biafra and Benin, and the island of Fernando Po', 27 September, 1875. The agreement was signed by Prince Eyamba for Archibong III, and by others representing the Archibong, Duke, Eyamba and Henshaw families. The peace meeting was held on board the *Matilda*.

54 CALPROF 4/1, Vol. 6, Statement of Henshaw Town, with reference to their Memorial to Lord Derby, 30 December, 1877, para. 16.

55 F.O. 84/1455, No. 11, W. A. McKellar to F.O., 29 February, 1876, encl. Henshaw III and six others to Earl of Derby, 18 February, 1876.

56 CALPROF 4/1, Vol. 5, J. Henshaw to W. A. McKellar, March, 1876; the British government was informed in F.O. 84/1455, No. 26, W. A. McKellar to F.O., 11 April, 1876.

57 Vide CALPROF 3/1, J. B. Walker (Chairman, court of equity) to W. A. McKellar, 9 March, 1876; CALPROF 3/2, Archibong III to European gentlemen, Old Calabar, 14 March, 1876; and CALPROF 3/1, Walker to McKellar, 17 March, 1876.

58 CALPROF 4/1, Vol. 6, Statement of Henshaw Town, with reference to their Memorial to Lord Derby, dated 30 December, 1877, 20 August, 1878.

59 For the text of the agreement, see CALPROF 5/7, Vol. 2, 'Agreement Between Henshaw Town and Duke Town', 6 September, 1878.

60 W. Marwick, op. cit., p. 564. There is a footnote reference at the bottom of the page just quoted to Dickie's *Story of the Mission in Old Calabar*, p. 98, where the six articles ('the notes of triumph of our mission') are given.

61 F.O. 84/1508, Agreement dated 6 September, 1878, encl. in Hopkins to F.O. 28 August, 1878, cited in E. A. Ayandele, op. cit., p. 86. It should be pointed out here that the date 28 August, 1878 given by Dr. Ayandele is apparently incorrect as can be seen from the date on which the agreement was concluded. I have not been able to trace the correct date of the despatch to which reference has here been made. Vide also CALPROF 5/7, Vol. 2, 'Rules and Regulations for the management of Henshaw Town', submitted to Consul David Hopkins, and approved by him, 6 September, 1878.

62 CALPROF 5/7, Vol. 2, 'Agreement between Qua Town and H.M. Government', 6 September, 1878.

63 CALPROF 4/1, Vol. 6, Statement of Henshaw Town, with reference to their Memorial to Lord Derby, dated 30 December, 1877, 20 August, 1878, para. 18.

64 Chief Michael E. Henshaw, interview, 18 November, 1865 and Chief Joseph E. Henshaw, interview, 6 December, 1965.

65 Information from a case of appeal heard at the African Court of Appeal, Lagos, 1937, between Henry Cobham (plaintiff) of Calabar and Idiok Une (respondent) who represented himself and the people of Uruyan.

66 R. L. M. Keown, *In the Land of the Oil Rivers*, pp. 29–30.

67 For a fuller treatment of George Watts and of his association with John Holt and Messrs. Irvine and Woodward, see C. Gertzel, 'John

Holt' et seq.; I have depended on Gertzel's account for factual information relating to the trade of the Qua Ibo and its environs, ibid., pp. 174–181.

68   Ibid., p. 177; also P. A. Talbot, *Life in Southern Nigeria*, pp. 289–299.
69   P. A. Talbot, ibid., pp. 289–97.
70   C. Gertzel, 'John Holt' et seq., pp. 176–77.
71   For some account of the activities of Ibuno middlemen, both at the coast and inland, see R. L. M. Keown, op. cit., p. 34.
72   P. A. Talbot, *Life in Southern Nigeria*, p. 292.
73   Ibid.
74   Ibid., p. 293.
75   F.O. 84/1630, Ja Ja to Lord Granville, 3 April, 1882.
76   Ibid.
77   F.O. 84/1630, Holt to Granville, 16 February, 1882.
78   J. C. Anene, op. cit., pp. 52–53.
79   F.O. 84/1634, No. 2, Hewett to Granville, 5 February, 1883, and its several encl.
80   Information from a case of appeal heard from the African Court of Appeal, Lagos, 1937, op. cit. It does not appear that any of Henshaw's sons continued to trade at Qua Ibo after him; Chief Michael E. Henshaw, interview, 1 November, 1965.
81   CALPROF 2/1, Vol. 33, F.O. to John Holt, 18 February, 1885.
82   CALPROF 2/2, Vol. 5, No. 12, H. H. Johnston to F.O., 1 August, 1887.
83   F.O. 84/1569, No. 30, Easton (acting consul) to F.O., 23 April, 1880.
84   Ibid.
85   Ibid., No. 22, F.O. to Consul Hewett, 19 October, 1880.
86   Letter of Anderson, 6 August, 1881; W. Marwick, op. cit., p. 579.
87   F.O. 84/1569, No. 22, F.O. to Consul Hewett, 19 October, 1880. It may be assumed that the Foreign Office would not disavow their agent on such slim evidence as this. But the records available on the Easton succession dispute affairs are silent on the matter.
88   For a fuller account of Consul Hewett's visit to Calabar and the unsettled political condition of Duke Town, see a letter by Rev. Anderson, 6 August, 1881; W. Marwick, pp. 579–80.
89   See, for instance, CALPROF 5/8, Vol. 2, Petition of George Duke, 13 July, 1883 and its encl.
90   CALPROF 5/8, Vol. 2, Petition of Chief Henshaw and others, 13 August, 1883. The petition, drawn up E. H. Henshaw, was commented upon by Hewett.
91   CALPROF 3/2, Prince Eyamba V to James Munro, 1 January, 1885.
92   E. E. Offiong Private Papers; Judgement Book, 'Consul's decision in the war between Henshaw Duke and Archibong Edem and people, 9 January, 1885.
93   Chief Ene Ndem Ephraim Duke, interview, 9 December, 1965.
94   CALPROF 4/1, Vol. 10, Prince Archibong III to Harold White (acting consul), 13 March, 1885.
95   CALPROF 4/1, Vol. 10, King Duke IX to H. White (acting consul) 16 March, 1885, and CALPROF 5/8, Vol. 11, 'Acting Consul's decision regarding recent disturbances in Old Calabar', April, 1885.
96   Vide *The Hart Report*, op. cit., pp. 151–52 where the question of the independent status of the Etim Effiom house is discussed.
97   King Duke IX's death was officially announced on November 19,

1896, though it is possible that he died about six days previously. He was the last king of Duke Town before the British take-over. Vide W. Marwick, op. cit., p. 574n.

98 G. I. Jones, *Trading States* et seq., Chapter 12 and Appendix A, passim. Vide also Chapter 1 in this volume.

99 This was a result of the 'population drift' theory explained earlier. G. I. Jones has argued that violent faction fights such as those which characterized Bonny politics never occurred in Calabar because the latter did not produce dominant rulers; G. I. Jones, *Trading States* et seq., pp. 76–77.

100 D. Simmons, op. cit., p. 14, states, however, that marriage was forbidden between parallel and cross cousins. But G. I. Jones maintains that cousins could inter-marry.

101 Chief Etim Ekpenyong, interview, 9 December, 1965.

102 Chief Okon Ma Ikot, interview, 20 January, 1966.

103 Vide *The Hart Report*, p. 108.

104 Ibid., pp. 107–08.

105 For details of the incidents, vide H. Goldie and J. T. Dean, op. cit., pp. 210–13.

106 The relationship of these kings with the Atai or Ambo was as follows: Eyo II was a son of Inyang Essien, the Mbarakom princess; Eyo III, as Eyo II's son, was also connected by blood with Mbarakom. Eyo VII was the grandson of the lady Mkanem Ita Okpo of the Ibijam family of Otung.

107 King Eyo IV died in 1865, Eyo V in 1867, Eyo VI in 1871.

108 For Goldie's account of how Henshaw Tom Forster was chosen as king, and for a biography of him, see his *Memoir of King Eyo VII* et seq. For the instrument conferring recognition of King Eyo VII, dated Creek Town, Wednesday, 25 February, 1874, vide *The Hart Report*, p. 102.

109 CALPROF 4/1, Vol. 3, Samuel Ambo, John Ambo, Hogan A. Ambo and Young H. Bassey of Ambo Town to Hartley, 6 October, 1874.

110 CALPROF 4/2, Hopkins to Rev. Goldie, (Sierra Leone), 7 May, 1879.

VI

The New Structure of Power, 1885–1906

The history of Anglo-African relations in the thirty years before 1885 encouraged Consul Hewett to advance the argument that it was but the logical consummation of British policy toward the coastal states that they be annexed and brought under direct British authority. In those thirty years or more, consular authority had on several occasions intervened in the domestic affairs of the states to settle disputes between British and African traders, or between African traders themselves. The Efik kings had been unable to impose their authority on European traders when either the price or quantity of palm oil fell and when competition between European traders was anything but orderly. Even more significant was the fact that the kings, and in particular the Duke Town kings, invited extra-territorial elements to settle the domestic disputes of the day.

The effect of such intervention was often to leave the situation more confounded. Duke Town in the mid-1880s is a good illustration in point. We have seen that the atmosphere in the town was charged with tension following the injudicious intervention in 1879 of the acting consul, Easton, into the succession dispute. Although Hewett, who succeeded Easton, had allowed the chiefs to elect their king independently, no candidate was able successfully to claim the throne. The struggle for the title raged on among the contestants, and the Efik political pundits were without the means to stop the 'jockeying' for power that went on.

Owing possibly to the incapacity of the political process to resolve a dispute of this nature, or to the self-interest of the disaffected party, some of the Efik chiefs petitioned the British government urging a take-over of the country.[1] Hewett found the situation an opportune one to suggest to the British government that peace could only be restored if Calabar was taken over completely by the British and he supported his case with the petitions received from the Efik.[2] The suggestion was renewed in the following year when Hewett urged the Foreign Office to consider the annexation of Calabar. He wrote:

No nation has taken the interest in the welfare of the natives that
we have nor has anyone shown a disposition to improve them
except ourselves . . . by slave trade treaties putting down human
sacrifices and cannibalism and twin murders . . . We have been the
most active agents fostering the palm oil trade and trade in other
products . . . Until recently English gunboats were almost the only
ones that natives ever saw . . . There has been a British Consul for
many years . . . We have led the natives to rely on us. To assume
a Protectorate would be simply a consummation of our policy on
the coast for many years . . .[3]

There is an implicit assumption in this statement which is interesting to note, namely that the colonial period was regarded as
merely the next logical step in Anglo-Efik relations.

The British government was not convinced of the wisdom of
annexation. Its chief interest in Calabar was the encouragement of
legitimate commerce between her traders and the Efik. The assumption of political responsibilities, such as undertaking to provide a
government to rule over the Efik, was frowned upon, or kept to a
minimum. The desire for economy in overseas expenditure, emphasized by the Parliamentary Committee of 1865, held good till
1884–5. Britain was on the coast to trade and her desire was to
expand this trade and protect her traders.[4]

The Protectorate

In the 1880s with the beginnings of the 'scramble' for valuable
portions of Africa the situation underwent a change. Consul
Hewett's assignment in 1885 was to negotiate treaties with the
coastal kings in order to prevent them from signing treaties with
other powers. Having responded so well to European commercial
intercourse it was felt that Calabar could offer little resistance to the
new British demands. However, while Creek Town under King Eyo
VII—a man whose admiration for the European knew few bounds[5]
—assented at once to the proposal, Duke Town under King Duke
IX was more sceptical of the provisions of the treaty. Whether
King Duke IX's cautious approach serves to destroy any suspicions
that may be felt about the extent to which the Efik understood
Hewett's treaty one cannot say for sure; if it is true that the Efik
rulers understood what they signed, what could one say about King
Eyo VII's understanding of its implications?[6]

Most of the provisions of the treaty[7] which received the sanction
of King Duke were those which only confirmed what had in fact
been the practice. For example, it was agreed that the kings and
chiefs were to manage the conduct of their internal affairs, settle
disputes affecting the Efik, and allow the British jurisdiction over

their own and foreign subjects enjoying British protection. But there were other provisions which were novel. By the terms of article five, the rulers of Creek Town and Duke Town agreed to assist the British consular officers and to act upon their advice in matters relating to the administration of justice, the development of the resources of the country, the interests of commerce, peace, and good government and the general progress of 'civilization'. Efik kings had the right to appeal against having to act upon the advice of the consular or other officers.

What gave rise to the apprehension of King Duke IX were the terms of article six. This article, it is interesting to note, was not agreed to by the kings and chiefs at the final ratification of the treaty. H. Goldie states that the Duke Town chiefs hesitated until they were assured by the British that there was no intention of disturbing their social relations.[8] The explanation attempted here, in terms of trade interests, appears to be a more likely reason not only for the hesitation expressed, but also the outright objection to agree to the clause. The article enjoined that

> the subjects and citizens of all countries may freely carry on trade in every part of the territories of the kings and chiefs parties hereto, and may have houses and factories therein.

British motivation in prescribing this clause was easily perceived. Hewett had intended to reintroduce the principle of 'free trade' and freedom of movement in the country. No doubt in the anti-slave trade treaties this freedom of movement for British traders had been assured. But the commercial agreements signed between British and African traders thereafter had laid down regulations regarding the payment of comey and trust, the settlement of disputes by courts of equity and the restriction of the movement of Europeans beyond certain limits from the port. As the oil trade developed the Efik kings were careful to see that European penetration into the interior was effectively prohibited.

King Duke IX probably realized that what the British intended by 'free trade' was the sweeping away of the monopolies Efik middlemen had enjoyed. The free trade clause, if agreed to, would throw open the markets of the interior to the Europeans and eliminate the commercial and political position of the middlemen. The controversy over the sixth article of the treaty indicated that political annexation coincided with an incipient commercial revolution—the up-country movement of European traders and the by-passing of the Efik house system. The British could not in all seriousness have expected the chiefs to surrender their source of livelihood and the basis of their economic and political power. The

Efik chiefs signed only a preliminary treaty agreeing not to enter into treaty relations with other powers. For the purposes of the British case at the Berlin West African Conference of 1884–5, an expression of acquiescence in her protection was sufficient for Britain to gain a position in the rivers and to keep out the French. The Protectorate government over the Oil Rivers came into being on 5 June, 1885, when notification to that effect was published in the London *Gazette*.[9]

The five years following the establishment of the protectorate passed by uneventfully and the administration during that period came to be referred to as 'a paper protectorate'. The headquarters of the protectorate (which was defined to include the coastline between Lagos and the right bank of the Rio del Rey and the banks of the Niger from Lokoja to the sea) were established at Calabar (Duke Town). The site was chosen presumably owing to the British consular offices, which had already been established there in 1872, and support needed to be given to the Christian missionaries who had resided in Calabar since 1846.

The next action was to determine after enquiry the form of government best suited to the area. A British special commissioner, Claude MacDonald, was sent out in 1889 on the errand. The re-action of the Efik was a mixed one. The chiefs of Creek Town, presumably under the influence of King Eyo VII, advocated annexation by Britain. The idea of annexation had been put earlier to the British government in 1887 by Prince E. J. Eyamba and others of Calabar in a petition that survives among the British official records. Whether this petition was a forged document or was prompted by tensions in domestic politics is not clear, but Hewett had again used this petition to recommend annexation.[10] The British government was unwilling to entertain the idea of annexation and did not approve of Hewett's recommendation.[11] The inadequacy of the British administrative machinery was all too evident and Johnston, who acted for Hewett between June, 1887 and May, 1888, called the attention of the British government to it.

The Duke Town chiefs opposed annexation and expressed a preference to rule themselves and be left alone.[12] When MacDonald told them politely that the alternative was really between a pro-tectorate by Britain and annexation to the territory of the Royal Niger Company, the Duke Town chiefs chose the protectorate. Some others, fearing for the security of their life and property, actually fled into the bush and did not return to Calabar for some time.[13] It was eventually decided by the Colonial Office to continue the consular administration (with improvements) until such time that a crown colony system was introduced.[14] In July, 1891 Claude

MacDonald was despatched to Calabar as Commissioner and Consul-General of the Oil Rivers and adjacent territories.

The administrative paraphernalia of the protectorate[15] need not be dwelt upon here. The facts concerning the diplomatic transactions, the theoretical and moral fiction with regard to protectorate relationship at the Berlin West African conference of 1884–5, and the details of the administrative system that was eventually set up on the coast have already been examined by other writers.[16] One must rather examine the extent to which Efik participation in government was encouraged, the position of the traditional rulers under the new government and the extent to which the traditional political structure of Calabar was retained or modified by the protectorate administration. Certainly the inauguration of the colonial system precipitated a series of political, judicial, social and economic changes which struck at the roots of time-honoured traditions in Calabar. It is a defensible argument that although tradition was modified by the introduction of colonial innovations, the Efik retained rearguard control over those areas of political and social life in which their interests were immediate; reforms which the Efik did not resist were largely those which were ultimately beneficial to them. This was simple enough, but it is noteworthy that in those areas of traditional life where innovations were made, the effectiveness of the new reforms was gradually lost and the way paved for a resurgence of tradition.

Major (later Sir) Claude MacDonald's orders were defined by the Foreign Office as follows:[17]

> Your object should be, by developing legitimate trade, by promoting Civilization, by inducing the natives to relinquish inhuman and barbarous customs, and by gradually abolishing slavery, to pave the way for placing the territories over which Her Majesty's protection is and may be extended directly under British rule. It is not advisable that you should interfere unduly in tribal government, the chiefs should continue to rule their own subjects and to administer justice to them; but you should keep a constant watch so as to prevent injustice and check abuses, making the chiefs understand that their powers will be forfeited by misgovernment. If you should in special cases, find it essential for the benefit of the natives, you will be authorized to insist on the delegation to you of a chief's judicial and administrative powers, which you will then exercise in their interest. You should be careful, however, not to arouse discontent by attempting too abrupt reform.

MacDonald was to take under his immediate control the 'inter-tribal' and foreign relations of the African chiefs. But during the first five years of the 'paper protectorate' Britain had the semblance but not the reality of power. Although control over the external affairs of the state had passed from the Efik chiefs to the new administration, the chiefs still resisted changes in their immediate external relations with the hinterland producers. They refused to allow European traders entry into their oil markets, and Britain had no means of forcing the issue of free trade. In the 1880s the price of palm oil had dropped, the competition between European firms for the produce was stepped up, and the Efik middlemen were determined to keep all European traders out of their markets. On 1 January, 1888, the British declared that all markets throughout the protectorate were to be thrown open without reservation for all traders alike. It was a move to break the monopoly claimed by Ja Ja at Opobo and to allow Bonny and Opobo traders to move freely between the two markets, and to restore trade with Europeans on terms more acceptable to the latter. In fact, however, the authority of Efik middlemen lived on among their people for a long time; and in the second place, there was hardly any alternative to the African commercial organization which had for long transported the produce of the interior to the seaboard.[18]

Nor could the British government disregard the traditional political machinery of Calabar in the early years of British administration. For at least the first five years of the protectorate, the Efik government was the only effective government in Calabar. The British had neither an adequate government, a police force nor had she revenue or a proper staff to run an administration of her own. The consul had no gunboat of his own although he had executive powers, but he could not get away to visit other parts of the protectorate except when a chance gunboat came into Calabar.[19]

MacDonald was also required to give his immediate attention to the question of raising revenue to cover the expenses of administration. The system hitherto in force, under which the coastal chiefs had exacted comey from traders, was to be finally abolished. This was done on 10 August, 1891. Duties were to be raised by a regular system on spirits, tobacco, gunpowder, 'Dane guns' and salt, and the chiefs who lost comey dues were to receive subventions from public revenue. It it possible that once comey was abolished and replaced by subsidies the general effect was to make the Efik political system less absolute.

Efik political agents as part of the new power structure

After 1891, when the administration was streamlined and the 'paper protectorate' came to an end, the political traditions of the Efik underwent a series of modifications. A new category of

British appointed officials called 'Native Political Agents' was established as part and parcel of the new power structure. This had the important effect of reducing the traditional chiefs to the status of political subalterns of these agents, particularly in the non-ritual aspects of public life. Their role in Efik society was similiar to that of the warrant chiefs of the Eastern region of Nigeria,[20] and enjoyed a position unprecedented in the political experience of the Efik. In the colonial service they came to be the most important African officials. At a time when the British wished to strengthen the administration, but lacked either adequate staff, revenue, intelligence information or knowledge of local languages and traditions, the system of appointing African political agents was an indispensable one.

Who were these 'Native Political Agents' and how did they come to be chosen? What were their duties and how faithfully did they perform them? The most important of these agents were Magnus Duke, Henry Black Davis, Eyo Eyo Ita, Joseph Henshaw, Richard Henshaw, David Henshaw, Coco Otu Bassey and James Egbo Bassey. They were chosen from amongst those who for one reason or other held wide local influence in their communities.

Many of them were important traders whose influence with the regions where they traded was valuable to the colonial administration. The agent, Henry Black Davis (Effa Ewa), who belonged to the Etim Effiom family, combined both education and lavish wealth, having been a trader in palm produce, rubber and ebony. He is said to have acquired his name by trading with a European trader called Davis. Black Davis wanted to buy up all Davis's goods, and since he was wealthy enough to do so, Davis called him his namesake.[21] He had estates at Oban and at Akpabuyo near Okoi. Prince Eyo Eyo Ita, the eldest son of King Eyo III, was chosen political agent because of his influence as a wealthy trader.[22] He owned land (on the site of St. Margaret's Hospital at Duke Town) and was a member of the Eyo household in Creek Town. Thus he was placed in charge of the courts in that town. He had been administering the affairs of the Eyo household when he was appointed a political agent. He later became a clerk of the Native High Court of Calabar at Duke Town. Daniel Henshaw was another agent who owed his position to his wealth for he had inherited his father's (Joseph Henshaw's) land at Oron where cocoa was grown.

Coco Otu Bassey, one of the best known of the political agents, and at one time president of the Itu court before the Aro Expedition of 1902, rose to political office because of his economic activities. The life story of Coco Bassey is extremely interesting. His original name was Okereke Okereke,

the son of a big chief, Okereke Ebru, at Inokon Town. Four
years after the death of his father he was stolen by traders
passing through his town, and taken to another Inokon town,
Amasu, where he was sold to an Enion man, Ekpo Nta. When
Ekpo Nta could not meet the debts he owed an Enion trader, Otu
Bassey Ofion, he gave to him Okereke Okereke. Otu Bassey Ofion
feared the release of Okereke by the latter's people and he therefore sent him away to Duke Town to an old man, Bassey Africa.
Africa was extremely sympathetic, having been a slave himself at
one time, and gave him the name Coco. Coco Bassey was handed
over to a European trader at Fernando Po, called Wood, and he
later worked in a ship, the *Almanta* under a Robert Murray. He
attended school twice a day and learnt English. Murray obtained for
Coco Bassey the 'freedom paper' from Consul Livingstone. He
later attended school at Accra, worked in hulks, and on his return
home entered into business. A successful and influential trader, he
was later selected by the government as a political agent for the
Cross River.[23] He was not only a large trader but had plantations
at Itu, cultivated cocoa, coffee, palm oil and nuts which he sold
to the factories, owned his own canoes, and employed several
hands to help in the enterprise. Coco Bassey had control over the
entire area stretching northwards between Itu and the German
frontier and on both banks of the Cross River. He was connected
by marriage with a large number of the Cross River peoples, and
was in the best position to assist in maintaining government control over the river.[24]

Political agents were also recruited from amongst men for whom
education had opened new avenues of employment. Richard Henshaw had been one of the fortunate Efik men of his time to gain
an education in England after his schooling in a mission establishment in Calabar. Upon the death of his father in about 1899 he
returned to Calabar and worked under Chief E. E. Offiong[25] in
the Upper Akpa Iyefe River (Ododop) area. He was subsequently
appointed a political agent. Magnus Duke, a relative of the Henshaws[26] and one of the most colourful personalities of the early
colonial period in Efik history, was another political agent who had
gained an overseas education. His father Efiom Edet Nsa, through
the help of British traders, had seen to the education of his son in
England. Oral tradition has it that while still in England, Magnus
Duke had an audience with Queen Victoria, at which he discussed
the situation in Calabar and offered his services to the British
government. The Queen acceded to his kindly gesture, and on his
return home he was appointed a clerk of a Native Court (the first)
at his home at Edet Nsa Street.[27] This oral tradition should be

treated with suspicion, for Magnus Duke might have enhanced his importance by relating stories of this nature to credulous villagers.

The attributes—sound education and/or the semblance of wielding great influence in their local communities—were significant, for the main duties of political agents involved the conveying of orders of the district officers to the local communities and acting as a liaison between the two polarities. They acted as interpreters to British officials on tour. They had oversight of special projects such as road making, the peaceful conduct of trade and the eradication of causes of civil unrest. Their problem was one of making British rule effective by securing the co-operation of the traditional rulers regarding the imposition of British authority over them.

They helped to achieve continuity in administration, and acted in many cases as a buffer between the angry people and the European officials. As European officials feared the debilitating effects of climate and of touring in the hinterland, African political agents were used for explaining government policies and heading expeditions into the interior. This prevented the European officials from having to do much of the mischief, which could be conveniently left to the Efik agents. The agents were employed at little expense and were provided with little clerical assistance or means of transport.[28] In fact for a long time their office was an honorary one and it was only later that they received remuneration for their jobs. This was one reason why they were allowed to trade on their own account. In 1899 they were entitled to an increase in their salary and henceforth not allowed to engage in trade.[29] But their salaries, according to the civil establishment list for 1904–1906, were not really far above that of the other clerical staff; they were paid between £80–£100 a year.[30]

It was the intention of the colonial administration to delegate the routine work of Calabar to the political agents so that the district commissioners would be left free to attend to the more important work of their offices. The political agents were placed in charge of 'Native Courts' and were also given some executive authority. Their intimate knowledge of traditions and customs, and of the country in general, was useful to the district commissioners who often consulted them on these points.

The manner in which Efik political agents enforced their executive authority was a political novelty. The authority conferred on the agents did not have the traditional sanction of the Efik chiefs or people. They enjoyed power and prestige over and above those sanctioned by tradition. In Efik tradition, no man except the king or the head of a house had the right to 'issue' orders to his town or kinsmen. A lineage head could be deposed if he failed to command the support of the majority in his particular lineage. Traditional Efik society was democratic in that the political leader depended upon popular support. Once he lost it he was replaced by another, and at times by one who had worked the agitation against him. But the political agent was above the traditional sanctions of the society in which he lived. In the colonial system, traditional democracy lost its sway since the political agent was only responsible to the colonial administration. And the agent had behind him the force of an alien but powerful government with its police and army. The very fact of appointment by a British authority was sufficient for him to coerce his fellow men without fear of traditional reprisals.

The essential point here is that the African political agents were regarded by the Europeans as part of the European administration and treated in many ways like European officials. But they were also Efik, part of the new power structure, and the reaction of the people to them depended more on this than on their being European officials. This is significant for it helps to explain the nature of the political crisis they caused. Their authority, though feared, was not always readily accepted by the communities over which they were placed in charge.

The political agents cannot justly be blamed for incompetence since they had hardly had any experience in performing the functions of such a non-traditional political office. The nature of their responsibilities was such that although they had the firm support of the British government on most issues they still needed to exercise a fair amount of coercion on the Efik in order to get them to do the biddings of the government. Even where the head chief of a town was a political agent he was not always considered a tradiional political officer on account of his new position. It is not surprising, therefore, that a political agent, E. E. Offiong III, once wrote to James Watts, a district commissioner, that he was compelled to tender his resignation as head chief of Old Town because he could not successfully convey government orders to the people. He therefore wished to free himself from any blame that might arise from this responsibility.[31]

There was also substantial suspicion that the agents were able to use their official position in order to seek their own self-aggrandizement to an extent unknown in the political experience of the Efik. The most notable exception was the diligent and honest Magnus Duke who is said to have died an insolvent man.[32] Even the district commissioners at times called upon their agents to display 'greater intelligence and grasp of their work'[33] and described Henry Black Davis[34] and James Egbo Bassey[35] as not being 'very

P

shining examples' of Efik political agents. A few examples will illustrate the resistance that the Efik and the Cross River people launched against the men who had become part of the new power structure.

In August, 1897 the people of Uyana village brought at Duke Town a suit against the political agent, Effiom Otu Ekon.[36] The committee, headed by Magnus Duke, which heard the case, found most of the allegations against Effiom Otu Ekon to be true. The latter had needlessly fined innocent men, intimidated others, taken law into his own hands, seized property when his personal debts had not been settled and acted in a fraudulent manner. Chief Effiom Otu Ekon was removed from his position as African political agent and as vice-president of the Uwet Minor Court.[37]

The man who replaced him at Uwet as political agent was Chief Young Egbo Bassey.[38] To what extent the allegations made against him were well founded it is difficult to tell since Young Egbo Bassey denied them all. The Umon people spoke of fines being imposed on their traders, of seizure of their merchandize, of flogging and wounds being inflicted upon them.[39] If this evidence is accepted, the hypothesis may be drawn that people 'broke' political agents as they did kings—not by law but by politics.

The king of Idua, Asam Inyan Ete, and his chiefs brought against Daniel Henshaw, the political agent at Idua, the complaint that Henshaw had taken their Old Town grounds and farms away from them by force. This was in addition to the piece of ground that had been sold to his late father. They expressed the fear that eventually more land would be seized from them; they lost confidence in his court and begged a replacement 'who was not a relation to him [Daniel Henshaw]'.[40]

It is not known if Coco Bassey ever used his official position to further his private interests. From the evidence of laudatory remarks about his service contained in the official records, this seems hardly likely to have been the case. But there were, nevertheless, persons like King Eyo Honesty VIII of Creek Town and his chiefs, who reported that Chief Coco Bassey hindered the trade of the river by requiring those who used it (at Itu) to pay a toll of four boxes of brass rods.[41] It was reported that the toll applied equally to all traders—Efik, Umon or Akunakuna. Subsequent enquiries, conducted for Gallwey by another Efik political agent, E. E. Offiong III, revealed that no such tolls had ever been collected by Coco Bassey or his boys on the Cross River.[42] Only a tax was paid by traders as entrance fee for any newly-founded markets to regulate and maintain their peace. At Umon market and at adjacent markets such as Ikpa, founded by King Eyo VII of Creek Town, tolls of 120 brass rods were paid by users to the king and his chiefs. Coco Bassey founded the market of Okori after the Ekoi expedition of 1898, and the traders there had paid tolls (to Coco Bassey?) of twenty brass rods each at the rate of four shillings.

There is no doubt that Coco Bassey was one of the main pillars of the British administration in the Calabar hinterland. In 1896, Moor paid him a glowing tribute in which he said:

> Without him [Bassey] the same amount of success could not have been attained and I consider that without his active co-operation and goodwill the difficulty of carrying on the work of opening up the Cross River . . . effectively would be increased to an enormous extent.[43]

In 1899, shortly after Coco Bassey's death, Moor eulogized:

> I cannot speak too highly of the assistance rendered by this chief to the Government. He employed all the means at his disposal, monetary and otherwise, and also used all his influence in furthering the establishment and control of the Administration . . . his death at a comparatively early age is due to the untiring energy which he displayed in the assistance of the Government . . . the expenditure he made in administration was by no means limited to the amounts which he received.[44]

Another source of dissatisfaction was the method used by the colonial power to recruit 'voluntary' labour for the construction of roadways. If a traditional authority, like a house head, had called for voluntary labour, there might have been less resistance to it, but the new men had no traditional authority to do so. To harness voluntary labour for a project the bidder had to be popular with those whose labour he sought to conscript. More often than not political agents were held in fear and suspicion, since the word of these 'uncrowned kings' had the effect of law. Joseph Henshaw, who became a court official under Magnus Duke, earned the reputation of a hard task master because of the way in which he demanded free labour in 1906 to build the Akpabuyo Road leading to Akpabuyo, beyond the terminus of the ferry at Atimbo. Each family was required to send out a contingent periodically to build the road over the swampy area. Although the road was useful in that it provided an urgently needed facility for the Calabar chiefs to get to their plantations at Akpabuyo, the force used to obtain free labour was intensely disliked.

On another occasion when Major Winn Sampson, district commissioner in Calabar,[45] was anxious to open a road between Oron and Eket, he made use of Richard Henshaw to win the support of the chiefs and other powerful people along the route. The chiefs, who controlled many neighbouring towns besides their own, put before the colonial administration their understanding that government always brought war upon a country when a road had once been allowed to pass through. The chiefs finally consented, but only after Sampson and Henshaw had sworn that they would never bring war. The road, which was finally constructed and opened to traders and mail-runners, owed much to Richard Henshaw. The Oron-Eket road[46] was full of adventure for European commissioners who tried to push their way along and away from it. They came upon unfriendly inhabitants, and on one occasion it was Chief Henshaw who had to save the lives of a group of English officers at the risk of his own.[47]

It is not exactly true that what increased the resistance of the traditional communities towards the men of the new power structure was that the latter were generally young men of great ambition.[48] Certainly the older traditionalists had no great desire to venture long distances to attend court, or to please others; nor were they always equipped with the knowledge required to understand and interpret British rule and court processes. In Efik society young men might have risen in that way, attended by all the traditional political complexities. The crucial factor was that the political agents symbolized the might of an alien government. There is ample evidence that the opposition to European officials was as great as it was to Efik agents. For instance, in September, 1895, A. A. Whitehouse, consular agent at Eket, Qua Ibo, reported to Moor that the people of Ikotaparta had persistently refused to recognize his authority and would not pay up their fines.[49] The political agents, like those mentioned above and Daniel Henshaw, the agent at Oron who did the translations for visiting officers and who broke a conspiracy that was planned against the district commissioners,[50] performed as far as the British government was concerned a most useful function in that they played the role of intermediaries between the British government and the African communities.

Efik kings under the new power structure

This situation of course raises the fundamental question of the place of the traditional Efik kings in the new structure of power. The British did not lose sight of the fact that though the political agents were an integral part of their power structure, the traditional chiefs held great power and influence over their people and that once they were confided in and their fears and mistrust removed they would probably agree to use their positions to open up the country. At any rate, this was what was outlined in MacDonald's

report of 1889. One method used to invite the participation of
Efik rulers and chiefs was to give them a place in the native councils
that were instituted. These replaced the 'governing councils' of
Acting Consul Johnston who had in 1887, recognizing the need for
practical government, introduced the councils. In effect, they were
a development of the court of equity. These native councils, set up
by MacDonald, operated as administrative and judicial bodies.
Chiefs also sat on native courts and dispensed justice. In July,
1895 MacDonald instituted the 'High Court of Native Councils of
Old Calabar', of which he was president. It should be noted that
though the chiefs were in one way or another brought into the
administrative and judicial apparatus of the colonial administration,
the legal status of the councils and courts of which they were members was not classified by the British government.[51]

Though the kings retained some measure of judicial authority
by virtue of membership of the courts, the traditional powers and
authorities they were accustomed to enjoy were frequently over-
ridden so that they were not in fact independent sovereigns. It
would be a piece of legal fiction to suggest that the kings alone
possessed the final powers and responsibility of government since
they were not free from the weight of the colonial yoke. The British
assumed that they could appropriate a few essential and superior
attributes of the powers of the traditional ruling elite and still expect
that power to function within its new limits as if unchanged, both
in essence and in the eyes of the subject. This becomes extremely
clear when the implications of the Old Calabar Native Council
Rules (No. 4) of 1902[52] are examined.

In essence, the rules of 1902 reduced the status of the kings.
Indeed, the title of 'king' (Edidem) was dropped, and instead that
of Obong was substituted for the heads of Duke Town and Creek
Town.[53] Of all three titles of Etinyin, Edidem and Obong used by
the Efik to describe their rulers and persons of consequence in
Calabar, the least important was Obong. In traditional parlance
Obong was equivalent to a 'lord', and prior to the twentieth century the Efik meaning of the word did not include the rank of
king or revered natural ruler. The reason for the change in the
traditional rank order is not difficult to understand: it was considered improper to retain the title of Edidem for the Efik paramount rulers when the Queen of England was sovereign ruler over
them. In an attempt to increase the value of the title, it was made
a punishable offence to use the title of Obong other than with
reference to an Efik paramount chief.[54]

The new rule also democratized the institution of Obongship.
By articles three and four, it declared that the right of every free

Efik family to contest for the Obongship was recognized. In other words, all etuboms (heads of families) were eligible for appointment as Obong. Strictly speaking, this right to kingship of the various Efik towns or families was justified in tradition. As stated in an earlier chapter, every Efik family was considered equal to the other and each lineage had a right to elect one of its own candidates to the highest position in the town. Owing to the numerical superiority, wealth, and the favour of European supercargoes, certain lineages were able to monopolize the office of king. Thus, the Okoho group in Duke Town and the Eyo group in Creek Town were able successfully to capture the kingship. Only on rare occasions did other lineages supply the kings of their respective towns.

With the advent of the colonial government, it is natural to expect that the less privileged houses would agitate for a restoration of their traditional right to produce a candidate for the highest office and that the colonial government's action would be welcomed by them. To make clear which families were eligible to produce candidates for the two Obongs of Calabar, some of the segmentary areas were combined. Mbiabo and Adiabo were combined with Creek Town to form Creek Town division, while Old Town and Duke Town were combined into a second, called Old Calabar. 'Old Calabar' meant Duke Town, which included Archibong Town, Cobham Town (which included James Town), Henshaw Town, Eyamba Town, Old Town, and their dependencies. It should be noted that the Muri of Efut and the Ntoe of the Qua, though they represented distinct communities, were placed under the Obong of Calabar. 'Creek Town' meant Creek Town, Ikoneto, Ibonda (Efut), Ikot Offiong, Mbiabo and Adiabo, and their dependencies. These areas conformed to the reality of their traditional standing vis-à-vis Old Calabar and Creek Town. The etubom of the Eyo, Ambo, Ibitam, Ikoneto, Ikot Offiong and Adiabo families were eligible for election to the post of Obong of Creek Town. The etubom of Duke (including Archibong and Ntiero), Cobham, Henshaw, Eyamba, and Old Town families were eligible for election to the position in Old Calabar.

In practice, however, despite the legislation, no other families besides the Okoho (Duke) and Eyo were able to compete successfully for the 'Obongship'. Though each town was equal to every other in status there were generally more Dukes and Eyos present at the election of an Obong and they succeeded in voting in their candidates.[55] The law came into effect at a time when, particularly at Duke Town, there was no king on the throne. When King Duke IX died in 1897 there was no ruler on the throne until Edem Effiom, a descendant of Effiom Okoho, succeeded to the throne as the first Obong of Duke Town (date not clear). The first Obong of Creek Town was Etubom Eyo Honesty VIII, who had been a signatory to the 1902 rules.

The most disconcerting feature of the new arrangement was that the Obongs held office at the pleasure of the high commissioner. This once again underlined the fact that the British were keenly interested in the conservation of the traditional status symbols and their incorporation into the administrative hierarchy, and not only because they had to lean for support upon such groups as possessed local power at a given moment. Even where the chiefs were not men of moment it was still useful to retain them before the populace as the nominal centres of power, reinforced by quiet but firm support for the traditional polity as long as no part of it was prejudicial to British interests. The general effect of requiring the Obongs to hold office at the pleasure of the high commissioner was hence to deny them the status of independent sovereigns and make them dependent upon the goodwill of the colonial administration. Also in restoring the democracy of the traditional political system the British were astutely giving themselves greater powers. The increase in competition between the several rival lineages might be expected to give the British government a greater say in any crisis precipitated by the elections, and the kings eventually elected would be less able to take independent action.

House heads under the new power structure

If all that was left of the kings was a show of pomp, ceremonial pageantry and charismatic influence rather than effective wielding of political power, the position of the heads of houses vis-à-vis the members was strengthened by the British administration. In order to seek a logical explanation for what seems to be an ironical situation it is necessary to examine the immediate problem of labour supply in Calabar. It would then be seen that what dominated the thoughts of the policy makers was not altruistic but merely a matter of economic expediency.

After the decision to abolish slave dealing in all parts of the Protectorate as from 1 January, 1902 the first concern of the administration was to avert any serious shortage of labour that might arise as a consequence of this decision. It was necessary to the development of the export economy, which rested in part on a net increase of labour, that domestic slaves in the houses be retained as a labour force. It was they who had always provided the motive power for trade in Calabar as in the Niger Delta. The formation of labour policy of course posed an awkward problem for the

colonial administration.[56] This was largely because it had to recon-
cile its previous stand against slave dealing and unmitigated forms
of slavery with the new need to retain slaves in order to provide
the necessary labour facilities to continue the oil trade. It had to
prevent the danger of provoking political and social unrest consequent upon the total removal of the old system, while ensuring
that there was no disturbance to the economy. The result was
a compromise: gradual abolition of domestic slavery, and the
retention of the traditional house system in such a way that the
position of slaves was ameliorated. High Commissioner Moor felt
that the only way in which slaves could be prevented from running
away from the houses was to improve the conditions of slaves
within them.

Since it was the heads of houses who controlled the labour of
the members of those houses it logically followed that it would be
impossible to administer the country and recruit the necessary
labour force for development purposes without the assistance of
the heads of houses. Thus if free or communal labour were required in order to build roads, public works or other projects the
government would have to depend on house heads to supply it with
the necessary labour.

The British government knew that it could count on the support
of the middlemen chiefs and house heads for any legislation which
increased the powers of the masters over the members.[57] This was
largely because the house heads were, towards the end of the century, victims of the revolution in trade by which enterprising
domestic slaves freed themselves of some of the controls of the
house heads and engaged in commerce independent of the houses
to which they previously belonged. One notable example of a rich
slave who had risen according to the traditional system and fended
for himself was Yellow Duke, who traded in oil and kernels. He
sent his traders far away into the regions between the basins of
the Cross River and Cameroons to gather the produce of the area
and traded it at Calabar. He owned a fleet of canoes in which
he and his traders sailed through the maze of creeks between the
Cameroons and Calabar. Several slaves had secured their emancipation as a result of Moor's policy in 1895 to increase the number
of free papers issued to slaves. Free papers guaranteed the absolute
freedom of the holders in disposing of their property and services.[58]

In 1901 Moor wrote a long treatise on the subject of slavery in
Southern Nigeria in which he alluded, after lengthy digression, to
the enforcing of a Slave Dealing Proclamation.[59] He doubted
whether it would be possible to maintain and efficiently carry on
the business of middlemen carriers unless additional labour was

recruited. He even went to the extent of suggesting (this was disapproved of by the Secretary of State) the establishment of a system by which, for a consideration, children from the interior might be apprenticed to Calabar for a period of years for general instruction in trade.

A direct effect of the coming into operation of a Slave Dealing Proclamation, coupled with the closing of the slave markets, which would result from a proposed expedition against the Aro, would have been to liberate in fact, if not in law, the domestic slaves currently held by chiefs and heads of houses. Some action had to be taken to prevent slaves from freeing themselves from the control of the chiefs and heads of houses. Moor's suggestion was that when the proclamation came into effect slaves would be under the same obligations and rights as free members of the houses. No member (including slaves) would have the right of obtaining employment, either from an African or a European, except with the consent of the house head. Traders who wanted to obtain labour could do so in the same way as they had done heretofore, by approaching the house heads. The Slave Dealing Proclamation would not hence interfere with the work of the European factories.

Once having settled the question of whether the house system was to be maintained or be allowed to go into decay it became evident that the house system could be fortified only if the heads of houses retained absolute control over the members whose conditions had been legally, if not in practice, improved. The two means that rationally justified this control were firstly, the recognition of the traditional laws and customs which stipulated that a member of a house may not trade without the consent of the head of his house and secondly, the enforcement of the rule that slaves were subject to the same obligations as the freemen in the house.[60]

This may reasonably be accepted as the background to the passage of the Native House Rule Proclamation of 1901.[61] The rule was essentially intended to maintain the control of the chiefs, and consequently prevent the existing labour system from being entirely dislocated. The proclamation laid down that each member of the house was subject to the law and custom relating to houses (so long as these were not repugnant to natural justice); that runaway members of houses might be arrested and restored; that no one might employ members without the consent of the house heads; and it also provided for the interest of members.

Since the proclamation sought to maintain intact the government of the house system and to hold the economic and political position of the house head, it also declared that every member of a house who refused to submit 'to the control, authority and rule of the head of his house' was liable to prosecution, and on conviction to a fine not exceeding fifty pounds or to imprisonment of not more than one year. Clause eight enjoined that a house member found wandering abroad 'without any visible means of subsistence' could be arrested without a warrant by any court official and sent to the District Commissioner for forcible return to the house head.

Colonial administrators had of course to defend the proclamation on grounds other than the protection of labour. It was advisable, they said, to preserve the traditional order of society since it was impossible to substitute the house system for any other without upsetting the social structure. Also 'the advantages and the guarantees afforded by it [House Rule] for the thrifty management of property and the resulting absence of pauperization among the lower social grades of the natives' justified the government in strengthening the 'quasi paternal authority' of the representatives of houses.[62] That the protection of labour was the chief motive behind the proclamation is confirmed by the fact that it was extended also to the hinterland where house rule did not exist. Colonial officers there used the new rule to demand labour for porterage and other purposes through the local headman using the prescribed penalties under the ordinance for sanction.[63]

The proclamation was nevertheless not a one-sided document since it laid down also the responsibilities and obligations of the heads of houses. In the first place, it made a house head who failed to discharge his duties liable to punishment of a fine not exceeding fifty pounds; secondly, it reduced the 'topping percentage' to chiefs from twenty-five percent to ten percent on trade profits,[64] and thirdly, it made it necessary for employers of labour to obtain the prior consent of a house head.

On the other hand, however, it can scarcely be denied that the new proclamation was in an anomalous position with the Slave Dealing Proclamation of the same year. Slavery, which was made a penal offence under the latter proclamation, was blithely overlooked in the House Rule Proclamation, which strengthened the slave institution by arresting runaways and giving house heads full authority. In fact, the new proclamation was almost a connivance at slavery. One newspaper actually called it the 'Southern Nigeria Slavery Ordinance'.[65] As Morel put it, the rule prevented natural evolution toward a 'higher state' by 'sterilizing healthy influences' making for modification.[66] House heads could not be destroyed, nor could one interfere with slavery.

The House Rule Proclamation also had the effect of making the old system so harsh that many of the house members began to flee from the houses or became disobedient toward their masters. Such members were handed over to the law courts and punished. In the case arising between a member, Omin Iso, and his master, Okon Akan, on a charge of disobedience, the former was found guilty and sentenced to a month's imprisonment.[67] In another case a woman, Iquo Duke Henshaw, who deserted the head of her house, was given six strokes and returned to her mistress, Efana Anwan.[68] Desertions of this nature were evidence of the unpopularity of the new proclamation among house members. A second way in which labour was mobilized by the colonial administration was by a Masters and Servants Proclamation of 1903.[69] This proclamation represented an attempt to carry into effect the system of apprenticeship mentioned earlier. The object was easy to conceive: now that the chiefs could no longer recruit boys by purchasing slaves, a method had to be devised by which they could obtain apprentices, either for instruction in local industries or as domestic servants, from the people of the interior. The system enabled chiefs to obtain apprentices in place of 'bought' domestic slaves. Children under sixteen years of age could be hired as apprentices for up to twelve years provided a contract to that effect was signed. This was to give chiefs some security of tenure for the services they had hired. Another object of the new proclamation was to make the provisions of the original one of 1901 applicable to government contracts of service, and thereby enable the government to introduce a business-like system of apprenticeship.[70] Thus whatever the objects, in effect the proclamation was a compromise between slavery and free labour, and a method of mobilizing labour.

In 1903 another proclamation, 'Roads and Creeks Proclamation', mobilized forced labour to clear public roads and waterways. It enabled chiefs to call upon forced labour up to six days in three months.[71] This proclamation added legal validity to the conscription of labour that was permitted under the traditional age grade system. The interesting fact that emerges from a survey of the economic policy regarding labour, and the various forms in which it was raised and used, is that the possibilities for progress and development were not lacking in traditional life. But the way in which the colonial administration went about the problem, even if its actions were a transitory panacea, did not have much to commend it.

It is not possible here to enter into the full story of the proclamation (later ordinance) until its repeal in 1914–15 by Lugard.[72] The government was bitterly criticized by the Aborigines Protection Society for the way in which local government recruited labour for all its projects, its oppressive nature, and its indiscriminate extension beyond the coast. Within the houses, too, as we have noted above, desertion became common; those who deserted either joined government service or commercial firms, and refused to give any part of their earnings towards the house. Effectively, the Masters and Slaves Proclamation became a dead letter after some time.

The land tenure system under the new power structure

If Efik tradition underwent many vicissitudes during the early colonial era, the chiefs made successful attempts to counter the floodtide of change so far as decisions regarding land tenure policy were concerned. The Efik chiefs claimed that the traditional land tenure system forbade the sale of land to foreigners, and with this argument the chiefs resisted the break-up of the customary forms of land tenure. The British had hence to subscribe to the idea that land was inalienable, and preserved its ownership for the people against any form of freehold. The official view became that indirect administration necessitated that Africans retain control of land. To open up the country, it was declared, would lead to an influx of European money and ideas and the consequence would be that land would be taken up by capitalists and speculators. Peasant agriculture therefore continued to exist where Africans had not taken to plantation agriculture. Though the importance of developing the agricultural sector was not completely overlooked by colonial administrators, it was not until June, 1910 that a director, W. H. Johnson, was appointed to supervise agricultural activities.

However, local government could appropriate or rent land for public purposes after compensation had been paid. Where communal land was required, the chief concerned (as trustee of the land) had to sell the area required to the government notwithstanding any customary law to the contrary.[73] In Qua Town, for instance, Chief Edim Ebana agreed to let to the protectorate, for a rent of ten pounds per annum, a piece of ground known as Rifle Range near the Qua River.[74] Similarly a chief of Old Town, Okon Etim Asiya Adim, on behalf of his people let out some land in the town to the protectorate in 1895. The rent payable in this case was also ten pounds per annum.[75] In the same year, another piece of Qua Town was rented out to the government.[76]

In addition to government acquisition, some private firms also rented land, especially areas along the beach, for trading purposes. In 1898, for instance, Essien Etim Offiong III of Duke Town rented out a parcel of land, situated at Henshaw Town beach, at a yearly rent of sixty pounds for seventy-five years. The tenant was a German firm, Ulrick Peterson of Berlin, which was doing business at Calabar.[77] But no land was leased out by chiefs for large-scale capital exploitation by European agents.

The legal system under the new power structure

As a general rule it was only in those areas of the body politic where the traditional structure met the demands of the British that the changes were minimal. Ekpe, traditionally the most important judicial body in Calabar, being inimical to the European sense of justice, had to lose its former significance. Henceforth, although it was still embedded in the lineage system of the Efik, it could be permitted to survive only as a ritual oracle with no place in the new political and judicial system.

The judicial system established by the colonial administration represented an important transition in the change from the pre-servation of the social equilibrium by chiefs to the impersonal justice of the courts acting under the rule of law. In the old régime, councils of elders and chiefs listened to civil disputes brought before them and expressed their opinions, stating the traditional rules of behaviour or conduct of the community. It was up to the plaintiff himself to assert his rights with the support of his kin and friends, and the general outcome normally consisted of a reconciliation of the disputing parties in the light of the merits of the case. What was most crucial in this form of justice was the reconciliation and delimitation of conflict, rather than the punishment of an offender. Only when an individual was persistent in flouting approved norms of behaviour did his kin withdraw their support, and every man rose against him. Ekpe, under the aegis of the chiefs and the important cases, recovered debts and protected the property of its members.

The introduction of a modern system of legal procedures did away with the traditional legal system. The ultimate object of law was no longer the application of the idea of reconciliation between conflicting interests or the idea of obtaining reciprocity but the punishment of the offender. No longer was the right to take life vested in the lineage or family but in formally instituted judiciaries. Indeed, to many laymen of that time the advent of colonial admin-istration invariably meant the advent of the European judicial system.

But for all the merits claimed for it,[78] the new judicial system did not function effectively nor did it inspire much confidence in the Efik. It has been claimed that the number of cases tried by these courts was an indication of their popularity.[79] There is no doubt that the figures indicate that large numbers of civil and criminal cases were heard before the 'native' and consular courts. For ex-ample, in forwarding the judicial returns for the year 1896 the attention of Moor was called to the large number of cases heard in the consular court, which added up to 504 (criminal and civil), in that year. This represented a substantial increase over that of

1894 when the figure was 286.[80] Between March, 1899 and March, 1900, 244 civil and 120 criminal cases were tried before the High Court. The minor courts tried 613 civil and 141 criminal cases.[81] Successive reports[82] always spoke of an increase in the number of cases heard by the various courts, and attributed it to the increased confidence the Efik and the Cross River people had in the newly established courts.

However, one ought not to confuse an increase in litigation with the effectiveness of the courts system. The major reasons that account for an increase in litigation in Calabar may be outlined as follows: in the first place, more cases were heard in Calabar than anywhere else in the protectorate because the population of Calabar (particularly Duke Town, which according to the colonial office list was the largest and most important town in the protectorate), was much larger than in other places. The presence of many 'foreigners' (the stranger element from other parts of West Africa and West Indies), whose disputes with the Calabar people and with each other were not inconsiderable, increased the number of palavers. Moreover, the soldiers and their women at the barracks (which became a town by itself) were also said to be the cause of no small number of cases, since the former were in such close proximity to Duke Town.[83] Secondly, the work of the 'Native' High Court after 1899 was greatly increased by the transference to it from the District Commissioner's court of cases between the people of Calabar and Africans from outside Calabar. Thirdly, from the nature of the civil cases, the increase in litigation indicates a growing desire for judicial adjustment of trade accounts between Africans and Europeans, rather than an increase of litigation in the usually understood sense of the term.

The balance of evidence seems to point to the fact that all was not well with the effectiveness of the courts system. The decisions of the court, as the official records indicate, do not seem to have been enforced. One court dignitary, E. E. Offiong III, for instance, reported the 'apparent indifference and negligent manner' of the 'Native' High Court to the implementation of decisions and orders of the court which were not always carried out.[84] There is a proliferation of such instances in the records. The more important question to ask would apparently be what rendered the judicial system apparently ineffective.

In this respect, it was the limitations of the system[85] that were most decisive. Only a few of these need to be examined here. In the first place the members of these courts were not always traditional authorities. They consisted also of non-traditional educated Africans who had gained the favour of the British.[86] Efik clerks did the clerical routine work, and Efik vice-presidents (political agents) received a sitting fee of ten shillings, while each of the three members, summoned by the clerks, and a special member representing the district where the case was heard received five shillings sitting fee per day.

The membership of the courts was not constant. In the High Court of the 'Native' Council of Old Calabar Courts (established in 1895) there were seven sitting members on 11 April, five on 21 October and twelve on 11 November, 1897. But while the 'native' councils were presided over by European political officers the Minor Courts, created in 1900, were presided over by Efik authorities or by a local chief.

These authorities derived their powers not from tradition but from those delegated to them by the British government. They were not always persons who enjoyed the full status of freemen and this factor often prejudiced their effectiveness.[87] Their western education enabled them to understand the regulations of the 'Native' Courts and often they assumed powers not assigned to them by law. For a bribe they were willing to use their powers to choose the sitting members, so that they were able to interfere with the proceedings of the case and influence its outcome. As one missionary put it,

> the fact that in more than one case these [court officials] were removed from their position on its being discovered that they took advantage of it to aggrandize themselves at the expense of their neighbours, did much to impress the people with the justice of the Government.[88]

The fact that some of the members of these courts had no traditional authority also made the work of executing laws difficult. When, for instance, a court messenger went up to a head chief of a town or village, where a particular defendant lived, he was not always influential enough to coerce him to attend court. Many defendants stayed away from the courts with impunity. In other cases the court messengers had no one but themselves to blame for the opprobrium in which they were at times held by the chiefs. The messengers woefully neglected the procedure governing the conduct of their duty and would not carry out their instructions nor report themselves to the head chief of the town before they proceeded to their business. In the case of an arrest they would not call upon the head chief to produce the person mentioned in the warrant but insisted that, as a rule, they should visit the house of the person wanted and seize him or her. Such rash acts naturally caused friction between the African officials and the rest of the community. Further, they 'demanded women' and interfered with the performance of traditional dances. Incessant complaints of the way police and court messengers behaved were brought to the notice of European officers.[89] Complaints were also made with regard to the behaviour of soldiers. The latter were accused of seizing articles in the market after paying nominal prices for them, and of robbing yam stacks and cutting sticks without permission.

The second structural weakness of the courts system was that they were not always located with cognizance taken of ethnic lines nor did they always take into account the differences in language and customs that divided certain communities. In attempting to erect a superstructure within which the various intensely patriotic self-centered little communities could be brought into some form of administrative and judicial organization, the British erred in their judgement of the social and cultural dynamics of the peoples with whom they were concerned. Areas which were widely different in their customs were grouped together in an ethnically incomprehensible manner. This is evident from the following list of towns represented on the 'native' council of Old Calabar in 1903:

LIST OF TOWNS REPRESENTED ON THE 'NATIVE' COUNCIL OF OLD CALABAR, 1903

Efik Name	English Name	Head Chief
Atakpa	*Old Calabar Town*	*Obong Adam Ephraim Adam*
Ufok Eden Ume	Duke Town	do.
Ukpri Okoretonko	Cobham Town	James Egbo Bassey (Etubom)
Ufok Offiong Okoho	Eyamba Town	—
Nsidung	Henshaw Town	Daniel Henshaw (Etubom)
Obutong	Old Town	Efiom Otu Ekong (Etubom)
Aqua Okoretonko	*Creek Town*	Obong Eyo Honesty
Adak Uko	—	do.
Otung	—	Itam Itam (Etubom)
Mbarakom	—	Esien John Ambo (Etubom)
Ibonda	—	Okon Nsubong (Etubom)
Adiako	*Adiabo Town*	Otu Ita (Etubom)
Akani Obio	—	Okon Efa
Okurikan	—	Ewa Asako
Usukhode	—	Otu Isa (Etubom)
Ikoro Ukpa	—	Ikot Ukpa
Ikot Mbo	—	Ikot Mbo
Mbiako Usuk	*Ikoneto Town*	
Mbiabo	—	Ansa Okon Offiong (Etubom)
Ikoroyak	—	Offiong Awat (Etubom)
Ito	—	Okon Itri
Ekon	—	Ukpon Esien

Efik Name	English Name	Head Chief
Mbiabo Edere	*Ikot Offiong* **Town**	
Ekot Offiong	—	Eyo Etim Ntuk (Etubom)
Mbiabo	—	
Abakpa	*Qua Town*	
Akwa Obio	—	Edim Ebana
Akim	—	Abasi Tata

In traditional society, the largest unit of effective government and justice was the village but the new courts were intended to cover not villages but clans. One result of transferring cases affecting the Calabar people and the stranger element from the District Commissioner's Court to the 'Native' Courts was that the different laws affecting the stranger elements often provided a stumbling block to the orderly working of the 'Native' Court. 'Native' Courts that tried cases between Efik and Efik worked far more smoothly. In the Cross River, where communities were heterogeneous, the weaknesses of the new legal system were also correspondingly greater. Although one of the members of the court was generally summoned with the express object of representing the traditions of the village or district in which the dispute arose, the accused had no real confidence in him.

The results of the new judicial system in the hinterland may be illustrated with reference to the Mbiabo, a large community in the Cross River. They had three main towns of which two were in Calabar Division and the third in Enyong. Of these three towns, the town of Mbiabo Edere attended court at Uwet, twelve hours' journey away, though there was a court at Ikot Offiong, only fifty minutes paddle from Mbiabo. The people of Ikoneto attended court at Creek Town with other Efik. Creek Town was about three hours away from Ikoneto by road or canoe. Ikot Offiong was the only Mbiabo town in Enyong Division which had its own court and served the Oku and Ayadeghe.

The disadvantage of Mbiabo Edere was that their co-attendants at court were a mixture of peoples with whom they had little social or commercial intercourse. In the case of Ikoneto the disadvantage was that, though they had commercial and social intercourse with their co-attendants, they were not joined with their fellow clansmen. In the case of Ikot Offiong, though advantageously situated from the point of view of territorial jurisdiction, there were differences in the customs between the Oku, Ayadeghe, and Ikot Offiong.[90] The court at Ikot Offiong had many points of custom to settle. When the four court members came from different clans

Q

and tried to settle a case upon a point of law of which only one could claim to have authoritative knowledge, difficulties might be anticipated.

Problems such as these were inevitable in an area of such great ethnic heterogeneity. They could have been eased a little, however, if the rightful rulers had come to the aid of the government in the initial stages of British administration. There were two reasons why the older gentry were reluctant to do this. The chiefs knew that many of their old customs would have to be given up. The head chiefs, who actually officiated at some ceremonies in connection with these customs, were not prepared to offend tradition. In the second place, there were unpleasant duties to perform. The chiefs knew that they would have to enforce the orders of government and it was more than likely that such orders would not meet with popular approval. The chiefs preferred to keep their old positions even if they had not now the influence and authority that they once possessed.

To the structural weakness of the system must be added other limitations in the actual dispensation of justice. One of the common criticisms of the judicial system was the ignorance of the members (and especially the European ones) of customary laws as long as the latter remained uncodified.[91]

But even where the laws were common knowledge there were, as T. O. Elias had indicated,[92] still difficulties in interpretation. The way law was administered made the courts neither African nor European, but essentially alien to the people. For how could 'Native Law' not be opposed to the principles of English jurisprudence, when in the former distinctions were made between certain types of crimes and attempts made to propitiate the supernatural elements? In the case of witchcraft, for instance, it was easier to abolish witchcraft by legislation than to define it. For it was difficult to distinguish in a case between a pretence of possessing occult power (which the law forbade), and trying to cure an ailment by means of medicinal herbs (which the law did not). Witchcraft was an amorphous concept and, as pointed out by Elias, eluded legislative precision as much as it defied judicial exposition.

Polygamy, which struck at the root of family life, was lawful but there were also three types of lawful marriage under the Marriage Ordinance, namely marriage in a recognized church, before a registrar at court, or by traditional custom. If a statutory marriage was mixed with a marriage by customary law the question of bigamy where it arose could pose an awkward problem.

Similarly, the institutions of slavery and of slave dealing were abolished by express legislation; yet their subtler manifestations sometimes eluded the vigilance of the courts. When a case of slavery came up in court, only masters who bought or captured slaves were punished; those who had slaves in personal subjection as domestics born into their houses were not easily handled before the courts. The most intractable problem was not just ignorance of the laws but lack of certainty in the detailed rules of customary law.

The number of ways in which these problems could be further complicated by those who were no longer part of the old tradition or by those who sought deliberately to misrepresent customary laws need hardly be imagined. Little wonder, therefore, that in many instances, force or the threat of it had to be employed in order to make court decisions effective.[93]

Another factor which rendered the courts ineffective was the form of punishment meted out to offenders. In many cases, the punishments were not effective deterrents to crime compared with punishments that would have been traditionally sanctioned for them. A few examples will illustrate this point.[94] In the new courts, the punishment inflicted upon a man found guilty of administering the poison ordeal was 60 strokes or a month's imprisonment; of calling another a witch, 120 rods fine or a month's imprisonment; of adultery, 60 strokes and a month's imprisonment for the man and 36 strokes and a week's imprisonment for the woman, and if the woman was found responsible for the invitation to commit adultery, she was subject to the same punishment as the man. In the traditional form of justice, if proven, almost all these crimes would have been punished with either death or slavery. The method of execution was slow and painful. The propensity to commit crime was hence very much diminished in traditional society. The punishment meted out by Ekpe was certainly far more dreaded than that of the new courts.

Tradition and 'modernization'

The predominant purpose of colonial activity was to transform Efik society into a new political, social and economic order. The result might briefly be stated as follows. The traditional political and social organization of Calabar underwent modification with the advent of colonial thraldom. The institution of kingship was retained but the powers and authority of the king no longer extended to the control of external relations. Ekpe as a political and judicial organization diminished in importance as a new legal system came into being. While the powers of the king declined those of the house heads were strengthened as a result of legislation passed to that effect. A category of western-educated Efik officials, namely the African Political Agents, who formed part of the new power structure, emerged in Calabar with powers and authority which were not derived from the traditional ranking in their society.

Colonialism altered the framework by which the Efik interpreted and evaluated the desirability of social change in a western direction. Prior to colonial rule certain facets of Western or Christian civilization were incorporated into Efik traditional life. But the introduction into the traditional society of Calabar of new and alien political and judicial systems, and the colonial-directed drive to the interior through political agents and 'consul men', which replaced the traditional method of controlling inland trading partners, ushered in an era of revolution rather than of gradual change. Many facets of this revolution were inimical to Efik interests and met with resistance, albeit unsuccessful.

However, a basic stimulus to change came with the opening of new avenues of opportunities such as salaried employment, a cash economy and aids to social mobility. This was especially true after the reorganization of the protectorate in 1891 when several government departments—customs, postal, treasury, marine, military, botanical, medical, sanitary and several others[95] came into being thus opening up new even if limited opportunities for local talent. It was from then on that there developed a great demand for trained African clerks and artisans, messengers and labourers in government and trade. As more and more territory was brought under effective government control there was at the same time an increase in the need for trained African personnel to help run the administration. Though it is true that the employment of wage earning Efik clerks and of unofficial wage earners such as gardeners, servants, tailors, watchmen, launderers and the like who congregated in Calabar produced in itself little social change, yet the establishment of colonial rule created other new needs and developed crafts such as printing, carpentry and construction works which helped Calabar to be a centre of economic opportunity, of political influence, and of education and attracted the Efik and other West Coast Africans to become involved in a new economy.

One of the paradoxes of colonialism was the Efik attitude to the challenge of the new times. They realized the necessity of coping with 'modernization' and the need to acquire western secular education in order to ensure that they were not left behind in the exploitation of some of the new opportunities for social progress. In this respect the revolutionary effects in some of the educational, sanitary and medical fields were wholly welcomed by the Efik. But they maintained tenaciously the status quo in those aspects of their life where changes would have led to economic catastrophe. They fought, for instance, for the retention of the traditional land tenure system and the traditional economic organization based on the middleman system. The economic and social development of Calabar depended on the control of these factors. The Efik were successful in upholding the idea that land was inalienable. The support the colonial powers gave to the preservation of traditional forms of control over land had the effect of strengthening the traditional role of the patrilineage head.

The real resistance to colonial rule in Calabar was economic rather than political. The land tenure issue was only one aspect of this resistance; the other equally important one was the resistance offered to changes in the Efik middleman system. The clashes between the Efik and European traders for control of the all-important middleman system of trade in the Calabar hinterland are examined in detail in the next chapter.

REFERENCES

1 Petitions of a similar strain to that of the Efik were also received from the Cameroons; vide F.O. 84/1617, Hewett to F.O., 17 April, 1882, and F.O. 84/1634, Hewett to F.O., 3 November, 1883.

2 F.O. 84/1634, Hewett to F.O., 17 February, 1882.

3 F.O. 84/1634, Hewett to F.O., 3 November, 1883; also, A. C. Burns, *History of Nigeria*, pp. 152–3.

4 C. 4279, London, 1885; T. V. Lister to Bramston, 5 October, 1883; and C. 4279, London, 1885; T. V. Lister to Hewett, 16 May, 1884.

5 Vide H. H. Johnston, *The Story of My Life*, p. 206; and H. Goldie, *Memoir* et seq., passim.

6 For a discussion of African and European treaty motives during the period of partition vide Saadia Touvall, 'Treaties, borders, and the partition of Africa', *J.A.H.* Vol. 7, No. 2, 1966.

7 E. Hertslet, op. cit., Vol. 17, pp. 154–157, 'Treaty with kings and chiefs of Old Calabar, September 10, 1884'.

8 H. Goldie and J. T. Dean, op. cit., p. 349.

9 Vide *London Gazette*, 5 June, 1885, p. 2581; E. Hertslet, *The Map of Africa by Treaty*, Vol. 1, pp. 117–8. The essence of the proclamation is reproduced in J. C. Anene, *Southern Nigeria* et seq., p. 67.

10 F.O. 84/1828, Hewett's 'Observations', 15 October, 1887, on a petition from Prince E. J. Eyamba and others of Old Calabar for the annexation of their territory to Great Britain.

11 For the reasons explaining the hesitant conduct of the British government, vide S. M. Tamuno, 'The Development of British Administrative Control of Southern Nigeria, 1900–1912', unpublished Ph.D. thesis, London, October, 1962, p. 29.

12 These chiefs wanted no further social changes, and desired the preservation of their systems of slavery, polygamy, land tenure and so on. For the reaction of various groups, vide F.O. 84/1940, MacDonald to Salisbury, 12 June, 1889, (his report on the Oil Rivers), encl. 8, Eyo Honesty to MacDonald, 16 April, 1889; also, encl., Henshaw III to MacDonald, 16 April, 1889; King Duke IX to Mac-

Donald, 17 April, 1889; Ikot Offiong and Ikoneto to MacDonald, 16 April, 1889; Cobham V to MacDonald, 16 April, 1889. For Mac-Donald's report of 1889, vide F.O. 84/2109, encl. in MacDonald to Salisbury, 13 January, 1890.

13   H. Goldie and J. T. Dean, op. cit., p. 350 and p. 353. It might be wondered whether the reason for the petition for annexation was drawn up by an anti-King Eyo party who feared Eyo would secure the full paraphernalia of British police, law courts and become a more powerful king.

14   C.O. 147/78, Lister to C.O., 17 July, 1890, encl. and C.O. to F.O., 21 July, 1890.

15   The protectorate was divided into three administrative divisions: Eastern Province—area: 29,056 sq. mls.—capital: Calabar; Central Province—area: 20,564 sq. mls.—capital: Warri; Western Province—area: 27,644 sq. mls.—capital: Lagos. The Eastern province, which was the largest, comprised Akpayafe, Akwa, Calabar, the Cross River and Qua Ibo. E. D. Morel, *Nigeria, its People and its Problems*, p. 63.

16   For more recent studies on the subject, vide J. C. Anene, *Southern Nigeria* et seq.; S. M. Tamuno, op. cit., J. C. Anene, 'The International Boundaries of Nigeria, 1884–1906', unpublished Ph.D. thesis, London, 1960.

17   C.S.O. 1/14, Vol. 1, No. 2, F.O. to Major MacDonald, 18 April, 1891.

18   C. Gertzel, 'John Holt' et seq., p. 298. For Hewett's (and later Johnston's) encounter with Ja Ja, vide ibid., pp. 259ff.

19   H. L. Galwey, 'Nigeria in the Nineties', *J.A.S.*, Vol. 29, No. 115, April, 1930, p. 224.

20   Vide A. E. Afigbo, 'The Warrant Chief System in Eastern Nigeria, 1900–1929', unpublished Ph.D. thesis, Ibadan, September, 1964. Although the Native Political Agents were not referred to in government papers as Warrant Chief there was little difference in their functions.

21   Chief Nicolas Efa Nsa, interview, 17 January, 1966.

22   The private papers of Eyo Eyo Ita (E. E. Offiong III) reveal that though he had extensive commercial dealings with European firms along the coast and with other parts of West Africa, he did not really succeed too well in this respect. But he was certainly an important trader of his time; E. E. Offiong III papers in possession of Chief L. A. Essien Offiong, 10 Edgerley Road, Calabar; also CALPROF 6/3, Vol. 3.

23   There is extant an autobiography (undated) of Coco Bassey among the Coco O. Bassey papers in the private collection of his son, Chief John Coco Bassey of 17, Coco Bassey Street, Calabar. I am indebted to the latter for allowing me to see these papers, and for the interviews of 11 and 15 January, 1966.

24   The E. E. Offiong private papers (Agreement Book A) contains agreements signed to the effect that certain people sold themselves to Coco Bassey in return for support and protection.

25   An application for the appointment made on 24 December, 1898, survives in the E. E. Offiong private papers (Correspondence Book).

26   The grandmother of Joseph Henshaw, another political agent, and the father of Magnus Duke are said to be descended from common parents; Chief Joseph Ewa Henshaw, interview, 6 December, 1965.

27 Joseph Ewa Henshaw, interview, 6 December, 1965. Due to the death of an aunt of Magnus Duke, it has not been possible to trace the papers of Magnus Duke which were in her possession. Magnus Duke's premises at Edet Nsa Street were built in his memory.

28 CALPROF 9/3, Vol. 1, Ani Eniang Offiong Eniang (political agent for Ikpa district) to District Commissioner, Old Calabar, 1 April, 1901, and 28 October, 1901.

29 C.S.O. 1/13, Vol. 2, Moor to C.O., 91, 14 June, 1899.

30 *Protectorate of Southern Nigeria Blue Books, 1904–1906.*

31 E. E. Offiong III private papers (Entry Book), E. E. Offiong III to James Watt, 19 July, 1902.

32 CALPROF 9/2, Vol. 1, R. Moor to Messrs. Elliot and Fry, London, 22 February, 1902.

33 CALPROF 10/3, Vol. 1, 'Old Calabar District—Report for quarter ending June 30th, 1900' by James Watt (Acting District Commissioner).

34 Ibid., 'Report upon Old Calabar District for the quarter ending September 30th' by Watt, dated 29 September, 1900, and 'District Report for the quarter ended 30 September, 1900' by A. A. White-house, dated 23 October, 1900.

35 Ibid.

36 CALPROF 8/1, People of Uyana vs. Effiom Otu Ekon, 27 August, 1897.

37 Ibid., Chief Effiom Otu's abuse of his position of Political Agent at Uwet—memo of 22 November, 1897; R. Moor to District Commissioner, 22 November, 1897; Law Officer to District Commissioner, 20 November, 1897.

38 Imid., Memo from A. A. Whitehouse to R. Moor, 24 November, 1897, and R. Moor to District Commissioner, 25 November, 1897.

39 E. E. Offiong Papers (Entry Book), Memo from the clerk, Native High Court, and Clerk Superintending Minor Courts to Young Egbo Bassey, 18 October, 1898, and the latter's reply, 19 October, 1898.

40 CALPROF 6/3, Vol. 3, King of Idua, Asam Inyan Ete, and chiefs to A. A. Whitehouse, 25 April, 1899. After the death of Daniel Henshaw, there was endless litigation between the Idua and the Henshaws over the disputed land acquisition of Daniel Henshaw. For further details vide the Appeal from the High Court of Calabar to the West African Court of Appeal, Lagos, 1937; the plaintiff was Henry Cobham of Calabar and the defendant was Idiok Une, who represented himself and the people of Uman.

41 CALPROF 6/1, Vol. 4, A. G. Griffith (Ag. District Commissioner) to Major H. L. Gallwey (Ag. Consul General), 26 July, 1898, encl. 1, Obong Eyo Honesty VIII and his chiefs to A. G. Griffith, 22 July, 1898.

42 CALPROF 8/1, Gallwey to E. E. Effiong III, Memo of 5 August, 1898, and reply, E. E. Effiong III to Gallwey, 9 August, 1898.

43 C.S.O. 1/13, Vol. 6, No. 36, Moor to F.O., 5 May, 1896.

44 Ibid., Vol. 2, No. 80, Moor to C.O., 30 May, 1899.

45 It is interesting to note that the head and chiefs of Calabar (who had formed themselves into an Efik National Committee by the turn of the century) complained about Major Sampson's high-handed measures towards African rulers; E. E. Offiong private papers (Letters' Entry Book), Head and chiefs of Old Calabar to R. Moor, 10 January, 1902.

46   For a short history of this road, vide P. A. Talbot, *Life in Southern Nigeria*, pp. 256–71.
47   Ibid., p. 266.
48   Cf. S. M. Tamuno, op. cit., pp. 375–76.
49   CALPROF 6/1, Vol. 2, A. A. Whitehouse to Moor, 15 September, 1895. Bedwell, another European agent, and his party were attacked by Npok Town, Qua Ibo River, during the execution of their duties; CALPROF 8/2, Vol. 1, H. Bedwell to Capt. H. L. Gallwey, 18 September, 1896; and CALPROF 5/8, Vol. 3, Regina vs. King Ofon of Ukpok, 2 October, 1896.
50   P. A. Talbot, *Life in Southern Nigeria*, pp. 265–69.
51   Vide S. M. Tamuno, op. cit., p. 60; F.O. 2/84, MacDonald to Salisbury, 12 July, 1895, incl. 5; and F.O. 2/100, Moor to Sir Clement Hill (private), 19 April, 1896.
52   It was made under the Native Courts Proclamation, 1901, and published in Gazette, No. 1 of 31 January, 1903. For a reproduction of the rule vide the 'Intelligence Report on the Calabar Division with special reference to the Efik clan' by N. Mylius, C.S.O. 26/3, file 27627, Vol. 1, Appendix D.
53   Vide *The Hart Report*, p. 74.
54   In September, 1903, for instance, the chiefs of Duke Town wrote to the editor of the *Old Calabar Observer* objecting to the political agent, Daniel Henshaw, referring to himself as Obong. As head of Henshaw Town, he was not entitled to the use of Obong which was reserved for the supreme heads of Duke Town and Creek Town; E. E. Offiong private papers (Letters' Entry Book), letter to editor of *Old Calabar Observer*, 5 September, 1902, encl. in Duke Town chiefs to District Commissioner, 15 October, 1902. The title Obong attached to Henshaw appeared in the *Observer* et seq. of 1 September, 1902, Vol. 1, No. 4, p. 28.
55   For a discussion of the diversity of interpretation that may be attached to those qualified to elect an Obong under the terms of the rulers referred to, vide *The Hart Report*, pp. 99–106.
56   Vide T. N. Tamuno, 'Native House Rule of Southern Nigeria', *Nigeria Magazine*, No. 93, June, 1957, pp. 162ff.
57   F.O. 84/1940, MacDonald to F.O., 12 June, 1889, and incl.
58   C.S.O. 1/13, Vol. 5, Moor to F.O., 25 December, 1895.
59   C.S.O. 1/16, Vol. 3, J. Chamberlain to Officer Administering the Government of Southern Nigeria (Confid.), 20 August, 1901, encl. R. Moor to C.O. (Confid.), 7 July, 1901.
60   C.S.O. 1/15, Vol. 2, No. 9, Moor to C.O. (Confid.), 14 September, 1901.
61   C.O. 588/1, No. 26 of 1901. It was made an ordinance after 1908.
62   *Annual Report on Southern Nigeria for 1901* (Colonial Reports, No. 381, Cd., 1388) cited in A. C. Burns, op. cit., p. 220.
63   M. Perham, *Native Administration in Nigeria*, p. 30.
64   'Topping' was a trade tax. After a trader had served a probationary period of three to five years, during which time he traded for his master, he was allowed to trade for himself. But he had to pay a tax to his master. This was normally ten shillings per puncheon of oil, four shillings per cask of kernel, or fifty per cent on the articles sold.
65   *Nigerian Times*, 16 August, 1910. 'The Southern Nigeria Slavery Ordinance' was the title of its leader for this issue.

66   E. D. Morel, *Nigeria, its Peoples and its Problems*, pp. 62–63.
67   Omin Iso vs. Okon Akan, 7 May, 1903, before the 'Native' Council of
     Calabar, 'Judgement Book, Native Council of Calabar' (available at
     the Calabar Customary Court).
68   Iquo Duke Henshaw vs. Efana Anwan, 8 May, 1903, before the 'Native'
     Council of Calabar, ibid.
69   C.O. 588/1, No. 12 of 1903, 'Masters and Servants Proclamation'. It
     amended the original 'Masters and Servants Proclamation' of 1901.
70   C.S.O. 1/13, Vol. 18, No. 83, Moor to C.O., 26 February, 1902.
71   C.O. 588/1, No. 15 of 1903, 'Roads and Creeks Proclamation'.
72   Vide T. N. Tamuno, 'Native House Rule' et seq., p. 164ff.
73   C.O. 588/1, No. 5 of 1903, clauses 3 and 4.
74   E. E. Offiong private papers, 'Agreement between Chiefs Edim Ebana
     of Qua Town and Niger Coast Protectorate, 28 June, 1894' (Agree-
     ment Book A).
75   Ibid., 'Agreement between Chief Okon Etim Asiya Adim of Old
     Town and Commissioner and Consul General, 10 August, 1895' (Agree-
     ment Book A).
76   Ibid., 'Agreement between Chief Etim Ebana of Qua Town and
     H.B.M. Government, 10 August, 1895' (Agreement Book A).
77   Ibid., 'Agreement between E. E. Offiong IV and Ulrick Peterson of
     Berlin, 13 December, 1898' (Agreement Book A).
78   The colonial administration, in its local government policy, thought
     that the courts system was a means of enabling educated Africans to
     govern themselves, dispense justice and establish peace and order;
     C.O. 520/18, Moor to C.O., 7 January, 1903. It also made for a
     reduction in the prohibitive costs entailed in establishing a full judicial
     system.
79   G. I. Jones, 'From Direct to Indirect Rule in Eastern Nigeria', *ODU*,
     Vol. 2, No. 2, January, 1966, p. 75.
80   CALPROF 8/2, Vol. 1, A. G. Griffith, Acting District Commissioner,
     to R. Moor, 16 June, 1896.
81   CALPROF 10/3, Vol. 1, 'Report upon the work of the Native Courts
     of the Old Calabar District during the year ending March 31st, 1900',
     dated 31 July, 1900, by J. Watt.
82   CALPROF 10/3, Vol. 1, 'Old Calabar District—Report for quarter
     ending June 30th, 1900' by James Watt; CALPROF 10/3, Vol. 6,
     'Administrative Report' by J. Watt, District Commissioner, Old Cala-
     bar, dated 1 April, 1903. Also, *Annual Report of the Niger Coast
     Protectorate for 1897–98*, Africa No. 2, January, 1899, (C—1924) by
     H. L. Gallwey.
83   CALPROF 8/2, (Vol. 1), A. G. Griffith to R. Moor, 16 June, 1896.
84   E. E. Offiong III private papers (Entry Book), E. E. Offiong III
     to the District Commissioner, n.d. (possibly early 1902); see also
     CALPROF 6/3, Vol. 2, Efiom Ama to District Commissioner, 4
     April, 1898. Both letters speak of non-compliance with court orders.
85   For studies of the constitution and variety of these courts vide J. C.
     Anene, *Southern Nigeria* et. seq., Chapter 7; Tamuno, op. cit., pp.
     86–100; A. E. Afigbo, op. cit., pp. 100ff and passim. Also C.O. 588/1.
     The Supreme Court, Criminal Procedure, Commissioners, Native
     Courts Proclamation Nos. 6, 7, 8 and 9 respectively of 1900.
86   For details, and for the difficulties encountered in distinguishing,
     from government gazettes, between traditional chiefs and 'warrant'

chiefs, see Tamuno, op. cit., p. 96. In 1902 the sub-chiefs of Henshaw Town objected to certain members being elected as members of the 'Native' Council; CALPROF 9/3, Vol. 2, Sub-Chiefs of Henshaw Town to District Commissioner, 25 April, 1902.

87   H. Goldie and J. T. Dean, op. cit., p. 352.

88   Ibid., also A. C. Burns, op. cit., p. 271.

89   C.S.O. 1/13, Vol. 29, No. 154, Egerton to C.O., 11 April, 1904, encl., 'Annual Report on the Cross River Division for the year ended 31st March, 1904' by A. B. Harcourt; also, CALPROF 9/2, Vol. 2, Moor to Divisional Commissioner, Cross River Division, 22 May, 1902.

90   Vide H. J. M. Harding, 'Intelligence Report on the Oku, Mbiabo and Ayadegbe Clans, Enyong Division', dated 19 October, 1832; C.S.O. 26/3, file No. 28862.

91   In the private papers of E. E. Offiong III, there were three statements of 'native laws and customs', one relating to Calabar adultery law, dated 3 March, 1900, another relating to Calabar marriage law and custom, dated 4 August, 1904. They were all drawn up presumably either by the 'Native' High Court, Calabar, or by a body known as the 'Efik National Committee'.

The punishments to be inflicted upon offenders, however, seem to have been fairly regularly established in Calabar, vide Judgement Book of Ison-inyan court (near Itu), 1898, which states the court procedure of the 'Native' Council of Calabar and some of the regulations governing it (dated 7 March, 1898). These and other records may be seen at the Customary Court of Calabar. I am indebted to Chief L. A. Essien Offiong, a member of the Calabar Customary Court, who translated the judgement books from Efik to English.

92   T. O. Elias, *Government and Politics in Africa*, and ibid., *Nature of African Customary Law* (Manchester, 1956).

93   J. S. Coleman, *Nigeria: background to nationalism*, p. 170.

94   Examples of the scale of punishment given here are based on the regulations governing the Esop (Court) Ison-inyan (near Itu) contained in the records kept at the Customary Court of Calabar, op. cit.

95   The number of departments that were established was certainly an imposing list. One writer remarked that in the early days there were about as many departments as there were individuals in the service; A. N. Cook, *British Enterprise in Nigeria*, p. 70.

VII

The New Economic Forces, 1885–1906

Until the last two decades of the nineteenth century European political, economic and missionary contact had only marginal significance to the peoples beyond the coastal fringes of Calabar. No doubt the European traders and their firms had consistently attempted to break the monopoly of the Efik middlemen and gain direct access to the rich palm producing belt but these efforts had been forestalled by the Efik political authority on the coast—which was declining in its efficacy through the century. Had it succumbed to British commercial pressure to open the trade of the river to all alike and permitted European intrusion into the hinterland the position of the middlemen kings would have been grossly undermined by European economic forces. In the 1880s and the decades that followed the colonial administration renewed its determined efforts to break the control of the Efik trading chiefs over the traditional middleman system and to extend its political control to the rich hinterland. These efforts were bound to have the largest economic and social consequences because political penetration into the hinterland went hand in glove with a breakthrough into interior markets.

Dynamics of relations between Calabar and the hinterland
It is worthwhile to begin the story by examining the dynamics of the relations between Calabar and its hinterland. The hinterland that is being referred to here may be defined as including the lineage plantations of Akpabuyo and Odukpani, the country known as Ibibio which for a long time traded its produce through Calabar, and most important of all the Cross River area which covered as much as a sixth of the total area of Eastern Nigeria and which was noted for its rich palm and other agricultural produce. We shall in this chapter be concerned largely with the Cross River area.

Calabar was the natural port for the produce of its Cross River hinterland. The Efik in Calabar set themselves up as the middlemen in this trade and derived their wealth from the trade of the water highway rather than as landowners, producers or manufacturers which was only of secondary importance.[1] In this respect they controlled land and river rights at Calabar and exploited the competition between European firms to inflate the prices.

It would however be erroneous to draw from the fact that the Efik controlled the trade of the coast the conclusion that Calabar exercised control over the interior markets in the Cross River area. In this respect it ought to be pointed out that the commercial relationship between Calabar and its Cross River hinterland differed in one important respect from that between the Delta states of Warri, Bonny, Brass and their hinterlands. Unlike the Delta states, Calabar did not exercise extensive control over its Cross River hinterland. No doubt some of the Cross River towns which had purchased the titles of the Calabar Ekpe order had theoretically close relations with the metropolitan towns of the coast. But this state of relations belonged to the period before the protectorate administration came into effective being. Once the protectorate administration truncated the legislative and executive powers of the Ekpe and erected in its place the 'native' councils, the influence of the traditional fraternity was virtually destroyed. There was no other element in the social structure of Calabar which gave it any semblance of authority over the hinterland.

On more than one occasion Calabar had to learn the hard lesson that it could not necessarily extend political authority to those areas which were under its cultural influence. The office of kingship did not confer effective or centralized authority over such areas; if anything tradition dictated the areas of jurisdiction of each Efik king. It was on the strength of the tradition that the effective jurisdiction of the Calabar kings did not extend beyond the coastal towns, the dependencies and the kingship lineage farms, that Adiabo rejected the enforcement of missionary reforms on them by Calabar. It is perhaps not entirely untrue to suggest that traditions of this nature could be invoked by the Cross River towns if it was economically expedient to do so at any particular point of time. For example, in the 1880s, feelings had run high between an Enyong village and Umon over what was ostensibly a criminal offence. An Umon man had been caught and killed in an Enyong village, which lay between Calabar and Umon. Enyong charged a Calabar man with the deed, thus causing Umon to seize and threaten to behead some Calabar men. At that time Umon held a large quantity of European goods in trust from Calabar traders, and it is not impossible that it was thought a convenient opportunity for obliterating the debts by exterminating Calabar creditors.[2] Thus, even before Ekpe was reduced to mere ritual significance by the British administration, there was already a movement by some of the Cross River towns to reduce the authority that the Calabar towns tried to exert upon them.

It is also untrue to suggest that the Efik waxed powerful and wealthy because they seldom took risks as British firms did when they advanced capital to the Efik traders. The Efik were in exactly the same position as the European firms. Since the interior markets were not effectively controlled by Calabar any trust payment made in the interior markets by the Efik middlemen contained an element of risk which could not be overlooked. The European firms provided the global capital for all Calabar, but they did not continue to back individual traders who did not invest trusts profitably. Efik traders who borrowed capital from the European mercantile capitalists sometimes found that although they could buy the produce of the interior at low prices, they lost on the transaction if unpredictable price fluctuations at the coast forced them to sell the produce at lower than anticipated prices. At other times, Efik traders who had given trust in the interior discovered that their profits were lower than they had originally expected. Similarly, European traders, who hoped to buy cheaply in Calabar and sell at a high price in England, found, too, that when they arrived in England price fluctuations in the English markets worked against them. It was hence possible for both Efik and European traders to get into bad debt if market conditions altered unfavourably for them.

Thirdly, it must be realized that just as Calabar had hardly any territorial authority over the Cross River towns, the latter, too, had no legal jurisdiction over Calabar. It might have been imagined that this hinterland, large, productive and populous as it was, might have been able to exert the weight of its power over the port. This was not the case. The Cross River country was not a single, homogeneous, political unity but a multiplicity of towns which vied with each other for control over parts of the river.

Each Cross River town retained its own areas of monopoly and warded off intruders, both African and European. For most of their history they were rivals in trade; and traditional political bonds, as it were, had worn thin during the boom period of European trade. The upriver peoples had their own commercial code, they raided Calabar canoes and made Efik traders pay tolls. The Akunakuna of the Aweyong tributary of the upper Cross River traded their produce with the Umon; the Umon in their turn traded with Enyong further down river, and the Enyong traded with the

Efik at the mouth of the river. The African commercial system in the Cross River, therefore, involved not a single, but multiple, groups of middlemen each of whom was a link in the chain of trade going down the river.

It is necessary to understand the complex ethnic heterogenity, the non-existence of large politically cohesive groups and the sturdy independence of each of the larger trading towns of the Cross River in order to see why it was that when Calabar easily succumbed to British political control the hinterland resisted colonial dominaation. Unlike the Itsekiri country, for instance, where the detention of the powerful Nana created a political vacuum and allowed the hinterland not only to degenerate into a free-for-all 'scramble', but to be brought under the European thumb, Calabar was in a somewhat different situation. In the latter instance, each Cross River town had to be independently brought under British control, more often than not by the direct imposition of British power. This meant that only through the exercise of force could the British control the links in the chain of middlemen.

Extension of the frontiers of British commerce

The predominant concern of the British government in the decades following the 1880s was substantially to increase the volume and value of British trade with West Africa. This meant, so far as Calabar was concerned, that the commerce hitherto transacted at the port of Calabar would be extended to the hinterland of that state. When therefore Consul Hewett was appointed to his office in 1882, his primary duty which was defined as the promotion of trade was interpreted not merely as meaning the maintenance of peace in the Cross River but the stimulation of British trade with the interior of Calabar.

At first the task of extending the frontiers of British commerce to the hinterland was left to individual British traders or trading firms. In 1883 John Holt approached Harry Hartze to 'make treaties and acquire concessions' in Calabar and up the Cross River, on behalf of the African Association.[3] It was feared that if territorial and trading rights in this region were not secured rapidly enough other commercial interests would compete with them for the same. Hartze was to win over the Calabar chiefs with the promise that European traders would not trade in the immediate markets of Calabar, but in the markets that lay beyond the town of Umon on the Cross River. In December, 1883 Hartze issued a notice to Henshaw III and other chiefs of Henshaw Town indicating his intention to open the Cross River to trade and to build trading stations at each market.[4] He requested Henshaw III to allow him

the hire of a beach where he could store his produce while awaiting shipment. Henshaw, like other Efik middlemen of the coast,
was opposed to any European commercial intrusion into the interior and presumably refused to accede to the request. Indeed as
we have seen earlier, Henshaw had himself been interested in the
opening of the Qua Ibo country to trade and had collaborated with
Watts to achieve that objective. In April, 1884 Holt began to entertain the idea of a chartered company for the Bights.[5] The proposal
received the sympathetic attention of Hewett who suggested an
amalgamation of all the trading firms in the river which would
make it easier for them to request an Oil Rivers Charter. Had
this grandiose scheme not fallen through it would have operated
against the spirit of the free trade principle enunciated by the
British in that year. It would have meant the British breaking the
middleman system in the name of free trade and reserving that
trade for British traders alone. But the danger of this abuse of free
trade was postponed rather than checked as later events were to
indicate.

In the early 1890s the manner in which the frontiers of British
commerce were to be extended underwent a change. The intensity
of the opposition unleashed by the Efik middlemen to their replacement by British merchants and trading stations was too great
for individual traders or firms. It was natural that the Efik middlemen would be hostile to British traders who sought to penetrate
the closely-guarded treasure houses and undermine the position of
African traders and interfere with marketing arrangements. Mac-
Donald, in his report of 1889, had put forward the view that British
traders could extend the frontiers of commerce 'and civilization'
into the interior country only if British officials protected them.
MacDonald's idea was to utilize the powers of the various middlemen to open up the country while British officials ensured the
protection of the trade. It was not at all an easy matter to win
over the chiefs to MacDonald's policy of pacific expansion and
the development of trade through the cultivation of friendship
with the chiefs.

It became clear that in the circumstances a modification of the
policy of pacific expansion of trade was urgently required. Political
penetration into the hinterland had to precede the advance of
European traders. With the establishment in 1891 of an Oil Rivers
Protectorate administration under MacDonald and the consequent
movement of the centre of effective political power away from the
Efik middlemen-kings to the British administration, the way was
paved for radical changes to be effected. The new administration,
armed with greater powers than the previous one, was directed to

look towards the hinterland by penetrating beyond the seaboard. Travelling commissioners, vice-consuls and African political agents (the most notable of whom was Coco Otu Bassey) were appointed to establish contact with the people of the Cross River towns, to search and assess the latent commercial resources and assert British authority in areas of strategic economic interest. The hinterland, which had remained a country sealed to the outside world, was to be visited by traders and officials alike and MacDonald himself went up the Cross River in 1893 to settle a dispute.[6]

Much of course was dependent upon the temperament and outlook of specific British officers, especially the vice-consuls who were on the spot. One of the most well known of the vice-consuls and whose contribution towards the promotion of commerce must be emphasized was Mary Slessor, the missionary who became popularly known as the 'White Queen of Okoyong'. Owing to her unique position and influence among the Okoyong, she was made a vice-consul in 1892 with powers to organize and supervise a 'native' court. We shall be concerned here only with her work as a government agent at Okoyong and with her role in promoting the commercial life of the Okoyong.

It is important to note that Mary Slessor differed from other British vice-consuls in that she was motivated by the social rather than economic benefits of trade. She had long been interested in trade matters even before she became a government agent, and as a missionary she felt that if the Okoyong became successful traders, they would be able to overcome their isolation from Calabar and 'be civilized'. She saw that an increase in trade would work towards peace by creating interdependence among ethnic communities and overcoming the isolation engendered by parochialism. Improvements in communication resulting from a proliferation of the trade network would enlarge the area of individual freedom, and limit the exercise of absolute rule once the rulers knew the liberating effect of the cash nexus. Increased prosperity, Mary Slessor believed, would identify the gospel with temporal advancement, and thus increase its attractiveness.

The trade barrier between Calabar and Okoyong had done little to encourage friendly relations between the two peoples. The Okoyong lived in very hilly country intersected by small streams, palm trees were fairly numerous but scattered through the bush; the people farmed for their own needs and little or no farm produce was sold, though some palm oil and kernels were sold in Calabar.[7] Mary Slessor attempted to break the isolation of the Okoyong by fostering in them an interest in trade, and by appealing to Efik traders in Calabar to bring acticles of trade up to Okoyong.[8] King

Eyo VII of Creek Town invited the suspicious chiefs of Okoyong to a palaver in his town and opened trade with Okoyong. Oil and kernels were sold in Calabar in return for European goods which were sent to the Okoyong. Missionaries like Slessor aided the efforts of the British Government to open inland countries such as Okoyong to the Efik at the coast. Trade from the Upper Cross River undoubtedly began to pass through Okoyong freely, but it is not known exactly what the increase in trade might have been.

What is not often emphasized, but explains subsequent events in the Cross River towns after the breakdown of the trade barriers, is that British attempts to control areas of strategic economic importance involved a substantial loss of revenue for the heads of the interior towns. Tolls could no longer be collected by the chiefs. The chiefs who had to resort to other forms of earning not only revenue but also a livelihood began to move further inland. In Okoyong, for instance, Slessor found in 1895 that the population was diminishing.[9]

The most plausible hypothesis is that the Okoyong were moving to richer agricultural lands elsewhere in order to earn a better living. A new market was opened at Akpap, further inland and nearer to the Cross River. Farms and villages grew up around the town. Slessor and the mission station were forced to move away from the old site to Akpap and Ikoneto (six miles away from Akpap) respectively. Henceforth, Akpap became the trading centre of the Okoyong. The occupation by the Okoyong of Akpap began an era of boundary disputes with the Ikoneto.[10] The Ikoneto and Okoyong had never been on friendly terms, and in September, 1867 they had waged war on each other. Calabar, resolved to reduce Okoyong to a dependency of hers, had in that year obtained its surrender by force.[11] Mary Slessor had encouraged trade between the two enemies—Calabar and Okoyong—to reduce their hostility.

It may be queried whether the missionaries, traders and government officials were opening up the country and breaking down 'tribal barriers of fear and prejudice' as they believed, or were in fact producing a new set of political combination. In any case, they seemed hardly to have taken into account the injurious effect that their actions might precipitate. The abolition of tolls, which the new trade system involved, undermined the power of the leading chiefs of the river who were naturally reluctant to open their towns to trade with Europeans and desisted from doing so as long as it was possible to hold out against the Europeans. The result was the continual recurrence of palavers and petty hostilities which interrupted the trade of the river. What accounted for the interruption in trade was the frequent blockades of the river by the middlemen chiefs who exacted tolls from vessels passing through their towns. These chiefs were not willing to stand by and see their economic and political fortunes swept away in the tide of a British forward movement.

Trade in the 1890s

The respective attitudes of the British government and the Efik merchant princes of the period are explained by the general state of trade in Calabar in the 1890s. Although the trade figures relating specifically to Calabar are not available, the trend may be assumed to reflect the total trade position of the Protectorate which, except for certain peak years, did not show any steep rise in the annual value of the trade:[12]

NIGER COAST PROTECTORATE

Year	Imports £	Exports £	Total Trade £	Revenue £	Expenditure £
1891–92 (half year)	295,529	269,238	564,767		
1892–93	729,890	843,500	1,573,390		
1893–94	929,333	1,014,089	1,943,420		
1894–95	739,864	825,099	1,564,963		
1895–96	750,975	844,333	1,595,308	155,513	145,044
1896–97	655,978	785,603	1,441,583	122,441	128,411
1897–98	639,698	750,223	1,389,921	153,181	121,901
1898–99	732,640	774,648	1,507,288	169,568	146,752
1899–1900	725,798	888,955	1,614,753	164,108	176,140

The outlook for trade in the early colonial period was therefore not good, although not entirely bleak. H. H. Johnston, who went to Calabar in about 1886, described it thus: 'Old Calabar in those times was sufficiently prosperous and the firms trading there sufficiently enlightened not only to maintain for their employees well built, bright, well furnished houses, but to support a first-class doctor, who rose in time to be Principal Medical Officer of the Protectorate'.[13] The British government had entertained the hope that the development of West Africa would attract British capital and that the Protectorate would provide an outlet for the desire of the British wealthy classes for investment overseas. This hope was based on the fact that the profits on British capital in England at that time were low. But the prices for palm oil available for the 1880s and 1890s suggest a series of fluctuations as the following selling prices per ton in Liverpool indicate:[14]

PALM OIL PRICES (LIVERPOOL)

1881	Apr.	£30 10s.	1889	Aug.	£22 15s.
1885	Dec.	£22	1890	Nov.	£24 15s.
1886	Jan.	£23	1891	Mar.	£24 10s.
	Mar.	£20		Nov.	£22 10s.
	Apr.	£19	1893	Aug.	£24
	May	£18 10s.	1895	Apr.	£20
1887	Apr.	£18	1896	Apr.	£18 10s.
1888	Oct.	£21 10s.			

It is thus not difficult to see that the colonial administration was interested in making concerted attempts to push the traders up the river, ostensibly to neutralize the palm producing areas in the name of 'free trade' and cause an abundant flow of oil direct to the river terminals at Calabar. The British could also, by outlawing the middleman system, control the system so that it was made to operate in favour of the British.

MacDonald's policy for peaceful expansion and the development of commerce through courting the friendship of the middlemen kings had now to give way to a new and more vigorous policy. It was not sufficient, from the British point of view, merely to despatch small expeditions in all directions to explain the aims and objects of the government, set up courts in the hope of establishing confidence between the different peoples and facilitate the course of trade, pay attention to the opening of land trade routes to the waterways and markets[15] and appoint travelling commissioners to act as 'feelers' for the British administration.[16] While these were important and had to go on, other and more vigorous steps were being contemplated by the British administration.

Punitive expeditions

The man who spearheaded the change in British policy was R. D. R. Moor, who was High Commissioner and Consul General of the Oil River and the Niger Coast Protectorate for various periods from 1892 to 1900. Moor's administration came to the conclusion that Efik economic resistance could be effectively subdued only if the British resorted to forcible intervention in the trading mechanism. Efik resistance had to be met by British military action and Moor believed in the effectiveness of punitive expeditions as a means of achieving the goal he had in mind. Punitive expeditions became part and parcel of the mechanism to establish and consolidate British control in the hinterland. Side by side with the setting up of administrative and judicial apparatus by Roger Casement and others (such as at Itu, Unwana, Okoyong and Uwet), a build-up of force was considered necessary at several strategic points. A constabulary force was raised with headquarters at Calabar and barracks located at Itu, Ekanem Essien and Uwet. The force was placed at the disposal of the consuls and was to be deployed whenever the need arose; it was this force which was used in the various punitive expeditions undertaken by Moor. The two areas where the nature and effects of the punitive expeditions were best seen were (a) Ibibioland, Qua Ibo up to Itu, and (b) the Cross River area.

(a) *Ibibioland, Qua Ibo up to Itu*

European consular agents had for many years been interested in journeying beyond the upper waters of the Qua Ibo in order to open up trade routes into the Ibibio interior. Ibibio country was known for its superior soft palm oil most of which had been evacuated originally through Calabar. The Ibibio oil trade was exceedingly profitable. Efforts were made by the British government in the 1890s to march from the Cross River to Itu, through the Inokun country to the upper waters of the Opobo River, but these often met with the sturdy resistance of the Ibibio. Though perfectly willing to welcome European travellers into their country, the Ibibio did not take kindly to the idea of European traders upsetting the economic organization and adversely affecting their economic livelihood. In 1895, consular agent A. A. Whitehouse reported that the Nensai people, whom he met on the upper waters of the Qua Ibo, allowed European traders no further than their town.[17] The Nensai chiefs were evidently fearful of the harmful effects it would have on their trade if they consented to throw open to others the creek leading to the upper river. In the following year they permitted nothing more than an exploration of the creek.[18]

The traditional practice, of the towns strategically located on the trade routes, of raising revenue by the levy of tolls on trade passing through them continued in spite of the opposition of the British. Some of the less viable towns might more readily have surrendered to the technological superiority of British arms than resisted advance, but it must be remembered that these weaker towns were often at the mercy of the larger and more powerful towns which were determined to forestall British penetration. Two examples may be mentioned to illustrate the situation. The chief of a Qua Ibo district called Issiet was known to make a practice of interrupting the trade passing through his town to the beach. The British government, upon investigation, was flabbergasted to discover that the traders most affected, the M'buta, were afraid to admit that their trade was interrupted or taxed.[19]

The Eket people too, were quite willing to befriend the British and allow them passage through their country into the interior. But they were threatened and intimidated by the Obium, whose country bordered very closely on Eket. The result was the British expeditions of February and March, 1906, resulting in the destruction of several Eket farms and compounds.[20] Hence the towns which seemed to offer resistance to British inland penetration could not as a rule be said to have done so by their own voluntary decision.

Where middlemen offered stiff resistance to British ideas of re-organizing trade the result invariably was the destruction of the town. The Qua Ibo chief, king of N'pok, for instance, violently attacked the government and found himself captured in a punitive expedition and imprisoned for seven years.[21] By such stern measures it was hoped the roads between the Cross and the Opobo rivers would eventually be opened, and the entire tract of country in that direction brought under effective British control.[22] Ibibio reaction to British moves continued, however, to be characterized by a spirit of unrest. As Divisional Commissioner Gallwey put it in a semi-official despatch to the High Commissioner: [23]

> The practice of calling chiefs to meetings, and then seizing them, and of calling in guns to mark and then destroying them had resulted in general distrust of the government and its policy.

Amaury Talbot, relating the experiences of British officials and African political agents engaged in opening up Ibibio land to European trade, provides an interesting account of the resistance met with by the exploratory teams.[24]

There is little doubt that the principal fear entertained by the middlemen chiefs was that the 'opening' of Ibibio land to Europeans spelled the end of a profitable revenue originating from the trade of the river. Thus, while middlemen were ready even to go so far as to welcome individual European traders, like John Harford who opened a station at Qua Ibo following favourable assurance that his trade would be secure, they were not willing to surrender to the British administration their legitimate sovereign rights.

Not only were the Ibibio concerned about the consequences of European economic intrusion into their country but in addition they had to be on guard against the commercial ambitions of the Efik. The relations between the Ibibio and the Efik had not been entirely cordial. In 1895 the town of Itu, situated on the fringe of Ibibio country and inhabited by a large number of peoples of Efik origin, was raided by the Ibibio from Use and Edidep. About forty to fifty settlers were slain and the rest driven off.[25] Those killed included not only Efik but also Itu, Enyong and Umon traders, and numbered about fifteen. Itu was reinstated with the aid of a trained armed force under Vice-Consul Gallwey and a band of Efik irregulars led by the political agent, Coco Bassey. Calabar kings Archibong and King Duke also came to rescue Itu from Ibibio terror.

The friction between the Ibibio and the Efik might be analysed in terms of the economic and social relationship between the two peoples. The Ibibio were oil producers and the Efik, as the middlemen in the transaction, thrived on the profits accruing from the sale of Ibibio oil. The Ibibio were naturally resentful of a relationship in which they were always the losing partner and were desirous of marketing the oil by themselves. Itu had throughout its history presented the picture of a small, but highly successful group which by reason of its commanding situation and association with the slave and later oil trade had become greatly influential in the region. A very large number of traders at Itu were of Efik origin, and the Efik at Calabar in their determination to keep the trade in their hands for as long as possible encouraged the Itu to think that Europeans were good for them.[26] To complicate matters further, there were in fact groups within Ibibio land, such as the Ikot Obong, who were friendly to the Efik and to Itu and who, in 1895, assisted in keeping back the unfriendly Ibibio. Some of the inland peoples were anxious to drive away the Ikot Obong in order to make a path to the riverside. Naturally, the Ikot Obong were friendly to Itu and to Calabar.[27]

Whatever the confused circumstances of the attack on Itu, it is clear that the Ibibio were prepared to defend their trading rights and destroy those of others. In Ibibio land, as in the Cross River, very little of the country had been 'pacified' by the turn of the century. At Itu, the number of European traders remained small. After the Aro expedition of 1902, a few Europeans arrived on the scene. They opened their first factory, Russells, at Okopedi in 1903; in 1905 and 1906 Miller Brothers and the African Association opened other stations at Itu.[28]

(b) The Cross River[29]

The British position in the Cross River towns did not differ greatly from that in Ibibio land. The country was far more productive than Ibibio land in natural resources. The upper Cross River lay in the belt of the richest palm-producing country in that part of the Protectorate. Palm oil and kernels were the basis of the economy; on the banks of nearly every stream, deep enough for a canoe, could be seen puncheons both empty and full, large boiling pots and canoes. Besides oil and kernels, the people also grew a whole series of staple crops such as yams, cassava, coco yams and maize. Plantain trees were planted round every house while other crops such as fruits and vegetables were also grown. Cocoa was grown in patches here and there on the banks of the Cross River. Though it was grown in parts of the Oku and Uman country, the important cocoa growing centre was at Ikot Offiong on the Cross River.[30] It was felt to be of the utmost urgency to the colonial administration that this rich agricultural tract of land be brought under British control and the trade in agricultural produce be regulated so as to favour British commerce.

The great link between Calabar and the upper waters of the Cross River was the water highway. A series of government stations were established at strategic points along this highway. A gunboat, the *Jackdaw*, was used not only for the carriage of passengers, mails and stores but also for the patrol of the river from Calabar to the Anglo-German boundary.[31] But in the dry season the gunboat was useless beyond Itu. Apart from the *Jackdaw*, government-owned steam launches and steel canoes[32] were also used to penetrate into regions fed by creeks from the main river. It was hoped that in this way effective British authority would be exercised over the entire hinterland once the rivers had been opened to European trade. To secure the latter aim, a series of punitive expeditions were undertaken against those who resisted the idea of throwing open their country to European commercial designs.

The first of these major expeditions in the Cross River was against Ediba in early 1895. Though the town was shelled, British aims were far from being achieved. Ediba refused to attend a palaver called by the British to discuss the causes of the bombardment of the town. Instead, the people called out to the African agent who had come to convey the message: 'We hear you and see the Consul go back and tell him our answer is NO if you come again we shall fire on you'.[33] Though eventually Ediba and the other Ikomorut towns made their peace, and undertook not to cause any further disturbances or stop trade in the river, they did not have the slightest intention of honouring their promises. As soon as the detachment of troops with the two officers stationed at Unwana were withdrawn in November, 1895, and the water in the river fell, Ediba commenced to seize trade canoes and traders passing up river. In 1896 both Umon and Ediba were again destroyed; Umon, it was alleged, was supplying arms and ammunition through Ikon to the Ediba. Two patrol canoes, with eighteen

armed men in each, were placed on the river at Ebom and at Iti-
gidi, both of which were close to Ediba. The canoes of traders
were convoyed up and down by these patrol canoes. Ediba continued to attack these canoes, several of whose occupants were
from time to time killed or wounded.[34]

Ediba was considered to be a convenient point for the establishment of a permanent British post from which to open up the
country around the Upper Cross River. Once communications
were opened with the Afikpo and Inokun peoples, it was optimisti-
cally hoped that matters would be judiciously handled and lead
eventually to the opening up of those areas to British trade. A
political officer, a medical officer, and a force officer with at least
fifty troops, were to be stationed at Ediba.

But a little distance beyond Ediba, serious difficulties had arisen
in 1896 and 1897 owing to a combination of four peoples—the
Ibo, Arun, Asiga and Ekuri—preventing the people in the interior
coming down to trade at the waterside. The Ibo fell upon the
traders—amongst them were the Nko, Ugep and others—and
slaughtered nineteen of the Nko.[35] The waterside people found it
profitable to go to the inland towns and purchase the produce at
their own price and subsequently sell it at inflated prices at
the riverside. This practice was a violation of the official British
declaration that trade routes and waterways were to remain free
'to all traders'.

A punitive expedition to open the interior routes to European
traders and to punish the offending towns was mounted in January,
1898. The Ekuri held out against the British for as long as possible;
the fighting that ensued was severe.[36] The losses to the Ekuri were
about 309 killed, including two sons of the head chief.[37] The British
now declared the country to the east of the Cross River freely
open to European trade. Earlier, in September and October, 1895,
a considerable force had gone up the Cross River to deal with
troubles in the Afikpo, Ikomurut and Igbo countries, and higher up
in Obubura. Ediba, as we have noted, was destroyed during this
expedition. A heavy blow had been dealt to the new middlemen—
the Arun, Asiga, Ekuri and others—who had emerged along the
banks of the river and established markets for inland produce. But
the way in which these middlemen had set up their trade rendered
the work of the two expeditions in 1895 and 1896 entirely futile. It
also indicated the hostile and truculent attitude of the Upper Cross
River traders to British intervention and commercial designs. One
result of the punitive expeditions in the Cross River was that they
created further unrest and bitterness among the people.

It must also be noted that it was not merely the palm oil producers but also growers of other agricultural primary products who expressed hostility against European economic penetration. For example, the Eastern Ibo, who inhabited large areas of the western bank of the Cross River (for instance Afikpo, particularly Ezza) and parts of Aro Obubura, and who were renowned food-crop farmers, growing yam, cassava, coco yams, maize, peppers, beans, okra, gourds and other subsidiary crops, were hostile towards European intrusion. Some surplus palm oil was exported through Calabar[38] from these areas but it was food crops rather than oil which provided the mainstay of the economy.

As we have seen from the trade statistics available for the period there was no significant expansion in the volume and value of the trade except during certain peak years. Perhaps the demand in England for oil especially up to 1897 was low primarily because the English economy was not in a position to absorb the large quantities of palm oil that had already been imported into the country.[39] In any case what is significant is that the use of military strength did not fulfil British hopes that trade would increase. Also, the stations and outposts that were progressively established in Ibibio land and up the Cross River did not really consolidate British influence in the areas under their jurisdiction. From the point of view of winning African confidence, nothing could have done greater damage to the cause than the punitive expeditions undertaken between 1896 and 1906. The rash actions of Moor neither won the goodwill of the chiefs nor provided any long term solution to the problems facing the administration. Instead, they left behind a trail of smouldering unrest which did not take long to break out into hostilities.

The great disillusion

The anticipation of the colonial administration that once the hinterland was pacified trade would naturally flow to the coast, uninterrupted by Efik middlemen, and result in a general trade boom, was not realized. Why was it that, in spite of the professed opening up of the country by force and diplomacy, trade from the interior to the coast did not increase on a larger scale?

In the first place, the hinterland expeditions had not finally settled the persistent struggle that went on between the trading groups in the hinterland, each competing with the other for control of the river routes and the markets at the river banks. Various intrigues were employed by the competing trading groups to outwit or stop the trade of the river. The Ikwe, for instance, who covered a large territory of the country, were an inland people well known for the stoppage of trade routes in the country between Ogruide and Idigiri. Though complaints were frequently lodged against them by the affected traders[40] the British government could do little because the Ikwe were not given to treat government messengers with much consideration. Like the Ikwe, the Ekuri treated British political officers rudely. Though they had been subdued in 1898 they had hardly settled down peaceably to accept the new order, and on one occasion one of the British political officers, E. P. S. Roupell, found the attitude of the Ekuri so threatening that he was 'thankful to get away safely out of their country'.[41] What emboldened them to resist British incursions effectively was the temporary alliance concluded occasionally between certain of the Cross River towns. The Ikwe, who were described as the principal creators of the trouble in 1899, were supported by the Inokun (Aro). They laughed Roupell to scorn when he remonstrated with them, adding that the Ikwe country belonged to them and that they allowed Europeans no further than the beach.[42] But the Ikwe were, in their turn, harrassed and raided by the people of the Azar country for control of the waterway.[43]

The British policy in this regard was to support those towns which might prove useful in opening up the country to British trade. But this general principle could not be put into practice because towns which were considered so useful were in the habit of subjecting others to continual depredations. The important town of Akunakuna is an apt illustration of this dilemma. The British were keen to support Akunakuna against its rivals since its people were venturesome traders who travelled long distances in their canoes to bring down oil, rubber and ivory. As an agricultural and industrious people[44] the Akunakuna would be useful in opening up the country as they had the necessary trade links. But they fell out with the Afikpo Ibo. This was because in 1893 a chief of the Akunakuna, named Akpotem Akpan, residing at the town of Oke-rike, had, in order to avenge a misdeed done him, fallen upon the Afikpo Ibo and caught many of them like rats in a trap. The Afikpo Ibo were important food suppliers, cultivating immense quantities of yams and Indian corn. The British feared that if the Afikpo Ibo were not appeased, they might refuse to trade through hostile country, with the result that the lower river might run short of necessities.

In the circumstances, therefore, the British administration believed that the trade could be kept going only if the two important economic groups—Akunakuna and Afikpo Ibo—were brought together in peace. Coco Bassey was to arrange a meeting to settle their outstanding differences. MacDonald destroyed the town of Okerike in order to capture and hand over the Akunakuna chief at Afikpo.[45] It is not clear from the records if feelings in Akunakuna were injured as a result of this action, but certainly the Afikpo were grateful to the British. In later years, however, Akunakuna was protected against raiding people from Abini.[46]

A study of the competing trading groups up the Cross River makes it clear that no one middleman group could be absolved from blame for stopping the trade. The Afikpo, who complained against the Akunakuna, were themselves guilty of seizing canoes and traders passing through their area of influence. The people beyond these areas, access to which was possible only when heavy rains increased the water level of the river, had little fear of British expeditions until the next rainy season. The water level was generally high enough for canoes to venture up the Cross River between the months of August and December.[47] During the dry season, not only the larger but the smaller towns as well took advantage of the generally disturbed state of the river to seize canoes and trading goods.

It was to 'protect' trade that military posts were established. Detachments of the Southern Nigeria Battalion were stationed at Unwana, Obubura, Obukun, Oluni, Ediba and Arochuku in the Cross River district at the turn of the century. But it was inevitable that as long as the attention of the government was confined to rendering the waterways secure for life and property, very little could be done to develop and open up the country interior to these waterways. The hold of the government on the Cross River was so precarious that it was not in a position to offer protection to anyone. The peoples to whom it promised protection and who were bound by treaty were being regularly raided, their men killed and their women and children carried off; and on their appealing to the government for the guaranteed protection, no security was forthcoming. Roupell complained that it was 'absolutely painful' for him to listen to the petitions for help and protection.[48]

British inability to fulfil their promises naturally resulted in the African population's loss of confidence in the efficacy of the new administration. The divisional commissioners often spoke about the indifference or insolence of the hinterland people toward them. Visiting Ibibio towns in 1902, Richard Morrisey described how he was shouted at to leave the town because the Ibibio wanted to see no white men.[49] The Aro Expedition of 1902—the most spectacular and the last of the hinterland expeditions—was calculated to induce fear of the administration among the Cross River peoples. It had the desired effect on the smaller towns which were petrified by the way in which the Aro power had been reduced. The British did not believe that Afikpo which it aided in 1893 and whose gratitude it won as a result of British intervention in the Afikpo-Akunakuna dispute would work against British interests. In fact the District Commissioner, Major Crawford Cockburn, even went so far as to deny that there was any truth in the reported warlike attitude of the Afikpo.[50]

The wool was removed from British eyes when they tried to establish at Afikpo a government station to further the work of political consolidation.[51] Though a site for it was given by the head chief of Endibe, the rest of the Afikpo refused to allow the British to come to their country. 'I talked to them on every side of the question', said one officer, 'but they [the Afikpo] were very determined in their attitude and I failed to get them to accept my views on the subject'.[52] He was, however, determined to have the station established, adding: 'They seem an independent cheeky lot of devils these Afikpos, but no doubt once we are in there, butter won't melt in their mouths . . .'[53] The attitude of the Afikpo must have surprised the British at first because they realized that the Afikpo were not only against a government station being established in their town but resisted the idea of Europeans entering into their country at all.[54]

The British felt it essential that the government should have control in this strategic area in order to ensure the safety of the friendly people at Unwana, the mission station, and also to effectively control the Ediba and the country south west of Afikpo to Bende. Extensive control was necessary to open up the whole of Ibo country lying between the Cross River and Niger to trade and induce the inhabitants to develop the natural resources of the country.[55] The British were inclined to believe that Afikpo resistance to the establishment of a station was due to coercion by certain declared enemies of the government. It was decided, however, that if it was found impossible to effect the foregoing objects by peaceable means resort to force would be made and the Calabar troops would be used to carry through the necessary operations.[56]

The Afikpo issued a direct challenge to the government by attacking the waterside town of Anofia (which had come to the British under a white flag) and refusing to receive British messengers.[57] As a result Britain undertook operations for the 'pacification' of the Afikpo country.[58] Afikpo resistance to British advance was supported by the Ezza Ibo, who lived north of the government headquarters at Obubura hills. The Ezza were soon subdued by a military expedition directed against them and the others who controlled the Aweyong tributary of the Cross River.

In the short run, therefore, the punitive expeditions into the hinterland did not achieve more than the physical opening of new markets and the introduction of the right of Europeans to engage in the trade of the Calabar hinterland. There was no substantial increase in the volume of exports between 1884 and 1906.

A second important reason for the situation just described is that the Efik middleman system was partially undermined and weakened but was not completely replaced by a new trade system. One of the factors responsible for the weakening of the traditional middleman system was the drastic measure taken to force the use of cash rather than the use of trade goods (barter). The ostensible reason for this measure was the difficulty of obtaining the local currency, which was brass rods. The rods were imported by the trading firms for exchange against produce in the interior. As the difficulty of obtaining them was not likely to decrease, the colonial administration found it desirable to reduce the importation of brass rods. It was hoped that this step would increase the price of brass and cash would be more generally used. Inflation was evidently a device used to build up trade. English coinage was gradually introduced, and African traders were forced to acknowledge the par value of British coins.

The practice of introducing British coins in lieu of the brass rods was begun in the late 1890s.[59] In 1897 it was envisaged that an ordinance should be passed compelling trade to be carried out on a cash basis, and prohibiting the import of any articles to be used as coinage other than English cash.[60] Sets of coins were left in the towns on the banks of the river and their usage explained to the riverside folk.[61] But the riverside people were reluctant to accept the new currency. In Duke Town, for instance, the Efik traders were reluctant to adopt the new coinage as the local markets refused to accept foreign currency. In order to understand the reasons for the objections that were raised it is necessary to examine the mechanics of the trading system. This is illustrated in the diagram overleaf.

The system in vogue was for the Calabar trader to sell his goods for rods with which he bought produce; this produce was again sold to the Europeans so that the middlemen made three profits on the round trip. The people who brought the rubber would take nothing but rods or guns as English money was not current in the German territory whence came most of the money.[63] It was noticed that where silver was not accepted in the markets brass rods were readily received. In the higher reaches of the river it was common practice for the middlemen to sell gin against rods at rates actually below the Calabar selling price, in order that they might use the rods for the purchase of produce at low rates down river. At Umon, gin was being sold against rods at prices under

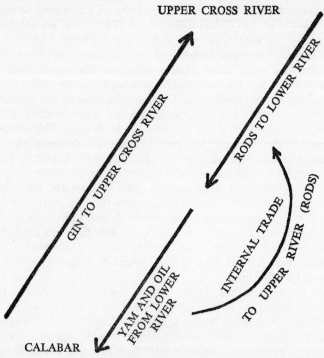

UPPER CROSS RIVER

GIN TO UPPER CROSS RIVER

RODS TO LOWER RIVER

INTERNAL TRADE

TO UPPER RIVER (RODS)

YAM AND OIL FROM LOWER RIVER

CALABAR

cost, and yams were bought with the rods at rates which allowed a hundred percent profit when sold in Calabar at the current market price. Though the trader got a low price for his produce he benefited from the inflated purchasing power of the rods which he received in exchange.

It can be seen from the above account that if the government restricted the importation of rods, the rods would become scarce and therefore more valuable. Hence the refusal to change to another form of currency. Also, since the market transactions of small traders did not amount to much at each transaction, the brass rods, which were available in very low denominations, were preferable to British coins, whose lowest denomination was still too high for the daily needs of the Efik.

In Lagos the currency policy was somewhat different. There, cowries were introduced in such large quantities that they continually depreciated and hence there was a greater willingness to switch over to a coin currency. In Calabar, on the other hand, both the European traders and the African market-man were against the introduction of a new currency system. The objection of the European traders is understandable: they profited from the old system, for when selling brass rods and manillas to Africans they fixed one rate, and when taking them in exchange for trade goods they charged another, more exorbitant rate. Thus the selling price of rods when newly imported might be about four to the shilling, but when used by Africans for purchasing trade goods, five were required to represent a shilling. The traders therefore opposed the introduction of a cash currency, hoping to gain from the old system as they had previously done, while the African market-men felt that so long as 'African currency' was used as a medium of exchange, they could not be exploited by their European counterparts.

The British government was anxious to introduce legislation which would place silver on a parity with the rod. It was even suggested that restrictions should be placed upon the area of their operations so that other traders might step in. This was to be done in two ways: to enforce separate spirit licences for areas north and south of Itu respectively, and to charge a registration fee for all canoes trading from Calabar.[64] The idea here, in all probability, was to obtain from the Calabar traders a definition of the markets they frequented. A trader could have as many licences as he pleased, but since he now had to pay for licences it would restrict him to certain districts. New traders could, therefore, be given a better chance of competition in other districts. The British also expressed the belief that the change to silver would not only make currency convenient and elastic but also increase the volume of trade[65] through the handy and manageable nature of the new currency. There is, however, little doubt that the measure was intended as a means of breaking the supremacy of the middleman system.

Although it did undermine the traditional system of trade it did not prove a complete success. The area of circulation of British coinage in Calabar was very limited, for it was only the salaries of African employees of the government that were paid in British coin. The salaries of European officers were almost entirely spent in England. The importation of British coin could only be permitted to the extent of real demand. If silver was imported beyond the extent of that demand, the government would be saddled with the responsibility and expense of repatriating the redundant coin.

The essential point about the introduction of cash currency was that it could not take place except in consequence of an increase in the volume of trade on a cash basis.[66] Hence, the new currency met with seriously embarrassing difficulties. Rods had to be exchanged for silver. The government could not easily obtain newly minted silver whenever required from the mint, and was not, therefore, in a position to supply traders with adequate currency until a special West African currency was introduced.[67] The result of all these attempts reinforces the argument made earlier, namely that the old Efik system was not removed successfully, nor was a new one imposed. Injury was nevertheless done to the trade of the river.

Another factor responsible for the break-up of the monopolistic position of the middlemen was the inauguration of the *Jackdaw* steam vessel service from the hinterland to the coast. This was bound to have a ruinous effect on the Efik middlemen since what it meant in effect was the transportation of interior producers of foodstuffs such as yam, corn and smoked fish, and their products from the hinterland to the seaboard by the *Jackdaw* at low passenger rates. It could be supposed that the hinterland producers would quickly learn to take advantage of these facilities and free themselves from the middleman.[68] This implied the disruption in this area of an existing differentiation of function between traders and farmer producers. If the *Jackdaw* were to carry farmers down, the traders were certainly going to have their positions undermined. This was a short-term policy, it being considered wiser and more conducive to progress for the merchants to provide their own canoes.

Thirdly, the trade mechanism was also changing. A great deal of the trade passed from Duke Town to Creek Town. Boys of the Duke Town houses, said one report, preferred to stay in town and get what work they could find there rather than go to the market. New ways to the interior markets were being devised to bypass middlemen, but the middlemen themselves were being offered more lucrative employment within the town. In Creek Town there were fewer opportunities for casual work and the chiefs had kept a closer hold on their houses with the result that the factory of the African Association at Creek Town did a larger trade than any factory at Duke Town.[69]

The fourth factor which impeded trade at the turn of the century was the position of affairs on the German boundary. During the Anglo-German boundary agreements in 1886, the British had bartered away the north eastern Calabar markets to the Germans in return for concessions elsewhere. The Calabar hinterland market at Ekol and Rumbi country[70] passed out of the hands of the Calabar kings. As the boundary followed no natural or ethnic divisions Calabar traders who had interests beyond it[71] could not prosecute their trade. Consequently, there was some interruption of trade, and the Calabar traders were reported to have been rather badly treated by the Germans.[72]

The British government failed to afford protection and security to

Efik rulers for their trade as promised in the Protectorate treaties. Indeed the German governor, on receiving the protest of the British consul in April, 1889, thought it strange that when he arrived at Calabar he found neither the consul nor any other representative to speak on behalf of the British government.[73] This was all the more serious because Calabar traders had supplied capital to the inhabitants to exploit the resources of the hinterland north-east of Calabar. Consequently, the latter were indebted to Calabar chiefs. When King Eyo VII arrested two men from this region to stand as sureties for the repayment of debts due to Calabar from the inhabitants, the German governor in 1889 ordered a German warship to arrest and remove Eyo VII. In fact the king was not released until two Calabar men were surrendered to the German governor.[74]

The fifth factor partly responsible for the trade situation was price. As long as the trade goods brought up to the upper Cross River by European traders consisted of the usual gin, salt, tobacco and a poor assortment of cotton goods,[75] there was little inducement for the small producer to increase his output and bring new people in to work the produce of the country. Better trade goods, and a greater variety of them, were certainly to be desired in order to increase profit incentives. British traders did not see the advantages of increasing the purchasing power of the primary producers.

Also, the prices paid for certain export produce were far from encouraging to the producers. For instance, although a large supply of oil went down to Calabar, the kernel trade was not worked to its full extent. This was due to the extremely low rates paid by the middlemen, viz. about six pounds per ton in the middle river, and four to five pounds in the upper reaches.[76] Once the powerful bargaining position of the Efik merchants was undermined the Efik were at the mercy of the Europeans. Valuable natural resources such as timber abounded on the banks of the Cross River and along the Anglo-German boundary. But in 1904 there was no trade at Calabar for rubber which was abundantly available in the Cross River. The reason given was that the price offered was not remunerative enough,[77] and some portion of it doubtless found its way to the German frontiers across the boundary.

The economic decline of Calabar

The sixth factor accounting for the state of trade, and certainly the most important in its long-term consequences, was the transport and communications factor. The development of transport can be viewed from two aspects: road construction in the towns of

s

Calabar and the means of transport between Calabar and the hinterland.

Within Calabar there were hardly any roads at all before 1885.[78] The various Efik settlements were all connected by 'bush paths' and these were used by the traders from the hulks and factories along the coast in order to reach their customers. The paths kept to the high ground in the neighbourhood of the present-day Calabar Road but as more permanent structures were built on shore after 1885 the necessity for access roads became noticeable. Roads were constructed but the majority of them were too steep, and often had flights of steps to their courses, and brick drains on both sides. The tracks of the more important of these roads are traced in the map on p. 257. Some of the roads were said to have been lit, however inadequately, by paraffin lamps set in ornate cast-iron lamp standards. The Marina (Akwa Esuk Street) was not built till 1907–1910 and was opened officially in 1910. Until that year the only access from Duke Town to Government Hill was by a ford, and later by 'Annesley's Bridge' in the neighbourhood of the present Tete Street. From this ford a proper road ran up past the present police headquarters to the Old Residency.

But what was even more urgently required, from the point of view of developing the economic resources of the country, was the development of good transportation facilities from the hinterland markets to the coastal town. Waterways had provided the main artery of transport and canoes had long been used to transport oil from the interior markets to the metropolitan towns. The colonial administration tried to raise the necessary finance to open up other lines of communication. In 1902, Moor approached European agents at Calabar to provide transport between the coast and the hinterland. But the traders showed reluctance, not because the economic value of such transportation was lost on them, but because they were not willing to invest money and wait for long-term results. They looked instead to the government for the provision of these amenities. British economic interests in Calabar were dominated by traders and shippers, already making some profits simply transporting and marketing African produce, and they showed no inclination to take risks by investing capital in new methods of production or in industrial development. We shall return to this essential point later but it is necessary meanwhile to note that the dynamic economic forces seem to come not from the British traders as such but from the colonial administration.

The question is often asked when exactly the economic decline of Calabar began. To determine a definite point in time for this is not easy. Already early in the century there were indications, as stated earlier, that the trade of Ibibio country was being directed to Bonny. As a background to this important story, however, one may say that a reason for the decline when it did come was to be found in the scant attention paid to Calabar when considering the railway proposals for the Protectorate. Moor was of the opinion that railways should run in such a way that the branch lines would supplement water transport in dry season.[79] This guided his railway policy east of the Niger, but no attempt was made to connect

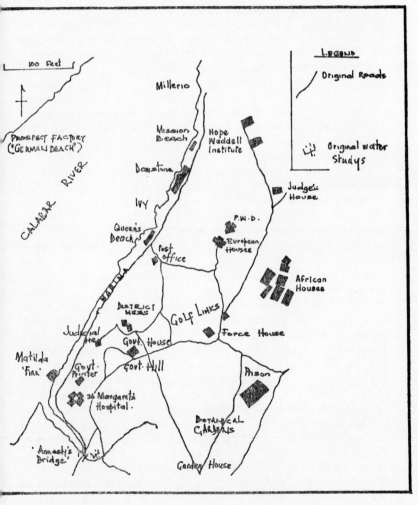

Central Calabar (after the Admiralty Chart of 1903)

that line with Calabar.[80] Instead, in February, 1903 Moor recommended the construction of a light electric railway, twenty-five to
thirty miles long, to tap the Cross River basin. The route was to
be surveyed and the hope was expressed that this line might later
be extended south to Calabar.

Between the Niger and the Cross River, the greatest waterways
of Southern Nigeria, lies a hundred miles of thickly populated
country, the lower portion of which was the richest palm oil belt.
The plan was to construct a railway from Itu to the middle of this
rich tract and northwards to Benue, and later on to Bauchi where
tin was said to be found in commercially payable quantity. Itu
was chosen as one terminus because navigation on the Cross River
for all but shallow boats stopped there for eight months a year.[81]
It was again hoped that when the traffic justified it the line would
be extended from Itu to Calabar. Another reason for the reluctance
in building the line was the knowledge that the country between
Calabar and the Cross River was almost unpopulated, mountainous
and neglected.[82] It was considered that the line would be expensive
to construct and that there would be little traffic on it until extended
beyond the Cross River.[83]

The value of a railway linking Calabar, the port, with its hinterland cannot however be over-emphasized. Not only would bulky
palm produce have been transported down to Calabar with ease
and speed, it would also have given a great boost to the development of the valuable forests containing quantities of rubber. The
tendency of peasant farmers was to establish their economic activities along the waterways where there was transport. A railway to
Calabar could have opened up the area and brought foodstuffs
to the towns lower down the river.

The Calabar harbour was still superior to most others at the
beginning of the present century. It was described as the 'finest
port on the Bight of Benin'[84] until the Lagos bar was removed.
Large steamers of 5,000 to 6,000 tons, and measuring nineteen
feet by twenty-one feet draught, carrying exports, imports and
passenger traders to and from Europe could enter Calabar. Many
of the vessels then built for the trade were of large capacity for
their draught. Lagos, which later superseded the other ports, had
a huge bar in front of it; none of the larger boats could enter it
and they had to be served by means of 'branch boat' (steamers of
900 to 1,200 tons and measuring nine by twelve feet draught) services to and from Forcados, where cargo was transhipped from
the larger steamers. Calabar gave twenty-one feet of draught at
the harbour.[85] It could not therefore have been Calabar as a port
which discouraged the railway builders.

The real decline of Calabar began when the railway proposals were turned into realities after 1916. The directions in which the lines were built were closely related to the factor of decline, for the eventual consequence was to siphon off the trade of the Cross River area westwards rather than southwards to Calabar. The eastern line was built between the coalfields of Udi, near Enugu, and Port Harcourt, about forty miles up the Bonny creek. The route was surveyed in 1913 and the construction was begun the same year but was not completed till 1916. The line stretched for about 151 miles and was intended to transport Udi coal to the coast. Port Harcourt was originally created to serve the Enugu coalfields[86] and the wider hinterland when the railway was extended northwards to Makurdi on the Benue (in 1924), to Kafanchan (1927), to Kaduna and to Jos (1927).[87]

The thin steel threads that ran between Enugu and Port Harcourt drew the trade of the Cross River when the latter was connected to the palm oil belt by rail. If it is realized that the most important fact about the economic development of Calabar is that it developed from the coast inwards, it will be clear how a diversion of trade would have adversely affected the economic position of Calabar.

The creation of Port Harcourt in 1913 and the removal of the bar at Lagos in the first decade of the present century hit Calabar badly. Until then there was still some hope that Calabar might be chosen from amongst Warri, Onitsha and Asaba as a likely port for Southern Nigeria. The colonial office did at one time support a line from Calabar but the crown agents who were finally responsible for authorizing the construction preferred an extension from Lagos, and Lugard wanted it to commence from the Niger. When the Colony of Lagos and the Southern Protectorate joined in the one government of 1906, the scheme for opening the entrance to Lagos harbour had begun, and all other plans were shelved.

It had been suggested in 1905, for instance, that though the Cross River could still transport most of the produce[88] a line should be built southwards. Egerton, who confessed that when Sir Ralph Moor recommended the survey very little was known of the country between the Cross River and the Niger, added that the administration now knew that the country behind Itu was one of the richest in the protectorate. 'The bulk of its products', he revealed, 'rots on the ground owing to the want of transport.' He suggested a tramway or railway to run between Itu and Oguta near the Niger (a distance of about a hundred miles covering the rich oil tract spoken of earlier). From Itu a line might be built to Calabar, once a bridge across the Cross River was built. From this bridge a line could be constructed to Creek Town, where another bridge could carry the line to the right bank of the Calabar River and opposite to the town of Calabar.

Alternatively, a line could have run from Itu to Uwet and thence on to Odukpani and to Calabar. Not even a survey of this route was proposed[89] and the idea was later abandoned. It was about this period, too, that there was a conspicuous growth of large settlements at Onitsha, Owerri and Aba. These grew at a tremendous rate and became important commercial centres. Their important position on the main highways that crossed the eastern region contributed to their rapid growth and urbanization. In 1905 it was hoped that when a road was constructed from Calabar northwards to Itu, Owerri, Oguta and similar places, it would result in great trade improvement in some of the lesser known parts of the protectorate. The trade would then pass through Calabar rather than through the other ports. As the situation stood in 1905, the trade that came from the district at the back of the Enyong Creek near the new station of Ikot Ekpene did not, as it should have done, come to Calabar but went down to Eket, Egwanga and Bonny.[90] The tendency in Ibibioland was to look outwards to Ikot Ekepene, Aba and Onitsha as cultural and commercial centres.[91]

The difficulties in transport and communications, which Moor claimed British firms did not help to alleviate, were crucial to the development of trade in the hinterland. They explain why the Efik middleman system was not fully replaced by a new European orientated trade network at the turn of the century. As late as 1905 Calabar traders were still going all the way up to the Cross River without fear of being attacked[92] and armoured canoes were used to patrol the river and to keep marauders from interfering with the flow of trade.[93]

One of the reasons why European traders were not very willing to do anything regarding transport problems was the initial inability of the government to give any guarantee that an increase of trade would follow from large capital outlays in the interior trade establishments. Moreover the fear was entertained that the big companies, having incurred all the heavy risks required, would not be able to prevent others (at a later stage when risks became minimized) from depriving the pioneering firms of their profits.

Hence, the big companies preferred to remain in Calabar and manœuvre the trade coming down the river to their own advantage. For example in 1902, the agents changed the basis on which the purity of palm kernels was determined. They stated that no kernel containing over two per cent of extraneous matter would be purchased by them. In fact the produce market in England allowed five per cent as refuse matter in clear kernels. The result of the new regulation was that the Efik were forced to sell the kernel in 1902 at a price forty per cent lower than they had obtained at the same time the previous year.

A large fall-off in the kernel trade resulted. The increase in the oil shipments from Calabar during the first six months of 1902 amounted to about 200 tons, whereas the actual decrease in kernels was 1,120 tons.[94] The rapid increase in the volume of trade expected to result after the pacification movements, therefore, failed to materialize.

Thus, while the representatives of the firms at home gave public expression to their desire to see the country opened up and to assist in the work, the local firms entered into an agreement binding on all of them not to take any active measures for opening up the Cross River and the inland markets. Even the German firms established at Calabar were drawn, with Messrs. Miller Brothers and the African Association, into the scheme. These firms desired no more competitors, were satisfied with the volume of trade, and paid large dividends without taking any further risks whatever. This was a continuation of the policy by which older traders in the Niger Delta safeguarded, or tried to safeguard, their interests by collaborating with each other against newcomers seeking to penetrate inland.

From the point of view of increasing trade what was most essential was an increase in prices. But the traders argued that it was most essential to establish trading stations at four points: one at Itu, one at the mouth of the Enyong Creek, one near Afikpo, and two others at suitable points between Afikpo and the German boundary.[95] The Itu factory, they believed, would be accessible at all seasons of the year and would tap an enormous amount of produce. The other stations, it was supposed, would benefit from the rich producing areas of Afikpo, and the ebony and rubber trade from the German border. It was nowhere explained by the traders why they believed that the establishment of these stations would open up the trade any more than forcible interference with the trading mechanism had done. European firms, said Miller Brothers, did not want to risk their enterprise without a British guarantee that firms would be in secure possession of the regions around the stations for a specific period of years.[96] The British government later agreed to give the firms the guarantees sought and in particular sent an assurance to George Miller and the African Association. Moor wrote to the African Association about the prosperous trade that could be carried on near the German border, and warned that if British firms did not show an early initiative German firms would open up establishments in British territory.

Moor held meetings with the African Association and Arthur Miller Brothers with reference to the opening up of the Cross River. He revealed German plans to establish a transport service on the Cross River paying a small transit rate to the chiefs for the same. It was highly probable that having established such a system the German company at the border would see the advantage of establishing trading stations in the Protectorate in the lower river, and provide freight services to render it remunerative. If this issued in action, the German factories would no doubt obtain a great deal of the trade which now found its way by middlemen carriers to Calabar and would result in considerable loss to English merchants.

Moor illustrated his point by referring to the case of the Niger. The enterprising and younger firms that became established in the upper Niger practically ruined the older firms which maintained their depots in Brass. Although there was no possibility of any firm or group of firms obtaining control on the Cross River, such as the Royal Niger Company obtained on the Niger, he stated that the enterprising firms, which established upriver with a view to developing new trade, would eventually obtain both the new and the existing trade. No doubt there were great difficulties in establishing any system of transport on the Cross River when trade was hardly opened up at all; nevertheless, there were large areas, both above and below the Cross River rapids in British territory, where trade could be developed. Already, the Germans were about to make an offer to develop this trade.[97]

This warning had the intended effect. Hitherto, the British mercantile firms had been reluctant to take on additional risks. They had opposed the punitive expeditions on the grounds that they ruined trade. It is interesting to note that it was a new line for the traders to preach pacificism instead of bombardment. Mercantile thinking at the turn of the century was therefore tremendously changed from that of the 1870s. Now they argued that

> commercially, it is not practical to shoot your customer. Politically, it is not practical in a country like West Africa to destroy the native form of society, break the power of the chiefs. Financially it is not practical, for it means the piling up of debts . . . and the ultimate impoverishment of the country.[98]

The change in the thinking of traders after 1901 was due to the security promised them by the government in opening up the Cross River. Soon after Moor's warning, the Calabar mercantile community despatched two representatives, Messrs. McFarlan and O'Neill, to the Cross River in September, 1902 to investigate the trade position there.[99] In March, 1903 two other representatives, Messrs. Fynn and Cowan, went up the Cross River to inquire further into the prospects of trade. Based on these reports, the African Association and Miller Brothers decided to commence a joint enterprise on the lines suggested by Moor, provided necessary inducements to do so were offered by the British government. Traders required assurances from the government that the two companies, which were prepared to finance the heavy outlays to begin trade and to provide the necessary transport, would not be interfered with by outside parties for a period of years till they had covered their initial losses.[100] In reply, the government was willing to guarantee that it would not grant to other European traders within a period of six years any site within fifteen miles by waterway on either side of each of the four trading stations selected.[101]

The implications of the arrangements sanctioned by the government for its earlier declaration of 'free trade' principles were serious. The situation had changed, and the British government was now using the economic aim of expansion to secure purely political ends. The pressing reason for the government's flagrant abandonment of free trade principles is not difficult to perceive. While the best way to break the Calabar monopoly was to encourage more firms inland, Moor was more interested in ensuring that the Germans did not seize the Cross River trade. And the period between 1902–1904 was just when anti-German feeling was beginning to emerge in Britain, because of the development of the German High Seas Fleet.

The basic problem was that there was no real burst of enthusiasm among the British mercantile capitalists to bring about a revolution in Cross River trade. Circumstantial evidence points to the fact that the idea was almost entirely that of Moor. He discovered that the Germans were going to use the Cross River to communicate with the Cameroons. He became anxious that once the Germans began to sail regularly up the river they would commence trade on its banks. Trade would lead to political influence; politics would lead to local conflict or friction. It would result in a query from the Colonial Office, and Moor would have to account for his *naïveté* in allowing the Germans into his area.

Moor had to work out how he could let the Germans use the river (as by international agreement they could) without allowing them to establish trading stations on its banks. He decided to get in touch with the mercantile firms but found the traders complacent because they were doing well where they were. They were not keen to upset an unstable equilibrium just to get Moor out of his predicament. Moor presumably decided then to draw Miller aside from other traders and make a deal with him. He requested him to open trading stations up the river and agreed to keep other traders off his grounds. Miller, a hard bargainer, promised to go up the river if he was given a big inducement. He wanted four stations to be opened to make it worth his while but he wanted to be assured of returns on his investment. Moor agreed to give this guarantee.

Deals such as these could not be kept secret. The concession met with the opposition of the Chambers of Commerce in Manchester and Liverpool, who argued that for all practical purposes the Cross River was closed to outsiders, and made a monopoly area. The distance between Itu and the German frontier was 157 miles. Of this, about 90 miles were to be absorbed by the proposed concessions, leaving about 67 miles for unrestricted competition. Moor's actions constituted government interference with trade, an iniquitous monopoly. The fact that Itu was included meant that a large portion of the trade of Calabar derived from Itu would be lost to others. At the end of the six years' period, other firms allowed to establish trading stations in the restricted area would find that the concessionaries had already obtained all the best trading sites. The concessionaries had it in their power to purchase African produce at less than its true market value by forcing producers to accept smaller quantities of European manufactures for a given quantity of African produce than the current market prices.

The colonial office refuted these arguments on the grounds that the associated firms were not given a monopoly; Africans were free to take their produce to any station they desired, or to Calabar. The Itu trade might still continue to go to Calabar if the Itu traders so wished. There was, in fact, a debate between the government and mercantile firms as to whether trading facilities should be granted to any European on the stretch between Calabar and Itu and on Enyong Creek. It was said that to do so was to neglect protection for Calabar middlemen, for if merchants began trading directly with the producers, thus taking the place of the Calabar middlemen, the latter would lose their means of livelihood. Eventually, however, no such special consideration was given by the British government to Calabar middlemen.[102] The colonial office further argued that some concessions had to be given to initiate firms to pioneer in this direction.[103]

The arguments by the colonial administration reinforce the point made earlier, that the principle of 'free trade' had undergone a change. For it is easy to see that the government did not allow a similar concession to Efik middlemen or to other British middlemen. To permit trading stations to establish themselves along the river was equivalent to asking them to take over the functions of the Efik middlemen. Granted that producers could go to any of the trading stations to sell their produce, the fact was that the location of these stations at strategic points along the river would make it necessary for the producers to bring their produce to the nearest station. This would be true for at least the fifteen-mile radius allowed to each of the stations.

Conclusion

The imposition of colonial rule is a convenient point to end an account of the political and social history of Calabar in the nineteenth century. For it marked in one sense the climax of more than half a century of active British political and social penetration into Efik society, while in another it marked a transition in the process of political and social development. What was most remarkable in this transition was the resilience in Efik and hinterland society. In this respect it was the primacy of economic factors which was crucial in the resistance to colonial rule. Though it was part of colonial policy to unleash new economic forces into the hinterland with a view to exploiting more profitably than before the abundance of raw material, and to substitute Efik middlemen with European trading stations, the results did little to warm the hearts of the colonial officials. The colonial administrators learnt the hard lesson that the resistance of the Calabar traders could not be overcome for any length of time either by the use of force, by the charm of smiles, or by the display of white umbrellas.

REFERENCES

1 A few families were specialists in certain crafts or functions, such as brass tray decoration. Some have alleged that the Efik were averse to manual labour and believed that their amour propre as a commercial people did not permit them to dirty their hands in manual toil.

2 Vide also H. Goldie and Dean, op. cit., p. 331. For a narration of Enyong tradition, vide M. D. W. Jeffreys, *Old Calabar* et seq., pp. 27–29.

3 C. Gertzel, 'John Holt' et seq., p. 319, Holt papers 26/3a, Holt to Hartze, 9 January, 1885.

4 Holt Papers 13/5, Hartze to Henshaw III, 12 December, 1883; cited in C. Gertzel, 'John Holt' et seq., p. 188.

5 C. Gertzel, 'John Holt' et seq., p. 306ff.

6 F.O. 2/85, MacDonald to F.O., 26 October, 1895.

7 L. Sealey-King, 'Intelligence Report on the Okoyong Clan, Calabar Division', dated 11 June, 1931; C.S.O. 26/3, file 276/674, pp. 1–2.

8 D. M. McFarlan, op. cit., p. 97.

9 W. P. Livingston, *Mary Slessor of Calabar*, p. 160.

10 CALPROF 8/1, Memo from A. G. Griffith (Ag. District Commissioner) to Ag. Consul-General, 18 November, 1896; the District Commissioner, A. A. Whitehouse, drew a boundary between the Ikoneto and Okoyong but it was never observed by either side; CALPROF 6/3, Vol. 2, Clerk of the Native Court of Ikoneto to Ag. District Commissioner, 13 April, 1898; CALPROF 6/4, Ag. District Commissioner to Clerk of the Native Court of Okoyong, 14 April, 1898; CALPROF 6/3, Vol. 3, Ikoneto chiefs to Ag. District Commissioner, 17 October, 1898.

11 Vide H. Goldie and J. T. Dean, op. cit., pp. 225–229.

12 A. F. Mockler-Ferryman, op. cit., p. 126. See also MS. C. C. Wrigley, 'The External Trade of Nigeria, 1901–1960'.

13 H. H. Johnston, op. cit., pp. 166–7.

14 Source: C. Gertzel, 'John Holt' et seq., pp. 615–616, where the John Holt papers are cited.

15 C.S.O. 1/13, Vol. 6, No. 50, Moor to F.O., 14 June, 1896.

16 CALPROF 8/2, Vol. 1, Arthur G. Griffith (Ag. Vice-Consul) to Consul-General, 3 April, 1895.

17 CALPROF 6/1, Vol. 2, A. A. Whitehouse (consular agent) to R. Moor, 15 August, 1895.

18 CALPROF 8/2, Vol. 1, A. G. Griffith (Ag. District Commissioner) to Moor, 5 June, 1896.

19 CALPROF 8/2, Vol. 1, H. Bedwell (Asst. District Commissioner) to Capt. H. C. Gallwey (Ag. Commissioner and Consul-General), 17 September, 1896.

20 C.S.O. 1/15, Vol. 7 (Confid.), encl. 6, Report by C. Hungerford (medical officer), dated 3 March, 1905, in High Commissioner to F.O., 17 June, 1905.

21 C.S.O. 1/13, Vol. 6, Phillips (Ag. General) to F.O., 25 November, 1896; also vide Gallwey to F.O., 24 September, 1896.

22 C.S.O. 1/13, Vol. 7, Moor to F.O., 20 May, 1897.

23 CALPROF 9/1, Vol. 1, Gallwey to High Commissioner, 19 January, 1900.

25 P. Amaury Talbot, *Life in Southern Nigeria*, Chapters 19 to 24.

25 R. K. Floyer, Itu Intelligence Report on the Itu Clan, Itu District File No. 31013, 1935, Appendix V. Memo from M. D. W. Jeffreys (District Officer at Itu) to the Resident, Calabar Province, dated 12 February, 1929, entitled 'Condition of Land Tenure in Itu', M.P. No. P.C. 52/1929, p. 36.

26 C. Partridge, *Cross River Natives*, p. 49.

27 Vide CALPROF 6/1, Vol. 2, A. G. Griffith (Ag. Vice-Consul) to C. MacDonald, 1 March, 1895, and its several encl.; CALPROF 6/3, Vol. 1, A. Graves to Vice-Consul, Old Calabar, 14 April, 1895.

28 R. K. Floyer, op. cit., Appendix V, p. 3.

29 Vide frontispiece for the location of the towns mentioned in the discussion.

30 Vide Capt. Hanitsch, 'Assessment Report, Uyo District, Calabar Province', dated 18 August, 1927, C.S.O. 26/3, file ref. 20682.

31 C. Partridge, op. cit., pp. 40–45.

32 For a description of the comfortable canoes, vide C. Partridge, op. cit., p. 47. There was also a stern wheeler, *Beecroft*, which was used for controlling the Cross River and keeping trade open, but it was lost at the mouth of the Cross River in May, 1895; and for a long

time afterwards the finances of the Protectorate did not admit of the purchase of a new one; C.S.O. 1/13, Vol. 2, No. 80, Moor to C.O., 30 May, 1899.

33 CALPROF 6/1, Vol. 3, Ekpensin(?) of Orok House to Moor, 10 March, 1896.
34 C.S.O. 1/13, Vol. 6, No. 36, Moor to F.O., 5 May, 1896.
35 C.S.O. 1/13, Vol. 7, No. 140, R. Moor to F.O., 13 November, 1897.
36 C.S.O. 1/13, Vol. 8, No. 26, Gallwey to F.O., 9 February, 1898, encl. Memo with regard to the Cross River Expedition, January, 1898, by R. Moor, dated 8 January, 1898. Vide also C.S.O. 1/13, Vol. 8, No. 850, R. Moor to F.O., 17 May, 1898.
37 C.S.O., 1/13, Vol. 8, No. 29, Gallwey to F.O., 15 February, 1898.
38 D. Forde and G. I. Jones, *The Ibo and Ibibio speaking peoples of Southern Nigeria*, op. cit., pp. 13 and 58; for Obubura, vide C. Partridge, op. cit.
39 Vide, for example, C. C. Wrigley, 'Economic and Social Developments', in J. F. A. Ajayi and I. Ispie (ed.); *A Thousand Years of West African History*, (Ibadan, 1965), p. 423ff.
40 C.S.O. 1/13, Vol. 6, No. 79, Gallwey to F.O., 22 September, 1896; C.S.O. 1/13, Vol. 9, No. 162, Gallwey to F.O., 10 October, 1898.
41 CALPROF 8/2, Vol. 2, E. P. S. Roupell (Political Officer, Ediba) to Consul-General, 20 May, 1899.
42 Ibid.
43 C.S.O. 1/13, Vol. 2, Moor to C.O., 14 June, 1899.
44 Ibid., Vol. 3, No. 23, MacDonald to F.O., 12 October, 1893.
45 Ibid.
46 CALPROF 6/1, Vol. 4, E. P. S. Roupell to Moor, 30 December, 1899.
47 C.S.O. 1/13, Vol. 5, No. 38, R. Moor to F.O., 11 September, 1895.
48 Ibid., Vol. 12, No. 78, Moor to C.O., 23 March, 1900, encl. extracts from Roupell to Moor, 8 March, 1900.
49 CALPROF 10/3, Vol. 4, Richard Morrisey (Ag. Divisional Commissioner, Cross River Division) to High Commissioner, 1 August, 1902.
50 CALPROF 10/1, Major W. A. Crawford Cockburn (District Commissioner, Cross River) to the Divisional Commissioner, Cross River Division, March, 1902.
51 CALPROF 9/4, R. Morrisey to Divisional Commissioner, Cross River Division, 6 April, 1902.
52 Ibid., Arthur W. Biddell to Divisional Commissioner, Cross River Division, 20 April, 1902.
53 Ibid.
54 CALPROF 9/1, Vol. 3, Divisional Commissioner, Cross River Division, to High Commissioner, 22 April, 1902.
55 Vide C.S.O. 1/16, Vol. 4 (Confid.), 14 September, 1902, encl. The London *Gazette*, Friday, 12 September, 1902, No. 27473.
56 CALPROF 9/2, Vol. 4, Memorandum of instruction with regard to patrol and possible operations for the establishment of government in the Afikpo territory, by Moor, dated 29 November, 1902.
57 C.S.O. 1/13, Vol. 23, No. 2, Moor to C.O., 2 January, 1903, encl. Divisional Commissioner to High Commissioner, No. 18, 27 December, 1902.
58 C.S.O. 1/14, Vol. 32, No. 149, J. Chamberlain to Officer Administering the Government of Southern Nigeria, 16 April, 1903.

59   The evidence for this is contained in the records of the courts. The court fines were evidently paid in both brass and sterling, and an exchange rate was established. One box of rods equalled 120 rods which was valued at 30 shillings. One rod was therefore worth 3d.; 'Regulations governing the Esop Ison-inyan (near Itu), 7 March, 1898' kept at the Calabar Customary Court; and C.S.O. 1/13, Vol. 15, Moor to C.O., No. 14b, 6 June, 1901, encl. notes confirm that 4 rods were equal to a sterling shilling. Also 20 copper wires were equal to a brass rod. Brass rods continued to be accepted in order to show that the old currency had not been rendered totally useless. It also taught the Efik the value of the new currency.

60   C.S.O. 1/13, Vol. 7, No. 140, R. Moor to F.O., 13 November, 1897.

61   Ibid., Vol. 9, No. 162, Gallwey to F.O., 10 October, 1898.

62   Note that rods being currency cannot move entirely in one direction. Perhaps the use of gin creates the same effect as a bimetallic currency with varying exchange rate producing large scale transfers of one or the other.

63   CALPROF 8/2, Vol. 2, E. P. S. Roupell (Political Agent, Ediba) to Consul-General, 20 May, 1899.

64   C.S.O. 1/13, Vol. 34, No. 238, Egerton to C.O., 6 June, 1905.

65   C.S.O. 1/14, Vol. 21, J. Chamberlain to Officer Administering the Government of Southern Nigeria, 5 October, 1901, encl. 'Currency in Southern Nigeria', dated 9 September, 1901.

66   The importation of brass rods and other African currencies were prohibited under the revised tariff of April, 1902; C.S.O. 1/14, Vol. 25, Chamberlain to Moor; No. 158, 17 April, 1902, and C.S.O. 1/13, Vol. 20, R. Moor to C.O., 29 May, 1902. For further problems connected with the currency question vide C.S.O. 1/13, Vol. 20, R. Moor to C.O., No. 268, 12 June, 1902, and C.S.O. 1/13, Vol. 22, Moor to C.O., No. 498, 11 November, 1902.

67   C.S.O. 1/13, Vol. 16, Acting High Commissioner to C.O., No. 305, 14 September, 1901.

68   Ibid., Vol. 34, No. 238, Egerton to C.O., 6 June, 1905.

69   CALPROF 10/3, Vol. 1, 'Old Calabar District—Report for quarter ending June 30th, 1900' by J. Watts, n.d.

70   F.O. 84/1828, Petition from Old Calabar, 19 July, 1887, and F.O. 84/1941, No. 17, Hewett to F.O., 30 April, 1889.

71   Johnston's exploration of 1886–1888 revealed the extent of Efik commercial activities. The Germans expelled Efik traders on their side of the provisional boundary; see J. C. Anene, 'The Nigeria–Southern Cameroon Boundary', *J.H.S.N.*, Vol. 2, No. 1, December, 1961, p. 192.

72   CALPROF 10/3, Vol. 1, 'Report upon Old Calabar District for the quarter ending September 30th, 1900', by J. Watts, dated 29 September, 1900.

73   F.O. 84/1941, No. 17, Hewett to F.O., 30 August, 1889.

74   J. C. Anene, *Southern Nigeria* et seq., p. 101.

75   One report in 1905 stated that at Umon, one of the largest goods markets, there were counted 209 cases of gin, 60 of rum, 71 bags of salt and several small boxes of soap, matches, etc. The value of the spirits equalled the whole of the other goods together, excluding yams and foodstuff; C.S.O. 1/13, Vol. 34, No. 238, Egerton to C.O., 6 June, 1905, encl. 1 (Confid.), 'Cross River Trade' by G. A. Birtwistle, dated 24 May, 1905.

76 Ibid.
77 C.S.O. 1/13, Vol. 29, No. 154, Egerton to C.O., 11 April, 1904; and ibid., 'Annual Report on the Cross River Division for the year ended 31 March, 1904', by A. B. Harcourt.
78 The description of Calabar roads here is based on Appendix C of B. B. Dean and N. M. B. Dean, op. cit.
79 C.O. 520/7, Moor to C.O., 17 January, 1901.
80 Ibid.
81 NIGERIA, *Further Correspondence relating to Railway Construction in Nigeria* (H.M.S.O., March, 1909) Cd. 4523, p. 4, para. 18. Vide Egerton to C.O., 26 June, 1906, encl. 1, 'Memo on Railway and Motor Road Construction in Nigeria with proposals for loan works to be at once undertaken'.
82 C.S.O. 1/13, Vol. 23, No. 94, Moor to C.O., 9 February, 1902.
83 NIGERIA, *Further Correspondence relating to Railway Construction* ... encl. 1, et seq., p. 4, para. 18.
84 Ibid. 'Benin' should in fact have read 'Biafra' here.
85 High Commissioner of Northern Nigeria to Secretary of State, No. 16, 30 May, 1907, encl. 'Report on Transport Policy of Nigeria' in *Further Correspondence* ... et seq., pp. 55–60.
86 These fields covered about 2,000 sq. mls., *Nigeria Handbook*, 1933, p. 22.
87 Vide map in K. M. Buchanan and J. C. Pugh, *Land and People in Nigeria* (London, 1962), pp. 208–210.
88 The trade of Calabar in 1904, which included all the trade from the right bank of the Cross River, was estimated at 2,338,025 gallons of palm oil and 18,429 tons of kernels, both being export figures; C.S.O. 1/13, Vol. 34, No. 267, Egerton to C.O., 30 June, 1905.
89 C.S.O. 1/13, Vol. 34, No. 267, Egerton to C.O., 30 June, 1905; also earlier a steam tramway from Calabar to the upper waters of the Cross River was to be surveyed; C.S.O. 1/14, Vol. 34, Moor to C.O., 29 September, 1903. But there was always considerable apprehension expressed about the traffic that would use these facilities when they were provided; C.S.O. 1/14, Vol. 41, No. 21, C.O. to Egerton, 19 January, 1905, encl. 'Southern Nigeria Railway Survey' by E. E. Blake, 9 January, 1905.
90 C.S.O. 1/13, Vol. 34, No. 239, Egerton, C.O., 11 June, 1905.
91 Vide for example, Udo-Ekong Etuk Obuo-Offiong, *An Introduction to Nait History: A First Step to the Study of Ibibio History*, passim.
92 C.S.O. 1/13, Vol. 34, No. 238, Egerton to C.O., 6 June, 1905.
93 CALPROF 10/3, Vol. 2, A. W. Biddell (Ag. District Commissioner, Cross River Division), 'Report on Division for quarter ending December 31st, 1901', dated 1 January, 1902.
94 C.S.O. 1/15, Vol. 20, No. 394, Moor to C.O., 25 August, 1902.
95 C.S.O. 9/2, Vol. 3, Moor to the Ag. Divisional Commissioner, Cross River Division, 12 September, 1902.
96 Ibid., encl. Extract from High Commissioner to George Miller, 22 August, 1902.
97 CALPROF 9/2, Vol. 1, High Commissioner to African Association and A. Miller Brothers, 21 February, 1901, and CALPROF 9/2, Vol. 3, R. Moor to African Association, 6 September, 1902.
98 *West Africa*, 12 October, 1901, p. 1184 (editorial); S. M. Tamuno, 'British Administrative Control' et seq., p. 105. The same arguments

had been put forward by the Aborigines Protection Society to the British government in March, 1897; C.S.O. 1/13, Vol. 7, No. 53, F.O. to Moor, 25 March, 1897, encl. Aborigines Protection Society to the Marquis of Salisbury (Confid.), 3 March, 1897.

99   CALPROF 9/1, Vol. 5, Chairman of Agents, Calabar to Moor, 12 September, 1902, and encl.; C.S.O. 1/13, Vol. 22, No. 465, Moor to C.O., 14 October, 1902, and encl.

100 C.S.O. 1/14, Vol. 34, No. 307, J. Chamberlain to Officer Administering the Government of Southern Nigeria, 14 August, 1903, and encl.

101 C.S.O. 1/13, Vol. 34, C.O. to African Association, 14 August, 1903; C.O. to Officer Adminstering the Government of Southern Nigeria, 9 October, 1903, No. 369, encl. 1, African Association to C.O., 26 August, 1903, and encl. 2, C.O. to African Association, 8 September, 1903.

102 For the full story, vide C.S.O. 1/14, No. 162, C.O. to Officer Administering the Government of Southern Nigeria, 25 May, 1905, encl. Alex Miller and Co. to C.O., 19 April, 1905; C.S.O. 1/13, Vol. 34, No. 238, Egerton to C.O., 6 June, 1905; C.S.O. 1/13, Vol. 34, No. 239, Egerton to C.O., 11 June, 1905; C.S.O. 1/14, Vol. 43, C.O. to Officer Administering the Government of Southern Nigeria, 28 July, 1905.

103 C.S.O. 1/14, Vol. 37, C.O. to High Commissioner W. Egerton, 8 April, 1904, encl. 1, Chamber of Commerce, Manchester, to C.O., 19 January, 1904; encl. 2, C.O. to Chamber of Commerce, Manchester, 8 April, 1904, encl. 3, Chamber of Commerce, Liverpool, to C.O. 19 January, 1904.

VIII

Conclusion: the Primacy
of Internal Factors

The principal conclusion derived from an examination of the factors which conditioned the political and social development of Calabar is that although in fact much of the change and development in Efik society was, either by direct or indirect processes, precipitated by its involvement in external trade, or initiated by the activities of European traders, missionaries and consuls, it was the logic of the internal politics and structure of the society which in pre-colonial days determined the areas and depth of change that external factors were able to effect.

External trade and internal developments

The economy of Calabar was heavily geared to external trade in palm oil and it was on the prosperity of this trade that much of the fortunes of the towns depended. The Efik, who were primarily the middlemen in the trade organization, owed their livelihood to the trade they transacted with the European supercargoes and firms. The political authority of the kings and the social structure of the society had their roots in external trade. Since the palm oil trade dominated the economy, economic and political changes in the fortunes of the oil trade had significant consequences on the broad spectrum of political, social and economic developments in the Efik towns.

It was shown that some of the most momentous changes in the social structure of Calabar took place as a consequence of the transition from the slave to the oil trade in the early decades of the nineteenth century. The prosecution of the new trade necessitated a restructuring of the house system in order to incorporate into its membership a large reservoir of enterprising slaves. In the slave trade days, the houses had consisted of only the immediate polygamous family, dependents of the headmen and those of adult kinsmen. With slaves being made members of the houses the term ukpuk (lineage), which was originally used to express blood relationship (or consanguinity), virtually disappeared among the Efik. The term was replaced by the new term ufok (house), and it symbolized the integration between the town-dwelling slaves and the free members of the houses. But slave members of the houses had only fictional rather than agnatic relations with the free members of the houses and remained for the most part outside the traditional rank system of society. Nevertheless, slave members improved their economic and social positions and towards the middle years of the nineteenth century they outnumbered the free agnates of the houses to which they belonged. They engaged in trade and, later in the century, some of them gained legal emancipation from their previous masters.

But not all the slaves were equally acculturated into the house or lineage system. Town-dwelling slaves who lived in the compounds of their masters were in a far better economic and social position than their counterparts who lived in the plantations at Akpabuyo and Odukpani. The plantation-dwelling slaves, although members of the lineage farms, remained in effect outside the house system proper and were less prosperous than the town-dwelling slaves.

Calabar society thus divided into vertical and horizontal social strata. It was internally divided between nobles and slaves, town-dwelling slaves and plantation-dwelling slaves, between town and country, privileged and underprivileged and between the rich and poor. It was in order to resolve some of these dichotomies and to assert the right of the plantation slaves to closer and more meaningful acculturation into the house system that the plantation slaves organized themselves into a movement. It was in Duke Town that 'slave power', if the term may be forgiven, became a formidable political instrument. It took advantage of the politics and tensions within the lineages of the town to place the interests of slaves in the forefront. In 1850–51 they mobilized their strength and under their powerful leaders, such as Eyo Okun, worked for the abolition of the custom of human sacrifices and other social disabilities. Certain Duke Town kings, such as Archibong II, who did not hold high Ekpe offices rallied with the Bloodmen movement (as the plantation slave movement was known) in order to ensure their support for their throne. Leaders of the slave movement and other wealthy slaves attached their signatures to treaties signed between Efik kings and European traders or British consuls.

The traditional socio-political institutions underwent structural and functional modifications in order to accommodate the less privileged but rich slave element into their framework. We have noted, for instance, how Ekpe changed during this period from a fraternity that oppressed the slave class to one that accepted them.

The Ekpe was characteristically a hierarchical, graded, exclusive and authoritative body. When trade was not expanding changes were made in the system of Ekpe grades in order to increase their number and thereby enrol more members. It has been noted, too, how the house system encouraged the town-dwelling slaves to work harder for material benefits and how the house heads had come to rely on slaves in order to increase the prosperity of their houses.

Two significant facts should be noted here. The first is that it was not the external traders but external trade which led to a restructuring of Calabar society in the middle decades of the nineteenth century. The other is that the events took place within a well established social framework, and that they led not to the overthrow but a restructuring of the traditional political framework. The new economic opportunities open to slaves merely re-arranged the patterns of social stratification. Individuals rose to importance and social recognition not on the old basis of birth and consanguinity but on merit measured by wealth. The freemen tried to retain the importance of free birth in the corporate kinship units as a means of sustaining their prestige among the slaves. What the slaves attempted to do—and they were partly successful —was to use the hierarchy to produce a stable meritocracy in place of the old aristocracy.

The political results of the expansion of the oil trade are best seen in the stimulation it provided to commercial and political rivalry between the major towns, namely Duke Town and Creek Town. It is a significant fact that Efik politics and society were dominated by the principle of lineage segmentation. The political system provided for each of the towns to be more or less central-ized in its government. Lineages formed the building blocks of the political system and each of them exercised influence over a par-ticular area. This was particularly true of Duke Town where there were a number of ward segments of local settlements (such as Cobham Town and Henshaw Town) which formed sub-units of the principal group. These sub-units were made up of wards or compounds. The history of the segmentary nature of Calabar society goes back to the days of the original founding ancestors when various families broke away to form secondary and tertiary segments as new generations arrived. Each of these segments had their own internal head (Akpan) and in time organized themselves into an Efik town.

As the external trade of the towns developed, rivalry between towns and within lineages sharpened. The Great Duke Ephraim (1814–1832) succeeded in centralizing political and economic power at Duke Town. After his death and especially during the period examined in this study, the political history of Calabar was marked by conflicts in, and the disintegration of, the old political structure. Also, with the death of the Great Duke in Duke Town and the accession to the rival Creek Town throne of the powerful and wealthy King Eyo II, the political balance was heavily tilted in favour of the latter. The result was the renewal of the conflict between Duke Town and Creek Town for a larger share of the trade and for the favour of extra-territorial elements.

Although the towns competed with one another for commercial and political supremacy, and looked towards the extra-territorial elements to buttress their respective political positions, the structural weaknesses of Efik society were not always exploited successfully by the foreigners. A distinction ought to be made between the political fortunes of Duke Town and Creek Town respectively.

Duke Town was internally divided into a number of rival lineages so that it became a preoccupation of the leadership of that town to expend its energy in containing the rivalries. As a result the Duke Town kings relied far more than Creek Town on extra-territorial elements for support to the ruling lineage. The kings succeeded to the throne, except in a few cases, as a result of an election by supercargoes. The political leadership of the town was thus more open to European intervention or pressure than that of Creek Town. Often the person chosen by the supercargoes to succeed a late ruler was not acceptable to the other lineages which had vied for the position. Discontented candidates began to name themselves 'king of all black men' if the successful one was 'king for the white men'. But reliance upon European supercargoes did not necessarily lead to the Duke Town kings sanctioning the free entry of traders into the interior markets.

While the immediate pressure in Duke Town was such as to engage the kings in internal politics, Creek Town under the rule of the powerful Eyo lineage was spared any extensive involvement in internal politics and concentrated on the exploitation of the oil trade. Eyo II made Creek Town the centre of that trade. Moreover, since Eyo II had served his apprenticeship under the Great Duke Ephraim he was not without political influence in Duke Town. Hence when there was a political crisis in Duke Town, Eyo was often summoned from Creek Town to help in resolving it. In a system of internal conflict and rivalry the ability to settle disputes was highly rated and Eyo's position in Duke Town was thus strengthened. Indeed in 1847 he had declared himself king of all Calabar. But in spite of the proclamation, he dared not overstep the traditional bounds of his authority which was confined to Creek

Town, its hinterland plantations and dependencies of the town. He refused, for instance, to 'blow Ekpe' on Old Town in 1850, although he was ready to use traditional sanctions on towns which he considered to be part of Creek Town (the case of Ebunda and Adiabo mentioned earlier being an example of this form of political action).

After 1858 (the year of King Eyo II's death) the centre of trade moved from Creek Town to Duke Town. But as trade began to stagnate after that year the distribution of the powers within the town precipitated a political crisis as well. It has been argued in this study that the noticeable decline in the efficacy of Efik political leadership at this time cannot be explained merely in terms of a consolidation in the position of the supercargoes and consuls but also by the economic stress which is shown to have developed in the country. The Efik political leadership was thus in a difficult position to redress shifts in the balance of power between the European and Efik traders. In the first place, the European traders found in the trust system of trade a means of weakening the Efik polity. Secondly, the Sierra Leonean traders, who had been invited to collaborate with Efik middlemen in fighting the Liverpool monopolists, began to consider themselves above the sanctions of Efik laws. They were a community owing allegiance to no local government since they claimed to be British nationals. In fact British policy was to consider them neither as Efik nor British subjects but to appeal to the goodwill of the Efik government. Thirdly, the distribution of free papers to slaves who bought their freedom had its own effect on the house system. Those who had the papers were legally emanicipated from the control of the house heads. Finally, there were certain centrifugal tendencies in vogue in the political system. The economic strain also altered the internal distribution of political power between the various towns, and within the towns between the principal lineages. This was most evident in the last quarter of the nineteenth century when the Duke house experienced further segmentation. Henshaw Town began to feel that its old ties with Duke Town had become obsolete and that it had nothing to benefit from them. Duke Town, keen to keep the trade at this time, used traditional sanctions on Henshaw Town (which it considered not as an autonomous town like Old Town or Creek Town but as part of itself) to monopolize the trade in salt. Henshaw Town thought in terms of its own economic interests and, as we have seen, defied the force of tradition by seceding from Duke Town. The Henshaws were originally supported by the missionaries who hoped to gain from separating the potentially Christian Henshaw Town from the 'heathen' Duke Town. But the supercargoes, who had their interests vested in Duke Town and were committed to supporting the ruling lineage, threw their weight in Duke Town's favour. Henshaw Town was finally defeated and made to trade through Duke Town.

The conflict between the Henshaws and the Dukes was symptomatic of the centrifugal tendencies that had begun to characterize the Duke Town political system. Soon other lineages in Duke Town, namely the Archibong, Eyamba and Etim Effiom began to break away from the Duke and found their own separate houses. The segmentation of the Duke house into these autonomous lineages was made possible partly because the party which wielded effective political authority was no longer the ruler of Duke Town (then King Duke) but the colonial government.

European traders and Efik political authority

Though the commercial and quasi-political activities of European traders were such as to challenge Efik political authority, the European supercargoes respected Efik trading chiefs because, like them, they too were capable of imposing a general trade boycott on all trade that passed down the river to the coast. Trade co-ordination between Europeans and Africans was provided by the kings who established personal contact with captains of trading vessels. They alone had the right to call out Ekpe for the settlement of debts owed by Efik traders to European supercargoes; this fact made the latter co-operate with the Efik chiefs who wielded enormous powers over their traders and the trading system. It was also for this reason that European traders, who had joined Ekpe in order to be able to enforce trust obligations, quarrelled with the missionaries when the latter agitated to truncate the powers reposed in Ekpe. The European traders had no alternative but to accept the commercial organization of the coast. They paid harbour dues to the chiefs and in addition honoured the levy of customs duties on every barrel of oil they bought.

There grew on the coast, therefore, a system of convention in which there was a healthy respect for each other's likes and dislikes. Efik chiefs certainly considered themselves to be the equals, if not the superiors of the European traders. This is hardly to be wondered at considering that the middlemen rulers, being the carriers and possessors of produce, had the entire African trade of the Calabar and Cross Rivers in their hands. Moreover, the Efik chiefs could all speak English and some of them even wrote it; they had in many cases sent their sons to England to be educated. They were also exceedingly keen and intelligent traders. Indeed, MacDonald in his report of 1890 seemed to think that they were quite half a century ahead of the chiefs of the Niger 'in point of civilization'. They were treated with considerable deference by European agents. They dined in state with the supercargoes either on board the trading vessels or in the houses of the rivers. There was an exchange not only of goods but of ideas relating to clothes, food and behaviour. They admired European wealth and technology and adopted European trade goods as status symbols. But they never allowed their culture to become Europeanized in any deeper sense. What developed instead was a strong sense of partnership in the profitable exploitation of trade.

But the problems of Efik political authority vis-à-vis European traders during periods of rapid economic and social progress such as the early 1850s differed from those during periods of stagnant or declining trade such as the 1860s and 1870s. It has been shown that the increase in competition between various categories of traders (European supercagoes, independent European traders and Sierra Leonean traders) coincided with a period in which trade remained essentially static. Controls required for a system of free trade and competition did not always exisit.

Efik rulers used their political and economic authority to safe-guard their own commercial interests. They worked to increase their profits by exploiting the competition and destroying the mono-polistic hold Liverpool buyers had over Efik suppliers. In the long run, however, the economic strain worked against the interests of Efik middlemen who lost control of the situation. Partly as a result of this Efik leadership became less effective. European traders tried to beat off the competition from the independent traders and the Sierra Leonean merchants and exploited the weakness in Efik leadership to become the dominant influence. The trust system of trade made society and government vulnerable to pressures from without. European traders demanded their trust payments when they knew that trade was at a standstill and fomented much of the misgivings in Anglo-Efik relations in the 1870s.

The fact of economic strain, which has hitherto not been recog-nized, was a major explanation for the breakdown in Anglo-Efik political relations. It did not, however, spell the downfall of the old system. Supplementary institutions were created by European traders to combine their interests and secure their agreement for a common commercial code. The court of equity, formed in 1856, was resurrected in 1862 with additional provisions. The commercial treaties signed between Efik chiefs and European traders trans-ferred responsibility for the settlement of trade disputes from the kings to the supercargoes who sat in council with the kings and chiefs. But even though the court worked on the principle of association with Efik leaders in the adjustment of trade claims it was in fact an organized pressure group of the European traders. Archibong II tried not unsuccessfully to counter the pressure by holding out against the machinations of Europeans and to effect trade laws to his advantage. It has been shown how Archibong used his traditional powers to stop the trade of the river when the supercargoes in April, 1862 reduced the price of oil on the plea that the English oil market prices were falling. Certainly the European traders had consolidated their position during the period of economic strain. Yet the court was only a supplementary body to Efik political authority and it really never functioned well enough to be a formidable weapon of European traders. It might be noted once again that what enabled the European supercargoes to consolidate their position was their successful exploitation of the weakness (or more specifically the vulnerability) of a commercial organization based on the trust system of trade.

Christian missionaries and Efik political authority

The extra-territorial element which benefited most from the political rivalry between Duke Town and Creek Town was the mission. It has been argued in this work that the influence of the missionaries went further in Calabar than elsewhere on account of this rivalry. Each town was equally keen to have Christian missionaries to strengthen it materially and benefit from the new knowledge of skills and language the mission was expected to spread. So keen was their desire to have missionaries live and work in their respective towns that the kings were anxious to preserve a monopoly over missionary enterprise. The kings were willing to use traditional sanctions and laws to show favour to the church if such favours did not threaten to undermine social and political solidarity.

Missionaries were fortified by an unquestioning belief in their own righteousness and in the depravity of most indigenous institutions. For the most part they condemned what they failed to understand. But missionary enterprise did not radically upset authorities. King Eyo II in particular took a rational view of missionary enterprise and used his powers to direct the 'winds of change' which the missionaries were anxious to set in motion. It was he who moderated the zeal of the missionaries and handled wisely the new and old ideas that were flowing through the life of the community at this time. Some changes which the missionaries proposed Eyo readily sanctioned, for instance, he outlawed human sacrifice, restricted trial by ordeal to public trials, ruled out Sabbath markets, permitted twins to live, stopped the killing of wives at the funerals of their husbands and sanctioned the proper burial of slaves.

Although the missionaries tended to claim much of the credit for abolishing certain traditional customs and beliefs, it has been argued that what the Christian missionaries did was in fact to tip the balance already swinging towards reform in certain areas of traditional life. For example, by 1849 Ekpenyong symbols had lost their traditional ritual importance; the office of the priest of the ndem Efik was less sought after since it conferred no economic benefits on the holder; and human sacrifice became uneconomic in a system that depended on slave labour, and was already under fire by the Bloodmen movement. This is an extremely important point to be borne in mind. The supercargoes and the missionaries thought it possible to end these customs because there was a body of opinion in Calabar, headed by King Eyo II of Creek Town, favouring reform of one kind or another. Some customs either died a natural death or were, as in the case of human sacrifice, abolished by Ekpe.

But Eyo was not prepared to do anything to antagonize the elderly chiefs who saw their closed cosmology threatened by the preachings of missionaries. Despite the steady downpour of Christian denunciations on the traditional way of life and institutions, and despite attacks or attempts to subvert the grass roots of Efik political and social authority, the Efik kings were able to check the excesses to which missionaries resorted at times. In 1851, Eyo, a genuine friend of the mission, forbade the movement of missionaries into the interior without his prior consent.

When the missionaries discovered that King Eyo would not sanction reforms which he believed would upset society and create anarchy and chaos they fell out with him. After 1851 or thereabouts the records indicate a growing incompatability between the reforming zeal of Waddell, the chief missionary, and the cautious, rational approach by Eyo to reform. This soon developed into a crisis in the relations between the mission body and the state, particularly at Duke Town. The establishment of a Mission House in 1856 was significant, for it set itself up as an institution concerned with the sanctions of Efik law and jurisdiction. It harboured fugitives from Efik law and refused to yield them to the evil authorities on the ground that Efik civil authorities were 'ungodly'. Moreover, once the Mission House was built the missionaries no longer relied upon Ekpe for assistance. Goldie believed that Ekpe had been quite useful in the past but for the present and future it was no longer relevant. The tendency of the missionaries was therefore to ignore, discourage or undermine Ekpe, but the poor results were disheartening.

But some of Waddell's strictures on Ekpe were merely a re-flection of the opinion of the oppressed but rising class of affluent slaves who desired not so much the abolition of the society as the widening of its membership to slaves. When Waddell noted that the Ekpe could not be rooted out of the cosmos of the old tradition he began, after 1850, to agitate for the improvement of the con-ditions of slaves. It was noted earlier that by that date there were certain changes in Efik society which weakened the more fragile institutions. Missionary reforms of traditional customs, where they succeeded, were primarily in those areas which had begun to lose their effectiveness rather than in those which were jealously pre-served by Efik kings. For instance, missionaries had no success in outlawing polygamy; the importance and the relevance to the lineage and political system of this institution has already been explained in this work. In a society where kinship and the ability to perpetuate one's lineage were accorded marked prestige, poly-gamy and concubinage or adoption of children (especially sons) helped to assure the attainment of large families. Divorce was not an index of social disorganization since the partners to the mar-riage remained within the kinship group.

Nor did the missionaries have any success when they preached that for the Efik to be saved he had to acquire a new sense of sin. Waddell and his fellow missionaries who tried to convert the whole society only succeeded in exposing rather than converting it to Christianity. In its attempts to abolish witchcraft, too, the mission had little success. The practice of witchcraft was central to a political system which used it in order to destroy rivals within it. The death of a ruling king was an occasion for the release of tension between rival lineages. In order to remove potential rivals there was a general purge from time to time, especially following the death of a king. Witchcraft was a useful device with which to charge a potential candidate and thus be rid of him. Chiefs there-fore organized defence against the wiles of witches believed to attack the community from within. Since witchcraft had relevance to the political machine the missionaries could not persuade the practitioners to surrender it.

The chief contribution of the missionaries lay, therefore, in the promotion of literary activities such as the translation of Biblical literature and hymns into Efik. Even so their educational pro-gramme left much to be desired. The missionaries valued scriptural lessons and the teaching of Efik; the Efik on the other hand saw education in relation to trade. Their economic system did not provide the leisure necessary to acquire the kind of formal educa-tion the missionaries had in mind.

In areas where missionaries were able to effect reforms or changes, the Efik rulers who had sanctioned these changes soon used them to serve their own political ends. It was noted that in 1850 Duke Town and Creek Town tried to exert their authority over Ebunda and Adiabo by legislating against the custom of human sacrifice which continued to prevail in the latter town. Efik rulers used the new laws to build some houses and to break others. It had been suggested that the Sabbath day observance could well have been a very useful political weapon if some Calabar houses dealt regularly in markets which were held on the equivalent of Sundays while others did not.

The consul and Efik political authority

In their relations with the British consuls, the kings of Creek Town and Duke Town were generally fortunate. For it was part of British policy on the coast in the consular days to support African political authority where it appeared to be effective. Archibong II, for instance, was supported by Consul Beecroft in his attempts to contain the Bloodmen movement and to strengthen the political authority of the state. It must be remembered that the powers of the consuls were limited and that, although the primary aim of establishing consulate government was to safeguard British trade, the consul had no jurisdiction over British subjects. British traders could appeal to him when the Efik government broke down or when trade was endangered. But as he lived on the Spanish island of Fernando Po and had no regular means of transport Beecroft only rarely visited the Calabar coast. The court of equity that the European traders formed was in part to overcome the inability of the consul to regulate trade and to provide the local government of European traders.

Although Beecroft and some of the other consuls kept away from Efik politics in line with official British policy, some of the other consuls did not. Also, with the death of King Eyo in 1858, the centre of effective political power moved from the Efik kings to the supercargoes and consuls. Consul Hutchinson, for instance, defended the mischief of the supercargoes in 1856 and blamed the Efik government alone for the breakdown in law and order largely fomented by the supercargoes. But by and large the consul, until colonial times, tried to remain outside Efik political authority and intervened in local politics only when he was summoned by the Efik kings or by European supercargoes. The missionaries and the supercargoes often tried to drive a hard bargain with the Efik kings and chiefs by threatening to summon the consul to the coast. But the consuls did not seriously challenge the internal or external policies of the kings although they tried to bring pressure to bear upon them when the British felt that there was a need to do so.

* * *

The peoples of Calabar were approached by Europeans from three angles: economically, as traders desiring a profitable exchange with the commodities produced in the hinterland of the Calabar towns; socially, as missionaries seeking to replace those institutions, traditions and values which had in the past maintained the social and religious fabric of society, with Christian morality and an alien religion; politically, as representatives of the British government desiring the promotion of British commercial interests in the Bights and rivers of the coast. Though these groups were more or less organized there were often conflicts between the members of each group. However, conflicts were not based on the ends they sought to achieve but on the best means to attain them.

Yet what must be emphasized in the political and social development of Calabar in pre-colonial times is the crucial importance of the 'internal logic and structure' of Efik society. Calabar was a politically ordered society with all the necessary apparatus for the administration of government and trade. A working system of political and social co-operation provided links in the mechanisms which connected the structure of kingship and clans, of political and religious authorities with the normal organization of daily life. Reliance was placed on informal controls exerted by kinships, Ekpe and the imposition of supernatural sanctions. Ekpe preserved the stability of society by checking rather than preventing civil strife and internecine squabbles, and by making laws and enforcing them. Though there was great rivalry between Efik towns there were also devices to resolve disputes between them. Once a candidate to a disputed election was successful there was an efficient system of checks and balances which prevented the political heads from abusing their powers. The king as a member of the highest grade of Ekpe was in a position to mobilize the lower grades to do his bidding. But because his decision-making powers were embedded within the heavily ritualized company of his high grade numbers, there was a strong antidote to abuse of his power and authority. He could be removed from office if he was found guilty of abusing his office. The etubom (head of the house) could be similarly deposed by the house members.

In addition, there was also a well developed economic system based not on barter, as contemporary traders described it, but on capital and credit. The internal economy was managed by various ranks of chiefs on a corporate basis, the principle being that all Efik traders traded through their house heads who in turn dealt with the king of the town. Wealth was distributed through multiple reciprocal obligations based on kinship and other ties. The road to power lay through not only external trade and support from European traders but also through a chief's ability to secure the loyalty of his kinsmen and other members. There were regular markets and seasonal fairs and the lines of trade and cultures radiated into the hinterland. The towns were therefore not only political units but also nodal points of a widespread trading system.

Because the Calabar towns were politically, socially and economically well ordered, and their rulers autonomous in their relations with one another, change and development in pre-colonial times took place largely within an existing framework. Rulers controlled the pace and direction of change and modified the traditional institutions to ensure that externally initiated changes did not disrupt the orderly working of the system. It was generally only in times of great economic strain, when the economic and political foundations of Efik authority were threatened, that the political system found it difficult to contain the strain imposed upon it by external agents. It was on these occasions that European traders consolidated their position and the rivalry within towns and lineages was greatest.

The colonial order

The climax of more than half a century of active British political and socio-economic activities was the imposition of the colonial order. A crucial single explanation for the dramatic transformation that Calabar underwent in the years after 1891 is that in the colonial situation, the Efik kings and chiefs were not in control of the extent of change they were willing to accept. Though they retained some of the political authority vested in them in the traditional system, the kings and chiefs were no longer in a position to determine the direction and depth of change. The Efik political authority lost its supremacy in the colonial situation. Once regarded by the Efik as a limited power group, the British merchants and consuls were now beginning to be seen as an ultimate political menace. In the pre-colonial era the Efik were no doubt apprehensive of the intentions of the missionaries whom they suspected, as early as 1846, of taking the land away from them. Relations with European traders were seen as economic. This pattern endured until colonial times and reached an equilibrium with the formation of the court of equity.

When Calabar came under colonial rule (effectively after 1891) there was a change in the political fortunes of the state. The kings became powerless once their right to comey was replaced by subsidies. The kings were also stripped of their power over external trade and diplomatic relations, and Ekpe as a political and judicial organization gave way before a new and alien judicial system. Colonialism seemed to alter the framework by which the Efik had hitherto interpreted and evaluated the desirability of change in a Western direction. The political and economic basis of the house system suffered with the passage of two ordinances in 1901. The first of these abolished domestic slavery and the second—the Native House Rule Ordinance—was intended to keep the houses intact even though domestic slavery had been abolished. The ordinance disturbed the delicate balance which traditionally existed between the house heads and their members. In its operation, the powers of the house heads over their members were increased. It also tended to remove the system of checks and balances. Slaves were encouraged by the passage of the Slave Ordinance to abscond from the house and the consequent social malaise affected both house heads and members alike.

Besides, the appointment of Efik political agents, who formed part of the new power structure, meant in practice the emergence of a new category of Efik with authority not derived from traditional ranking in society. The new demand for clerks and an educated literate group led to a burst of enthusiasm for education. What mattered in the colonial period was not to become kings or house heads, for they were not any longer able to effectively mobilize the political system, but to be recruited into the colonial administration as clerks or political agents. The colonial period became, as it were, a period of oligarchy rather than one of monarchy.

Imperialism also raised the Europeans to a ruling caste. Intimacies between colonials and the Efik were incompatible under the structure of colonial authority. Life as it was for the early pioneers was at an end. The missionaries welcomed colonialism because it facilitated religious change by shedding an aura of prestige and authority over the religion of the conquerers, and the opening up of new areas for missionary endeavour. Even so, the hinterland Efik regarded Mary Slessor, for instance, not so much a missionary or a government agent but as a person useful in settling disputes between the Okoyong and other peoples and in placing their town in the political forefront rather than a 'bush relation' of Creek Town.

But colonialism did not entirely wipe out all the old traditions; vicissitudes of the past still remained in certain areas of Efik tradition. A good example of this was the land tenure system. Although the Efik were enmeshed in a new economy they continued to maintain rearguard control over land tenure rights and their economic position as middlemen in the trade system. When, after 1891, the colonial administration tried to break the control of the Efik and the hinterland chiefs over the middleman system and extend its political authority to the hinterland it met with the sturdy resistance of a determined people. Thus the greatest resistance to colonialism was not so much political as economic. In this the Efik were of course assisted by the fact that the European firms, until the end of the first decade of the present century, were not willing to risk their capital in establishing inland trading stations. The British attempted to counter Efik resistance with punitive expeditions and to employ technological superiority and military power to attain dominance over the unwilling peoples of the hinterland.

*   *   *

The external factors in Calabar history must hence be examined in close relation to the internal factors. Fluctuations in trade, internal political rivalries and the social structure turned the wheels of fortune and determined the course of political and social development. To some extent it is true that any society in transition permits ranges of 'structural substitutability' consistent with the requisites for its survival as a system. Within some range, changes in the way particular functions were performed in Efik society made little difference to the total structure, but beyond that range it had wide ramifications. Efik politics and society were characterized by a remarkable syncretic capacity in which accommodation and modification, rather than conflict and anarchy, were the keynotes of historical development.

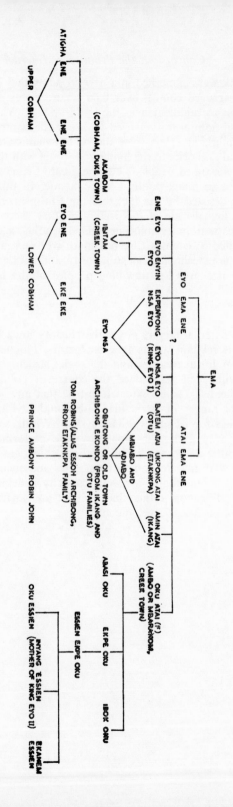

APPENDIX A
STRUCTURAL GENEALOGY OF THE EFIK
(i) THE EMA GROUP

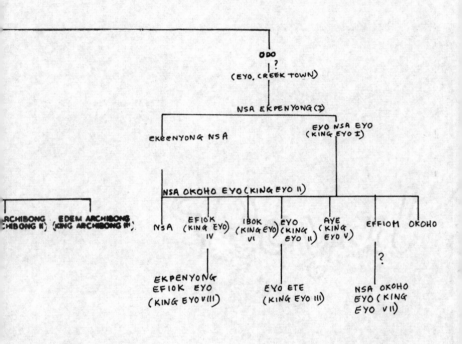

ODO
?
(EYO, CREEK TOWN)

NSA EKPENYONG (I)

EKEENYONG NSA

EYO NSA EYO
(KING EYO I)

NSA OKOHO EYO (KING EYO II)

ARCHIBONG (CHIBONG II)　EDEM ARCHIBONG (KING ARCHIBONG IV)

NSA　EFIOK (KING EYO IV)　IBOK (KING EYO VI)　EYO (KING EYO II)　AYE (KING EYO V)　EFFIOM　OKOHO

EKPENYONG EFIOK EYO (KING EYO VIII)

EYO ETE (KING EYO III)

?

NSA OKOHO EYO (KING EYO VII)

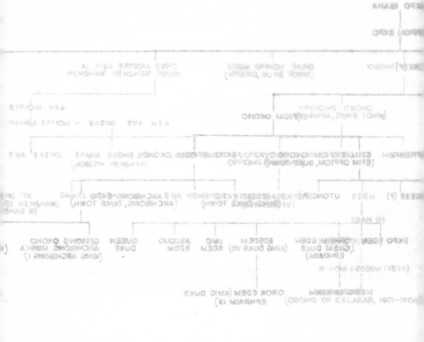

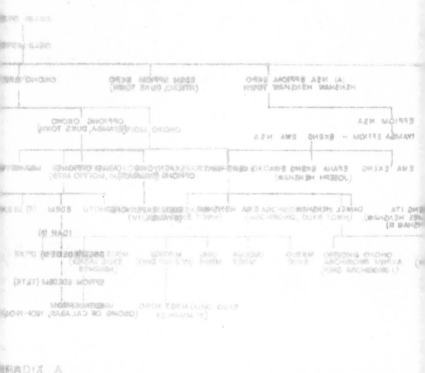

APPENDIX B

A NOTE ON EFIK NAMES

Traditional names

The Efik, like the Ibo and Ibibio, followed the custom of naming their children according to the week days which invariably fitted into the market day system of their areas. The Efik calendar consisted of an eight-day week. The week was divided into a 'big week' (akwa) and a 'small week' (ekpri), each of which consisted of four days. The following table shows the market week and the corresponding names of children born on any four of them.

Day of Week	Name of male child born on that day	Name of female child born on that day
Akwa Ederi	Edet	Edit (Arit)
Akwa Efion	Effiong	Afiong
Akwa Ikwo	Asuquo	Iquo
Akwa Iyibio	Etim	Atim

The same names held true for those who were born during the 'small week'.

Other names were subsequently conferred on the Efik child, and these tended to displace the week-day names. A person born on the day, Akwa Ederi, and called Edet, may take on another name, such as Offiong or Asibong. In time the second names stick fast to the original and become just as popular as the first. Also, the time of the day might determine the name of a new-born child. The names Okon (for boys) and Nkoyo (for girls) are given to children born at night. It is also common to have names relating to the circumstances of the parents, the community or the child itself, at the time of birth. The name Akpan is given to the first-born male. The posthumous child might be named Edem (meaning 'behind' or 'later on') whether or not his father had that name. The name Asibong or Obong might be given to children born during the installation of the father or anyone else in the community to the title of chief or king (the Efik word for which is Obong). The names of secret societies such as Ekpe, and deities such as Adem, Anansa, Ekpenyong and Inyang also feature among Efik names.

Anglicization of traditional names

Though Efik names have much in common with Ibibio and Annang names, they have developed certain peculiarities which mark the Efik as a distinct people. The distinctiveness is due to European influence which was brought to bear on the Efik much earlier than their neighbours farther away from the coast.

As a result of the early contact, traditional Efik names became more anglicized in form than either Ibibio or Annang names. Europeans, who found it difficult to pronounce Efik names, modified them in spelling and pronunciation to suit their convenience. The name Orok (or Aduk) was

U   287

anglicized to Duke, Asibong to Archibong, Edem to Adam, Effiom to Ephraim, Awabom to Cobham, Ansa (or Nsa) to Henshaw, Okon to Hogan and Ene to Henry. Today, most Efik spell their names in the anglicized form. For easy reference, it is in this form that their names appear in this study, but where the traditional names are known they are given in brackets.

APPENDIX C

THE SEVEN EFIK COMMUNITIES
(and a list of houses)

1.	Iboku	Duke Town
		Eyamba Town
		Cobham Town
		Henshaw Town
		Creek Town
2.	Obutong	Old Town
3.	Adiabo and Ibonda	—
4.	Mbiabo	Mbiabo Edere
		Ikot Offiong
		Ikoneto

presently in Duke Town. These being
unable to stand have given themselves up
to the other brother towns, chiefly Duke
Town, but are still in existence although
subordinate.

5. Enwan
6. Usuk Akpa
7. Aba Eyen

No.	Town or District	Family/House	Sub-House
1.	Duke Town	Duke Family	Ikot Ene or Duke Ephraim
			Ephraim Adam (Tete)
			King Duke IX
			Black Davis
			Yellow Duke
			Adam Duke or Edet Nsa
			Etim Effiong Duke Nsisuk
			Efiong Essien
			Nakanda
			Adam Iron Bar
			Queen Duke
			Hogan Iron Bar
			Effana Offiong Efana Nsa
			Okon Idem
			Eyo Edem
2.		Archibong Family	King Archibong I
			King Archibong II
			Yanabo
3.		Ntiero	Eyo Ndem
			Offiong Efiwat
			Efio Esien
4.	Eyamba Town	Eyamba	Obong James Eyamba
			Joseph Eyamba
			Adam Eyamba
			John Eyamba
			Ntiere Ekpenyong
			Ekpenyong Okon

289

No.	Town or District	Family/House	Sub-House
			Minika Efiom Okoho
			Ekpa Essien Bassey Offiong
			Mkponam Esien
			Otu Bassey
			Etim Bassey Offiong
			Efiom Okoho Essien
5.	Cobham Town	Cobham Family	Egbo Bassey
			John Boco
			Antikha Ene
			Ene Uyi
6.	Henshaw Town	Henshaw Family	Eken Ewa
		A. Ewa Ekeng	Inyan Ewa
			Ansa Ewa
			Ewa Eken Ewa
			Akun
		B. Ekeng Iwat	Efana Eken
			Ekanam Eken
			Ered Eken
			Efana Ikpon
			Ekpo Nsa
		C. Efana Offiong	Efana Efana
			Edem Efana
			Ekpo Nsa
		D. Anden Ankoi	Eken Abia Ndem
			Abasi Ukpon
			Andem Ukpon
7.	Old Town	Old Town Family	Ikot Otu
			Ikan
			Itak Ukpa
8.	Creek Town	Eyo Family	King Eyo II
			King Eyo III
			Ako Eyo Nsa
			Aye Eyo Nsa
			Efiok Ekpenyon Nsa
			Efiok Eyo Nsa
9.		Ibitam Family	Ibitam Ibitam
			Okpo Ibitam
			Ekpo Enyi
10.		Ambo Family	Antikha Esien
			Oku Esien
			Ekpenyon Esien
			Etim Ared
			Hogan Bassey
			Ema

No.	Town or District	Family/House	Sub-House
11.	Adiabo District	Adiabo Family	Ikot Ubo Ikot Ukpa Usukhode Okut Ikan Akani Obio
12.	Ibonda Town	Ibonda Family	Ibonda
13.	Ikoneto Town	Ikoneto Family	Ikot Ukpo Ikot Ani Ikot Ukpon Ikot Ukotebi Ikot Ayok Ikot Ito
14.	Ikot Offiong Town	Ikot Offiong Family	Ikot Eton Ani Ikot Offiong Ani
15.	Mbiabo Town	Mbiabo Family	Offiong Inyan Iwat Eniang Owon

List of the houses belonging to Duke Henshaw sold by Archibong family to King Duke IX after the death of Duke Henshaw:

1. House of Asuquo Ete Mbom.
2. House of Inyan Ibuno (or Isokop).
3. House of Asuquo Ene.
4. House of Eshien Abasi.
5. House of Owono.

APPENDIX D

THE VOLUME AND VALUE OF TRADE AT
THE BIGHTS OF BENIN AND BIAFRA
IN THE NINETEENTH CENTURY

Year	Vol. of Exports (in tons)	Value of Exports (in £)	Vol. of Imports (in tons)	Value of Imports (in £)
1834	13,945[1]			
1837	11,000[1]	400,000[9]		
1845	25,000[1]			
1846	18,000[1]	750,000[10]		
1850	21,723[2]			
1851	29,000[2]			
1853	30,000[1]			
1854–5	26,630[3]			
1856	25,060[4]			
1857	21,592[5]			
1859	16,102[6]			
1864	26,000[7]	800,000[7]		
1871	25,000[8]			
1891–2		780,000[11]		740,000[11]
1892–3		800,000[11]		960,000[11]
1893–4		820,000[11]		960,000[11]
1894–5		740,000[11]		825,000[11]
1895–6		—		—
1896–7		650,000[11]		785,000[11]
1897–8		639,000[11]		750,000[11]
1898–9		730,000[11]		770,000[11]

REFERENCES

1 *Parl. Pap.*, 1854, Vol. 65 (296), Quantities of Palm Oil imported into United Kingdom, 1844–53.
2 K. O. Dike, *Trade and Politics*, et seq., p. 100.
3 N. H. Stilliard, op. cit., p. 77. This figure is for the Bonny and Kalabari trade alone.
4 *Parl. Pap.*, 1857, Vol. 16 (2201), Report by T. J. Hutchinson on the Trade of the Bight of Biafra for 1856. The figure shown in the table does not, like the other figures, include that of the Bight of Benin.
5 N. H. Stilliard, op. cit., Chapter 5.
6 Ibid., p. 78.
7 F.O. 2/45: Confidential, Fernando Po, Burton to Russell, 15 April, 1864 (private), printed for the F.O.
8 F.O. 84/1356, No. 371, Consul Livingstone's Memo. Received by F.O., 3 December, 1871.
9 R. Jamieson, *Commerce with Africa* (London, 1859), p. 5.
10 *Parl. Pap.*, 1842, Vol. 12, Part 11, Appendix and index, palm oil trade, pp. 33–36. Cf. with *Parl. Pap.*, 1842, Vol. 11, Part 1, appendix and index, No. 7, pp. 574–84, Memo. on British Trade with Africa.

Also *Parl. Pap.*, 1842, Vol. 11 (551), Hutton's evidence, question 3811.

11 Annual Reports for the Niger Coast Protectorate, 1891–99 (financial year ending 31 March). Cf. these figures derived from the annual reports with those given by A. F. Mockler-Ferryman, op. cit., reproduced on p. 240, above.

APPENDIX E

LIST OF TOWNS REPRESENTED ON THE NATIVE
COUNCIL OF OLD CALABAR, 1903

Efik Name	English Name	Head Chief
Atakpa	*Old Calabar Town*	*Obong Adam Ephr. Adam*
Ufok Edem Umo	Duke Town	do.
Ekpri Okoretonko	Cobham Town	James Egbo Bassey (Etubom)
Ufok Offiong Okoho	Eyamba Town	—
Nsidung	Henshaw Town	Daniel Henshaw (Etubom)
Obutong	Old Town	Efiom Otu Ekong (Etubom)
Aqua Okoretonko	*Creek Town*	Obong Eyo Honesty
Adak Uko	—	do.
Otung	—	Itam Itam (Etubom)
Mbarakom	—	Esien John Ambo (Etubom)
Ibonda	—	Okon Nsubong (Etubom)
Adiako	*Adiabo Town*	Otu Ita (Etubom)
Akani Obio	—	Okon Efa
Okurikan	—	Ewa Asako
Usukhode	—	Otu Ita (Etubom)
Ikoro Ukpa	—	Ikot Ukpa
Ikot Mbo	—	Ikot Mbo
Mbiabo Usuk	*Ikoneto Town*	
Mbiabo	—	Ansa Okon Offiong (Etubom)
Ikoroyak	—	Offiong Awat (Etubom)
Ito	—	Okon Itri
Ekon	—	Ukpon Esien
Ibiabo Edere	*Ikot Offiong Town*	
Ekot Offiong		Eyo Etim Ntuk (Etubom)
Mbiabo		
Abakpa	*Qua Town*	
Akwa Obio	—	Edim Ebana
Akim	—	Abasi Tata

APPENDIX F

BRITISH CONSULS AND HIGH COMMISSIONERS IN THE BIGHTS

1. *British Consuls of the Bights of Benin and Biafra, 1849–1891*
1849   John Beecroft
From 1853 onwards there were separate Consuls for the Bights of Benin and Biafra.

Consuls of the Bights of Biafra (Fernando Po)
1853   John Beecroft
1855   T. J. Hutchinson
1861   Capt. F. R. Burton
1864   C. Livingstone

Consuls of the Bights of Benin and Biafra
1867   C. Livingstone
1873   G. Hartley
1878   D. Hopkins
1880   E. H. Hewett

2. *High Commissioner and Consuls-General of the Oil Rivers and Niger Coast Protectorate*
1891   Major C. M. MacDonald
1896   R. D. Moor

3. *High Commissioners and Consuls-General of the Oil Rivers Protectorate (Headquarters: Calabar)*
1891   Major C. M. MacDonald
1892   R. D. R. Moor (Administration)

4. *High Commissioners and Consuls-General of the Niger Coast Protectorate*
1893   Major C. M. MacDonald
1894   R. D. R. Moor (Administration)
1895   Sir C. M. MacDonald, K.C.M.G.
1896   R. D. R. Moor, R.C.M.G.
1897   J. R. Philips
           Major H. L. Gallwey (Administration)
           Sir R. D. R. Moor, K.C.M.G.
1898   Major H. L. Gallwey (Administration)
1899   Sir R. D. R. Moor, K.C.M.G.
1900   Major H. L. Gallwey (Administration)

5. *High Commissioners of the Protectorate of S. Nigeria (Headquarters: Calabar)*
1900   Sir R. D. R. Moor, K.C.M.G.
1901   L. Probyn (Administration)
1902   Sir R. D. R. Moor, K.C.M.G.
1903   W. F. W. Posbery (Administration)
1904   W. Egerton, C.M.G.
1905   J. J. Thorburn (Administration)
1906   Sir W. Egerton, K.C.M.G.

6. *Provincial Commissioners of the Eastern Province, 1906–1914* *(Headquarters: Calabar)*

1906   A. B. Harcourt (Ag.)
          H. Bedwell

7. *Officers in Charge, Calabar District*

1896	H. Bedwell	Asst. Dist. Comm.
1897	H. Bedwell	Ag. Dist. Comm.
1898	H. M. Douglas	Ag. Dist. Comm.
1899	J. Watts	Asst. Dist. Comm.
	H. M. Douglas	Ag. Dist. Comm.
1900	J. Watts	Ag. Dist. Comm.
1901	J. Watts	Ag. Dist. Comm.
	A. W. Biddell	Asst. Dist. Comm.
	W. C. Syer	Asst. Dist. Comm.
1902	J. Watts	Dist. Comm.
	E. D. Simpson	Ag. Dist. Comm.
	C. Partridge	Asst. Dist. Comm.
1903	J. Watts	Dist. Comm.
1904	J. C. Colton	Asst. Dist. Comm.
	R. A. Roberts	Dist. Comm.
1905	H. P. Chamley	Dist. Comm.
1906	H. P. Chamley	Dist. Comm.
	Capt. H. R. H. Crawford	Asst. Dist. Comm.
	A. W. Biddell	Dist. Comm.

BIBLIOGRAPHY

I. PRIMARY SOURCES

A. GOVERNMENT RECORDS

(i) CALABAR PROVINCIAL OFFICE PAPERS, catalogued 'CALPROF', deposited in the National Archives, Ibadan and Enugu. The records cover the main phases of the administrative history of the country; they contain the despatches of the Foreign Office and the British consuls, the records of the court of equity, account papers, treaties and agreements, proclamations and Native Court papers. The details of the pre-1906 records, the bulk of which are unbound papers, are as follows:

(a) **Pre-Consular Records** (pre-1849). These records are the earliest in the CALPROF series, and they span the years 1846–1849, and are classified as CALPROF 1—Pre-Consular papers: Correspondence (five bundles).

(b) **Consular Papers** (1849–1891), classified as:
CALPROF 2—Consular Papers: Despatches (47 bundles).
CALPROF 3—Consular Papers: Court of equity records (5 bundles).
CALPROF 4—Consular Papers: Correspondence (13 bundles).
CALPROF 5—Consular Papers: Miscellaneous (11 bundles).

(c) **Records of the Oil Rivers and Niger Coast Protectorate** (1891–1899), classified as:
CALPROF 6—Correspondence: Commissioner (11 bundles).
CALPROF 7—Despatches: Commissioner (2 bundles).
CALPROF 8—Miscellaneous (8 bundles).

(d) **Records of 'Southern Nigeria'** (1900–1906), classified as:
CALPROF 9—Correspondence: Commissioner (18 bundles).
CALPROF 10—Miscellaneous (16 bundles).

Apart from the above ten in the CALPROF series deposited in the Ibadan headquarters, there are some others preserved in the Enugu branch of the archives. The references made in the book to CALPROF papers refer to the Ibadan collection. It might be added that the classification of CALPROF papers in the Ibadan and Enugu archives differs in respect of the serial numbering.

(ii) COLONIAL SECRETARY'S CORRESPONDENCE, known as the C.S.O. series, available in the National Archives, Ibadan. The colonial secretariat was a single organization functioning under the direction of the Chief Secretary to the government, through whom all papers passed en route to and from the governor. The papers cover the period 1891–1951, and for the period covered in this study they consist largely of despatches, registers, reports, administrative instruments, letter books, proclamations and treaties. Those pertinent to the period examined in the study are:

Archives Ref.	Covering dates	Despatches	Volumes
C.S.O. 1/13	1891–1906	Oil Rivers, Niger Coast Protectorate, and Southern Nigeria despatches to the F.O. and C.O. (first ten	40

Archives Ref.	Covering dates	Despatches	Volumes
		volumes addressed to the F.O.)	
C.S.O. 1/14	1891–1906	Oil Rivers and Niger Coast Protectorate and Southern Nigeria despatches from the F.O. and C.O. (first 29 volumes issued from the F.O. and next 21 from the C.O.	49
C.S.O. 1/15	1900–1907	Southern Nigeria Confidential despatches to the C.O. (Secretary of State)	12
C.S.O. 1/16	1899–1907	Southern Nigeria Confidential despatches from the C.O.	13
C.S.O. 1/18	1890–1904	Southern Nigeria Circular despatches (open and confidential) from the C.O.	5
C.S.O. 2/20	1904–1913	Registers of Southern Nigeria despatches from the C.O.	10
C.S.O. 2/22	1874–1891	Register of Nigeria despatches from the C.O.	5
C.S.O. 3/2	1906–1912	Telegrams: Governor of the Colony and Protectorate of Southern Nigeria to and from the C.O.	13
C.S.O. 4/1	1886–1937	Governor's Inspection Notes	6
C.S.O. 4/2	1872–1933	Statistical Returns	25
C.S.O. 4/3	1864–1946	Miscellaneous Reports	27
C.S.O. 5/1	1852–1914	Treaties	47 originals and copies
C.S.O. 5/2	1842–1914	Agreements	47 originals and copies
C.S.O. 5/3	1842–1868	Deeds of Conveyance	8 originals and copies
C.S.O. 5/4	1892–1952	Proclamations	10 pieces
C.S.O. 5/5	1863–1960	Orders-in-Council	138 originals and copies
C.S.O. 5/6	1886–1951	Letters Patent	31 originals and copies
C.S.O. 5/7	1862–1943	Commissions and Warrants	64 originals and copies
C.S.O. 5/8	1862–1960	Royal Instructions	50 originals and copies
C.S.O. 5/9	1886–1895	Declarations and Undertakings	24 originals and copies
C.S.O. 5/10	1887–1888	Conventions	7 originals and copies

Archives Ref.	Covering dates	Despatches	Volumes
C.S.O. 8/2	1896–1909	Governor of Lagos and Southern Nigeria Letter Books of Incoming Local Correspondence	10 Volumes
C.S.O. 8/4	1874–1904	Governor of Lagos and Southern Nigeria Letter Books of Incoming Correspondence from firms (local and foreign), Chiefs, British consuls and Governors of Neighbouring British and French territories	3 Volumes
C.S.O. 8/5	1862–1923	Outgoing Correspondence	29 Volumes
C.S.O. 8/7	1889–1936	Governor . . . Miscellaneous Correspondence	10 Volumes

(iii) FOREIGN OFFICE PAPERS (on microfilm, University of Ibadan library).

F.O. 2 (Fernando Po): African Consular. This series covers the period between 1849 and 1872 and deals with the activities of British consuls in the Bights.

The papers relevant to this study in the F.O. 2 series, available at Ibadan, are as follows:

F.O. 2/3,   1839–1846
F.O. 2/9,   1853
F.O. 2/13,   1855
F.O. 2/15,   1856
F.O. 2/16,   1856
F.O. 2/19,   1856–1857
F.O. 2/29,   1859
F.O. 2/35,   1860
F.O. 2/40,   1861

F.O 84 (Slave Trade). This series includes consular despatches, from the Board of Trade, the Admiralty, the Treasury and the Colonial Office.

The papers relevant to this study in the F.O. 84 series, available at Ibadan, are as follows:

F.O. 84/858,   1851
F.O. 84/1061,   1858
F.O. 84/1176,   1862
F.O. 84/1265,   1866
F.O. 84/1290,   1868
F.O. 84/1308,   1869
F.O. 84/1377,   1873

(iv) COLONIAL OFFICE PAPERS

C.O. 84 (Fernando Po). This series consists of original correspondence and entry books and covers the period of the British occupation of Fernando Po, but has a good deal of material on Calabar during that period.

(v) PARLIAMENTARY PAPERS AND REPORTS

(d) **Parliamentary papers** (University of Ibadan library).

1842, (551) Report from the Select Committee on the West Coast of Africa, 5 Aug. 1842.

1849, Report from the Select Committee on the West Coast of Africa.

1865, (170) Sir Harry St. George Ord: Report into the condition of the British Settlements on the West Coast of Africa, Colonial Office, 28 Mar. 1865.

1865, (412) Report from Select Committee on Africa (Western Coast), 26 June, 1865.

1873, LXV, GREAT BRITAIN, Report by Consul Livingstone on the Trade and Commerce of Old Calabar for the year 1872 in *Reports from Her Majesty's Consuls on the Manufactures, Commerce, of their Consular Districts*, No. 4, c–828, Aug. 1873 (London, 1873) pp. 693–700.

(b) Confidential Prints (University of Ibadan library).

GREAT BRITAIN, *Correspondence respecting the Oil Rivers District and the Question of a British Protectorate, 7 Aug. 1879–31 Mar. 1884*. C.P. 4824–5, 4865, 4955, 4962.

GREAT BRITAIN, *Correspondence respecting Affairs in the Oil Rivers District of the West Coast of Africa, and the Increase of Consular Supervision and British Responsibilities, 20 Nov. 1883–Dec. 1884*, C.P. 5004, 5021, 5063.

GREAT BRITAIN, Foreign Office. *Report by Major MacDonald of his visit as Her Majesty's Commissioner to the Niger and Oil Rivers*. C.P. 5913, Mar. 1890.

(c) Printed Reports (University of Ibadan library).

GREAT BRITAIN, Colonial Office. *Report on the Oil Rivers District, West Coast of Africa* (1 Dec. 1888) by H. H. Johnston. Also available in the F.O. 84/1882 series.

GREAT BRITAIN, Foreign Office. *Annual Reports on the Niger Coast Protectorate*.

NIGERIA, *Report of the Aba Commission of Inquiry* (Lagos, 1930) Appendix III (i) Memorandum as to the origins and causes of the Recent Disturbances in the Owerri and Calabar Provinces by C. T. Lawrence, Secretary, Southern Provinces, Enugu, 16.1.1930.

NIGERIA, *Report of the Commission appointed to enquire into the fears of minorities and the means of allaying them* (H.M.S.O., London, 1958), Part 3: The Eastern Region.

Jones, G. I. *Report of the Position, Status and Influence of Chiefs and Natural Rulers in the Eastern Region of Nigeria* (Enugu, 1956).

Hart, A. K. *Report on the Enquiry into the Dispute over the Obongship of Calabar* (Government Printer, Enugu, 1964). Official document No. 17 of 1964.

(d) Intelligence Reports (National Archives, Ibadan).

Mylius, N. A Report on the Calabar Division with special reference to the Efik clan, 5 Mar. 1932. C.S.O. 26/3, file 27627, Vol. 1. Report on the Native Organization of the Efik clan, Calabar Division.

Alderton, E. C. A Report on the Efut Fragments in the Calabar Division, with referenece to their representation in the Efik Native Authority, 21 Jan. 1933. C.S.O. 26/3, file 27627, Vol. 2.

Alderton, E. C. A Report on the Qua Clan, n.d. C.S.O. 26/3, file 27627, Vol. 2.

Floyer, R. K. Itu Intelligence Reports, 1935. File 31013.

Harding, H. J. M. and others. Intelligence Report on the Oku, Mbiabo and Ayadegbe Clans, Enyong Division, Calabar Province, 19 Oct. 1932. C.S.O. 26/3, file 28862.

Sealy-King, L. Intelligence Report on the Okoyong Clan, Calabar Division, Calabar Province, 11 June, 1931. C.S.O. 26/3, file 27674.

Harding, H. J. M. Intelligence Report on the Ibionos, Idoros and strangers upon Ibiono land in Itu District, 13 Feb. 1933. C.S.O. 26/3, file 28881.

(e) **Assessment and Re-assessment Reports on the Calabar Division by C. F. Colye (1927).** (National Archives, Ibadan.)

(f) **Documents of West African Interest from the National Archives of Rhodesia and Nyasaland.** (On microfilm at University of Ibadan library.)

Journals of Sir H. H. Johnston, 26 Jan. 1887–20 Jan. 1888 covering his service as H.M. Consul in the Niger Coast Protectorate. Charles Livingstone, 1821–1873. Seven letters written during his service as H.M. Consul at Fernando Po and Calabar.

B. MISSIONARY RECORDS

(a) **The Hope Waddell Journals.** (On microfilm, University of Ibadan library). Only five of the eleven volumes of Hope M. Waddell's private diaries are extant. For the period 1846–1856 they are a most invaluable treasure chest of information. The journals are in manuscript form and may be classified as follows:

Vol. 1 (1846)
Vol. 7 (1849)
Vol. 8 (1850–1851)
Vol. 10 (1853–1855)
Vol. 11 (1855–1856)

(b) **Other manuscripts and printed sources:**

Letter Books of the United Presbyterian Mission Board covering the period Dec. 1847–Aug. 1882, containing copies of letters to the principal missionaries.

Missionaries Letter Books No. 2, covering the period 31 Aug. 1856–29 Jan. 1875, dealing largely with financial matters.

United Presbyterian *Missionary Record* (printed), a periodical to interest supporters of the missionary society and containing estimates of expenditure.

Minutes of the Foreign Mission Committee (printed), which contains summaries of the transactions and business conducted by the committee.

Jones, Rev. E. Journal of a Voyage from Sierra Leone to Fernando Po in the Months of April, May and June, 1853, CMS Records, West Africa Mission, CA1/0129.

(c) **Records which were originally held by the Presbyterian Archives at Afikpo for the period before 1906, now deposited in the Enugu Archives.**

The records consist of minutes of local chuch meetings, church statistics and a station log book. They are of greater relevance to the internal workings of the Presbyterian Church, which fall outside the scope of this study.

The following is the list of articles available:

Minutes of the Presbytery of Biafra, continuous in five volumes from 1858–1926, in manuscript form.

Minute book from 1894–1898. Calabar Mission Council Minutes, four volumes, covering the period 1847–1884, 1884–1905.
Minute Book of the Up River Committee, 1890–1894. Letters from the Foreign Missions Committee, Scotland, 1856–1920.
Missionary Record of the United Presbyterian Church, 1846–1861, 1868–1873, 1878–1881.
Duke Town Church: Financial, Attendance and other Statistics, 1858–1917.
Creek Town Session Minute Book, 1858–1886, in English and Efik (not very legible).
Log of Ikot Offiong, 1870–1937.
A number of items on social questions, mostly undated, including some papers by Calabar people on land tenure and marriage.
Two envelopes relating to the Anderson-Ross quarrel.

C. PRIVATE PAPERS

(a) E. E. Offiong III papers (in the possession of Chief L. A. Essien Offiong, 10, Edgerley Road, Calabar):
  (i) Court Judgement Books, 1885–1910.
  (ii) Correspondence Books, 1898–1900.
  (iii) Letters Entry Book, 1898–1907.
  (iv) Agreements Book, 1869–1901.

(b) Coco Otu Bassey papers (in the possession of Chief John Coco Bassey, 17, Coco Bassey Street, Calabar):
  (i) Diary, 1878–1889.
  (ii) An autobiography of Coco Otu Bassey.

(c) The Hope Waddell Institute papers (in the possession of the Institute):
  (i) Minutes of the Session of the Institute's Church, 1905–1946.
  (ii) Log Book of the primary school for the period 1894–1908.
  (iii) The Hope Waddell Training Institute Magazine, No. 1–13, 1849–1855.

(d) Records kept at the Customary Court of Calabar, especially judgement books dating from 1898.

II. SECONDARY SOURCES

A. CONTEMPORARY SOURCES

There are a fairly large number of travel books which deal largely with the years between 1850–1890. They have to be used critically since most travellers wrote in lurid colours and dwelt, in an ethnocentric way, on the so-called 'evil habits' and 'obnoxious' customs of African middlemen. But there are other books which contain more objective and reliable information.

(i) Contemporary Books:

Adams, Capt. J. *Remarks on the country extending from Cape Palmas to the River Congo* (London, 1823; reprinted Frank Cass, London, 1966).
—— *Sketches taken during Ten Voyages to Africa, 1786–1800* (Liverpool, n.d.).
Baikie, W. B. *Narrative of an exploring voyage up the Rivers Kwora and Benue in 1854* (London, 1856; reprinted Frank Cass, London, 1966).
Barbot, J. *Description of the Coasts of North and South Guinea; and of*

Ethiopa Inferior . . . first printed from his original MS 1732; to be reprinted by Frank Cass, London. Reference to Calabar pp. 380–84; 461–66.

Bold, E. *The Merchants and Mariners African Guide* (London, 1819).

Bosman, W. *A new and accurate description of the Coast of Guinea* (London, 1705; 2nd ed., with a new introduction by Professor John Ralph Willis, Frank Cass, London, 1967).

Crow, Hugh. *Memoirs of the Late Captain Hugh Crow of* Liverpool (London, 1880; reprinted Frank Cass, London, 1970).

Esiere. *As Seen Through African Eyes* (London, n.d.) by Esien Esien Ukpabio.

Goldie, H. *Principles of Efik Grammar* (Edinburgh, 1868).

—— *Dictionary of the Efik Language* (Glasgow, 1890).

—— *Memoir of King Eyo VII of Old Calabar* (Old Calabar, 1894).

—— and Dean, J. T. *Calabar and its Mission* (Edinburgh, 1890, and Edinburgh and London, 1901).

Holman, J. *Travels in Madeira, S. Leone*, etc. (London, 1840). Extracts relating to Calabar republished also by the American Association for African Research in *Holman's Voyage to Old Calabar*, Donald C. Simmons, ed. (Calabar, 1959).

Hutchinson, T. J. *Impressions of Western Africa* (London, 1858; reprinted Frank Cass, London, 1970).

—— *Ten years' wanderings among the Ethiopians* (London, reprinted Frank Cass, London, 1967).

Jamieson, R. *Commerce with Africa* (London, 1859).

Kingsley, M. *Travels in West Africa* (London, 1897; 3rd ed., with a new introduction by Dr. John E. Flint, Frank Cass, London, 1965).

Laird, M. and Oldfield, R. A. K. *Narrative of an Expedition into the Interior of Africa*, Vol. II (London, 1837; reprinted Frank Cass, London, 1971).

Marwick, W. *William and Louisa Anderson* (Edinburgh, 1897).

M'Queen, J. *A Geographical Survey of Africa* (London, 1840).

Ranking, F. H. *The White Man's Grave: A Visit to Sierra Leone in 1834*, Vol. 2 (London, 1836).

Reade, Winwood. *Savage Africa* (London, 1863).

Robertson, G. A. *Notes on Africa* (London, 1819; to be reprinted by Frank Cass, London).

Smith, J. *Trade and Travels in the Gulf of Guinea, West Africa* (London, 1851).

Waddell, H. M. *Twenty-nine Years in the West Indies and Central Africa, 1829–1858* (London, 1863; 2nd ed., with a new introduction by G. I. Jones, Frank Cass, London, 1970).

Whitford, Rev. J. L. *Trading Life in Western and Central Africa, 1853–1875* (Liverpool, 1877; 2nd ed., with a new introduction by Dr. A. G. Hopkins, Frank Cass, London, 1967).

Wilson, Rev. J. L. *Western Africa: its History, Conditions and Prospects* (London, 1856).

(ii) Articles

Anon. 'King Eyo Honesty VII of Old Calabar, West Africa', in *The Christian*, issue for Oct. 15, 1891. A copy is attached to the back flap of H. Goldie, *Memoir of King Eyo Honesty VII*, op. cit. (University of Ibadan library copy).

Beecroft, Capt. and King, J. B. 'Details of Exploration of the Old Calabar River in 1841 and 1842', *J.R.C.S.*, Vol. 14, Part 2, 1844.
Coulthurst, C. H. 'Expedition to Old Calabar, etc', *J.R.C.S.*, Vol. 2, 1832.
Fyfe, C. 'Peter Nicolls—Old Calabar and Free Town', *J.H.S.N.*, Vol. 2, No. 1, Dec. 1960.
Johnston, H. H. 'A Journey up to Cross River, West Africa,' *P.R.G.S.* No. 10, 18888.
Oldfield, R. A. K. 'Ascent of Old Calabar River in 1836'; *J.R.G.S.*, Vol. 7, Part 1, 1837.
Walker, J. B. 'Notes on the Old Calabar and Cross River'; *P.R.G.S.*, Vol. 16, No. 2, 1872.
—— 'Notes of a visit in May 1875 to the Old Calabar and Qua River, the Ekoi Country and the Qua Rapids', *P.R.G.S.*, Vol. 20, 1876.
—— 'Notes on the politics, Religion and Commerce of Old Calabar', *Journal of the Anthropological Institute of Great Britain and Ireland*, Vol. 6, 1877.

B. LATER WORKS
(i) Books
Ajayi, J. F. A. *Christian Missions in Nigeria, 1841-1891—The Making of a New Elite* (London, 1965),
—— and Ispie, I., eds. *A Thousand Years of West African History* (Ibadan, 1965).
Alagoa, E. J. *The Akassa raid, 1895* (Ibadan, 1960).
—— *The Small Brave City-State; a history of Nembe-Brass in the Niger Delta* (Ibadan and Madison, 1964).
Anene, J. C. *Southern Nigeria in Transition, 1885-1906* (Cambridge, 1966).
Ayandele, E. A. *The Missionary Impact on Modern Nigeria, 1842-1914* (London, 1966).
Bascom, W. B. and Herskovits, M. J. (eds.) *Continuity and Change in African Cultures* (Chicago, 1959).
Basden, G. T. *Among the Ibos of Nigeria* (London, 1921; reprinted Frank Cass, London, 1966).
—— *Niger Ibos* (London, 1938; reprinted with a new bibliographical note by Professor John Ralph Willis, Frank Cass, London, 1966).
Beattie, J. *Other Cultures, aims, methods and achievements in Social Anthropology* (London, 1964).
Blyden, E. W. *West Africa before Europe* (London, 1905).
Brokensha, D. W. *Social Change at Larteh, Ghana* (Oxford, 1966).
Buchanan, K. M. and Pugh, J. C. *Land and People in Nigeria* (London, 1962).
Buell, R. I. *The Native Problem in Africa*, 2 vols. (New York, 1928; reprinted Frank Cass, London, 1965).
Burns, A. *History of Nigeria* (London, 1929).
Butt-Thompson, Capt. F. W. *West African Secret Societies* (London, 1929).
Coleman, J. *Nigeria—Background to Nationalism* (California, 1958).
Cook, A. N. *British Enterprise in Nigeria* (London, 1943; reprinted Frank Cass, London, 1964).
Crowder, M. *The Story of Nigeria* (London, 1962).
Curtin, P. D. *Image of Africa; British Ideas and action, 1780-1850* (Madison, 1964).
Davies, K. *The Royal African Company* (London, 1957).

Dean, B. B., *Diamond Jubilee: the story of the Calabar hospitals, 1897–1957* (Calabar, 1957).

Dent, H. C. *British Education* (London, 1949).

Dike, K. O. *Trade and Politics in the Niger Delta, 1830–1885* (Oxford, 1956).

Donnan, E. *Documents Illustrative of the History of the Slave Trade to America* (Washington, 1930–35; reprinted Frank Cass, London, 1966), 4 vols.

Elias, T. O. *The Nature of African Customary Law* (Manchester, 1950).

—— *Government and Politics in Africa* (London, 1961).

Ellis, A. B. *The Land of Fetish* (London, 1883).

Epelle, E. M. T. *The Church in the Niger Delta* (Port Harcourt, 1955).

Fage, J. D. *Introduction to the History of West Africa* (Cambridge, 1955).

Flint, J. E. *Nigeria and Ghana* (New Jersey, 1966).

Forde, C. D. (ed.). *Efik Trades of Old Calabar* (Oxford, 1956).

Forde, D. and Jones, G. I. *The Ibo and Ibibio-Speaking Peoples of South-Eastern Nigeria*, Part 3 in the series *Ethnograhic Survey of Africa* (ed. D. Forde), (London, 1962).

Fortes, M. and Evans Pritchard, E. E. *African Political Systems* (London, 1961).

Geary, N. M. *Nigeria Under British Rule* (London, 1927; reprinted Frank Cass, London, 1965).

Green, M. *Igbo Village Affairs* (London, 1947; 2nd ed., with a new introduction by the author, Frank Cass, London, 1964).

Greenberg, J. H. *Studies in African Linguistics Classification*, Part 1 (New Haven, 1955).

Groves, C. P. *The Planting of Christianity in Africa*, Vol. 2, 1840–1878 (London, 1954).

Hallet, R. *Records of the African Association, 1788–1831* (London, 1858).

Hertslet, E. *Map of Africa by Treaty* (London, 1895–1909; reprinted Frank Cass, London, 1967).

Hertslet, E. *A Complete Collection of the Treaties and Conventions between Great Britain and Foreign Powers* (London, various dates). Of special reference to Calabar see:

Vol. 8 (1851)
Vol. 9 (1851)
Vol. 10 (1859)
Vol. 11 (1900)
Vol. 12 (1905)
Vol. 13 (1877)
Vol. 14 (1880)
Vol. 17 (1890)
Vol. 18 (1893).

Hewart, E. G. *Vision and Achievement, 1796–1956* (Thomas Nelson, London, 1960). This is a history of the Foreign Missions of the Churches united in the Church of Scotland. Chapter 15 deals with the mission in Calabar.

Hilliard, F. H. *A Short History of Education in British West Africa* (London, 1957).

Hodgkin, T. *Nigerian Perspectives* (London, 1960).

Hunter, G. *The New Societies of Tropical Africa* (London, 1962).

Imona, Chief. *Chieftaincy in Calabar, the status of Big Qua Town and the Origin of Akim Qua Town* (Calabar, n.d.).

Ita, E. *A Decade of National Education Movement* (Calabar, 1949).

Jeffreys, M. D. W. *Old Calabar and Notes on the Ibibio Language* (H.W.T.I. Press, Calabar, 1935).

John Holt and Company (Liverpool) Ltd. *Merchant Adventure* (Northampton, n.d.). This is an account of the trading activities of John Holt and Co.

Johnston, H. H. *The Story of My Life* (London, 1923).

Jones, G. I. *The Trading States of the Oil Rivers* (Oxford, 1963).

Lander, R. and J. *Journal of an Expedition to Explore the Course and Termination of the Niger*, 2 vols. (London, 1832 and 1838).

Leonard, A. G. *The Lower Niger and its Tribes* (London, 1906; reprinted Frank Cass, London, 1968).

Lienhardt, G. *Social Anthropology* (London, 1966).

Livingston, W. P. *Mary Slessor of Calabar* (Garden City, 1923).

Lloyd, P. C. *Africa in Social Change* (Penguin, 1967).

Lowie, Robert. *Primitive Religion* (London, 1960).

Luke, J. *Pioneering in Mary Slessor's Country* (London, 1929).

McPhee, Allan. *The Economic Revolution in British West Africa* (London, 1926; reprinted Frank Cass, London, 1971).

Macrae, N. C. *The Look of the First Sixty Years, 1895-1955* (Calabar, 1956). It is a story of the Hope Waddell Training Institute.

Martin, Anne. *The Oil Palm Economy of the Ibibio Farmer* (Ibadan, 1956).

Mason, R. J. *British Education in Africa* (London, 1959).

McFarlan, D. M. *Calabar, The Church of Scotland Mission, 1846-1946* (London, 1957).

McPhee, A. *The Economic Revolution in British West Africa* (London, 1926; reprinted, with a new introductory note by Dr. A. G. Hopkins, Frank Cass, London, 1971).

Meek, C. K. *Law and Authority in a Nigerian Tribe* (London, 1937).

Mockler-Ferryman, A. F. *British West Africa: its rise and Progress* (London, 1900).

—— *British Nigeria* (London, 1902).

Moore, W. E. *Social Change* (New Jersey, 1963).

M'Keown, R. *In the Land of the Oil Rivers, the story of the Qua Iboe Mission* (London, 1902).

—— *Twenty-Five Years in Qua Iboe: the story of a missionary effort.* (London, 1912).

Morel, E. E. *Nigeria, its Peoples and its Problems* (London, 1911; 2nd ed., 1912; 3rd ed., with a new introduction by Kenneth Dike Nworah, Frank Cass, London, 1968).

Murray, A. *The School in the Bush—a critical study of the theory and practice of Native Education in Africa* (London, 1938; 2nd ed., 1938; reprinted Frank Cass, London, 1967).

Newbury, C. W. *British Policy towards West Africa, Select documents, 1786-1874* (Oxford, 1965).

Newland, Capt., H. O. *West Africa, a handbook of practical Information* (London, 1922).

Obio-Offiong, V. E. *An Introduction to Nait history: a history of Afagba Obio Offiong and a first step to the Study of Ibibio history* (Aba, 1958).

O'Brien, B. *She Had a Magic: the Story of Mary Mitchell Slessor* (London, 1958).

Ottenberg, S. and P. *Cultures and Societies of Africa* (New York, 1960).

Partridge, C. *Cross River Natives* (London, 1905).

Parrinder, G. *African Traditional Religion* (London, 1954).
—— *West African Religions* (London, 1961).
Perham, M. *Native Administration in Nigeria* (Oxford, 1937).
Seligman, C. C. *Races of Africa* (London, 1939).
Southall, A. *Social Change in Modern Africa* (London, 1961).
Talbot, P. A. *In the Shadow of the British* (London, 1912).
—— *Life in Southern Nigeria* (London, 1923; reprinted Frank Cass, London, 1967).
—— *The Peoples of Southern Nigeria*, Vol. 1. Historical Notes (London, 1926; reprinted Frank Cass, London, 1969).
—— *Tribes of the Niger Delta* (London, 1933; reprinted Frank Cass, London, 1969).
Thorp, E. *Ladder of Bones* (London, 1956).
Ward, Rev. W. J. *In and Around the Oron Country* (Harmmond, 1912?).
Weiler, Hans N., ed. *Erziehung und Politik in Nigeria* (Freibourg, 1964).
Williams, C. *History of the Liverpool Privatees etc.* (London, 1897).
Williamson, S. G. *Akan Religion and the Christian Faith* (Accra, 1965).
Wilson, J. L. *The British Squadron on the Coast of Africa* (n.d.), being a collection of reprints from various sources.
Wilson, Rev. J. *Western Africa* (London, 1886).
Wise, Colin C. *A History of Education in British West Africa* (1956).

(ii) **Articles**
Afigbo, A. E. 'Efik Origin and Migrations Reconsidered', *Nigeria Magazine*, No. 87, Dec. 1965.
Allen, W. 'Is the Old Calabar a branch of the River Quora?' *J.R.C.S.*, Vol. 7, 1837.
Amaku, E. N. 'Beauty Parlours at Calabar', *Nigeria Digest*, Vol. 1, No. 6, March, 1946.
Anene, J. C. 'The Protectorate Government of Southern Nigeria and the Aros: 1900–1902, *J.H.S.N.*, Vol. 1, No. 1, Dec. 1956.
—— 'The Foundation of British Rule in Southern Nigeria, (1855–1891)' *J.H.S.N.*, Vol. 1, No. 4, Dec. 1959.
Anon. 'Calabar', *Nigeria Magazine*, No. 52, 1956.
Brown, P. 'Patterns of Authority in West Africa', *Africa*, Vol. 21, No. 4, Oct. 1951.
Bushman. 'Symbolic Chiefs on the Cross River', *Nigerian Field*, Vol. 1, No. 5, 1932.
Clinton, J. V. 'King Eyo Honesty II of Creek Town', *Nigeria Magazine*, No. 69, August, 1961, p. 182.
Cotton, J. C. 'The Calabar Marriage Law and Custom' *J.A.S.*, Vol. 4, 1904–1905.
—— The People of Old Calabar, *J.A.S.*, Vol. 4 ,No. 15, April, 1905.
Cowan, A. A. 'Early Trading Conditions in the Bight of Biafra', Part 1 in *J.A.S.*, Vol. 34, 1935; Part 2, in *J.A.S.*, Vol. 35, 1936.
Daniell, W. F. 'On the Natives of Old Calabar, West Coast of Africa', *Journal of the Ethnological Society*, Vol. 1, 1848.
Dike, K. O. 'John Beecroft, 1790–1854', *J.H.S.N.*, Vol. 1, No. 1, Dec. 1956.
Dougall, J. W. C. 'The Development of the Education of the African in relation to Western Contact', *Africa*, Vol. II, No. 3, July, 1938.
Elliot, G. E. S. 'Some Notes on Native West African Customs', *Journal of the Anthropoligical Institute*, Vol. 23, 1894.
Ema, A. J. Udo. 'The Ekpe Society', *Nigeria Magazine*, No. 16, 4th Quarter, 1958.

308   *Bibliography*

Forde, D. 'The Conditions of Social Development in West Africa', *Civilizations*, Vol. 3, No. 4, 1953.

Gavin, R. J. 'Nigeria and Lord Palmerston', *Ibadan*, No. 12, June 1961.

Gertzel, C. J. 'Commercial Organization on the Niger Coast, 1852–1891', *Historians in Tropical Africa*, being proceedings of the Leverhulme Inter-Collegiate History Conference held at the University College of Rhodesia and Nyasaland, Sept. 1960. Mimeographed at Salisbury, 1962.

—— 'Relations between African and European Traders in the Niger Delta, 1880–1896' *J.A.H.*, Vol. 3, No. 2, 1962.

Henderson, R. N. 'Generalised Culture and Evolutionary Adaptability: a companion of urban Efik and Ibo in Nigeria', *Ethnology*, Vol. 5, No. 4, Oct. 1966.

Hopkins, A. G. 'The Currency Revolution in South West Nigeria in the Late Nineteenth Century', *J.H.S.N.*, Vol. 3, No. 3, Dec. 1966.

Horton, R. 'The Kalabari Ekine Society; a borderland of religion and art', *Africa*, Vol. 33, No. 2, April, 1963.

Jeffreys, M. D. W. 'Some Notes on the Ekoi', *Journal of the Royal Anthropological Institute*, Vol. 69, 1939.

—— 'Mary Slessor: magistrate', *West African Review*, Vol. 21, No. 273, 1950.

—— Review of *the Ibo and Ibibio Speaking Peoples of South-East Nigeria* by D. Forde and G. I. Jones (Oxford, U.P. 1950) in *African Studies*, Vol. 2, No. 1, March, 1952.

—— 'Fort Stuart; a lost site', *Nigerian Field*, Vol. 20, No. 2, 1955. It discusses the origin of the names 'Old' and 'New' Calabar.

—— 'Witchcraft in the Calabar Province', *African Studies*, Vol. 25, No. 2, 1966.

—— 'Efik Origin', *Nigeria Magazine*, No. 91, Dec. 1966.

Jones, G. I. 'Who are the Aro?', *Nigerian Field*, Vol. 8, No. 3 (1939), contains a description of the origin of the Aro and their relationship with the Ibibio and other peoples of the Cross River.

—— 'Being a description of the origin of the Aros and their relations with the Ibibio and other tribes of the Cross River', *Nigerian Field*, Vol. 8, 1939.

—— 'Dual Organization in Ibo Social Structure', *Africa*, Vol. 19, No. 2, 1949.

—— Review of '*Trade and Politics in the Niger Delta*', by K. O. Dike, *Africa*, Vol. 27, No. 1, Jan. 1957.

—— 'European and African Tradition in the Rio Real', *J.A.H.*, Vol. 4, No. 3, 1963.

—— 'From Direct to Indirect Rule in Eastern Nigeria', *ODU*, Vol. 2, Jan. 1966.

Kitson, A. E. 'Southern Nigeria: some considerations of its structure, people and natural history', *Geographical Journal*, Vol. 41, No. 1, 1913.

Little, K. 'The Study of Social Change in British West Africa', *Africa*, Vol. 23, 1953.

Malcolm. 'Notes on the seclusion of girls among the Efik of Old Calabar, *Man*, Vol. 25, Article 69, 1925.

Maxwell, J. 'Calabar Stories', *Journal of the Royal African Society*, Vol. 5, 1905–1906.

Milsome, J. R. 'Missionary extraordinary', *West African Review*, Vol. 32, No. 401, 1961. This is a biography of Mary Slessor.

Morrill, W. T. 'Immigrants and Associations: the Ibo in Twentieth-Century

Calabar', *Comparative Studies in Society and History*, Vol. 5, 1963.

Musgrove, F. 'Some reflections on the Sociology of African Education', *African Studies*, Vol. 2, No. 4, Dec. 1952.

N'idu, A. 'Ekpe, Cross River Cult', *West African Review*, Vol. 30, No. 384, Nov. 1959.

Oldham, J. H. 'The Educational work of Missionary Societies', *Africa*, Vol. 7, 1934.

Parkinson, J. 'A note on the Efik and Ekoi tribes of the Eastern Province of Southern Nigeria', *Journal of the Royal Anthropological Institute*, Vol. 37, 1907.

Rewner, W. 'Native Poison, West Africa', *J.A.S.*, Vol. 4, 1904–05.

Romilly, G. 'The Oil Rivers in the Nineteenth Century', *Progress* (a magazine of Lever Booklets), Vol. 41, No. 229, 1950–51.

Simmons, D. C. 'Fort Stuart, Calabar—a further note', *Nigerian Field*, Vol. 20, No. 3, 1955.

Tamuna, T. N. 'Native House Rule of Southern Nigeria', *Nigeria Magazine*, No. 93, June, 1967.

Thurnwald, R. 'The Social Problems of Africa', *Africa*, Vol. 2, No. 2, 1929.
—— 'Social Systems of Africa', *Africa*, Vol. 2, No. 3, 1929; and Vol. 2, No. 4, 1929.

T. L. H. 'An Efik Diarist', *West Africa*, Vol. 41, No. 2081, 2 March, 1957; this is a review of the diary of Antera Duke.

Watts, J. 'Notes on the Old Calabar District of Southern Nigeria', *Man*, Vol. 3, 1903.

Webster, J. B. 'The Bible and the Plough', *J.H.S.N.*, Vol. 2, No. 4, Dec. 1963.

C. UNPUBLISHED WORKS

(i) Mimeographed manuscripts

Papers read at the Seventh International African Seminar on 'The Impact of Christianity in Tropical Africa', held at Legon in April, 1965.

Robin Horton, 'From Fishing Village to City State', a paper read at a seminar on Non-written Sources for Nigerian History', University of Ibadan, Feb. 1967.

C. C. Wrigley, 'The External Trade of Nigeria, 1901–1960', MS., dated 18 Apr. 1967.

(ii) Theses

Afigbo, A. E. 'The Warrant Chief System in Eastern Nigeria, 1900–1929' (Ph.D. Ibadan, 1964).

Anene, J. C. O. 'The Boundary Arrangements for Nigeria, 1884–1906: An Objective Study in Colonial Boundary Making' (Ph.D. London, 1960).

Gavin, R. J. 'Palmerston's Policy Towards East and West Africa, 1830–1865' (Ph.D. Cambridge, 1959–60).

Gertzel, C. 'John Holt: A British Merchant in West Africa in the Era of Imperialism' (D. Phil. Oxford, 1959).

Knight, C. W. 'History of the Expansion of Evangelical Christian Mission in Nigeria' (D. Th. Southern Baptist Theological Seminary, U.S.A., 1951).

Morrill, W. T. 'Two Urban Cultures of Calabar, Nigeria' (Ph.D. Chicago, June, 1961).

Smythe, H. M. 'Patterns of Kinship Structure in West Africa' (Ph.D. Northwestern, 1945).

Stilliard, N. H. 'The Rise and Development of Legitimate Trade in Palm Oil with West Africa' (M.A. Birmingham, 1938).

Tamuno, S. M. 'The Development of British Administrative Control of Southern Nigeria, 1900–1912: A Study of the Administrations of Sir Ralph Moor, Sir William MacGregor and Sir Walter Egerton' (Ph.D. London, 1962).

III. ORAL EVIDENCE

Documentary sources do not do full justice to the rich variety and complexity of Efik political and social organization, the genealogical traditions preserved by the leading Efik families and houses, and vital background data on the Efik kings, chiefs, elders and evangelists important in the history of their times. Oral evidence, gathered in the course of field work in Duke Town, Henshaw Town, Creek Town, the hinterland plantations of Akpabuyo and Odukpani, and the towns and villages up the Calabar and Cross Rivers, has proved to be an indispensable supplement to evidence gathered from other sources. More than thirty informants, drawn from various walks of life and traditional status, were consulted regularly during the course of the field work done for this study. The reliability and authenticity in the interpretation of familial and other histories were closely cross-checked as the author was conscious of the controversies over the disputed succession to the stool (Obong) of Calabar in 1964.

INDEX

Aba, 260
Abakom Ene Eyo, 8, 10, 11
Abatim Otung Ema, 4
Abasi Offiong Okoho, 9
Abeona, 112n.77
abia idiong, 53, 59
Abini, 249
Aborigines Protection Society, 217, 270n.98
Abua, 3
Accra, 205
Acqua, King of Old Town, 85
Adams, Capt. John, 24, 29, 34n.68, 34n.85, 159
Adem, 288
Adiabo (Guinea Company), 2, 4, 88 (map), 106, 212, 234, 275, 280
Adiadia, 26
Adim Atai, 5, 8, 11
Adim, Okon Etim Asiya, 218
adultery, 225
afia-ifot, 52
Afikpo, 34n.82; people, 246, 247; Ibo, 248, 249; country, 250; British government station, 250, 261
Africa, 152n.25
African Association, 236, 244; Creek Town, 254, 261, 262, 263
African Steamship Company, 117
agriculture, 29; plantation, 37, 62, 85–6, 218, 258; produce, 233, 239, 245, 247, 248; *see also* commodities
Akim Qua Town, *see* Big Qua Town
Aku Akim, 8
Akpa, *see* Qua
Akpabuyo, 28, 29, 30, 34n.82, 37; manpower, 37, 41, 42, 81, 159, 181, 204, 209, 233, 272
Akpa Iyefe, Upper, 205
Akpan, 273
Akpan, Akpotem, 248
Akpap, 239
Akpayafe, 228n.15
Akpotem Akpan, 248
Akunakuna, frontispiece, 2, 27, 84, 85, 88(map), 208, 235, 248–9, 250
Akwa, 228n.15
Akwa Ete Kiet, 7

Alderton, E. C., 3, 31n.8
Almanta, 205
Amakiri, 11, 187
Amakiri group, 189
Amasu, 205
Ambo, family, 5, 7, 79, 197n.106, 189, 191–2, 212; blessing of Creek Town kings, 79; relations with Eyo I, 27, 79
Ambony Robin John, Prince, 8
Ambrosine, 111n.77
Anang, people, 183
Anansa, 99, 288
Anansa Ikang, 56
ancestor cult, 58
Anderson, Rev. William, 49, 57, 59; and trial by ordeal, 103, 104, 161, 164, 166, 167, 172, 173, 175, 176
Anderson, Mrs. William, 167
Andony River, 145
Anko, Chief, 163
Annang, 288
Annesley's Bridge, 256, 257(map)
Anofia, 250
Ansa, Efan, 174
Ansa, Effiom, 174
Ansa, Ekeng Ewa, 174
Ansa, Ekpo, 170, 174
Ansa, Ewa, 174
Ansa, Eyo, 190
Ansa, Nkoro, 174
Antelope, H.M.S., 101
Antera Duke, 66, 74n.67
Anwan, Efana, 217
Araminta, 156n.97
Archer, H.M.S., 111n.77
Archibong I, 49, 54, 95–8, 104, 111n.69
Archibong II, 57, 138–9, 140, 141, 155n.90, 156n.97, 160–3, 164, 175, 184, 272, 278, 281
Archibong III, 16, 55, 164–7, 168ff., 172, 176, 184–5, 186
Archibong, Ekondo, 8, 15
Archibong Ekpo, 170
Archibong family and lineage, 9, 160, 162, 169; and Duke Family, 76, 186, 187, 212, 276

318   *Index*

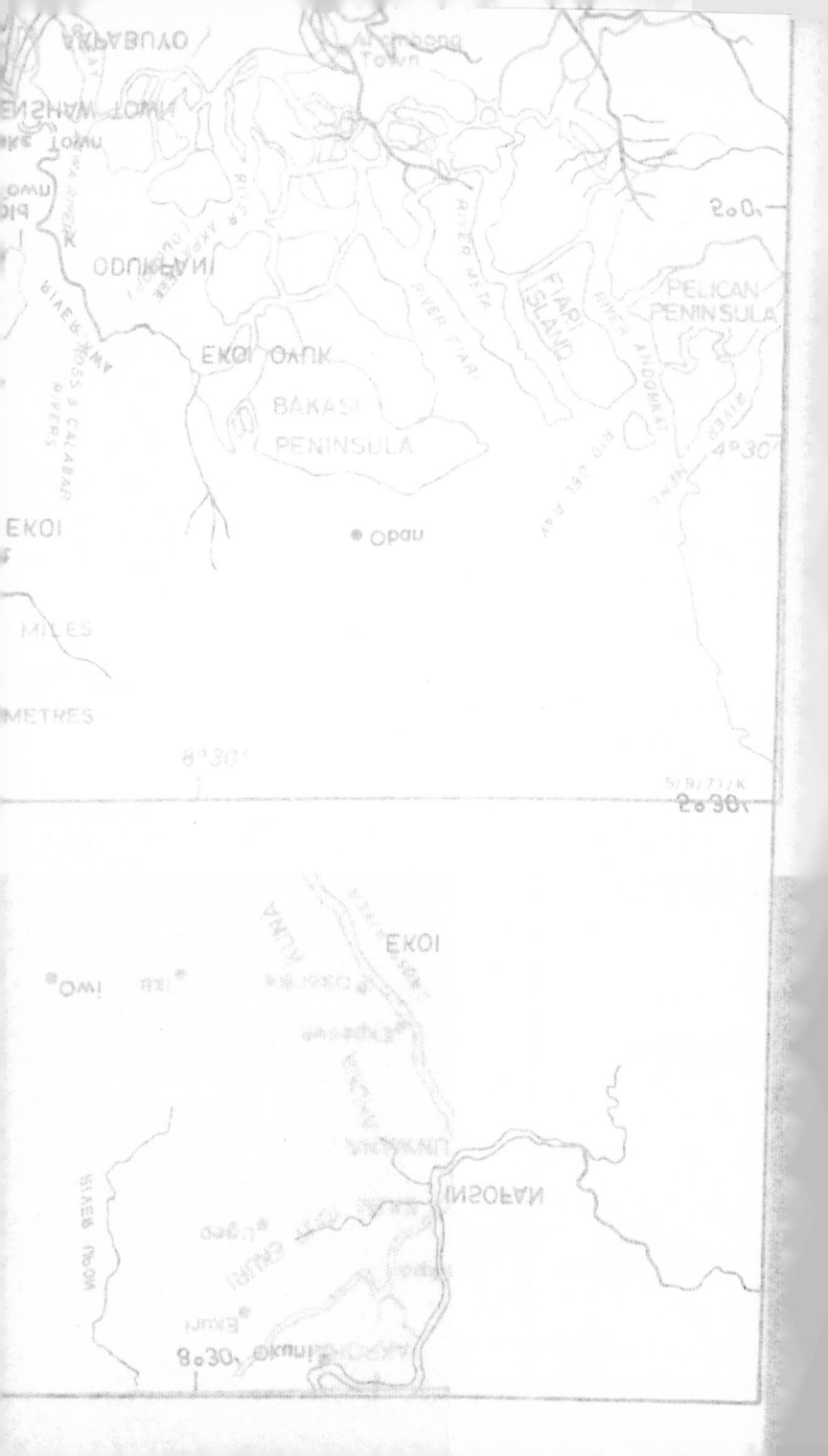

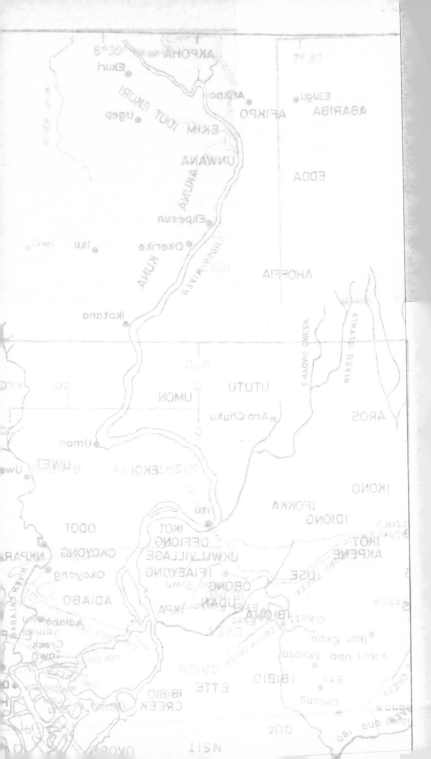